SĀMA VEDA

SĀMA VEDA

S. V. Ganapati

MOTILAL BANARSIDASS PUBLISHERS
PRIVATE LIMITED • DELHI

3rd Reprint: Delhi, 2016
First Edition: Delhi, 1982

ISBN: 978-81-208-1046-4 (Cloth)
ISBN: 978-81-208-1072-3 (Paper)

MOTILAL BANARSIDASS
41 U.A., Bungalow Road, Jawahar Nagar, Delhi 110 007
8 Mahalaxmi Chamber, 22 Bhulabhai Desai Road, Mumbai 400 026
203 Royapettah High Road, Mylapore, Chennai 600 004
236, 9th Main III Block, Jayanagar, Bangalore 560 011
8 Camac Street, Kolkata 700 017
Ashok Rajpath, Patna 800 004
Chowk, Varanasi 221 001

Printed in India

by RP Jain at NAB Printing Unit,
A-44, Naraina Industrial Area, Phase I, New Delhi–110028
and published by JP Jain for Motilal Banarsidass Publishers (P) Ltd,
41 U.A. Bungalow Road, Jawahar Nagar, Delhi-110007

CONTENTS

PART II
UTTARA ĀRCIKA

INTRODUCTION

1. (a) The Sāma Veda is one of four Vedas which had been handed to us over a period of thousands of years by oral tradition, without an error of even a syllable, before they were reduced to writing in very recent times. The Vedas are of varying lengths with varying number of mantras or hymns as stated below:

(1) Sāma Veda	1,875	mantras
(2) Yajur Veda	1,976	,,
(3) Ṛg Veda 1,028 hymns	10,552	,,
(4) Atharva Veda	5,038	,,

The mantras are mostly in the form of couplets of varying metres ranging from 24 to 40 or 50 syllables. The hymns in the Ṛg.Veda comprise groups of mantras ranging from 3 to 40 or 50 even. The Yajur Veda is partly in prose form.

(b) Although the Ṛg Veda is credited with 10,552 mantras, this number is reduced to 8,629, which represents its own contribution, if we deduct 1,442 mantras from the Sāma Veda and 481 mantras from the Yajur Veda which the Ṛṣis of the Ṛg Veda have quoted or adopted. This however is our view although it is generally erroneously believed that Sāma and Yajur Vedas have adopted from Ṛg Veda. This cannot be true as both Sāma and Yajur Vedas are very much more ancient as we will show later while discussing the antiquity of the Vedas.

2. Origin of the Vedas

It is generally believed, even by some scholars of repute, that the Vedas are eternal and were directly communicated to some inspired ṛṣis of old. This view is held because of the scholars not having been able to determine the period from which the oral tradition had been persisting. This belief is no longer true as we are now in a position to determine with some exactitude the dates of the Vedas. But, apart from this fact, the claim that the Vedas are direct utterances of God revealed to some ṛṣis arises from a confusion between the expression Veda meaning knowledge in general and "The Vedas" referring to the works discussed here. No doubt all knowledge arises only from God, otherwise how could creation have taken place which involves a vast amount of concealed knowledge divulged in the manifestation processes themselves. Knowledge was there which arose as ideas of the creator. Then it is unbelievable that God gave utterances to any knowledge. The process by which God reveals his ideas is to endow man with the faculty of speech and to inspire him with ideas through his brain and to induce him to the utterances. Such ideas as form the content of the Vedas are revealed only to profound thinkers who had gone through life's experiences and gathered wisdom.

3. (a) **Revelation—What it Means**

The expression "Revelation" used to indicate the source of the Vedas has been thoroughly misunderstood. What was meant to be conveyed by the word was that the knowledge which remained locked up in man's brain, before language had developed to such an extent as to enable one's thoughts and ideas to be translated cogently into speech, was revealed to the outside world when speech was perfected. Thus man himself was the author of the revelations and not God direct. This truth is borne out by the Ṛg Veda itself as stated in Maṇḍala X.71.1-2.

See *Call of the Vedas* by A. C. Bose, Bhavan's Publication.

> "Of the first and foremost speech that you sent
> Giving names to things, O Bṛhaspati,
> Whatever was noblest and stainless and secretly treasured
> With love you revealed.
> When sages have created the word straining it through
> Their spirits as flour through a sieve
> Therein have friends recognised their mutual friendships
> Whose blessed signs lay hidden in words."

So here we see what revelation signifies.

(b) This truth receives further confirmation by statements in Sāma and Yajur Vedas which declare repeatedly that the knowledge conveyed by them was derived by tradition. No authorship is mentioned in these two Vedas. The mantras then must have accumulated over a long period little by little. Knowledge is a growing experience and accumulates with the efflux of time. (See Appendix III)

(c) Thus it is seen that the Vedas themselves do not claim

divinity for the knowledge revealed by the mantras. Still people attributed divinity of origin to them. It can only be for all knowledge in general.

4. (a) Special Features and Content of Sāma Veda

Sāma Veda alone of the four Vedas is set to music and is intended to be sung. The present day music is derived from it. Evidently there was no script at the time and all knowledge had to be committed to memory and transmitted by oral tradition to succeeding generations. In musical form it is easier to commit to memory. The text of the Veda or Saṃhitā is divided into two sections namely: (1) Gaṇa or songs being the first part containing 640 mantras, some of which are based on musical notes. These mantras are again subdivided into two groups namely those which are to be sung in the villages and those which are meant to be sung only in the forests and not in the villages. (2) The second part containing the remaining 1,235 mantras is called Ārcika or prayers. The subject-matter of the two sections is the same and there are 222 mantras of the first part repeated in the second part often-times addressed to a different Deva or lending itself to be interpreted differently.

(b) Subject-matter

As regards the content or subject-matter of the Veda, it is to be noted that a number of translations are available with divergent trends and interpretations. The Veda lends itself to be so dealt with, because of the economy in words and brevity of expression devised for easily committing to memory. Oftentimes the mantras read like the Delphic oracle "the Greeks the Romans conquered", leading to different renderings.

(c) Transcriptions

Another circumstance which has accentuated the confusion is that the transcription to writing from oral tradition has been made several thousand years later when the Veda had become more or less a faint memory in the lives of the people. Again the transcription has been done from musical chanting in which the syllables are often tacked on to a previous or a succeeding word, which give different meanings altogether. In our translation we have resorted to this artifice to a great extent to arrive at proper ideas consistent with the trend of the subject-matter.

(d) Our Line of Interpretation

We hold that in whatever other ways the Veda may have been translated and presented, it lends itself to be correctly presented as we have done in our effort. This leads us to a cogent and consistent system of ideas bearing on two subjects principally, namely; (1) Evolution and (2) How the operations of the brain and the sense organs and the body take place and what Devas are responsible for carrying them out. All prayers for one's own welfare and prosperity are addressed to these Devas. The entire Veda is devoted only to these subjects.

5. (a) The Home of the Veda

The Sāma Veda as well as the Yajur Veda were the gift of the Deva race to us who along with the kindred Asuras were the inhabitants of the Arctic circle originally and were uprooted from their homes when they were invaded by glaciation. These races were mistakenly thought to be divine beings even in very early times and so represented by the Purāṇic writers. Actually they were human beings who, after they abandoned their original homes in the Arctic belt settled down in Central Asia, in the trans-Himalayan regions west of the Gobi desert up to and including the present day Iran. Of these two sections of a kindred stock of people, the Asuras after a ceaseless struggle with their kindred folk settled down in the present day Iran and imparted their culture to the local people the Parsees who have chronicled the memory of their past, their faiths and beliefs in their sacred books and religious writings similar to our Vedas.

(b) The Devas

The Devas on the other hand settled down towards the east of the Asura lands as in Afghanistan and further east known as Ilāvrata Varṣa in ancient times. They were hill lovers and so had their homes and settlements on the slopes of hills, where the plains were occupied by our own forefathers the patriarchs and their own people. That our forefathers were of a different stock from the Devas and Asuras has been made plain in all ancient writings and all our Purāṇas. The Devas and Asuras were in ceaseless warfare among themselves although they were on friendly terms with the local population and got on well with them.

(c) Deva Culture

The language Sanskrit called Devanāgarī originated from them and is their mother tongue i.e. of Devas and Asuras. Other expressions in current use like "deva gaṇa" "deva bhāṣā" all confirm that the Sanskrit language originated from them and also the Sāma and Yajur Vedas. The Devas had a superior culture which exercised a wholesome influence on our remote forefathers the patriarchs who seem to have absorbed the Deva culture in toto, their language, their customs and manners, their faiths and beliefs and also their Vedas, Sāma and Yajur. The Deva clans were headed by leaders like Indra, Agni, Mitra, Varuṇa, Vāyu, Yama, Brahmā and so forth, everyone of whom had his own distinct hill settlement in the Ilāvrata Varṣa. Brahmā was the supreme head and Indra a subordinate leader under him. Brahmā's residential area was known as Manovatī and on this hill every other leader had a place of residence to live in whenever he had to call on the supreme head. Indra's region was known as Amarāvatī. Here in their new homes the devas lived their lives amicably with the local people imparting their culture, language and art to them.

(d) Our Forefathers

The people of present day India whose distant forefathers were the Patriarchs Marīci, Atri, Pulastya, Pulaha, Kratu, Vasiṣṭha, Aṅgiras, Bhṛgu, Pracetas and Nārada and their followers were living in the plains of Central Asia among whom the Devas also lived but on the hills. There were 11 other Prajāpatis too making up 21 in all. That the Prajāpatis followed the Vedic way of life is evident from the Yajña which Dakṣa I arranged, to which he had not invited his own son-in-law Śiva, at which his daughter Satī felt insulted and immolated herself in fire and the dire consequences which befell Dakṣa himself. During this patriarchal period, peace seems to have prevailed between the Devas and Asuras—at least there is no record of strife between them. But at a much later period during the reigns of the Solar and Lunar dynasty kings, descendants of the patriarchs, the Devas frequently resorted to help from these kings in their wars against the Asuras. Ṛg Veda was unknown during the sojourn of the patriarchs in Central Asia. It had its origin in the Indian soil after the migration to India of the descendants of the patriarchs, owing to a great flood. The Ṛṣis of the Ṛg Veda spoke of the distant and forgotten forefathers when referring to the patriarchs, the originators of their race.

(e) The Arctic Home of the Devas and Asuras

That these people had their original homes in the Arctic belt is established from the mantras which refer to natural phenomena observable only in the Arctic belt. There are 7 such mantras in the Sāma Veda, 8 in Yajur Veda. Unless one has lived in that area and had been an eye-witness it would not have been possible to describe them. But these references have been made only to illustrate that similar phenomena take place in our own system. These two Vedas inculcate that the phenomena in the external world is similar to what takes place within us but on a magnified scale. Their conviction is that the external world is what one conceives as perceiving. So these two Vedas do not deal much with the external world separately.

(f) Peculiarities of Natural Phenomena in the Arctic Circle

The peculiar features of the Arctic region are:

1. A six-month long continuous day followed by a six-month long continuous night at the pole.
2. A period of 7 to 10 months of daily sunshine and darkness of varying durations as in other places, according to the latitude of the place.
3. A period of continuous darkness varying from 2 to 100 days according to the latitude of the place.
4. A revolving dawn of 2 to 30 days followed by the re-appearance of the Sun above the horizon succeeded by days and nights as in lower latitudes followed by a period of continuous sunshine.
5. The rising of the Sun from the South.

Independent of the mantras from Sāma and Yajur Veda Tilak has established beyond doubt quoting extensively from the Ṛg Veda and other sources that the home of the Vedas was in Arctic circle originally. But we have already mentioned that the Ṛg Veda originated from Ṛṣis on Indian soil who had only vague memories of their remote forefathers in the Central Asian plains. So, whatever references are made to the Arctic phenomena in the Ṛg Veda cannot be from personal experiences but gleaned from the older Vedas and from traditional knowledge. Thus Tilak's findings can be applied only to Sāma and Yajur Vedas and under no circumstances to Ṛg Veda, as the former had their homes in the Arctic belt while the latter in the Indian soil. Further they were so remote in time from each other, as will be shown presently.

6. (a) The Age of the Veda

The Sāma Veda gives us no sort of indication to determine its age except by references to the Arctic home. It has to be established only from indications given in the Yajur Veda and the Parsee scriptures. Although scholars try to fix the age of the Vedas with reference to Ṛg Veda considering it to be the oldest Veda, which however it is not, as pointed out above, we have to fall back on the sources stated by us which enable us to fix the date with great exactitude.

(b) Yajur Veda Mantras

Mantra XXX.18 reads as follows:

"The imperishable is the origin of all, now Kṛta (yuga) is gone (cheated us), Tretā is being witnessed by us newly to be followed by the closely connected Dvāpara, I determine from my immaculate gift from beyond that assemblies of men and plant life (stationary objects) will perish, hour of death will control men, hunger and destruction of cattle will follow, there will be deformity (internal transformation) begging and evil doings will be resorted to with sinful minds and robbery." This mantra is followed by a few more predicting dire calamities to people, breakdown of morality, society etc. and the resulting evils thereof. There will be endless wanderings in search of a new home. We have however no clues to know whether the prognostications did come out to be true, in our own ancient records. The only information left behind by the Veda is (1) that a dire calamity will overtake the race and (2) that it will be in the beginning of Tretā Yuga.

(c) Confirmation from Parsee Scriptures

The Parsee race who were originally in Iran and adopted the culture of the Asuras, of the same stock as Devas but with different beliefs and hostility to their kindred folk, confirms that what was foretold did come to pass. Their holy book *Zend Avesta* mentions that glaciation set in in the Arctic area and destroyed the homes of their forefathers who in consequence had to wander over many lands, as many as 16, and for several hundreds of years, suffering untold calamities and death and destruction until they finally settled in safe homes in Iran.

(d) Glaciation early in Tretā Yuga

Thus, if we fix the date of glaciation, we can be certain that the two ancient Vedas were current in inter-glacial times. The date of commencement of Tretā Yuga can be fixed only by settling the period covered by Mahāyuga. The Purāṇic writers assign a period of 43,20,000 years on the assumption that Devas were gods and that a year of 360 days is but a day for the Devas. But we know now that the Devas were human beings and so the period of time is the same for both and that a Mahāyuga of 12,000 years as fixed by Manu and Vyāsa is the same for both races and has not be multiplied by 360 to arrive at the human Mahāyuga period.

A Mahāyuga comprises four sub-periods comprising (1) Kṛta—4,800, (2) Tretā—3,600, (3) Dvāpara—2,400 and (4) Kali—1,200 including Sandhi periods of 10 per cent both before and after, making 12,000 years altogether. Since now 5,078 years have elapsed from the commencement of Kaliyuga, the date of commencement of Tretāyuga is 5,078+6,000=11,078 years. Glaciation then occurred about this time and the two Vedas had been accumulating their traditions earlier over several hundreds of years possibly.

(e) Glaciation—Other Determinations

Other Researchers have estimated the age of glaciation variously from 8,000 to 23,000 years. Tilak fixes the date from astronomical data and statements from Parsi scriptures at 8,000 to 10,000 years from now. A more recent determination appeared in the *Reader's Digest*, March 1974, pages 44-48 under the title "Solving the great Cornfield Mystery" by Ronald Schiller on the researches of archaeologist Stuart Struver. Explorations were made by him in the Koster Valley near the river Illinois in North America in 1969. The lowest layers of the excavations revealed Red Indian settlements of about 8,000 years old. Struver states that the earliest evidence of the presence of this tribe is variously estimated at from 13,000 to 26,000 years. These Red Indians are said to have migrated from Asia across the Behring Strait about 10,000 years ago as the glaciers receded and the climate turned warmer and drier in America. There is no doubt that these Red Indians were one of the races who fled from the Arctic area on the onset of glaciation. It appears to us that among all these determinations the Yajur Veda statement stands out as the most precise one.

7. Evolution According to Sāma Veda

(a) General

The conceptions of Sāma Veda on Evolution on earth are unique but at the same time most rational carrying the stamp of conviction. This Veda shares its views on this subject to a great extent with Yajur Veda. Since this creation had a beginning at some remote time it is natural to enquire what was there before. All this illimitable and vast space was filled completely with his presence. All that exists now and which may appear in the future are his manifestations (619). There can be nothing that is not he. Three parts of this Puruṣa of the nature of pure intelligence, named Savitā or Viṣṇu, and of the nature of activity also, constituting the heaven, beyond our perceptions, is all about us and filling all space. We are at his feet taking on repeated existences (mantra 618). The Puruṣa has a thousand heads, a thousand eyes and a thousand flights of imagination. He envelops the entire universe, transcends it and looks upon it as at a finger (617). Since the creator is of the nature of activity, he should have pursued that activity within himself i.e. he was in a state of browsing and planning for the future. From what followed this state of single blessedness, it is natural to infer that he was seized with a desire to know himself and as it is possible only in the presence of a multitude of others, he came out of his reverie, which may be called the state of cosmic sleep, and indulged in creating his objective states. This great and irrepressible zeal to externalize his activity and create his objective states as ideas is known as Agni in the mental world and he is represented on earth by fire, both possessed of the same qualities i.e. to devour everything to be identified with what is devoured.

(b) The World of Ideas

This Veda, in common with the Yajur Veda, holds the view, what everyone of us knows and experiences, that no activity or achievement is possible on earth or in heaven without prior thought or planning. Activity in the material world is only a transfer of ideas to matter. This universal truth is equally valid for the manifestation process on earth. What truly happens in manifestation is to provide a mantle or cloak to envelop the ideas received from heaven for their activity from within. Nothing new takes place on earth. Whatever happens here then is what has already happened in the world of ideas in heaven which surrounds us, though unseen. So, the manifested world was evolved first as ideas in heaven by the intelligent creator; the creator woke up from sleep to dream, what we call the cosmic dream.

(c) Ideas are only Objective States of Creator

Since there was only the creator present, he had himself to play the role of object. Intelligence in activity creates only ideas and these formed his objective states. But when he is an object there is no subject and when he next resumes his role of subject there is no object at that instant. During this activity several gods or Devas appeared on the scene. In the first place appeared the Aśvins with their twin arms, along one arm of which he passed on to be an object which he deposited in himself, as he was present all over, and returned by the other arm of the Aśvins to resume his subjective role. This activity spelt out two new ideas namely, (1) the sense of differentiation and (2) the sense of touch by which the objective states were constantly recharged. These two functions form part of the seven-pronged or -armed activity of Vaiśvānara called also simply Activity or the seven celestial rivers, the other arms being the other four sense perceptions and speech. And now an activity once initiated is repeated again and again to confirm the object unshakeably. This role of repeating activities was taken over by Ṛta. And now, from what we said above the object of the creator to know himself is not realised as this entails the simultaneous presence of both subject and object which however is not possible as it stands. So the creator was committed to unending activity which persisted even in the manifestation process.

(d) Evolution in the World of Ideas

The creator was compelled, therefore, by his own resolve, to produce ideas continually until the whole of the vast space was completely filled with ideas which were to take part in the subsequent manifestation. These ideas formed the foundation of knowledge. Knowledge furnished the basis for the evolution of creatures in the subtle world at first. Hundreds of the likenesses of all creatures were released from the depths of knowledge (321). This established the dharma for the subsequent manifestation. The Self or jīvas were born foremost in ancient times prior to Ṛta (594). Man was the first being to be created by Vaiśvānara possessing the sense of differentiation, the five sense perceptions and speech but without the scope to exercise these faculties till later (1,116). As manifestation was the ultimate goal and as that was not possible until the ideas reached the stage of matter, other creatures with less and less sense faculties were evolved. All the creatures which subsequently appeared on earth during manifestation were evolved now in prototype forms by suppressing at first speech, then hearing, then sight, smell and taste when the lowest forms of creatures were reached. Where only the sense of touch remained the stage of trees and plants was reached. The suppression of this sense too paved the way for the inanimate world. It must be borne in mind that the suppressed sense faculties remained latent in the creatures making the other faculties more acute. Agnideva sensed us in the story of creation and bestowed many creatures beginning with men (1,782). The Puruṣa bestows births of creatures first, unites with them, then he created the worlds (621).

(e) (i) Evolution of the Inanimate World of Ideas

Manifestation depends on matter or inertia equally with ideas, for life process is an association of both. But this matter of no external activity cannot be derived from ideas of unimaginable activity in one jump. Ideas have to slow down their activity in stages and it is during this process we come across the world of radiation and energies. Cosmic radiation, gamma, beta, alpha, x-Ray ultra-violet, light, infra-red, heat and sound are all varying forms of ideas more and more densely packed and in varied configurations accounting for their various properties. Then we come down to air, water and earth in which ideas are wholly deprived of external activity and in which the activity is internal with electrons spinning round a central nucleus. The Veda says that followers of Agni i.e. ideas were roped together to form impenetrable ignorance (matter) giving diverse guileless objects (1,748). The elements of the periodic table were formed in this manner, more and more ideas entering into the composition of the elements. Automatic radiation in elements like uranium indicates that excess of ideas had been packed in, leading to their escape from imprisonment. The world of energies and matter were evolved out of ideas thus. The external world of Stars, Sun, Moon and the planets with their contents were evolved thus. This external world is constituted only of the percepts of the creatures and hence it came into existence after the creatures. Anyhow all energies and all matter exist only as ideas at times. All the properties which they are endowed with are percepts of the creatures induced by the creator. (e) (i) The descent from ideas to matter *through energy* is our own inference and is not expressly stated in the Veda. But we consider it a reasonable inference. The stage was now set for manifestation.

(ii) Since man was the first creature to be created and since the manifestation terminated with man, the Veda considers man as having undergone the travails of experiences through the various stages of evolution.

(f) Time Involved in Evolution

We have some means of ascertaining with reasonable guesses the period that has expired since manifestation began. We assign it a period of 4,000 to 5,000 million years. But we have no means of even guessing at the period taken for evolution in the subtle plane. But ideas function with unimaginable rapidity, far superior to the speed of light and other radiations. So, the period involved must have been very very little, perhaps a 100 years or less in our reckoning. The ideas had not to contend with inertia.

(g) Manifestation

In manifestation the various types of Jīvas or creatures with varying number of sense activities already evolved are provided with a shelter enclosing them, for them to engage in activity with the outside world. This shelter is the body with the sense organs. Agni bestowed sense objects on the jīvas in heaven who were browsing in ancient times and he bestowed on them ideas. He bestowed many youthful creatures freeing them from their slumber in the fight for life and honoured them with gifts from sense activities (1,782). What was hindering manifestation was Vṛtra or inertia of matter. Indra overpowered him in water and laid the foundation for life-activity.

(h) Cell Life

Cell organisms were the foremost to be organised in water. They are the building blocks of organised life. Agni invoked water and announced his desire to them for supporting the bodies of creatures with its latent heat (18). Water was chosen for organising cell life as it was easier to split it up and as the latent heat furnished the energy requirements. The first step in producing creatures taken by the creator was in the ocean waters (529). Life-activity in the form of these cells came into being when Vṛtra (inertia) in water was overcome, which was a hindrance (1,429). In ancient times the intelligence of Prajāpati perceived homes (cells) in water and he bestowed Activity to control them (1,495). Consciousness bestowed protection on the cells like lightning and also existence (1,496). In very ancient births Agni adorned the lives of the species (1,711). The protector of creatures nourishes all cells like milch cow (1,720). Indra assaulted the water for the sake of the cells desiring existence to the jīvas (1,858). Indra cut off the head of Namuci with the foam from the water of the oceans and won him for the bodies of creatures (211). See the explanations given under the mantra. The cells sprouted from water, Indra bestowed them, enveloped and roused them up (1,327). These cells grew combined and finally developed to become the brain. Devas (ideas) from heaven bestow wealth from the waters by overflowing and riding them which the brain cells sip (55). The earliest creatures of ancient times were very odd which the sense activities brought to light, on whom the brain depended (1,494).

(i) Plant Life

The cells gave rise to plant life in the waters at first and by the combined action of the wind and waves they were wafted ashore and in due course established plant life on land as well. Birth is the dharma of the yonder world which unites with life and grows with existence (90). In ancient times when the cells were without a mind as in plants Indra used to move to release impulses (1,677). The plants in which only the sense of differentiation and sense of touch were active initiated the process of building up a physical body. Indra ruled over them, over the sense activity and consciousness (1,678). They furnished the food for survival of the forms of life which followed them. The stationary trees and plants are sunk in fearful dependence and they rejoice to grow collectively (1,698). The ruddy rays of the sun are helpful to the plant kingdom (1,783). Prāṇa was not the cause of delighting manifestation in ancient times i.e. in plants, the sense of touch was the comrade of the sap (1,010). Plants do not have a mind as this comes into existence only through sense organs which the trees and plants do not have.

(j) Mobile Creatures

(*i*) Since trees and plants with a stationary existence were so utterly dependent on help from the other world for their existence, the creator conceived introducing mobile creatures who to some extent can help themselves by their own activity. This thought brought out the mobile creatures on earth which exist already in heaven as idea groups. In these mobile creatures the sense activities and Uṣas together with the external world (Varuṇa) and sense organs play mighty roles.

(*ii*) Vṛtra

In these mobile creatures matter formed part of the existence of the creatures. Known as Vṛtra in the Veda, it formed the outer shell or body providing a shelter and armour for the ideas within to have scope for their activity. At the same time this inertia had to be overcome within in the brain, before sense activities or ideas can function. Consciousness honours sense activities and strikes down Vṛtra through Indra (89). Consciousness honours the head after striking down and pushing away Vṛtra (126). Indra bestows understanding and supports it by opposing Vṛtra whom he struck down to give newer and newer forms of creatures (179). Indra after striking down Vṛtra makes him form the other half of creatures (181). Indra cut off the head of Namuci i.e. inertia and won him for the bodies of creatures (211). Indra strikes down Vṛtra for newer and newer creatures to be created (913). Life-activity came into being when Vṛtra was overcome, who was hindering it (1,429). Life-activity was born out of it and consciousness also took a hand at it (1,430). After Vṛtra is shattered and devoured the Aśvins turn round to Activity for establishing the brain (1,719). But it was Agni who first put down Vṛtra when he established cell life and plants and offered sense objects (4).

(*iii*) Agni-activity

After inertia is overcome, Activity or Vaiśvānara controlled by Agni established the mobile creatures on earth after the plant kingdom. Agni from heaven visualised a variety of creatures in the waters through ideas (629). Agni in ancient times ran to create many forms of creatures and bestowed his favours on mind through the nerves (69). Vaiśvānara has his source in Agni and man is his guest (67). The sense activities from the source preside over the brain and bestow it mightily from heaven to bring out creatures (77). Various colourful creatures are born of sense activities and then man enters (352). The sense activities are bestowed by the Aṅgiras' (Agni-activity and Aśvins) (1,641). Sindhu (sense activities) envelops us, subdivides itself into the five activities and bestows on the head impartially (1,652). All paths of sense activities were released in the early morning of creation in the waking state; consciousness arose in midday in man (1,754). In the early morning of creation Agni let in the motley sense activities (85). When the brain cells were young Agni established mammoth creatures (359). In ancient times when the brain cells were young, Agni established odd creatures from the source (1,250). Agni churns the external world through sense activities. Aditi rains ideas from Varuṇa's dominion through Indra (1,857). Alone Indra ran to the conflict of life and bestowed many youthful creatures (325).

(*iv*) Sense-organs

The sense activities function through the sense organs. These organs are developed progressively with higher and higher forms of life with greater complexities of life. The Veda does not expressly mention the sense organs of the very low forms of life. But as food is the basis of their lives and activity we can infer that they are all provided with a mouth for consuming food and some sort of breathing apparatus for taking in air for oxidising the food. The sense of taste and smell for selecting the food must have been developed in course of time. As we ascend the scale of evolution the sense of sight was imparted to the creatures first both for searching prey and to look out for enemies. The great Activity chose the sense of sight as desired by the creatures (303). Later on the creatures were equipped with ears as a further protection bestowed by heaven disclosing concealed enemies (1691). The sense of smell also falls in this category. The brain drinks the intoxicating honey, sense perception and there Indra supports the sense of hearing (356). The sense organs constituted though of matter (or ignorance) themselves are gateways to knowledge. They open the doors to the external world. Lastly when man came on the world scene he was endowed with the faculty of speech. Indra supports us by uniting with us; he mixes with all for yoking them to speech. The function of speech is to reveal the ideas stored or received by the brain. The Vedas were said to be revelations and what was meant by this was that the knowledge stored in the brains of men was revealed to the outside world through speech. Speech is said to be Agni's minister and it is speech that tells us that we are born from the source and appeared first in water (1,382).

(*v*) (*a*) Sense-perceptions—Ideas

Sense activities only establish a physical connection between the creator and the objects he created in the external world or the creatures. They do not reveal anything more. The sense activities are however accompanied by ideas from heaven and they make their imprint on the objects they meet with and give a content to them, when they become sense impressions or perceptions contributing to knowledge stored by the brain. Agni! You cultivate (educate) the devotee with ideas (11). Indra arouses sense activities to bestow sense perceptions creating forms of objects. What is available in the external world a moment before the first sense perception of an object is formed is a group of unformed ideas pell-mell fashion. The idea from heaven gives them a form and consolidates them to a specific object. Such contacts are repeated by Ṛta and the shape and content stabilised. Further contacts give rise to sense impressions in the creatures of a pure nature. It is well-known that ideas attach themselves to the brain, unite with it and strive to help the brain cells (170). Ideas nourish the sense organs praiseworthily (324). Every organ of the body is a home of ideas i.e. it is constituted of ideas and responds to other ideas (636). Ancient creatures sought ideas and these hastened to mind. Such Ideas either induced them to activities, or constituted their sense perceptions or added to the store of knowledge. Indra rains ideas boldly with Aditi (sense activities) in Varuṇa's dominion vigorously (1,857). Troops of ideas move to Indra from beyond emulating sense activities (1,860). In ancient times troops of ideas supported the body watching it like a swan steadily and unperturbed (770).

(*v*) (*b*) Sense-perceptions Tinged and Untinged

Although the objects of the external world remain constant they arouse differing reactions in the observing creatures or men, primarily tinged and untinged. The tinged sense reactions arise out of desires for which ideas are furnished by heaven through Soma. Soma is universal mind who fulfils the desires of the individual mind. The individual mind cultivates desires from sense perceptions with which it is fed and its longings are fulfilled by Soma allied to ideas from heaven furnished by Agni. The latent heat in the brain fluids shines and pleases the sense activities releasing them untiringly (1,385).

(*vi*) Nervous System

A miniature nervous system is already in evidence in the cell organisms. As these developed to a complicated brain as evolution progressed with higher and higher scale of beings with increasing number of sense organs a complicated system of nerves grow apace organised by Indra first to receive the sense activities from heaven and then distribute them among the brain cells and from there to spread them out selectively to the mind and sense organs, then to receive the sense perceptions and reactions from the external world and redistribute them among the brain cells and finally to pass them on to mind also. Rudra is said to be in charge of this nervous system. He is considered the younger brother of Indra who is in overall charge and who receives the sense activities from heaven for distribution. Among these nerves, the spinal cord with two long nerves commencing in the region of the rectum and running parallel, crossing at the base of the spine to opposite lobes of the brain, are the most important. These two nerves at the sides are said to be controlled, one by Indra and the left one by Viṣṇu. Normally Indra functions in conjunction with the left lobe of the brain and only when this lobe is damaged and rendered useless the right lobe of the brain and Viṣṇu come into operation. The function of these two nerves is to energise the brain cells and prepare them to receive sense activities from heaven and sense perceptions and reactions coming from the sense organs. The central spinal cord conveys messages from the brain to all parts of the body and conveys the reactions of all bodily cells to the brain. The Veda says that above the spinal cord unites with the brain like a river, the source i.e. heaven unites with it (143). The footless brain cells release us from ignorance (145). All paths of sense activities i.e. the nerves were released in the early morning of creation in the waking state (1,754).

(vii) Consciousness—Uṣas

We are not aware of all that goes on in the brain, the centre of all activities. These are all however transferred to mind by Indra through the nerves and then Uṣas or Consciousness, her father, reveals them to the mind of the creatures. This is the second birth for ideas, the first birth being in heaven. Consciousness with his full blaze of light is associated only with man. The feeble light of Uṣas is associated with all other creatures. The Veda says that in the early morning of creation in ancient times the effulgent consciousness looked within the head which gave us the waking state (20). Consciousness as a relative of Activity draws out the image of Savitā for existence, as men (1,547). Uṣas terminated herself in favour of consciousness when man appeared (1,725). In ancient times Uṣas sought to cut off her own activities (1,728). The highest Deva is consciousness bestowing the variegated rays on the sense activities, Savitā likewise created night and day (sleeping and waking states) (1,749). Consciousness arose in midday in man. The ruddy light of Uṣas protects the paths of sense perceptions of the new creatures (1756). The motley sense activities eagerly bestowed powerful atmospheric creatures in the earlier half of creation. Soma tells us that we men have descended along the line of animals (boar) (524).

(*viii*) Evolving New Creatures from Existing Ones

How the successive species of creatures in bewildering variety came on the world scene remains a mystery. Modern Evolutionists attribute it to random mutation and goal directed activity. It does not explain how the phenomena took place. The Sāma Veda gives a rational explanation. Since most of the creatures are womb-born, transformation must take place in the brains of an existing creature to influence the genes to be transmitted to the new creature.

Ideas relating to the new species awaiting manifestation in heaven enter the brain of a selected existing species and effect transformations in the brain cells without the knowledge of the creatures themselves. This happens when prāṇa is not in contact with the brain cells i.e. when prāṇa is on its downward journey to the body. So, the Veda says that the paths of the ideas are below consciousness (172). Agni helps to produce transformations (1,348). Viṣṇu nourished the new creatures with oblations; Indra and the Aśvins approached the creatures with ideas. Indra fosters the growth of only such creatures which have to continue existence and lets others become extinct (1,639). Man is anxious not to suffer transformations himself and says "let not the form of my body be changed to another form by Activity" (1,625). Prāṇa carves out new forms in the home with Tvaṣṭā (440). Besides the transformations in the brain cells the bone structure is also changed through ideas. For, it is said, according to the sacred ordinances of old times the bones of creatures were split and jointed for new creatures (244). Indra fosters life-activity in whatever creature which subsists and which he envelops (121).

(*ix*) Mind

Mind appeared in evolution with the advent of mobile life on earth. The individuality of a creature is known only from its own private experiences which together make up its mind. Mind is not strictly necessary for existence, as we do exist during sleep when mind is dissociated from the brain. Men are known to continue in existence during the state of Samādhi stretching over several days or when men go into a state of coma extending over several years even. Mind's presence is however necessary on other counts. Mind is like a nagging wife. It forms desires and goes on complaining about its wants, inadequacies and so forth and in this way it was instrumental in the creation of higher and higher species of creatures, with increasing number of sense organs and better equipped to face the battle of life. Continued evolution depended on it. And then it plays an even more important role in continuing existence after death. The brain with all its experiences is buried or burnt and it is only the mind, which knows all the current experiences and which are conveyed for an after-life. It fulfils the creator's purpose of continued existence. The Veda says that the brain and sense organs bestow on mind (622). Ancient creatures sought ideas and they hastened to mind (1,264). Indra! You bestow a new gift on women for which you arouse the girl and bestowing it guide it. (1,460).

(x) The Jīvas from heaven were born in ignorance (467). They gather knowledge only on this earth through the sense organs from the external world and from heaven, all as ideas. In the state of ignorance the brain is restive like a horse, Agni bestows a variety of gifts on it (1,871). The source itself is glad that its activity depends on ignorance being devoured to establish existence on earth (1,872).

8. Man and his Internal Activities

Man as well as all other creatures are sustained by universal Devas whose functions we speak of in physiological terms alone forgetting the divinities behind them. We realise however that the activities go on in spite of ourselves and that we cannot control except at grave risk to ourselves. There are a large number of mantras spread out on this aspect, too numerous to be presented in brief, but they are the activities of the following Devas:—

(a) Savitā is the arbiter of the destinies of the universe and the creatures and the stimulator of their activities. He is also known as Viṣṇu or worker and the equivalent of the later Brahman. He is immanent in all both subtle and gross. Unlike Brahman who is conceived to be in eternal repose, Savitā is eternally and incessantly active, sustaining the activity of every creature, sustaining all energies and the inertia of matter. In fact he is all these at all times. His various attributes or activities are personified as various divinities mentioned below.

(b) The Aśvins

The Aśvins have twin arms and are said to be the vehicle of Savitā by whom the creator is enabled to play the part of both subject and object moving along one arm to be the momentary object and returning along the other arm to resume being the subject. The Aśviṇs also bridge two levels of activities transforming each other and assist the other Devas. They carry on the cooking of the various component parts of the body translating ideas into matter. By virtue of their twin arms they are often referred to by cloven footed animals like sheep, goat etc. in the Veda.

(c) Consciousness

The creator next brought consciousness into being to bestow all his beneficences on the creatures by revealing them and so consciousness is termed his hands. Consciousness brings out the identity of the universal with the particular and the differences among the particulars themselves. It is an instantaneous activity.

(d) Agni

Agni is the flaming zeal for activity and knowledge. This furnishes the basis for every activity of man and the creator included. This aspect of Savitā is the leader of the Devas and organiser of the creatures and the worlds.

(c) Activity

Activity also known as Vaiśvānara or seven Ṛṣis or celestial rivers, is the basic activity establishing the creatures and the worlds contributing to their knowledge. This Activity is constituted of seven limbs or illuminating principles namely: (1) sense of differentiation as subject and object; (2) the five sense perceptions also known as Aditi, Sarasvatī etc.; and (3) speech which releases ideas of the brain to the external world.

(f) Indra

Indra is the architect of the bodies of creatures. Agni inspires activity through the seven ṛṣis but it is Indra who is directly involved in breaking up matter, overcoming inertia and building up bodies with the help of Aśvins and ideas. Ideas are the building blocks of the body. He builds up the nervous system too and Indra's younger brother Rudra is said to be the leader of the nervous system. The spinal cord and the afferent and efferent nerves are together known as the three Ṛbhus who are said to be the first to reach heaven (head or brain) from the terrestrial world (body). Indra is also known as the Bull, Destroyer of a hundred forts etc. and is the universal prāṇa. Indra comprises the five prāṇas (1) Udāna, (2) Prāṇa, (3) Apāna, (4) Samāna, and (5) Vyāna.

(g) Soma

Soma is the universal mind sustaining Activity through his reacting with desires instructed by Agni. Activity and Soma sustain each other and neither can function without the other. Soma representing desires has sway over all creatures. So desires discarded by some take hold of others as their victims. Desires unfulfilled in the current life are carried over by Soma to the next.

(h) Prāṇa

Prāṇa is the controller of individual bodies representing Indra. Prāṇa controls the body by inciting the brain cells and functioning through the nervous system. We have explained under mantra 1,685 the five-fold activity of Indra of which prāṇa is one. This prāṇa actuates the brain cells towards receiving sense impressions from outside or calls from inside the body. Prāṇa does this by ascending along one of the two long nerves running parallel to the spinal cord on either side of it and cross each other at above neck level and ascend to both sections of the brain. The nerve on the right side of the spinal cord is traversed by Indra-Prāṇa and the one on the left, which comes into operation when the left section of the brain becomes inoperative due to damage to it, is under the control of Viṣṇu. Regarding the other prāṇas please see the explanations under mantra 1,685. The prāṇa is called the horse (aśva) which draws the chariot (body) and Indra is the charioteer.

(i) **Mind**

Mind is the individual man or creature sustained by the universal Devas who impart all their gifts to the brain and carry on their activities; impart knowledge and understanding to it. The brain in turn imparts all these to the Mind. Ordinarily we attribute all subtle activities to Mind whereas they all emanate from Soma who acquaints Mind with them through the brain. Mind comprises sense perceptions, sense reactions and desires.

(j) **Mitra**

Mitra is the brain comprising the brain cells variously referred to as grains, drops, caves and the nerve fibres referred to as grass, hair, threads etc. The brain too is referred to as fat, porridge etc. The brain may be said to be the computer of the creator who feeds the brain and sustains it to carry on life-activity through his assistants. The brain mediates between the universal Devas and the external world and acts as a central exchange between them. All the universal Devas enter the brain through the skull which is not impervious to them.

(k) **Varuṇa**

The whole of the external world, of land, seas and air is referred to as Varuṇa. Ideas of the external world conveyed by the perceptions are imparted to Mitra so that Varuṇa resides in Mitra as ideas and so these two Devas are always spoken together. Varuṇa is said to be a stern upholder of truth in the sense that he presents for cognition ideas invested with form and substance so that there can be no mistake about them.

(l) **Viśvedevas**

The brain-cells like the stars in the sky are referred to as Viśvedevas.

(m) **Devas Maruts**

Ideas are referred to by these names. Ideas form the building blocks of the non-material and the material worlds. Devas are said to have been slaughtered, by depriving them of their natural activity, in building up the bodies of creatures which need inertia to retain their forms.

(n) Vṛtra, Vala, Namuci etc.

These Asuras or non-Devas represent matter which is another class of ideas deprived of their natural voluntary activity by which they acquire inertia or inactivity which is so essential for life-activity to be carried on successfully. In the course of evolution in the subtle plane in heaven the jīvas shed one perceptive faculty after another, which successively became latent, until all seven became latent reaching the state of matter but still remaining an idea floating about in space like the rest of the ideas. A legend in the Purāṇas says that Indra smote down these floating inert ideas to settle down as land, mountains and rivers. It is evidently a picturesque way of describing what took place subsequently to the inert ideas by getting very densely packed by cohesive forces among them variously as land, sea and air of various groups of ideas. Perhaps the radioactivity of some of the higher elements of matter is an effort at breaking free from this repressed state presaging life-activity to follow with the cooperation of matter.

The characteristic of matter is that it preserves carefully what is entrusted to it. This essential feature contributes to memory in the brain cells without which life-activity would be impossible. This matter forms a protective shell in the shape of a head and body. Man and the other creatures represent a cooperative activity of ideas and matter. Incidentally light and other forms of energy are also degraded forms of ideas of less intensive activity and they occupy an intermediate place between ideas and matter.

9. Some Special Expressions

Some of the expressions used in the Veda have been misunderstood leading to wrong interpretations. Hence we give below some of the expressions and what they truly indicate.

(1) Head : This is referred to as heaven, the rock, hill, assembly and ocean.
(2) Body : cow, corpse, buffalo, earth, land, prison.
(3) Brain : hṛdaya, broth, porridge, sky
(4) Brain cells : stars, Viśvedevas, drops, corn
(5) Nerves : grass, hair, thread, snakes, reeds, cobwebs.
(6) Spinal cord : snake, pillar, ahi, crossbeam, tree.

(7) Skull : pipru
(8) Prāṇa : aśva (horse), trita; trita āptya means activity moving in all three states.
(9) Yajña, yaja, Soma yajña: life-activity.

10. Misconception about S.V. and Y.V. Originating from R.V.

The current belief among scholars is that the Ṛg Veda is the oldest Veda and that the other two Vedas have borrowed to a very great extent from it. Except for 75 mantras in S.V. and about 220 in Y.V. all the rest are ascribed to R.V. How wrong, these notions are can be seen from the following considerations.

(1) We have already shown that the S.V. and Y.V. spring from inter-glacial times whereas R.V. is of the period of solar and lunar dynasty kings say about 5,000 to 4,000 B.C. which separates them by 5,000 years.

(2) The two older Vedas are of Arctic origin and vested with the Devas and Asuras who were of a different race from the patriarchs and their descendants in whom the R.V. was vested in Indian soil.

(3) While the whole of the Ṛg Veda has been ascribed to some 400 Ṛṣis, the S.V. and Y.V. claim to be of traditional origin and no ṛṣis are mentioned about them.

(4) The three Vedas have wholly different outlook and goals and approaches to life. Sāma Veda stresses only prayers for release to the original home in heaven and had not conceived yajña. The Yajur Veda introduced the yajña ritual and believed in life on earth and prayed for return to this earth again and again. Both S.V. and Y.V. deal with evolution and the activities of the Devas in our brain and body. The S.V. deals more with perceptions whereas the Y.V. deals more with Mind. The Ṛg Veda comprises thoughts and aspirations of a more sophisticated age with different outlook on life and living. It deals with different paths for salvation such as bhakti, karma, mysticism, yoga and wisdom.

(5) The Ṛg Veda has adopted 1,443 mantras from Sāma Veda and 481 from Y.V. actually. In the Bhagavad Gītā Kṛṣṇa says "of the Vedas I am Sāma Veda". He did not cite Ṛg

Veda. Some of the mantras of Sāma Veda have been adopted by more than one Ṛṣi.

(1)	S.V. 1208	R.V. IX.25.6	Dṛḍahacyuta Āgastya
	do	„ 50.4	Ucathya Āṅgirasa
(2)	S.V. 1,167	VIII.11.8	Vatsa Kāṇva
	do	„ 43.21	Virūpa Āṅgirasa
(3)	S.V. 76	III.7.11	Gādhino Viśvāmitra
	do	do 15.7	Utkīla Kātya
	do	do 23.5	Devaśravā Devavātaśca
(4)	S.V. 169/682	IV.31.1	Vāmadeva Gautama
	do	VII.32.23	Maitrāvaruṇī Vaśiṣṭha

11. Repetition of Mantras

There are 222 mantras as given in App. VII which are repeated. But in many cases the mantras are addressed to a different Deva, sometimes a different meaning is conveyed when so addressed.

12. In App. IX, we have grouped the mantras according to each Deva which are not presented in one block but scattered over the whole Veda indicating that mantras about every Deva were added from time to time establishing a tradition. The number of mantras devoted to the various Devas are follows:—

(1) Savitā 29, (2) Aśvins 31; (3) Consciousness/Uṣas 125; (4) Agni 328; (5) Activity/seven Ṛṣis 80; (6) Indra/prāṇa 658; (7) Soma/Mind 251; (8) Mitra 53; (9) Varuṇa 8; (10) Jīva 72; (11) Ṛta 10; (12) Devas/Maruts 36; (13) Soma Juice 36; (14) Tvaṣṭṛ 3; (15) Water 3; (16) Vṛtra 8; (17) Speech 12; (18) Nerves 31; (19) Head and body 39, Miscellaneous 60. Total 1,873.

13. An Earlier Race of Men

The Veda mentions having known a race of men in Mantra 322 who appear to be a super-human type from the brief description given. This contradicts the Western anthropologists' view of early man as a semi-savage brute. We may pause to consider what must have really taken place in the course of evolution. The first men from a descendant of a gorilla were more of god-like type rather than savage. We know from our own experience that a dunce begets a genius and a genius begets a dunce. So, as the Veda says, the early man must have been a superman and his descendants degenerated to a savage state due to natural calamities as had been foretold in the Yajur Veda to the Devas and Asuras at the advent of glaciation in Tretã yuga. After all the same Intelligence pervades both the genius and the savage and how they come about depends on the creator and the environment.

14. The Brain

The Veda also admits of two halves of the brain, only one of which is in operation in normal waking hours. The other half affords a 100 per cent reserve. As we said earlier the left half of the brain is under the control of Indra and the right half under Viṣṇu. The left side of the brain holds only current life experiences while the right section holds both the current and the unfulfilled longings from the past life. External impulses arising from heaven or from the world of matter split into two and feed both halves of the brain. What is carried from previous life breaks out in a man's career suddenly when it is most propitious. This alone can explain sudden changes for the good or bad in every man's life time at some point of time. All repressed desires probably are also stored in the right half of the brain giving us a conception of a sub-conscious Mind. In dreams the right section of the brain comes into play bringing in experiences of earlier lives.

15. Translation of the Veda

There are no doubt a few translations of the Veda already in the field and some bhãṣyas (commentaries) in Sanskrit by Sãyaṇa and in Hindi by Bhagavadacharya and Satavalekar. The English translation is by R.T.H. Griffith who has largely been influenced by Sãyaṇa. There is also an English translation by Devichand which is a re-translation from Hindi by Swami Dayanand Sarasvati, founder of the Arya Samaj. These English translations, a few of which have been cited in Appendix VIII as examples, do not convey much sense most often. They are abstruse, distorted in sense and oftentimes absurd also. They do not present a consistent system of thought on which the Veda should have been based. They do not tell us definitely what the functions of the various Devas are. The Veda repeatedly affirms that the Devas are engaged in Yajña establishing the creatures and the worlds. Nowhere is this basic fact been brought out in these translations. Although this Veda has been acclaimed as the best among all the four books of knowledge, one cannot get this impression by reading these translations. We are struck with many absurdities in them. We, therefore, felt that the Veda should be rescued and restored to its proper preeminent place by a fresh translation. In whatever other ways a number of mantras could be translated, for which the Veda easily lends itself, both by reason of brevity of expression and improper transcription from chanting to writing, they would be valueless unless they jointly present a consistent picture. Our claim is that the Veda lends itself to be correctly translated as we have done which establishes the aims of the Veda unmistakably namely about the yajña (life-activity) conducted by the Devas for manifestation of the creatures and maintaining them. Our guiding light has been the belief in the wisdom of the ancients who desired to preserve their thoughts for future generations having been convinced of their eternal value.

16. The Destiny of Man

The Sāma Veda conceives of man's destiny differently from the Upaniṣads and later śāstras. These latter hold, what is to a large extent accepted by the Hindus even now, that man, after endless births and experiences secures wisdom and extinction by merging with the creator. If this is to be his destiny then why should the creator have taken the trouble to evolve him? At the same time it is argued by them that the individual self is at all times one with the Supreme Self, which remains unknown until wisdom dawns. This means only that there never is an individual soul, then who is to merge?

The Sāma Veda presents two different concepts namely: (1) that all that exists and that may come in the future too are nought but the Puruṣa known as Savitā or Viṣṇu. All activity belongs to him and he manifests himself as all creatures and the worlds. (2) He creates man in his own image as a subtle being endowed with all seven principles of activity, who degenerates to lower forms by shedding one activity after another in the subtle world until he is devoid of all seven activities and reduced to the state of inanimate matter. Then the universal Devas pull him up through low forms of life rising higher and higher in the scale of existence reaching the stage of man finally. In this state he undergoes many trials and tribulations and longs to go back to his original heavenly home. He prays for it continually and finally gets back. After a time he is seized with a desire to return to earth and is born again as a human being and undergoes the fortunes of earthly existence. He does not merge with the creator at any time. This second view may be considered as identical with the first if it is taken that the conception of a jīva makes it easy to explain the processes of creation. Anyway the sole purpose of the creator is to continue activity and unending existence and towards this end he has diversified the activity with increasing sense perceptions. Activity alone ensures existence.

17. Prayers

The sole means to be resorted to by man, according to Sāma Veda, is prayers. These prayers take the form of extolling the various universal Devas for their varied activities in establishing the creatures, evolving and maintaining them all impartially. The devotee prays for an unimpaired life of a hundred years, in welfare, keen in perceptions and sound of limbs and in understanding. The aim of prayers is to keep in touch with the creator continually. Whether one prays or not the activities are always of the creator but by ever-recurring renewal of contacts with him life's burden can be borne lightly.

S.V. Ganapati
28-9-78

SĀMA VEDA

PART I

Āgneya Kāṇḍa

BOOK I: CHAPTER I

D. I.

१. अग्न आ याहि वीतये गृणानो हव्यदातये ।
नि होता सत्सि बर्हिषि ॥

1. Agni moves and arouses the desires of the devotee for and bestows oblations.

He presides down below in existence and binds us with desires to the motley sense activities. (1)

२. त्वमग्ने यज्ञानां होता विश्वेषां हितः ।
देवेभिर्मानुषे जने ॥

2. Agni! You preside over yajña (life-activity) and bestow the desire for welfare on the home,

and support the homes of men eagerly through devas. (2)

३. अग्निं दूतं वृणीमहे होतारं विश्ववेदसम् ।
अस्य यज्ञस्य सुक्रतुम् ॥

3. Agni chooses great (or victorious) messengers to preside and gladdens the devotee by bestowing,

and to do good in our yajña. (3)

४. अग्निर्वृत्राणि जङ्घनद् द्रविणस्युर्विपन्यया ।
समिद्धः शुक्र आहुतः ॥

4. Agni strikes down Vṛtra (inertia) resoundingly to inspire us extensively through wealth and guide us,

and offers flaming fuelsticks (sense objects). (4), (1396)

५. प्रेष्ठं वो अतिथिं स्तुषे मित्रमिव प्रियम् ।
अग्ने रथं न वेद्यम् ॥

5. The guests (sense activities) bestow nourishment as desired praiseworthily with kindness like that of a friend.

Agni a hero controls knowledge. (5), (1244)

६. त्वं नो अग्ने महोभिः पाहि विश्वस्या अरातेः ।
उत द्विषो मर्त्यस्य ॥

6. Agni! You protect both (head and sense organs) greatly by arousing our homes and bestowing
the desires of men for both. (6)

७. एह्यू षु ब्रवाणि तेऽग्न इत्थेतरा गिरः ।
एभिर्वर्धास इन्दुभिः ॥

7. Agni! You behold the sense organs and tell them to cross over to the hill (brain).
They support and foster growth in brain cells. (7), (705)

८. आ ते वत्सो मनो यमत्परमाच्चित्सधस्थात् ।
अग्ने त्वां कामये गिरा ॥

8. They (the brain cells) control the child Mind in the assembly of the Supreme Intelligence.
Agni! The hill (brain) is your beloved. (8), (1166), (Y.V.12, 115)

९. त्वामग्ने पुष्करादध्यथर्वा निरमन्थत ।
मूर्ध्नो विश्वस्य वाघतः ॥

9. Agni! You produce prosperity through curds (sense reactions), then hasten below to churn and release them
in the head (brain) through the sense organs of the devotee. (9), (Y.V.11, 32)

It is the sense reactions which call for sense activities bringing prosperity. Like the milk turning to the irreversible form of curds, sense activities turn to sense reactions by the addition of desires.

१०. अग्ने विवस्वदा भरास्मभ्यमूतये महे ।
देवो ह्यसि नो दृशे ॥

10. Agni! You ride on us yourself, bestow on and support us and help us greatly,
with devas to look up and transform us. (10)

Agni is the leader of the devas and personifies the flaming zeal of Savitā, the creator, to activity to know himself. He is the flaming desire for life-activity.

D. II.

१. नमस्ते अग्न ओजसे गृणन्ति देव कृष्टयः ।
अमैरमित्रमर्दय ॥

1. Agni! Obeisances, You cultivate the devotee with ideas (devas) within vigorously,

like a friend of the brain (hill) of mortals in compassion. (11), (1648)

२. दूतं वो विश्ववेदसं हव्यवाहममर्त्यम् ।
यजिष्ठमृञ्जसे गिरा ॥

2. The messengers bestow all knowledges of the cosmos (Viśva), conveying them as oblations to mortals.

Desiring life-activity (yaja) they strive for the brain (hill). (12)

३. उप त्वा जामयो गिरो देदिशतीर्हविष्कृतः ।
वायोरनीके अस्थिरन् ॥

3. Above, prāṇa is born of you in the brain (hill) to whom you give command (direction) to produce oblations to the brain,

which he stabilises through the nerves (Vāyu) below. (13),(1570)

४. उप त्वाग्ने दिवेदिवे दोषावस्तर्धिया वयम् ।
नमो भरन्त एमसि ॥

4. Agni! You bestow on us from above day after day the home (brain) to cross over (ignorance) with satisfaction.

We make obeisances to you for supporting and binding us to the path. (14) (Y.V. 3, 22)

५. जराबोध तद्विविड्ढि विशेविशे यज्ञियाय ।
स्तोमं रुद्राय दृशीकम् ॥

5. Old age bestows understanding of it in various ways on man after man (home after home) in life-activity,

which the nervous system (Rudra) loves to let us see (or reveals) praiseworthily. (15), (1663)

६. प्रति त्यं चारुमध्वरं गोपीथाय प्र हूयसे ।
मरुद्भिरग्न आ गहि ॥

6. They are well-known to nourish us and make life-activity agreeable and strive to invoke sense activities to nourish us.

Agni arouses sense activities (ga) to support them with ideas (Maruts). (16)

७. अश्वं न त्वा वारवन्तं वन्दध्या अग्निं नमोभिः ।
सम्राजन्तमध्वराणाम् ॥

7. Prāṇa (aśvaṁ)! You make obeisances to Agni to release curds within as desired, in the enclosure.

You are the supreme lord within in life-activity. (17)

८. और्वभृगुवच्छुचिमप्नवानवा हुवे ।
अग्नि समुद्रवाससम् ॥

8. Matter (earth) gives support to the body well as usual and Agni invokes Activity and announces his desire for it. Agni bestows joy on the entire home (brain) (Alt.). Agni invoked and announced his desire to water to give support to bodies as usual with the latent heat,

which resides in the ocean waters. (18)

This indicates origins of cell organisms created from water with the help of its latent heat.

९. अग्निमिन्धानो मनसा धियं सचेत मर्त्यः ।
अग्निमिन्धे विवस्वभिः ॥

9. Agni kindles my Mind and bestows satisfaction by uniting with the motley sense activities of mortals.

Agni himself rides on us and kindles. (19)

१०. आदित्प्रत्नस्य रेतसो ज्योतिः पश्यन्ति वासरम् ।
परो यदिध्यते दिवि ॥

10. In ancient times in the early morning (of creation) in the beginning, the effulgent consciousness bestowed his rays to look within (in the head),

from beyond, which kindled the waking state by uniting (with the brain). (20)

D. III.

१. अग्नि वो वृधन्तमध्वराणां पुरूतमम् ।
अच्छा नप्त्रे सहस्वते ।

1. Agni bestows abundant desires to grow within in life-activity.

They are near at hand as good vehicles for understanding, victoriously. (21), (946)

२. अग्निस्तिग्मेन शोचिषा यं सद्विश्वं न्य३त्रिणम् ।
अग्निर्नो वंसते रयिम् ॥

2. Agni is mightily passionately glowing, controls the home and guides the three states in the cosmos.

Agni bestows support to wealth (of sense activities). (22)

३. अग्ने मृड महाँ अस्यय आ देवयुं जनम् ।
इयेथ बर्हिरासदम् ॥

3. Agni is greatly compassionate towards us, the pious (devoted) men.

He bestows so much to strengthen us in the home. (23)

४. अग्ने रक्षा णो अंहसः प्रति स्म देव रीषतः ।
तपिष्ठैरजरो दह ॥

4. Agni! Protect us from distress with might, indeed counter them by bestowing devas (ideas) as desired.

Bestow the desire for tapas and burn away the aging process. (24)

५. अग्ने युङ्क्ष्वा हि ये तवाश्वासो देव साधवः ।
अरं वहन्त्याशवः ॥

5. Agni! You unite with the brain (home) and bestow (sense activities). Prāṇa arouses you and achieves devas (ideas) to be bestowed.

He is well-known to convey them along the spokeslike nerves to the sense organs (body). (25), (1383)

६. नि त्वा नक्ष्य विश्पते द्युमन्तं धीमहे वयम् ।
सुवीरमग्न आहुत ॥

6. (Agni!) You approach the path to the home and bestow on us much understanding of heaven within.

Agni incites vigour in us and makes offerings. (26)

७. अग्निर्मूर्धा दिवः ककुत्पतिः पृथिव्या अयम् ।
अपां रेतांसि जिन्वति ।

7. In the head of Agni (ruled by Agni) Consciousness is the lord of the summit and the path to the body (sense organs).

He supports the rays of Activity and wins knowledge. (27)

८. इममू षु त्वमस्माकं सनिं गायत्रं नव्यांसम् ।
अग्ने देवेषु प्र वोचः ॥

8. Here you have bestowed on us sense organs (body) as gift which support sense activities newly.

Agni! the devas (ideas) nourish the missiles of speech. (28), (1497)

९. तं त्वा गोपवनो गिरा जनिष्ठदग्ने अङ्गिरः ।
स पावक श्रुधी हवम् ॥

9. Agni! You desire to protect the wishes of sense activities to the brain (hill) born of the Aṅgiras (Activity),

and bestow them on the head to drink, to cook understanding as oblations. (29)

१०. परि वाजपतिः कविरग्निर्हव्यान्यक्रमीत् ।
दधद्रत्नानि दाशुषे ॥

10. The lord of life-activity (Indra) goes around to guide the new oblations of the poet Agni, in due course,

and bestows valuable gifts eagerly on the devotees. (30)

११. उदु त्यं जातवेदसं देवं वहन्ति केतवः ।
दृशे विश्वाय सूर्यम् ॥

11. It is well-known that all knowledge takes its rise above (in heaven), devas convey us desires.

Consciousness (Sūrya) moves, perceives all and bestows on the home. (31), (Y.V. 7, 41)

१२. कविमग्निमुप स्तुहि सत्यधर्माणमध्वरे ।
देवममीवचातनम् ॥

12. The wise Agni is praised for arousing the sense of existence above in accordance with dharma of life-activity.

The deva moves to guide us also. (32)

१३. शं नो देवीरभिष्टये शं नो भवन्तु पीतये ।
शं योरभि स्रवन्तु नः ॥

13. The devi (Aditi) embraces us willingly (or as desired) if we are parched up (of sense activities), if withered we drink of her in existence (or for) within.

She toils extensively to flow and bind us. (33), (Y. V. 36. 12)

१४. कस्य नूनं परीणसि धियो जिन्वसि सत्पते ।
गोषाता यस्य ते गिरः ॥

14. Now she associates herself with our brain (head) and bestows to drink to satisfaction and wins the path for existence.

The sense activities sharpen it; it swallows them. (34)

D. IV.

१. यज्ञायज्ञा वो अग्नये गिरागिरा च दक्षसे ।
प्रप्र वयममृतं जातवेदसं प्रियं मित्रं न शंसिषम् ॥

1. In life after life Agni bestows satisfaction also on every man.

He nourishes and fulfils us mortals by letting all knowledge to be born in friendliness to the brain (Mitra) who praises him willingly. (35), (703), (Y.V. 27, 42)

२. पाहि नो अग्न एकया पाह्यु३त द्वितीयया ।
पाहि गीर्भिस्तिसृभिरूर्जाम्पते पाहि चतसृभिर्वसो ॥

2. Agni! You arouse us in the first place to drink (sense activities); secondly you show us also the path;

thirdly you are attached to the hill and arouse it to drink nourishment from the Lord of nourishment and; fourthly you support the home. (36), (1544), (Y. V. 27, 43)

३. बृहद्भिरग्ने अर्चिभिः शुक्रेण देव शोचिषा ।
भरद्वाजे समिधानो यविष्ठ्य रेवत्पावक दीदिहि ॥

3. Agni supports and honours the brightly shining deva consciousness.

He supports the kindling fuel (sense perceptions) in life-activity which love the brain-cells; he beams down on the wealth (of sense activities) and releases them in the head to drink. (37).

४. त्वे अग्ने स्वाहुत प्रियासः सन्तु सूरयः ।
यन्तारो ये मघवानो जनानामूर्वं दयन्त गोनाम् ॥

4. Agni! You have invoked yourself here, you bestow on us gifts in kindness arousing streams of them.

Indra (Maghavan) guides men extensively to sense activities to cross over (ignorance) in compassion. (38), (Y.V. 33, 14)

५. अग्ने जरितर्विश्पतिस्तपानो देव रक्षसः ।
अप्रोषिवान् गृहपते महाँ असि दिवस्पायुर्दुरोणयुः ॥

5. Agni! The Lord of the home (Activity) bestows protection on the devotees through the drinks (sense activities) offered by the devas.

The Lord of the home fulfils their desires eagerly; consciousness is great fulfilling extensively by uniting with the brain (head). (39)

६. अग्ने विवस्वदुषसश्चित्रं राधो अमर्त्य ।
आ दाशुषे जातवेदो वहा त्वमद्या देवाँ उषर्बुधः ॥

6. Agni! Uṣas (Dawn) rides over and achieves a variety of wealth of sweet perceptions to mortals.

You convey eagerly to the devotees knowledge which takes birth, through the sense perceptions wonderfully. (40), (1780)

७. त्वं नश्चित्र ऊत्या वसो राधांसि चोदय ।
अस्य रायस्त्वमग्ने रथीरसि विदा गाधं तुचे तु नः ॥

7. Agni! You help the home (brain) to achieve a variety of wealth which you support to rise up.

You are our king; you are the charioteer knowing the sense activities in the home to whom you bind the mind. (41), (1623)

८. त्वमित्सप्रथा अस्यग्ने त्रातर्ऋतः कविः ।
त्वां विप्रासः समिधान दीदिव आ विवासन्ति वेधसः ॥

8. Agni! You are a pillar to us and extend your support to us; you support Ṛta; you inspire and bestow on us sense objects (fuel-sticks) on which consciousness shines and riding on them bestows on devotees as gifts. (42)

९. आ नो अग्ने वयोवृधं रयिं पावक शंस्यम् ।
रास्वा च न उपमाते पुरुस्पृहं सुनीती सुयशस्तरम् ॥

9. Agni now fosters our growth, bestows wealth (of sense activities) to drink and controls praiseworthily.

He himself bestows highest gladness; they arouse and guide us with abundant eagerness to cross over (ignorance) excellently. (43)

१०. यो विश्वा दयते वसु होता मन्द्रो जनानाम् ।
मधोर्न पात्रा प्रथमान्यस्मै प्र स्तोमा यन्त्वग्नये ॥

10. Indra (Vasu) presides over the sense organs in compassion and skilfully allots (the sense activities of men) to them.

He supports and fulfils (our needs) munificently and is the most important deva for us he guides us praiseworthily, O Agni! (44), (1583)

D. V.

१. एना वो अग्निं नमसोर्जो नपातमा हुवे ।
प्रियं चेतिष्ठमरतिं स्वध्वरं विश्वस्य दूतममृतम् ॥

1. Then Agni bestows nourishment on the descendants (sense organs) who invoke and bow to him.

Then the immortal messengers themselves gladden the sense organs very brightly in kindness in life activity. (45), (749)

२. शेषे वनेषु मातृषु सं त्वा मर्तास इन्धते ।
अतन्द्रो हव्यं वहसि हविष्कृत आदिद्देवेषु राजसि ॥

2. (Agni!) You bestow on mortals all their residual desires through the missiles (rays) of the mother and kindle them.

You convey the oblations unweariedly; the ancient deva (Savitā) creates the oblations which control and bind us. (46)

३. अदर्शि गातुवित्तमो यस्मिन्व्रतान्यादधुः ।
उपोषु जातमार्यस्य वर्धनमग्निं नक्षन्तु नो गिरः ॥

3. Knowing the desires of the devotee you visit them and bestow his vows.

Man's desires for the sense organs are born hereabove, which Agni approaches on the hill (brain) and fosters. (47), (1515)

४. अग्निरुक्थे पुरोहितो ग्रावाणो बर्हिरध्वरे ।
ऋचा यामि मरुतो ब्रह्मणस्पते देवा अवो वरेण्यम् ॥

4. Agni presides over the motley sense activities (barhi) on the hill praiseworthily in life. Soma, lord of knowledge praises ideas (Maruts), his relatives, whom he favours us with excellently. (48)

५. अग्निमीडिष्वावसे गाथाभिः शीरशोचिषम् ।
अग्निं राये पुरुमीढ श्रुतं नरोग्निः सुदीतये छर्दिः ॥

5. Agni favours with oblations as desired by the devotees through the sharp and glowing rays (of sense activities).

Agni has control over abundant rewards; he listens to men. Agni beams down, arouses and bestows (vomits). (49)

६. श्रुधि श्रुत्कर्ण वह्निभिर्देवैरग्ने सयावभिः ।
आ सीदतु बर्हिषि मित्रो अर्यमा प्रातर्यावभिरध्वरे ॥

6. The ears hear sacred knowledge (tradition) and set up satisfaction. Agni conveys and supports the brain cells by bestowing ideas (devas). In the early morning of creation Indra (Aryamā) supported the brain cells (yāva) through his friends, the motley sense activities in the home. (50), (Y.V. 33, 15)

७. प्र दैवोदासो अग्निर्देव इन्द्रो न मज्मना ।
अनु मातरं पृथिवीं वि वावृते तस्थौ नाकस्य शर्मणि ॥

7. Agni nourishes his devotees with ideas (devas) through deva Indra's majesty.

Now the mother gladdens the sense organs, rides and envelops them and protects them from heaven. (51), (517)

८. अध ज्मो अध वा दिवो बृहतो रोचनादधि ।
अया वर्धस्व तन्वा गिरा ममा जाता सुक्रतो पृण ॥

8. Then Consciousness shines very brightly and bestows satisfaction by favouring us with the path (in life).

He himself grants us prosperity (vardha), guides on the hill; he does us good from the source and satisfies. (52)

९. कायमानो वना त्वं यन्मातॄरजगन्नपः ।
न तत्ते अग्ने प्रमृषे निवर्तनं यद् दूरे सन्निहाभुवः ॥

9. Prajapati (Kāya) is fond of the home (brain) and guides you (consciousness) to the mother bestowed on the world through Activity.

The ṛṣis (Activity) who are distant are turned down by Agni and he dances about and nourishes us and bestows gifts here for existence. (53)

१०. नि त्वामग्ने मनुर्दधे ज्योतिर्जनाय शश्वते ।
दीदेथ कण्व ऋतजात उक्षितो यं नमस्यन्ति कृष्टयः ॥

10. Agni! You bestow extensively on Mind down below; guidance flows constantly to men from the effulgent Consciousness.

The motley sense activities (etha) bestow on the brain cells; Ṛta from the source, strengthens them, controls, honours, guides and cultivates. (54)

BOOK I : CHAPTER II

D. I.

१. देवो वो द्रविणोदाः पूर्णां विवष्ट्वासिचम् ।
उद्वा सिञ्चध्वमुप वा पृणध्वमादिद्वो देव ओहते ॥

1. The devas bestow wealth from waters by overflowing and riding them which the dwellers (brain cells) sip gaining fulfilment.

That which is bestowed buzzes along above, which the two ancient devas bestowed for transformations (ohata). (55)

२. प्रैतु ब्रह्मणस्पतिः प्र देव्येतु सूनृता ।
अच्छा वीरं नर्यं पङ्क्तिराधसं देवा यज्ञं नयन्तु नः ॥

2. Soma (Brahmaṇaspati) nourishes with the motley sense activities; the sense activities nourish men by arousing them.

The deva guides the wealth of five sense activities of men within, in the yajña, to bestow vigour. (56)

३. ऊर्ध्व ऊ षु ण ऊतये तिष्ठा देवो न सविता ।
ऊर्ध्वो वाजस्य सनिता यदञ्जिभिर्वाघद्भिर्विह्वयामहे ॥

3. The brain (head) above helps the sense organs (in the body) as desired by them by stimulating ideas.

The brain bestows gifts on them in life which adorn and support the devotee with much oblations. (57)

४. प्र यो राये निनीषति मर्तो यस्ते वसो दाशत् ।
स वीरं धत्ते अग्न उक्थशंसिनं त्मना सहस्रपोषिणम् ॥

4. Agni! You control the nourishment which the mortals below desire, for whom you strive to serve in the home.

Agni! You bestow on them vigour praiseworthily and are spoken about; you yourself nourish them mightily with thousands of items. (58)

५. प्र वो यह्वं पुरूणां विशां देवयतीनाम् ।
अग्निं सूक्तेभिर्वचोभिर्वृणीमहे यं समिदन्य इन्धते ॥

5. You bestow abundant nourishment on the restless brain cells; the devas unite with them mightily in the home.

Agni praiseworthily supports speech and supports greatly to

nourish it; he controls and bestows on the brain, guides it and incites it. (59)

६. अयमग्निः सुवीर्यस्येशे हि सौभगस्य ।
राय ईशे स्वपत्यस्य गोमत ईशे वृत्रहथानाम् ॥

6. Agni is the path; he arouses vigour in us and rules arousing welfare in us.

He controls and rules along his path; he is rich in sense activities (cows); he rules after striking down Vṛtra (inertia). (60)

७. त्वमग्ने गृहपतिस्त्वं होता नो अध्वरे ।
त्वं पोता विश्ववार प्रचेता यक्षि यासि च वार्यम् ॥

7. Agni! You are the lord of the home; you preside over life-activity.

You fulfil and also you are wealth to the sense organs (viśva); nourish the mind and quicken his pace and bind him to the wealth. (61)

८. सखायस्त्वा ववृमहे देवं मर्तास ऊतये ।
अपां नपातं सुभगं सुदंससं सुप्रतूर्तिमनेहसम् ॥

8. You help the devas to envelop and bestow on us much and bestow help on the mortals.

Activity arouses the sense organs (descendants) to consciousness (bhaga) and arouses all wondrous things, nourishes them well to encourage and help the mind. (62)

D. II.

१. आ जुहोता हविषा मर्जयध्वं नि होतारं गृहपतिं दधिध्वम् ।
इडस्पदे नमसा रातहव्यं सपर्यता यजतं पस्त्यानाम् ॥

1. Mortals win oblations in life from the tongues (of sense activities) which preside below and gladden as lord of the home and run to give satisfaction.

They are the steps for oblations which they release and honour us, give us services in life in the home. (63)

२. चित्र इच्छिशोस्तरुणस्य वक्षथो न यो मातरावन्वेति धातवे ।
अनूधा यदजीजनदधा चिदा ववक्षत्सद्यो महि दूत्यां३ चरन् ॥

2. If desires dry up they cause a variety of them grow like

a tree, guided by the mother who releases desires and bestows knowledge.

Now they bestow what wins and gives to men, which build up (ci) and bestows, bestows to grow strong at once greatly and go around as messengers. (64)

३. इदं त एकं पर उ त एकं तृतीयेन ज्योतिषा सं विशस्व ।
संवेशनस्तन्वे३चारुरेधि प्रियो देवानां परमे जनित्रे ॥

3. Here you are one (i.c. sense activities), there is one beyond (Savitā), the third one is consciousness, all of them for the home itself.

All enter the home to bestow and guide; they gladden us kindly with prosperity; thc devas are born in yonder region. (65)

४. इमं स्तोममर्हते जातवेदसे रथमिव सं महेमा मनीषया ।
भद्रा हि नः प्रमतिरस्य सं सद्यग्ने सख्ये मा रिषामा वयं तव ॥

4. Here praises are appropriate for bestowing knowledge to be born like being conveyed in a vehicle; all of them gladden men.

They arouse welfare, bind us to nourishment for our understanding; they all help us at once, do not hurt us; we belong to you. (66), (1064)

५. मूर्धानं दिवो अरतिं पृथिव्या वैश्वानरमृत आ जातमग्निम् ।
कविं सम्राजमतिथिं जनानामासन्नः पात्रं जनयन्त देवाः ॥

5. Consciousness from the head above gladdens the sense organs; Vaiśvānara (cosmic man or Activity) the immortal has Agni as source.

In the sovereign region of poet Agni men are guests and competent to be near him; the devas guide men. (67), (1140)

६. वि त्वदापो न पर्वतस्य पृष्ठादुक्थेभिरग्ने जनयन्त देवाः ।
तं त्वा गिरः सुष्टुतयो वाजन्त्याजिं न गिर्ववाहो जिग्युरश्वाः ॥

6. Activity is not spoken of as the foremost to support us on the hill without you. Agni! The devas guide men.

You are desirous of the brain (hill), appropriately; it is well-known that you are victorious in life; prāṇa unites victoriously with the brain and conveys extensively to bestow. (68)

७. आ वो राजानमध्वरस्य रुद्रं होतारं सत्ययजं रोदस्योः ।
अग्निं पुरा तनयित्नोरचित्ताद्धिरण्यरूपमवसे कृणुध्वम् ॥

7. Rudra, the nervous system controls us in life, presides truly in life over both brain and sense organs.

Agni in ancient times ran to create many forms of creatures bestowing his favours and guided them (through the nerves) to Mind to satisfy and gladden him. (69)

८. इन्धे राजा समर्यो नमोभिर्यस्य प्रतीकमाहुतं घृतेन ।
नरो हव्येभिरीडते सबाध आग्निरग्रमुषसामशोचि ॥

8. The king (controller i.e. Rudra) kindles the assembly (brain); obeisances to him; the head (ka) offers him clarified butter for nourishment.

He supports the oblations of men and bestows soma juice (Sava), which Agni earlier bestows eagerly on us glowingly. (70)

९. प्र केतुना बृहता यात्यग्निरा रोदसी वृषभो रोरवीति ।
दिवश्चिदन्तादुपमामुदानडपामुपस्थे महिषो ववर्ध ॥

9. Agni is well-known to move towards the forms of objects greatly to nourish and Indra bestows on both brain and sense organs for their sake.

Consciousness bestows their images (upamā) on the mind within; Indra the charioteer gladdens by bestowing on him through the nerves and fulfils and fosters. (71)

१०. अग्निं नरो दीधितिभिररण्योर्हस्तच्युतं जनयत प्रशस्तम् ।
दूरेदृशं गृहपतिमथव्युम् ॥

10. Agni beams on men and satisfies by supporting and gladdening extensively letting sense perceptions from his hands (sense activities) by uniting with men praiseworthily.

He looks far ahead as lord of the home and churns us with sense activities. (72), (1373)

D. III.

१. अबोध्यग्निः समिधा जनानां प्रति धेनुमिवायतीमुषासम् ।
यह्वा इव प्र वयामुज्जिहानाः प्र भानवः सस्रते नाकमच्छ ॥

1. Agni awakes us to kindling fuel (sense objects) and nourishes men with them by letting the milch cow (sense activities) approach through the nerves eagerly.

They nourish us restlessly and victoriously; consciousness flowing from heaven nearby lets them nourish. (73)

२. प्र भूर्जयन्तं महां विपोधां मूरैरमूरं पुरां दर्माणम् ।
नयन्तं गीर्भिर्वना धियं धा हरिश्मश्रुं न वर्मणा धनर्चिम् ॥

2. The great consciousness bestowing inspiration on the sense activities won from the dull sense organs acute ideas of objects in ancient times in accordance with dharma.

He guides within and supports the hill (brain) and bestows satisfaction; the rays (beard) of the ruddy Consciousness bestowed protection and honoured the wealth (of the senses). (74)

३. शुक्रं ते अन्यद्यजतं ते अन्यद्विषुरूपे अहनी द्यौरिवासि ।
विश्वा हि माया अवसि स्वधावन्भद्रा ते पूषन्निह रातिरस्तु ॥

3. They (the sense activities) guide now the desires of life activity; they guide the forms of objects from all sides in day time (waking state), released from heaven; they bestowed and bound them (the objects).

They arouse the sense organs marvellously, bless their wishes at their own will for welfare; they gladden us here with prosperity. (75)

४. इडामग्ने पुरुदंसं सनिं गोः शश्वत्तमं हवमानाय साध ।
स्यान्नः सूनुस्तनयो विजावाग्ने सा ते सुमतिर्भूत्वस्मे ॥

4. Agni! the sense activities bestow gifts of oblations wondrously in abundance and accomplish to bestow desire for oblations in the home constantly.

They guide the mind within, they gush to bestow and they release good understanding to come into existence in us. (76), (Y. V. 12, 51)

५. प्र होता जातो महान्नभोविन्नृषद्मा सीददपां विवर्ते ।
दधद्यो धायि सुते वयांसि यन्ता वसूनि विधते तनूपाः ॥

5. The sense activities from the source preside, the great ones bestow mightily from heaven on men which Activity develops in the home. They bestow curds (sense reactions) on Mind, they support us, guide us who are in poverty, to wealth and protect us delicately. (77)

६. प्र सम्राजमसुरस्य प्रशस्तं पुंसः कृष्टीनामनुमाद्यस्य ।
इन्द्रस्येव प्र तवसस्कृतानि वन्दद्वारा वन्दमाना विवष्टु ॥

6. The material world of asuras (sense organs) praiseworthily nourishes man and cultivates him so as to be hailed.

Indra speeds up to produce nourishment for the brain cells through the nerves praiseworthily which the brain (home) praises for having gained by being ridden. (78)

७. अरण्योर्निहितो जातवेदा गर्भ इवेत्सुभृतो गर्भिणीभिः ।
दिवेदिव ईड्यो जागृवद्भिर्हविष्मद्भिर्मनुष्येभिरग्निः ॥

7. The nerves gladden through the welfare created by the birth of knowledge, the sense activities, as if they are the source; support them well like a pregnant woman.

Day after day Agni supports men with oblations from sense activities in the waking state. (79)

८. सनादग्ने मृणसि यातुधानान्न त्वा रक्षांसि पृतनासु जिग्युः ।
अनु दह सहमूरान्कयादो मा ते हेत्या मुक्षत दैव्यायाः ॥

8. Agni is associated with mortals from ancient times, to whom he moved to bestow gifts and protect and support them and united with them in fighting.

Now he overcomes and burns away the stupid inertia closely united with (yāda) the head (ka), by which the sense activities cause to make them strong through devas (ideas). (80)

D. IV.

१. अग्न ओजिष्ठमा भर द्युम्नमस्मभ्यमध्रिगो ।
प्र नो राये पनीयसे रत्सि वाजाय पन्थाम् ॥

1. Agni! Support me vigorously from heaven with the irresistible sense activities.

They strive admirably to control nourishment now; they bestow the paths in life and bind us. (81)

२. यदि वीरो अनु ष्यादग्निमिन्धीत मर्त्यः ।
आजुह्वद्धव्यमानुषक् शर्म भक्षीत दैव्यम् ॥

2. What is vigorously attached to Agni mightily is the understanding of mortals.

He bestows it on men in the head through his tongues (rays) which devour ideas and control us. (82)

३. त्वेषस्ते धूम ऋण्वति दिवि सं च्छुक्र आततः ।
सूरो न हि द्युता त्वं कृपा पावक रोचसे ॥

3. You desire them to agitate me to oblige me with understanding; the father (Activity) makes it all bright in waking state.

You arouse it vigorously from heaven in compassion and let it glow to bestow on the head to drink. (83)

४. त्वं हि क्षैतवद्यशोऽग्ने मित्रो न पत्यसे ।
त्वं विचर्षणे श्रवो वसो पुष्टिं न पुष्यसि ॥

4. Agni! You arouse the motley sense activities in the home to bestow speech from the brain (Mitra) and strive with the descendant (speech organ).

You are diligently active in listening and fatten us with wealth (Vasu) and make us prosperous. (84)

५. प्रातरग्निः पुरुप्रियो विश स्तवेतातिथिः ।
विश्वे यस्मिन्नमर्त्ये हव्यं मर्तास इन्धते ॥

5. In the early morning of creation Agni in all kindness to the brain (home) let in the motley sense activities as guests.

He bestowed through them oblations on the sense organs of mortals; they kindled the mortals and bound them to them. (85)

६. यद्वाहिष्ठं तदग्नये बृहदर्च विभावसो ।
महिषीव त्वद्रयिस्त्वद्वाजा उदीरते ॥

6. What was conveyed was at Agni's desire with which he honoured us greatly and through which he bestowed existence.

You bestow wealth, you bestow life-activity above and incite and bestow desires which gladden us. (86), (Y.V. 26, 12)

७. विशोविशो वो अतिथिं वाजयन्तः पुरुप्रियम् ।
अग्निं वो दुर्यं वचः स्तुषे शूषस्य मन्मभिः ॥

7. The guests (sense activities) bestow on man after man (home after home); they guide life-activity with abundant love.

Agni bestows the entrance on speech praiseworthily and resoundingly to my mind. (87), (1564)

८. बृहद्वयो हि भानवेऽर्चा देवायाग्नये ।
यं मित्रं न प्रशस्तये मर्तासो दधिरे पुरः ॥

8. Consciousness honours us by bestowing ideas from Agni and arouses us greatly.

He controls the brain (Mitra) praiseworthily, bestows curds (sense reactions) in the city. (88)

९. अगन्म वृत्रहन्तमं ज्येष्ठमग्निमानवम् ।
य स्म श्रुतर्वन्नार्क्ष्ये बृहदनीक इध्यते ॥

9. Consciousness honours the sense activities and strikes down Vṛtra (inertia) through Indra as desired, for Agni to bestow (vomit) on the home.

He moves indeed to hear us and hastens with food (sense perceptions) to make up for loss which unite and kindle what is in front greatly. (89)

१०. जातः परेण धर्मणा यत्सवृद्भिः सहाभुवः ।
पिता यत्कश्यपस्याग्निः श्रद्धा माता मनुः कविः ॥

10. Birth is the dharma of yonder world which unites with us and grows together with existence.

The father (Activity) unites with the brain, concealed like a tortoise. Agni has faith in mother who is the preceptor to Mind. (90)

D. V.

१. सोमं राजानं वरुणमग्निमन्वारभामहे ।
आदित्यं विष्णुं सूर्यं ब्रह्माणं बृहस्पतिम् ॥

1. Soma is king to whom we submit, through whom Agni seizes mind greatly to bestow (ideas of) Varuṇa.

Aditi controls him (mind). Consciousness works for knowledge as also Soma (Bṛhaspati). (91)

२. इत एत उदारुहन्दिवः पृष्ठान्या रुहन् ।
प्र भूर्जयो यथा पथोद्यामङ्गिरसो ययुः ॥

2. The motley sense activities spring up above; consciousness guides them foremost as he rises.

The sense organs win nourishment; likewise prāṇa gains the path above to release the Aṅgirā (sense activities). (92)

३. राये अग्ने महे त्वा दानाय समिधीमहि ।
ईडिष्वा हि महे वृषं द्यावा होत्राय पृथिवी ॥

3. Agni controls the brain cells with fuelsticks (sense objects) greatly.

He bestows oblations and arouses heaven (brain) powerfully to bestow on the sense organs over which he presides. (93).

४. दधन्वे वा यदीमनु वोचद्ब्रह्मेति वेरु तत् ।
परि विश्वानि काव्या नेमिश्चक्रमिवाभुवत् ॥

4. He runs to bestow; he bestows now what the motley sense activities release as knowledge through speech resoundingly.

He goes around the sense organs for knowledge (kāvya), approaches the summit to go around and bestow understanding in existence (or for existence). (94)

५. प्रत्यग्ने हरसा हरः शृणाहि विश्वतस्परि ।
यातुधानस्य रक्षसो बलं न्युब्जवीर्यम् ॥

5. Agni! You grasp the sense activities and convey them to arouse the sense organs going around and cook them.

You move to the brain cells to bestow protection, and forcibly restrain their vigour. (95)

६. त्वमग्ने वसूँरिह रुद्राँ आदित्याँ उत ।
यजा स्वध्वरं जनं मनुजातं घृतप्रुषम् ॥

6. Agni! You bestow wealth here, also the nervous system (Rudra) and Aditi.

In life activity, you besprinkle mind with clarified butter from the source. (96)

PART I

BOOK II : CHAPTER I

D. I.

१. पुरु त्वा दाशिवां वोचेऽरिरग्ने तव स्विदा ।
तोदस्येव शरण आ महस्य ॥

1. Agni! You bestow abundantly in graciousness; you sweat to release speech; you hasten us by goading and protect and gladden us. (97)

२. प्र होत्रे पूर्व्यं वचोऽग्नये भरता बृहत् ।
विपां ज्योतींषि बिभ्रते न वेधसे ॥

2. Agni! In olden times you presided over and nourished speech and supported it greatly.

Consciousness inspires the devotee without agitation. (98)

३. अग्ने वाजस्य गोमत ईशानः सहसो यहो ।
अस्मे देहि जातवेदो महि श्रवः ॥

3. Agni! Our sense activities rule us victoriously in life-activity and bestow speedily.

You bestow much knowledge to be born through much hearing. (99), (Y.V. 15, 35), (1561)

४. अग्ने यजिष्ठो अध्वरे देवान् देवयते यज ।
होता मन्द्रो वि राजस्यति स्रिधः ॥

4. Agni is desirous of life-activity and devas (ideas) devoted to life-activity; the devas unite with life-activity.

You preside over it pleasantly; you control wrong-doing by uniting with us. (100)

५. जज्ञानः सप्त मातृभिर्मेधामाशासत श्रिये ।
अयं ध्रुवो रयीणां चिकेतदा ॥

5. Knowledge is born of the seven Ṛṣis (Activity); the mother supports the mind with understanding, in existence for prosperity. (101)

६. उत स्या नो दिवा मतिरदितिरूत्यागमत् ।
सा शन्ताता मयस्करदप स्रिधः ॥

6. Also, this consciousness is come to make known understanding from Aditi.

He bestows benefits by bestowing protection to prāṇa from wrong, in producing Activity. (102)

७. ईडिष्वा हि प्रतीव्यां३ यजस्व जातवेदसम् ।
चरिष्णुधूममगृभीतशोचिषम् ॥

7. (Consciousness) bestows oblations and nourishes us with all knowledge from the source himself in life-activity.

He goes seeking the smoke (of knowledge), grasps it and glows with it. (103)

८. न तस्य मायया च न रिपुरीशीत मर्त्यः ।
यो अग्नये ददाश हव्यदातये ॥

8. Now he gladdens us marvellously by releasing it to rest in mortals.

Agni bestows his services to bestow the oblations. (104)

९. अप त्यं वृजिनं रिपुं स्तेनमग्ने दुराध्यम् ।
दविष्ठमस्य सत्पते कृधी सुगम् ॥

9. It is well-known that Activity envelops and is a conqueror and releases to man, Agni hastens to open the door to sip him (Activity).

The lord of existence is remote from us and yet creates understanding and welfare in us. (105)

१०. श्रुष्टयग्ने नवस्य मे स्तोमस्य वीर विश्पते ।
नि मायिनस्तपसा रक्षसो दह ॥

10. Agni gives willing services newly to us for vigour praiseworthily in the path to the brain (home).

He bestows protection on us warmly and marvellously and burns (the enemies). (106)

D. II.

१. प्र मंहिष्ठाय गायत ऋताव्ने बृहते शुक्रशोचिषे ।
उपस्तुतासो अग्नये ॥

1. The sense activities unite and nourish us munificently. Ṛta desires greatly to show it off brightly.

They praise Agni. (107)

२. प्र सो अग्ने तवोतिभिः सुवीराभिस्तरति वाजकर्मभिः ।
यस्य त्वं सख्यमाविथ ॥

2. Agni bestows nourishment, he helps us, arouses vigour in us to cross over (ignorance) and in the duties in life-activity.

You help them in difficulties (in these life-activities). (108)

३. तं गूर्धया स्वर्णरं देवासो देवमरतिं दधन्विरे ।
देवत्रा हव्यमूहिषे ॥

3. You desire to move to the devotee and bestow from heaven and gladden, bestow ideas; the devas gladden us; they bestow as if shot from a bow for our comfort.

The devas support with oblations which transform us. (109)

४. मा नो हृणीथा अतिथिं वसुरग्निः पुरुप्रशस्त एषः ।
यः सुहोता स्वध्वरः ॥

4. Let not the sense activities be worth for seeking wealth which flow from Agni very praiseworthily.

Seed up to preside well in your life-activity. (110)

५. भद्रो नो अग्निराहुतो भद्रा रातिः सुभग भद्रो अध्वरः ।
भद्रा उत प्रशस्तयः ॥

5. Agni offers us welfare; he is ready to bestow gifts for welfare and prosperity in the life-activity for welfare.

You are also praised for the welfare. (111), (1559), (Y.V. 15, 38)

६. यजिष्ठं त्वा ववृमहे देवं देवत्रा होतारममर्त्यम् ।
अस्य यज्ञस्य सुक्रतुम् ॥

6. You are desirous of life-activity; you envelop us and bestow (ideas) devas greatly; devas preside, support and gladden mortals.

You do us good in our life-activity. (112), (1413)

७. तदग्ने द्युम्नमा भर यत्सासाहा सदने कं चिदत्रिणम् ।
मन्युं जनस्य दूढ्यम् ॥

7. Thus, you support us from heaven; you unite with us and overcome in the home for the mind's desire for the 3 states.

Men are eager to control the ill-disposition (of mind). (113)

८. यद्वा उ विश्पतिः शितः सुप्रीतो मनुषो विशे ।
विश्वेदग्निः प्रति रक्षांसि सेधति ॥

8. What the lord of the home bestows by way of knowledge (whiteness) is out of kindness to the brain of men.

Agni bestows on sense organs and in turn protects and supports from a distance. (114)

Indra Kāṇḍa

D. III.

१. तद्वो गाय सुते सचा पुरुहूताय सत्वने ।
शं यद्गवे न शाकिने ॥

1. The sense activities thus move to the Mind and bestow by uniting with the warrior (Indra) who invokes them abundantly.

He toils thus with sense activities and bestows them to be helpful. (115), (1666)

२. यस्ते नूनं शतक्रतविन्द्र द्युम्नितमो मदः ।
तेन नूनं मदे मदेः ॥

2. Indra who did a hundred deeds strives now in heaven for the desires of the sense activities.

They now bestow me joyously. (116)

Indra of a hundred deeds refers to an Arctic phenomenon of the sun going down below the horizon for 100 days during the winter when the earth is in total darkness during the whole period, at a particular latitude. The sun is supposed to be kept in captivity by the nether powers. Indra is supposed to have fought with them, destroyed 100 forts and retrieved the sun at the end of 100 days to shine on the earth again.

३. गाव उप वदावटे मही यज्ञस्य रप्सुदा ।
उभा कर्णा हिरण्यया ॥

3. The sense activities bestow much on the brain cells above as information (speak to them) in life-activity they arouse and bestow whispering on the brain cells.

Prāṇa arouses both the brain sections (both ears) and gladdens them. (117), (1602)

४. अरमश्वाय गायत श्रुतकक्षारं गवे ।
अरमिन्द्रस्य धाम्ने ॥

4. Prāṇa gladdens sense activities by uniting the brain cells to hear what the sense activities release and they are gladdened.

The spokes-like nerves are in Indra's home. (118)

५. तमिन्द्रं वाजयामसि महे वृत्राय हन्तवे ।
स वृषा वृषभो भुवत् ॥

5. Indra is fond of life-activity; he strikes down Vṛtra (inertia) greatly.

Indra bestows, like raining, understanding in existence. (119)

६. त्वमिन्द्र बलादधि सहसो जात ओजसः ।
त्वं सन्वृषन्वृषेदसि ॥

6. Indra! You bestow satisfaction strongly and bestow vigour from the source at the same time.

You rain gifts and are powerful. (120)

७. यज्ञ इन्द्रमवर्धयद्यद्भूमिं व्यवर्तयत् ।
चक्राण ओपशं दिवि ॥

7. Indra fosters life-activity in whatever creature, which subsists, which he envelops.

Also he causes the cessation of the waking state willingly (Krāṇa). (121), (1639)

८. यदिन्द्राहं यथा त्वमीशीय वस्व एक इत् ।
स्तोता मे गोसखा स्यात् ॥

8. I am to Indra like what he is to the ruler and alone he bestows on the home.

He is praiseworthily the friend of my sense-activities. (122)

९. पन्यंपन्यमित्सोतार आ धावत मद्याय ।
सोमं वीराय शूराय ॥

9. Soma is admirable; admirably he has established Soma juice to bestow understanding through the sense-activities.

Soma is a vigorous hero. (123), (1657)

१०. इदं वसो सुतमन्धः पिबा सुपूर्णमुदरम् ।
अनाभयिन्ररिमा ते ॥

10. Here Indra lets the Mind drink stomach full when in ignorance.

He releases them for me, bestows them mightily from the source. (124), (734)

D. IV.

१. उद्वेदभि श्रुतामघं वृषभं नर्यापसम् ।
अस्तारमेषि सूर्य ॥

1. Indra bestows sense activities above for hearing to protect men.
Consciousness gladdens their desires in the home. (125), (1450)

२. यदद्य कच्च वृत्रहन्नुदगा अभि सूर्य ।
सर्वं तदिन्द्र ते वशे ॥

2. What now honours the head besides, after striking down and pushing away Vṛtra (inertia), for the sake of sense activities is consciousness.
All of them are desired (vaśa) by Indra. (126), (Y.V. 33, 35)

३. य आनयत्परावतः सुनीती तुर्वशं यदुम् ।
इन्द्रः स नो युवा सखा ॥

3. He (Indra) guides, understanding from beyond, for which he guides sense activities quickly to the home.
Indra bestows gifts on mind as a friend. (127)

४. मा न इन्द्राभ्या३ दिशः सूरो अक्तुष्वा यमत् ।
त्वा युजा वनेम तत् ॥

4. Indra directs in the home; the hero blesses it eagerly and bestows and controls it.
He desires life activity here. (128)

५. एन्द्र सानसिं रयिं सजित्वानं सदासहम् ।
वर्षिष्ठमूतये भर ॥

5. Indra is victorious in securing wealth and he wins desires constantly with might.
He rains them to us, helps and supports. (129)

६. इन्द्रं वयं महाधन इन्द्रमर्भे हवामहे ।
युजं वृत्रेषु वज्रिणम् ॥

6. Indra is to us a great treasure. Indra bestows much oblations on poor men like us.

He unites with the missiles of sense activities, envelops us and supports through the vigorous nerves. (130)

७. अपिबत्कद्रुवः सुतमिन्द्रः सहस्रबाह्वे ।
तत्राददिष्ट पौंस्यम् ॥

7. He hastens to the brain (head) to bestow on the Mind for drinking, the thousand-armed Indra.

There he bestows as desired and controls his prosperity. (131)

८. वयमिन्द्र त्वायवोऽभि प्र नोनुमो वृषन् ।
विद्धी त्वा३स्य नो वसो ॥

8. Indra! You bestow nourishment on our brain cells and honour them by raining (sense activities).

You acquaint us with understanding now in the home. (132)

९. आ घा ये अग्निमिन्धते स्तृणन्ति बर्हिरानुषक् ।
येषामिन्द्रो युवा सखा ॥

9. Agni induces you to attach yourself to the motley sense activities and bestow through the nerves.

The Mind desires (seeks) Indra as a friend. (133), (1338), (Y.V. 7, 32)

१०. भिन्धि विश्वा अप द्विषः परि बाधो जही मृधः ।
वसु स्पार्हं तदा भर ॥

10. Activity subdivides itself for the sense organs; goes around (looking for) the desires of both (brain and sense organs), so that tormentors may depart from fighting.

Indra (vasu) charmingly supports it. (134), (1070)

D. V.

१. इहेव शृण्व एषां कशा हस्तेषु यद्वदान् ।
नि यामं चित्रमृञ्जते ॥

1. He hastens here to crush (the tormentors) seeking them with whip in hand and bestows gifts of sense activities.

That the varied paths below (nerves) strive for me. (135)

२. इम उ त्वा वि चक्षते सखाय इन्द्र सोमिनः ।
पुष्टावन्तो यथा पशुम् ॥

2. You perceive and bestow on the home (brain) through them (nerves); Indra supports and binds Soma.

He bestows within to fatten him (brain) (like fattening) cows. (136)

३. समस्य मन्यवे विशो विश्वा नमन्त कृष्टयः ।
समुद्रायेव सिन्धवः ॥

3. He honours the sense organs and cultivates the brain cells in the home; at the same time the mind by speeding up Sindhus (the 7 celestial rivers) gladdens them. (137), (1651)

४. देवानामिदवो महत्तदा वृणीमहे वयम् ।
वृष्णामस्मभ्यमूतये ॥

4. The devas bestow us here mighty much and envelop us greatly.

Indra gives us help. (138)

५. सोमानां स्वरणं कृणुहि ब्रह्मणस्पते ।
कक्षीवन्तं य औशिजः ॥

5. Soma, the lord of knowledge, creates, arouses us and himself gladdens us.

He bestows to the brain cells within eagerly. (139), (1463), (Y.V. 3, 28)

While mind is a characteristic of individuals Soma is universal mind, who imparts ideas for desires and knowledge to individual minds. Soma reacts to sense activities in the subtle world and he releases them also. He assists Agni in these matters. He is named Bṛhaspati and Brahmaṇaspati also.

६. बोधन्मना इदस्तु नो वृत्रहा भूर्यासुतिः ।
शृणोतु शक्र आशिषम् ॥

6. He imparts knowledge to mind here. On Vṛtra's departure, he moves to the sense organs (bhūr) for the sake of mind.

He cooks them with the motley sense activities, as they (sense organs) desire food. (140)

Vṛtra represents matter or inertia. The Veda considers matter also as ideas as it is apprehended only as ideas by us. Matter is ideas deprived of external activity; its activity is internal. Ideas are very very densely packed in matter. Matter's characteristic is that it preserves whatever is given to its safekeeping. Our memory is dependant on matter being incorporated in our make-up.

७. अद्या नो देव सवितः प्रजावत्सावीः सौभगम् ।
परा दुःष्वप्न्यं सुव ॥

7. Now the deva Savitā has bestowed mind on men for their welfare.

Milk (sense perceptions) from beyond are admirably scattered and bestowed by stirring it (mind). (141)

८. क्व३स्य वृषभो युवा तुविग्रीवो अनानतः ।
ब्रह्मा कस्तं सपर्यति ॥

8. Wherever Indra is, the mind (youth) swallows (grīvā) always the sense activities powerfully.

The brain (home) in the head serves him with knowledge. (142)

It is the brain that feeds the mind with knowledge and everything. The mind is dependant on sense activities, Indra sense organs and the external world.

९. उपह्वरे गिरीणां सङ्गमे च नदीनाम् ।
धिया विप्रो अजायत ॥

9. Above the spinal chord (hvara) unites with the brain (hill) like a river.

The source (heaven) unites with it and inspires satisfaction. (143), (Y. V. 26, 15)

१०. प्र संम्राजं चर्षणीनामिन्द्रं स्तोता नव्यं गीर्भिः ।
नरं नृषाहं मंहिष्ठम् ॥

10. Indra is diligently active in his sovereign region and praiseworthily nourishes the brain (hill) freshly.

They flow munificently in men in the waking state. (144)

BOOK II : CHAPTER II

D. I.

१. अपादु शिप्रयन्धसः सुदक्षस्य प्रहोषिणः ।
इन्द्वोरिन्द्रो यवाशिरः ॥

1. The footless (brain cells) release us from cheekful of ignorance, arouse us and satisfy by nourishing us eagerly indeed.

Indra moves to the brain cells in the head and bestows (sense activities and perceptions). (145)

२. इमा उ त्वा पुरूवसोऽभि प्र नोनुनवुर्गिरः ।
गावो वत्सं न धेनवः ॥

2. Indra (Vasu) now bestows abundantly here to nourish freshly and extensively on the hill.

The sense perceptions bestow on mind (youth) like a milch cow. (146)

३. अत्राह गोरमन्वत नाम त्वष्टुरपीच्यम् ।
इत्था चन्द्रमसो गृहे ॥

3. There indeed Tvaṣṭā (sense of touch) lying hidden gladdens sense activities by bestowing (releasing) and guiding them to us.

Thus they are bestowed on mind from the home. (147)

४. यदिन्द्रो अनयद्रितो महीरपो वृषन्तमः ।
तत्र पूषाभवत्सचा ॥

4. What Indra guides to the brain (hill) greatly is Activity who rains desires.

There prosperity follows and comes into existence. (148)

५. गोर्धयति मरुतां श्रवस्युर्माता मघोनाम् ।
युक्ता वह्नी रथानाम् ।

5. The sense activities sip ideas (Maruts) extensively; we hear extensively through the mother as gifts.

She unites with the sense organs (vehicles) and conveys. (149)

६. उप नो हरिभिः सुतं याहि मदानां पते ।
उप नो हरिभिः सुतम् ॥

6. Above now, the tawny consciousness moves to the mind and arouses him for his lord the sense activities.

Above now the tawny consciousness arouses desires. (150), (1790)

७. इष्टा होत्रा असृक्षतेन्द्रं वृधन्तो अध्वरे ।
अच्छावभृथमोजसा ॥

7. Indra desiring to preside flows to the home to promote the growth of life-activity.

He favours it well and supports vigorously. (151)

८. अहमिद्धि पितुष्परि मेधामृतस्य जग्रह ।
अहं सूर्य इवाजनि ॥

8. The father goes round the brain (fat) in waking and supports it for understanding to be born in the home.

The waking state takes birth, like consciousness. (152), (1500)

९. रेवतीर्नः सधमाद इन्द्रे सन्तु तुविवाजाः ।
क्षुमन्तो याभिर्मदेम ॥

9. Indra bestows wealth to his comrade mind as gift mightily in life-activity.

He moves to him within to support him with sense perceptions as food. (153)

१०. सोमः पूषा च चेततुर्विश्वासां सुक्षितीनाम् ।
देवत्रा रथ्योर्हिता ॥

10. Soma also furthers the prosperity of mind vigorously through bestowing from the sense organs on the brain (home) by arousing it.

Devas (ideas) support the sense organs (vehicles) towards welfare. (154)

D. II.

१. पान्तमा वो अन्धस इन्द्रमभि प्र गायत ।
विश्वासाहं शतक्रतुं मंहिष्ठं चर्षणीनाम् ॥

1. Indra bestows the desire to be relieved of ignorance and fulfils and unites with sense activities to nourish us (for the purpose).

He produces hundreds of (ideas) and bestows from sense organs in waking munificently diligently. (155), (713)

२. प्र व इन्द्राय मादनं हर्यश्वाय गायत ।
सखायः सोमपाव्ने ॥

2. Indra honours sense activities and bestows them to nourish; prāṇa conveys the sense activities to unite (with the brain) or the tawny consciousness unites with sense activities).

They help Soma to drink as desired. (156), (716)

३. वयमु त्वा तदिदर्था इन्द्र त्वायन्तः सखायः ।
कण्वा उक्थेभिर्जरन्ते ॥

3. You have thus bestowed on us just their purpose; you guide and help us.

You support the brain cells praiseworthily till old age. (157)

४. इन्द्राय मद्वने सुतं परि ष्टोभन्तु नो गिरः ।
अर्कमर्चन्तु कारवः ॥

4. Indra goes around the brain (hill) praiseworthily on account of the desires of mind for sense perceptions.

He honours the brain (prison house) and bestows praiseworthily on it. (158)

५. अयं त इन्द्र सोमो निपूतो अधि बर्हिषि ।
एहीमस्य द्रवा पिब ॥

5. Indra is the path for Soma who enlightens and satisfies through the motley sense activities.

He hastens towards us and drinks up the flows (of sense activities). (159), (725)

६. सुरूपकृत्नुमूतये सुदुघामिव गोदुहे ।
जुहूमसि द्यविद्यवि ॥

6. Indra helps to arouse the good sense activities and approaches them to bestow sense perceptions creating (producing) the forms of objects.

It is the rays (tongues) which acquaint the brain and favour it and bind us to them. (160)

७. अभि त्वा वृषभा सुते सुतं सृजामि पीतये ।
तृम्पा व्यश्नुही मदम् ॥

7. Indra! You rain them to the mind to shine, you flow to your relative mind for him to drink.

The sense activities yield milk to satisfaction. (161)

८. य इन्द्र चमसेष्वा सोमश्चमूषु ते सुतः ।
पिबेदस्य त्वमीशिषे ॥

8. Indra moves to bestow desires for sipping from Soma who sips the sense organs for the sake of mind.

He bestows on us desires to drink. (162)

९. योगेयोगे तवस्तरं वाजेवाजे हवामहे ।
सखाय इन्द्रमूतये ॥

9. Soma! Every time you unite with the home you gladden it with much oblations in life after life.

Indra, your friend, moves to help you. (163), (743), (Y.V. 11, 14)

१०. आ त्वेता नि षीदतेन्द्रमभि प्र गायत ।
सखायः स्तोमवाहसः ॥

10. Soma! You lie in wait for (sad) the motley sense activities; Indra unites with the sense activities to nourish you.

The friend (Indra) moves, praiseworthily conveys and bestows them on you. (164), (740)

D. III.

१. इदं ह्यन्वोजसा सुतं राधानां पते ।
पिबा त्वा३स्य गिर्वणः ॥

1. The lord of wealth bestows afresh strongly from heaven on mind.

He drinks it willingly from our hill (brain). (165)

२. महाँ इन्द्रः पुरश्च नो महित्वमस्तु वज्रिणे ।
द्यौर्न प्रथिना शवः ॥

2. Indra is great and gladdens us abundantly; the vigorous nerves honour us much.

They spread out from the head to the sense organs (body). (166)

३. आ तू न इन्द्र क्षुमन्तं चित्रं ग्राभं सं गृभाय ।
महाहस्ती दक्षिणेन ॥

3. Indra! You grab a variety of foods; you seize them all. Through your great hands (nerves) coming from the south. (167)

४. अभि प्र गोपतिं गिरेन्द्रमर्च यथा विदे ।
सूनुं सत्यस्य सत्पतिम् ॥

4. Indra honours the lord of sense activities as enjoined on the hill to nourish him.
The lord of existence arouses men to existence. (168), (1489)

५. कया नश्चित्र आ भुवदूती सदावृधः सखा ।
कया शचिष्ठया वृता ॥

5. The messengers (ideas) constantly bestow in existence and promote the growth of their friend (mind) who attains thus a variety (of ideas).
They move to the head desiring to unite by enveloping it. (169), (682), (Y.V. 27, 39)

६. त्यमु वः सत्रासाहं विश्वासु गीर्ष्वायतम् ।
आ च्यावयस्यूतये ॥

6. It is well-known that they bestow on us in Soma yajña (life activity) victoriously and by themselves attach to the hill and unite with it.
They strive to help the brain cells. (170), (1642)

७. सदसस्पतिमद्भुतं प्रियमिन्द्रस्य काम्यम् ।
सनिं मेधामयासिषम् ॥

7. The lord of the brain cells (Agni) and the home bestows support cheerfully on Indra's desires (for new creatures).
He bestows his desires as gifts to the brain (medhā). (171), (Y.V. 32, 13)

८. ये ते पन्था अधो दिवो येभिर्व्यश्वमैरयः ।
उत श्रोषन्तु नो भुवः ॥

8. Their (the messengers') paths are below consciousness; they are supported by the Aśvins on the hill through prāṇa.
Also they cook eagerly (new creatures) within for existence. (172)

९. भद्रंभद्रं न आ भरेषमूर्जं शतक्रतो ।
यदिन्द्र मृडयासि नः ।।

9. Indra of hundred deeds supports the nourishment desired for welfare to shine and gladden.

In which Indra is compassionate and binds us to them. (173)

१०. अस्ति सोमो अयं सुतः पिबन्त्यस्य मरुतः ।
उत स्वराजो अश्विना ।।

10. Soma is the path for our mind; he drinks our ideas (Maruts).

Also from the Aśvins, who are their own masters. (174), (1785)

D. IV.

१. ईङ्खयन्तीरपस्युव इन्द्रं जातमुपासते ।
वन्वानासः सुवीर्यम् ।।

1. Indra does service to mind through Activity who shakes him up and guides within.

He bestows on him desires to which he is sewn, to arouse his vigour. (175)

२. नकि देवा इनीमसि न क्या योपयामसि ।
मन्त्रश्रुत्यं चरामसि ।।

2. There is no deva so mighty, not anywhere above who can control him (mind).

He (Indra) goes around and controls (compels) him to hear the sacred texts. (176)

३. दोषो आगाद् बृहद्गाय द्युमद्गामन्नाथर्वण ।
स्तुहि देवं सवितारम् ।।

3. If any blemish arises in him sense activities (perceptions) from heaven hasten to him then.

He (mind) then praises the deva Savitā. (177)

४. एषो उषा अपूर्व्या व्युच्छति प्रिया दिवः ।
स्तुषे वामश्विना बृहत् ।।

4. Dawn (Uṣas) in ancient days cut herself off kindly in favour of consciousness.

The lovely Aśvins were praised greatly for this. (178)

Dawn with its poor light could illumine only in the lower order of creatures. With the advent of man full consciousness blazed forth in him, which was when Dawn ceased. This was brought about by the Aśvins who are praised.

५. इन्द्रो दधीचो अस्थभिर्वृत्राण्यप्रतिष्कुतः ।
जघान नवतीर्नव ॥

5. Indra also bestows understanding abidingly and supports it by creating opposition to Vṛtra (inertia).

Whom he struck at his posterior to cross over to newer and newer species of creatures. (179)

६. इन्द्रेहि मत्स्यन्धसो विश्वेभिः सोमपर्वभिः ।
महाँ अभिष्टिरोजसा ॥

6. Indra awakes us from ignorance, like that of a fish, through the sense organs; Soma bestows to them from beyond.

The great one bestows what is desired vigorously. (180), (Y.V. 33, 25)

७. आ तू न इन्द्र वृत्रहन्नस्माकमर्धमा गहि ।
महान्महीभिरूतिभिः ॥

7. Indra strikes down inertia (Vṛtra) for our sake, who forms half of us (sense organs) for the sense activities to be aroused.

They (sense organs) are great ones and support and help us much. (181), (Y.V. 33, 65)

८. ओजस्तदस्य तित्विष उभे यत्समवर्तयत् ।
इन्द्रश्चर्मेव रोदसी ॥

8. They agitate both the brain and mind vigorously, by uniting with them and treating them alike.

Indra envelops both brain and sense organs like the skin. (182)

९. अयमु ते समतसि कपोत इव गर्भधिम् ।
वचस्तच्चिन्न ओहसे ॥

9. The paths to them (sense organs) from the brain also are alike; the source satisfies the sense organs like a young animal.

They undergo transformation and bestow thoughts for speech. (183), (1599)

१०. वात आ वातु भेषजं शम्भु मयोभु नो हृदे ।
प्र न आयूंषि तारिषत् ॥

10. The nerves bestow on them nourishment benevolently conducting to gladness from the brain (heart).

They nourish through life to cross over (ignorance) as desired. (184), (1840)

D. V.

१. यं रक्षन्ति प्रचेतसो वरुणो मित्रो अर्यमा ।
न किः स दभ्यते जनः ॥

1. Indra (Aryamā) controls and protects us from within, bestows nourishment on mind, gives help to brain (Mitra).

In uniting with men he does not hurt. (185)

२. गव्यो षु णो यथा पुराश्वयोत रथया ।
वरिवस्या महोनाम् ॥

2. Prāṇa conveys the sense activities to the sense organs in the same manner as he did with the motley sense activities in ancient times.

He moves in the home in the enclosure very greatly. (186)

३. इमास्त इन्द्र पृश्नयो घृतं दुहत आशिरम् ।
एनामृतस्य पिप्युषीः ॥

3. Indra draws out speckled clarified butter from the milk here in the head.

Then men drink it eagerly. (187)

४. अया धिया च गव्यया पुरुणामन्पुरुष्टुत ।
यत्सोमेसोम आभुवः ॥

4. Good fortune satisfies us; also the sense perceptions move abundantly to mind who praises them.

Soma unites with me and bestows on me existence. (188)

५. पावका नः सरस्वती वाजेभिर्वाजिनीवती ।
यज्ञं वष्टु धियावसुः ॥

5. Speech is bound to Sarasvatī and drinks of her who supports it in life-activity and leads vigorously to understanding.

Indra (vasu) bestows her in life-activity to win satisfaction. (189), (Y.V. 20, 84)

६. क इमं नाहुषीष्वा इन्द्रं सोमस्य तर्पयात् ।
स नो वसून्या भरात् ॥

6. Indra bestows to the Spinal cord from the head to satisfy Soma.

Indra bestows on him gifts, guides them and supports him. (190)

७. आ याहि सुषुमा हि त इन्द्र सोमं पिबा इमम् ।
एदं बर्हिः सदो मम ॥

7. Indra moves to the mind (child) and arouses him for his well-being, who drinks from Soma.

Behold the motley sense activities constantly with me. (191), (666)

८. महि त्रीणामवरस्तु द्युक्षं मित्रस्यार्यम्णः ।
दुराधर्षं वरुणस्य ॥

8. Indra (Aryamā) bestows on the brain (Mitra) heavenly gifts and blesses the three states by bestowing mightily.

He opens the door to flow to Varuṇa (the external world). (192), (Y.V. 3, 31)

९. त्वावतः पुरूवसो वयमिन्द्र प्रणेतः ।
स्मसि स्थातर्हरीणाम् ॥

9. Indra nourishes us with much understanding in the home through the motley sense activities.

He indeed binds us to the tawny consciousness to cross (ignorance). (193)

BOOK III : CHAPTER I

D. I.

१. उत्त्वा मन्दन्तु सोमाः कृणुष्व राधो अद्रिवः ।
अव ब्रह्मद्विषो जहि ॥

1. When it is sluggish within, Soma runs to produce wealth on the hill to bestow.

He blesses us with knowledge from desires aroused and born of both (brain and sense organs). (194), (1354)

२. गिर्वणः पाहि नः सुतं मधोर्धाराभिरज्यसे ।
इन्द्र त्वादातमिद्यशः ॥

2. Indra arouses the mind and binds him to the brain (hill) as desired to drink, he strives for clarified butter and supports wealth (of sense activities) abundantly.

Indra! You bestow grandeur to the brain. (195)

३. सदा व इन्द्रश्चर्कृषदा उपो नु स सपर्यन् ।
न देवो वृतः शूर इन्द्रः ॥

3. Indra bestows constantly, he goes around and bestows to cultivate (the brain), above now he bestows and gives his services.

The heroic Indra envelops the devas. (196)

४. आ त्वा विशन्त्विन्दवः समुद्रमिव सिन्धवः ।
न त्वामिन्द्राति रिच्यते ॥

4. Indra! You bestow on the brain cells in the home through the Sindhu, vast as the ocean.

She is released by Indra to unite. (197), (1660)

५. इन्द्रमिद्गाथिनो बृहदिन्द्रमर्केभिरर्किणः ।
इन्द्रं वाणीरनूषत ॥

5. Indra approaches the singer (devotee) and bestows, consciousness supports him much praiseworthily.

Indra follows Sarasvatī. (198), (796)

६. इन्द्र इषे ददातु न ऋभुक्षणमृभुं रयिम् ।
वाजी ददातु वाजिनम् ॥

6. Indra bestows desires through the Ṛbhus (the spinal system) on us, the Ṛbhus are wealth.

They bestow us in life-activity speedily. (199)

७. इन्द्रो अङ्ग महद्भयमभी षदप चुच्यवत् ।
स हि स्थिरो विचर्षणिः ॥

7. Indra's limb prāṇa gladdens us fearlessly by cooking understanding in the home as accustomed.

He is diligent in bestowing and stabilising it. (200)

८. इमा उ त्वा सुतेसुते नक्षन्ते गिर्वणो गिरः ।
गावो वत्सं न धेनवः ॥

8. Here you bestow also Soma juice on Mind by approaching him within, in the hill who is desirous of the hill.

The sense perceptions bestow on mind like a milch-cow. (201)

९. इन्द्रा नु पूषणा वयं सख्याय स्वस्तये ।
हुवेम वाजसातये ॥

9. Indra now assists in our prosperity in welfare.

We invoke him constantly in life-activity. (202)

१०. न कि इन्द्र त्वदुत्तरं न ज्यायो अस्ति वृत्रहन् ।
न क्येवं यथा त्वम् ॥

10. There is no one superior to you, Indra! in victoriously striking down Vṛtra (inertia).

There is none like you anywhere. (203)

D. II.

१. तरणिं वो जनानां त्रदं वाजस्य गोमतः ।
समानमु प्र शंसिषम् ॥

1. Indra rich in sense activities (cows) bestows on the three homes (states) of people in life-activity to cross over ignorance.

He nourishes them equally praiseworthily. (204)

२. असृग्रमिन्द्र ते गिरः प्रति त्वामुदहासत ।
सजोषा वृषभं पतिम् ॥

2. They flow before Indra to the brain (hill) and nourish him in existence before he departs.

Indra the lord acts in harmony. (205)

३. सुनीथो घा स मर्त्यो यं मरुतो यमर्यमा ।
मित्रास्पान्त्यद्रुहः ॥

3. He arouses and guides men indeed and controls, Indra restrains ideas (Maruts).

He fulfils the brain without hurting. (206)

४. यद्वीडाविन्द्र यत्स्थिरे यत्पर्शाने पराभृतम् ।
वसु स्पार्हं तदा भर ॥

4. Indra bestows and establishes them firmly, makes them abiding, the yonder world beholds, unites with them and supports.

Indra eagerly supports constantly. (207), (1072)

५. श्रुतं वो वृत्रहन्तमं प्र शर्धं चर्षणीनाम् ।
आशिषे राधसे महे ॥

5. He bestows hearing sense after striking down Vṛtra (inertia) as desired and diligently nourishes boldly.

The food (sense perceptions) bestow great prosperity as desired. (208)

६. अरं त इन्द्र श्रवसे गमेम शूर त्वावतः ।
अरं शक्र परेमणि ॥

6. Indra flows along the spokes-like nerves to come here to favour us with understanding, heroically.

The yonder world draws Indra along the nerves like a magnet. (209)

७. धानावन्तं करम्भिणमपूपवन्तमुक्थिनम् ।
इन्द्र प्रातर्जुषस्व नः ॥

7. Indra bestows on the brain cells, the porridge-like bake-house i.e. the brain bestows on us within (all ideas) praise-worthily.

In the early morning of creation Indra himself rejoiced resoundingly. (210)

८. अपां फेनेन नमुचेः शिर इन्द्रोदवर्तयः ।
विश्वा यदजय स्पृधः ॥

8. Indra cut off the head of Namuci (asura) with the foam of water in the ocean waters.

He won him for the bodies of creatures in the fight. (211). (Y.V. 19, 71)

The purāṇas have developed a story out of this mantra which runs as follows:— Indra wanted to forge an invincible weapon and consulted knowledgeable people. He was advised that the asura (matter) Namuci had a body hard as diamond and that he was such a charitable person that he never said 'no' to any request to him from anybody. So, Indra was advised to request Namuci's body as a gift. Indra, acting on the advice, immediately went to Namuci and made his request. Namuci told Indra that he may cut off his head and take away his body. Indra accomplished this with the foam of the ocean waves and took away Namuci's body for fashioning the outer shell for creatures.

The idea is that matter formed part of the creatures. Then ideas are so exceedingly fine that they penetrate the interstices of matter and break them down.

९. इमे त इन्द्र सोमाः सुतासो ये च सोत्वाः ।
तेषां मत्स्व प्रभूवसो ॥

9. Here Soma bestows on mind through Indra, who also bestows.

They are desired as masters in the home by us. (212)

१०. तुभ्यं सुतासः सोमाः स्तीर्णं बर्हिर्विभावसो ।
स्तोतृभ्य इन्द्र मृडय ॥

10. You two bestow on mind, Soma shines over the spread out nerves in the home.

Indra is praiseworthily compassionate. (213)

D. III.

१. आ व इन्द्र कृविं यथा वाजयन्तः शतक्रतुम् ।
मंहिष्ठं सिञ्च इन्दुभिः ॥

1. Indra bestows (on the brain) to cultivate, as he does in life-activity, with a hundred acts.

Munificently he tingles along to the brain cells. (214)

२. अतश्चिदिन्द्र न उपा याहि शतवाजया ।
इषा सहस्रवाजया ॥

2. Indra moves above towards the mind to arouse him to a hundred things in life.

He has a thousand desires in life-activity. (215)

३. आ बुन्दं वृत्रहा ददे जातः पृच्छाद्वि मातरम् ।
क उग्राः के हा भृण्विरे ॥

3. With Vṛtra's departure (Indra) bestows the rays (arrows of sense activities) from the source on the two enquirers (brain and sense organs) after the mother.

He gladdens the head powerfully, the head cooks and bestows for comfort. (216)

४. बृबदुक्थं हवामहे सृप्रकरस्नमूतये ।
साधः कृण्वन्तमवसे ॥

4. Very praiseworthily great oblations flow to help to nourish and produce.

They create a forest of desires in the home constantly. (217)

५. ऋजुनीती नो वरुणो मित्रो नयति विद्वान् ॥
अर्यमा देवैः सजोषाः ॥

5. Indra leads Varuṇa, truthfully he guides (ideas of) him to the brain desiring knowledge.

Indra (Aryamā) acts in harmony with ideas (devas). (218)

६. दूरादिहेव यत्सतोऽरुणप्सुरशिश्वितत् ।
वि भानुं विश्वथातनत् ॥

6. Very distant from here, the sun's rays in our existence unite with and release Activity to grow within.

Through his effulgence he guides the worlds. (219)

७. आ नो मित्रावरुणा घृतैर्गव्यूतिमुक्षतम् ।
मध्वा रजांसि सुक्रतू ॥

7. The sense activities help to sprinkle clarified butter from Varuṇa on the brain (Mitra).

They support the bestowal of varied sweet perceptions. (220), (663)

८. उदु त्ये सूनवो गिरः काष्ठा यज्ञेष्वत्नत ।
वाश्रा अभिज्ञु यातवे ॥

8. They (the sense activities) also arouse new (ideas) above on the hill, heaven bestows the desires in life-activity through them.

They move and bestow to cook knowledge. (221)

९. इदं विष्णुर्वि चक्रमे त्रेधा नि दधे पदम् ।
समूढमस्य पांसुले ॥

9. Here Viṣṇu perceives as he goes around me, in the natural course, and steps in the 3 states (homes) and bestows,

on such ignorant ones, like dust as we are, by grasping us. (222), (1659), (Y.V. 5, 15)

D. IV.

१. अतीहि मन्युषाविणं सुषुवांसमुपेरय ।
अस्य रातौ सुतं पिब ॥

1. He (Viṣṇu) arouses mind's eagerness and bestows mightily, he bestows and supports mind above after stirring him up.

He is gracious about our drinking Soma juice. (223)

२. कदु प्रचेतसे महे वचो देवाय शस्यते ।
तदिध्यस्य वर्धनम् ॥

2. He nourishes mind greatly always, devas (ideas) unite with the brain cells for the sake of speech.

They kindle and foster the growth of speech. (224)

३. उक्थं न च शस्यमानं नागो रयिरा चिकेत ।
न गायत्रं गीयमानम् ॥

3. The brain cells in the home gladden it praiseworthily by bestowing the wealth on the spinal cord perceiving its desire.

The spinal cord supports the sense activities so much from the home. (225)

४. इन्द्र उक्थेभिर्मन्दिष्ठो वाजानां च वाजपतिः ।
हरिवांत्सुतानां सखा ॥

4. When in a sluggish state Indra supports us praiseworthily in life-activity willingly (or as desired) and also the lord of life-activity,

consciousness releases them to mind his friend. (226)

५. आ याह्यु प नः सुतं वाजेभिर्मा हृणीयथाः।
महां इव युवजानिः ॥

5. Mind is closely united (with the brain) and bound to it, is supported in life-activity and (the brain) is not angry with it.

Mind is like a great being to the source. (227)

६. कदा वसो स्तोत्रं हर्यत आ अव श्मशा रुधद्वाः।
दीर्घं सुतं वाताप्याय ॥

6. Indra bestows praiseworthily the channels desired by the head to sustain both (brain and sense organs) and blesses them.

These (channels) are in friendship with mind abidingly. (228)

७. ब्राह्मणादिन्द्र राधसः पिबा सोममृतूंरनु।
तवेदं सख्यमस्तृतम्।

7. Indra bestows knowledge on mortals from the wealth (of sense perceptions) they drink, which is supported by Soma extensively.

Ṛta helps them here in the home. (229)

८. वयं घा ते अपि स्मसि स्तोतार इन्द्र गिर्वणः।
त्वं नो जिन्व सोमपाः ॥

8. It (knowledge) controls us indeed and we are bound to it also, Indra praiseworthily bestows it on the hill and binds us to it.

Soma wins it now and fulfils by bestowing. (230)

९. एन्द्र पृक्षु कासु चिन्नृम्णं तनूषु धेहि नः।
सत्राजिदुग्र पौंस्यम् ॥

9. Indra moves towards thoughts (ideas) to honour and nourish man (with such food) which he bestows delicately and binds us to them.

He wins prosperity for us in Soma yajña vigorously. (231)

१०. एवा ह्यसि वीरयुरेवा शूर उत स्थिरः।
एवा ते राध्यं मनः ॥

10. Vigorously you speed up extensively from heaven and bind us speedily and stabilise them heroically.

They speed up wealth to mind. (232), (824)

D. V.

१. अभि त्वा शूर नोनुमोऽदुग्धा इव धेनवः ।
ईशानमस्य जगतः स्वर्दृशमीशानमिन्द्र तस्थुषः ।

1. We now make obeisances to you as a hero, you are like a milch cow to the calves, you rule us in this world, to look up to heaven you rule us. Indra! You are abidingly eager. (233), (680), (Y.V. 27, 35)

२. त्वामिद्धि हवामहे सातौ वाजस्य कारवः ।
त्वां वृत्रेष्विन्द्र सत्पतिं नरस्त्वां काष्ठास्वर्वतः ॥

2. Indra! You bestow much oblations on the brain (fat) in the prison contiunally in life-activity.

You envelop and support by bestowing, as lord of existence, men praise you, you know the celestial course to heaven. (234), (809), (Y.V. 27, 37)

३. अभि प्र वः सुराधसमिन्द्रमर्च यथा विदे ॥
यो जरितृभ्यो मघवा पुरूवसुः सहस्रेणेव शिक्षति ॥

3. Indra honours the sense activities as enjoined to bestow nourishment to arouse wealth.

He is abundantly gracious to devotees and instructs them with thousands (of ideas). (235), (811)

४. तं वो दस्ममृतीषहं वसोर्मन्दानमन्धसः ।
अभि वत्सं न स्वसरेषु धेनव इन्द्रं गीर्भिर्नवामहे ॥

4. You desire to bestow the desires of men wondrously in waking state, Indra gladdens us by enabling us to bid farewell obeisances to ignorance. (236), (685), (Y.V. 26, 11)

The rays stream along to Mind themselves, Indra supports them much for fresh oblations.

५. तरोभिर्वो विदद्वसुमिन्द्रं सबाध ऊतये ।
बृहद्गायन्तः सुतसोमे अध्वरे हुवे भरं न कारिणम् ॥

5. He bestows to support us to cross (ignorance), Indra knows about wealth (Vasu) and helps to release us from distress.

He guides sense activities greatly, you invoke Soma in life-activity to support mind mightily from the brain (prison). (237)

६. तरणिरित्सिषासति वाजं पुरन्ध्या युजा ।
आ व इन्द्रं पुरुहूतं नमे गिरा नेमिं तष्टेव सुद्रुवम् ।

6. You bestow desires to cross (ignorance) in life-activity in existence and to sip from the brain (city) by uniting.

We make obeisances to Indra and invoke him much to bestow, as if he obtains (what he wants) from the rim (surface) of the brain he hastens to arouse it to bestow. (238), (867)

७. पिबा सुतस्य रसिनो मत्स्वा व इन्द्र गोमतः ।
आपिर्नो बोधि सधमाद्ये वृधे३ऽस्मां अवन्तु ते धियः ॥

7. Our Mind drinks with taste from our panting Indra, rich in cows (sense activities).

He also instructs us, he fosters the growth of his comrade mind, they favour us giving satisfaction. (239), (1421)

८. त्वं ह्येहि चेरवे विदा भगं वसुत्तये ।
उद्वावृषस्व मघवन् गविष्टय उदिन्द्राश्वमिष्टये ॥

8. Indra! You hasten to heaven (head) to arouse and bestow knowledge also, consciousness is gracious to you.

Indra (Maghavan) himself rains (his gifts) above on us desirous of sense activities, prāṇa desires Indra above (to bestow). (240), (1581)

९. न हि वश्चरमं च न वसिष्ठः परिमंसते ।
अस्माकमद्य मरुतः सुते सचा विश्वे पिबन्तु कामिनः ॥

9. You rouse up the home, also gladden it, you desire to reside, to gladden and go around supporting us.

Ideas (Maruts) unite with mind for us, the sense organs drink them lovingly within. (241)

१०. मा चिदन्यद्वि शंसत सखायो मा रिषण्यत ।
इन्द्रमित्स्तोता वृषणं सचा सुते मुहुरुक्था च शंसत ॥

10. Lead both from the brain and sense organs to mind and bestow them, help him praiseworthily, do not hurt him in uniting,

Indra praiseworthily establishes him by uniting him powerfully in an instant and is praised. (242), (1360)

BOOK III : CHAPTER II

D. I.

१. नकिष्टं कर्मणा नशद्यश्चकार सदावृधम् ।
इन्द्रं न यज्ञैर्विश्वगूर्तमृभ्वसमधृष्टं धृष्णुमोजसा ।

1. The head is desirous of fruitful activity, it achieves it immediately also, the brain (prison) constantly grows.

Indra praises the sense organs in life, on which the spinal cord bestows at the same time boldly on which the Sense activities boldly bestow. (243), (1155)

२. य ऋते चिदभिश्रिषः पुरा जत्रुभ्य आतृदः ।।
सन्धाता सन्धिं मघवा पुरूवसुर्निष्कर्ता विह्रुतं पुनः ।।

2. According to sacred ordinances in old times the bones (of creatures) were split and jointed (for new forms) of creatures.

Gifts were bestowed by Indra and united to them, Indra abundantly made diversions and restituted them. (244)

The mantra explains how new creatures were fashioned from existing ones by altering the bone structure, all internally of course. This shows that there was always pre-planning and that these ideas were injected into existing creatures.

३. आ त्वा सहस्रमा शतं युक्ता रथे हिरण्यये ।
ब्रह्मयुजो हरय इन्द्र केशिनो वहन्तु सोमपीतये ।।

3. Indra! You bestowed thousands of creatures uniting with hundreds of species of bodies (vehicles) and aroused gladness.

Indra conveys knowledge and unites it to us, he conveys Soma before the (bearded) consciousness who swells over to him. (245), (1391)

४. आ मन्द्रैरिन्द्र हरिभिर्याहि मयूररोमभिः ।
मा त्वा के चिन्नि येमुरिन्न पाशिनोऽति धन्वेव तां इहि ।।

4. Indra arouses the motley sense activities, like a peacock's plume, and supports them before consciousness.

You bestow thoughts (ideas) on the head, control them extensively which are akin to the arrows in a hunter's hand. (246), (1718)

५. त्वमङ्ग प्र शंसिषो देवः शविष्ठ मर्त्यम् ।
न त्वदन्यो मघवन्नस्ति मर्डितेन्द्र ब्रवीमि ते वचः ॥

5. Your limbs (nerves) nourish us with ideas (devas) praiseworthily with might and control mortals.

Indra (Maghavan)! There is none other like you in compassion for us, I tell men in my speeches. (247), (1723)

६. त्वमिन्द्र यशा अस्यृजीषी शवसस्पतिः ।
त्वं वृत्राणि हंस्यप्रतीन्येक इत्पुर्वनुत्तश्चर्षणीधृतिः ॥

6. Indra, lord of the sense organs (body) and brain cells! You are famed in rushing to them.

You went all alone in ancient days to oppose and strike down Vṛtra, you stood firmly invincible and active. (248), (1411)

७. इन्द्रमिद्देवतातय इन्द्रं प्रयत्यध्वरे ।
इन्द्रं समीके वनिनो हवामह इन्द्रं धनस्य सातये ॥

7. Indra! You bestow understanding through the brain, you unite with sense activities in life-activity.

Indra desires conflicts, he bestows much oblations of wealth on us continually. (249)

८. इमा उ त्वा पुरूवसो गिरो वर्धन्तु या मम ।
पावकवर्णाः शुचयो विपश्चितोऽभिस्तोमैरनूषत ॥

8. Indra, here, you foster growth in the brain abundantly and graciously for us.

You bestow varied (ideas) on the head to fulfil and shine, also you perceive the mind, who attaches himself to you praiseworthily. (250), (1607), (Y.V. 33, 81)

९. उदु त्ये मधुमत्तमा गिर स्तोमास ईरते ।
सत्राजितो धनसा अक्षितोतयो वाजयन्तो रथा इव ॥

9. You incite and bestow sense activities and desires also above on the hill praiseworthily.

You are victorious in Soma yajña, bestow wealth, help the brain (home), guide life-activity like a vehicle. (251), (1362)

१०. यथा गौरो अपा कृतं तृष्यन्नेत्यवेरिणम् ।
आपित्वे नः प्रपित्वे तूयमा गहि कण्वेषु सु सचा पिब ॥

10. Activity moves towards the brain cells (gauro—mustard)

and produces and leads ideas for the greedy cells mightily, and bestows.

Also you bind them, nourish them also quickly, arouse sense activities for the brain cells to unite with and drink. (252), (1721)

D. II.

१. शग्ध्यू३षु शचीपत इन्द्र विश्वाभिरूतिभिः ।
भगं न हि त्वा यशसं वसुविदमनु शूर चरामसि ॥

1. Indra! You are helpful in sipping the sense organs, you help the sense organs.

You now arouse the splendour of consciousness and now you go round like a hero to know the wealth of sense perceptions. (253), (1579)

२. या इन्द्र भुज आभरः स्वर्वा असुरेभ्यः ।
स्तोतारमिन्मघवन्नस्य वर्धय ये च त्वे वृक्तबर्हिषः ॥

2. Indra! You move now to help (the brain cells) to consume what heaven bestows as ideas (Sura) (or to the sense organs—asuras).

Praiseworthily Indra (Maghavan) fosters our growth mightily through the nerves which are spread out. (254)

३. प्र मित्राय प्रार्यम्णे सचथ्यमृतावसो ।
वरूथ्ये३ वरुणे छन्द्यं वचः स्तोत्रं राजसु गायत ॥

3. He moves to nourish the brain (Mitra), Indra (Aryamā) fulfils by uniting mortals to wealth (or graciously).

He protects what the body (Varuṇa) conceals and controls as speech, the sense activities unite with it, control and arouse it praiseworthily. (255)

The body here is referred to as Varuṇa as all its components are built of the products of Varuṇa.

४. अभि त्वा पूर्वपीतय इन्द्र स्तोमेभिरायवः ।
समीचीनास ऋभवः समस्वरन्रुद्रा गृणन्त पूर्व्यम् ॥

4. Indra! You cause it (speech) to swell earlier and praiseworthily release it from the brain cells.

The spinal cord (Ṛbhus) associate and are united with you,

at the same time Rudra announces the sounds from within which he controls from earlier on. (256), (1573)

Rudra is the controller of the nervous system under the leadership of Indra whose younger brother he is considered to be. The Ṛbhus comprise the three primary nerves i.e. spinal cord and the two long nerves rising from above the anus, running parallel, and crossing each other at about neck level terminate at the opposite lobes of the brain. They are terrestrial beings and are said to have reached heaven first after Indra.

५. प्र व इन्द्राय बृहते मरुतो ब्रह्मार्चत ।
वृत्रं हनति वृत्रहा शतक्रतुर्वज्रेण शतपर्वणा ॥

5. Indra honours knowledge greatly and bestows ideas (Maruts) to nourish it.

He strikes down Vṛtra, Vṛtra departs, and carries out a hundred deeds in hundred days. (257), (Y.V. 33, 96)

Once again the arctic phenomenon is referred to. We have already explained it under mantra 116. Vṛtra is supposed to have imprisoned the Sun below the ocean waters in the nether regions. One hundred forts were supposed to have been attacked during the hundred days and the Sun retrieved by Indra.

६. बृहदिन्द्राय गायत मरुतो वृत्रहन्तमम् ।
येन ज्योतिरजनयन्नृतावृधो देवं देवाय जागृवि ॥

6. Indra greatly united the sense activities to ideas (Maruts) after striking down Vṛtra as desired.

Consciousness released and guided them to take birth in men to promote their growth through ideas (devas), the devas move in the waking state. (258)

७. इन्द्र क्रतुं न आ भर पिता पुत्रेभ्यो यथा ।
शिक्षा णो अस्मिन्पुरुहूत यामनि जीवा ज्योतिरशीमहि ॥

7. Indra produces (ideas) by supporting like a father his son.

On our invoking him he instructs us in the path for jīvas abundantly and ties us on to consciousness greatly. (259), (1456)

८. मा न इन्द्र परा वृणग्भवा नः सधमाद्ये ।
त्वं न ऊती त्वमिन्न आप्यं मा न इन्द्र परावृणक् ॥

8. Indra envelops the home with sense activities from beyond for existence and binds it to them as a comrade.

You now help us, you control through Activity the home mightily, Indra envelops the head from beyond. (260)

९. वयं घ त्वा सुतावन्त आपो न वृक्तबर्हिषः ॥
पवित्रस्य प्रस्रवणेषु वृत्रहन्परि स्तोतार आसते ॥

9. Indra! Indeed you bestow and control us, you bestow Activity on mind within through the spread out nerves.

The missiles (rays) of sense activities flow to us beneficently and, after Vṛtra is struck down, go around us bestowing praiseworthily in existence (or for). (261), (864)

१०. यदिन्द्र नाहुषीष्वा ओजो नृम्णं च कृष्टिषु ।
यद्वा पञ्चक्षितीनां द्युम्नमा भर सत्रा विश्वानि पौंस्या ॥

10. Which Indra delivers to the spinal system willingly, to cultivate vigorously and courageously.

The five rays (fingers) from heaven support both (brain and sense organs) through it (spinal system) and bestow prosperity through the sense organs. (262)

D. III.

१. सत्यमित्था वृषेदसि वृषजूतिर्नोऽविता ।
वृषा ह्यु॒ग्र शृण्विषे परावति वृषो अर्वावति श्रुतः ॥

1. Indra! You rain (sense activities) to establish existence, you inspire and bless us by raining them.

Indra now powerfully cooks with the rays from beyond for understanding, the showers hasten with understanding from hearing. (263)

२. यच्छक्रासि परावति यदर्वावति वृत्रहन् ।
अतस्त्वा गीर्भिर्द्युगदिन्द्र केशिभिः सुतावाँ आ विवासति ॥

2. You control the production of understanding from beyond which hastens with knowledge after Vṛtra is struck down.

Then you support the hill (brain) for heaven to utter speech, consciousness through residing bestows it on Mind. (264)

३. अभि वो वीरमन्धसो मदेषु गाय गिरा महा विचेतसम् ।
इन्द्रं नाम श्रुत्यं शाकिनं वचो यथा ॥

3. The valorous Indra bestowed the missiles (rays) of sense activities to release from ignorance, the sense activities perceive all on the great hill.

Indra honours the sense of hearing and likewise he is helpful to speech. (265)

४. इन्द्र त्रिधातु शरणं त्रिवरूथं स्वस्तये ।
छर्दिर्यच्छ मघवद्भ्यश्च मह्यं च यावया दिद्युमेभ्यः ॥

4. Indra protects the three states, he guards them for their welfare.

He bestows to them and controls, he bestows wealth fearlessly also gladdens and bestows sense activities on the brain cells. (266)

५. श्रायन्त इव सूर्यं विश्वेदिन्द्रस्य भक्षत ।
वसूनि जातो जनिमान्योजसा प्रति भागं न दीधिमः ॥

5. As though consciousness is provided for the sense organs Indra lets him shine on them from the home.

The sense activities (women) from the source are born in the home through Indra (Vasu) and bestow vigorously on every part and give satisfaction. (267), (1319), (Y.V. 33, 41)

६. न सीमदेव आप तदिषं दीर्घायो मर्त्यः ।
एतग्वा चिद्य एतशो युयोजत इन्द्रो हरी युयोजते ॥

6. Somadeva protects the desires of man during a long life.

The motley sense perceptions are bestowed on mind, prāṇa releases them vigorously, through Indra, who indeed releases prāṇa vigorously. (268)

७. आ नो विश्वासु हव्यमिन्द्रं समत्सु भूषत ।
उप ब्रह्माणि सवनानि वृत्रहन्परमज्यां ऋचीषम ॥

7. Indra arouses the sense organs for oblations and ornaments all.

Above he bestows desire for knowledge by striking down Vṛtra, desires shine then to win it from beyond. (269), (1492)

८. तवेदिन्द्रावमं वसु त्वं पुष्यसि मध्यमम् ।
सत्रा विश्वस्य परमस्य राजसि न किष्ट्वा गोषु वृण्वते ॥

8. Indra! You give protection here graciously (or to wealth), you bestow prosperity through sense perceptions and control us.

In life-activity he controls the sense organs from beyond and bestows the sense activities to envelop the head for knowledge. (270)

> ९. क्वेयथ क्वेदसि पुरुत्रा चिद्धि ते मनः ।
> अलर्षि युध्म खजकृत्पुरंदर प्र गायत्रा अगासिषुः ॥

9. Whatever he moves, wherever he is, he bestows satisfaction on mind to a great extent.

He desires the tumult of battle for our sake and the destroyer of forts produces nourishment by supporting sense activities and bestowing their rays. (271)

> १०. वयमेनमिदा ह्योऽपीपेमेह वज्रिणम् ।
> तस्मा उ अद्य सवने सुतं भरा नूनं भूषत श्रुते ॥

10. He bestows mightily on the brain and controls it, through heaven and protects this here through the vigorous nerves.

Through them now he bestows the desires of the mind, supports it and adorns it from hearing. (272)

D. IV.

> १. यो राजा चर्षणीनां याता रथेभिरध्रिगुः ।
> विश्वासां तरुता पृतनानां ज्येष्ठं यो वृत्रहा गृणे ॥

1. He is the king (controller) and is diligently active and moves towards the sense organs (vehicles) to support them with the sense activities (gu) irresistably. (273)

> २. यत इन्द्र भयामहे ततो नो अभयं कृधि ।
> मघवञ्छग्धि तव तन्न ऊतये वि द्विषो वि मृधो जहि ॥

2. Indra unites, for the paths to shine indeed, the father now creates fearlessness and satisfaction.

Indra honours by giving food and satisfaction, you help and guide it through both its desires, you induce them to be born there without weariness. (274), (1321)

> ३. वास्तोष्पते ध्रुवा स्थूणांसत्रं सोम्यानाम् ।
> द्रप्सः पुरां भेत्ता शश्वतीनामिन्द्रो मुनीनां सखा ॥

3. You lord over the home eagerly (or you are eager) for the path to the home, firm, abiding in the life-activity to Soma.

Indra in ancient times subdivided the brain cells constantly, Soma, a sage, was his friend. (275)

The brain cells were allotted varying functions early in evolution.

४. बण्महाँ असि सूर्य बडादित्य महाँ असि ॥
महस्ते सतो महिमा पनिष्टम मह्ना देव महाँ असि ॥

4. Consciousness is a great (deva) very desirable (van), Aditi is powerful (bala) and great.

He gladdens us in the home very greatly, he is admirable to us, the majestic deva is a great one for us. (276), (1788)

५. अश्वी रथी सुरूप इद्गोमां यदिन्द्र ते सखा ।
श्वात्रभाजा वयसा सचते सदा चन्द्रैर्याति सभामुप ॥

5. Prāṇa the charioteer arouses the forms (objects) here through the sense activities in which Indra is helpful.

He bestow on us invigorating food to consume always by uniting, he goes on to mind from the assembly above. (277)

६. यद्द्याव इन्द्र ते शतं शतं भूमीरुत स्युः ।
न त्वा वज्रिन्त्सहस्रं सूर्या अनु न जातमष्ट रोदसी ॥

6. What Indra bestowed were sewed on (incorporated) in hundreds and hundreds of species of creatures.

You set in motion thousands of them in life-activity, consciousness now obtains from heaven (source) for both the brain and sense organs. (278), (862)

७. यदिन्द्र प्रागपागुदङ्न्यग्वा हूयसे नृभिः ।
सिमा पुरु नृषूतो अस्यानवेऽसि प्रशर्ध तुर्वशे ॥

7. What Indra fulfils with sense activities is for the sense organs to drink them (for milk i.e. sense perceptions) by guiding sense activities to them in men.

He binds men to them also abundantly what are new, nourishes them boldly and vigorously in the home. (279), (1231)

८. कस्तमिन्द्र त्वा वसवा मर्त्यो दधर्षति ।
श्रद्धा हि ते मघवन्पार्ये दिवि वाजी वाजं सिषासति ॥

8. Indra has his home in the head, he bestows on the home, he flows in mortals to bestow.

Indra (Maghavan) fulfils man faithfully with welfare, consciousness bestows existence speedily in life-activity as desired. (280)

९. इन्द्राग्नी अपादियं पूर्वागात्पद्वतीभ्यः।
हित्वा शिरो जिह्वया रारपच्चरत्त्रिंशत्पदा न्यक्रमीत् ॥

9. Indra and Agni bestow Activity whom they control, who comes to swell and bestow the steps to knowledge.

The sense activities arouse the head through their tongues. Activity goes around to the three states to bestow and guide them duly. (281)

१०. इन्द्र नेदीय एदिहि मितमेधाभिरूतिभिः।
आ शंतम शंतमाभिरभिष्टिभिरा स्वापे स्वापिभिः।

10. Behold Indra nearby, he helps and supports to establish understanding.

He desires to toil for it, he supports auspiciously and bestows as desired, he protects us himself, himself bestows to drink. (282)

D. V.

१. इत ऊती वो अजरं प्रहेतारमप्रहितम्।
आशुं जेतारं हेतारं रथीतममतूर्तं तुग्रियावृधम् ॥

1. He bestows on us help undecayingly, gladdens us by causing nourishment and nourishes us to welfare.

He wins quickly and gladdens, he is the cause of our gladness, he directs us to our desires quickly, he moves powerfully to envelop the home (or to foster growth). (283)

२. मो षु त्वा वाघतश्च नारे अस्मन्नि रीरमन्।
आरात्ताद्वा सधमादं न आ गहीह वा सन्नुप श्रुधि ॥

2. (Indra,) you are very eager about us devotees, you release gladness in us men, below.

You are ready to bestow on both brain cells and sense organs as comrades, you come here to bestow gifts from above and hear our satisfaction. (284), (1675)

३. सुनोता सोमपाव्ने सोममिन्द्राय वज्रिणे।
पचता पक्तीरवसे कृणुध्वमित्पृणन्नित्पृणते मयः ॥

3. Indra arouses and guides (sense activities) to fulfil the desires of Soma, Indra moves to Soma along the vigorous nerves.

He (Soma) cooks them, he bestows the cooked (sense activities), prāṇa runs to cultivate and establish them to nourish (the brain cells), the sense activities nourish them. (285)

४. यः सत्राहा विचर्षणिरिन्द्रं तं हूमहे वयम् ।
सहस्रमन्यो तुविनृम्ण सत्पते भवा समत्सु नो वृधे ॥

4. Indra speeds up to life-activity and is indeed very active, we desire to invoke him greatly.

He guides thousands (of ideas) to us powerfully and boldly, he is the lord of existence, he fosters the growth of mind with all. (286)

५. शचीभिर्नः शचीवसू दिवा नक्तं दिशस्यतम् ।
मा वां रातिरुपदसत्कदाचनास्मद्रातिः कदाचन ॥

5. He supports and binds us with might, Indra is mighty, day and night he directs and unites.

You two are ready to bestow on us above who are always in want, you are ready to bestow on us always. (287)

६. यदा कदा च मीढुषे स्तोता जरेत मर्त्यः ।
आदिद्वन्देत वरुणं विपा गिरा धर्त्तारं विव्रतानाम् ॥

6. What you reward us, mortals with always praiseworthily till old age are the motley sense activities.

The sense activities were praised in ancient times for scattering ideas of Varuṇa (external world) in the hill (brain) to support and gladden it according to their vows (duties). (288)

७. पाहि गा अन्धसो मद इन्द्राय मेध्यातिथे ।
यः संमिश्लो हर्योर्यो हिरण्यय इन्द्रो वज्री हिरण्ययः ॥

7. The sense activities arouse and fulfil us by releasing ignorance, Indra moves joyously to Aditi for understanding.

They speed up to mingle with all eagerly and extensively, Indra moves to arouse and gladden us through the vigorous nerves and the tawny consciousness. (289)

८. उभयं शृणवच्च न इन्द्रो अर्वागिदं वचः ।
सत्राच्या मघवान्त्सोमपीतये धिया शविष्ठ आ गमत् ॥

8. Indra controls both the brain cells and sense organs, cooks for them and bestows also and speeds here for speech.

In life-activity Soma drinks off Indra and comes to us to satisfy us in our desire for sense organs. (290)

९. महे च न त्वाद्रिवः परा शुल्काय वीयसे ।
न सहस्राय नायुताय वज्रिवो न शताय शतामघ ॥

9. You gladden us much on the hill by bestowing and strive to bestow from beyond for a price.

You bestow through the vigorous nerves wealth (of perceptions) in hundreds of hundreds to thousands nay myriads (of brain cells. (291)

१०. वस्यां इन्द्रासि मे पितुरुत भ्रातुरभुञ्जतः ।
माता च मे छदयथः समा वसो वसुत्वनाय राधसे ॥

10. Indra binds me to the paths to the home of the father (Activity) resoundingly who releases the mother.

The mother also is concealed and unites with me blessing at the same time, Indra guides and bestows the wealth. (292)

BOOK IV : CHAPTER I

D. I.

१. इम इन्द्राय सुन्विरे सोमासो दध्याशिरः ।
ताँ आ मदाय वज्रहस्त पीतये हरिभ्यां याह्योक आ ।।

1. Soma bestows curds (sense reactions) in the head of the devotee for his comfort through Indra here.

Longingly he (Soma) drinks sense activities from the vigorous nerves (hands) to which consciousness moves in the head (pot). (293)

२. इम इन्द्र मदाय ते सोमाश्चिकित्र उक्थिनः ।
मधोः पपान उप नो गिरः शृणु रास्व स्तोत्राय गिर्वणः ।।

2. Here Indra moves to the sense activities, knowing which Soma supports praiseworthily and binds them.

He protects and drinks them above on the hill, he cooks and bestows them praiseworthily on the brain desiring them. (294)

३. आ त्वा३द्य सबर्दुघां हुवे गायत्रवेपसम् ।
इन्द्रं धेनुं सुदुघामन्यामिषमुरुधारामरङ्कृतम् ।।

3. Now you invoke all those yielding milk (perceptions), support the sense activities to scatter them all.

Indra opens the eyes of the mind to the good milk from the milch-cow of varied hues which he supports extensively. (295)

४. न त्वा बृहन्तो अद्रयो वरन्त इन्द्र वीडवः ।
यच्छिक्षसि स्तुवते मावते वसु न किष्टदा मिनामि ते ।।

4. Indra bestows and establishes gifts within, they stream along from you for consumption.

You control and bind them to the home praiseworthily for understanding, you bestow understanding graciously on the head, you approach it and bestow what is desired. (296)

५. क ईं वेद सुते सचा पिबन्तं कद्वयो दधे ।
अयं यः पुरो विभिनत्योजसा मन्दानः शिप्रयन्धसः ।।

5. The mind unites with knowledge from the brain, he drinks what is bestowed on him, prāṇa bestows vigorously and mightily without shining and speeds them along the path to the home,

he releases the cheekful ignorance of the mind from the brain cells. (297), (1696)

६. यदिन्द्र शासो अव्रतं च्यावया सदसस्परि ।
अस्माकमंशुं मघवन्पुरुस्पृहं वसव्ये अधि बर्हय ॥

6. Which is Indra's command according to his vow (duty) for which he moves and goes around to the brain cells in the home.

Indra is very eager for Soma juice on our behalf and he moves to increase (barha) it in the home to satisfy us. (298)

७. त्वष्टा नो दैव्यं वचः पर्जन्यो ब्रह्मणस्पतिः ।
पुत्रैर्भ्रातृभिरदितिर्नु पातु नो दुष्टरं त्रामणं वचः ।

7. Tvaṣṭā (sense of touch) controls the ideas of speech, Soma (Brahmaṇaspati) rains them.

Aditi supports them as though they are her children or brothers and protects them, recognising it (speech) in the spokes-like nerves (aram), mind supports speech. (299)

८. कदा चन स्तरीरसि नेन्द्र सश्चसि दाशुषे ।
उपोपेन्नु मघवन्भूय इन्नु ते दानं देवस्य पृच्यते ॥

8. You gladden us always by releasing relishing (ideas) in the home, Indra unites with the devotees eagerly.

Indra (Maghavan) protects them above mightily in their existence, devas (ideas) unite with them nourishing them with gifts. (300)

९. युङ्क्ष्वा हि वृत्रहन्तम हरी इन्द्र परावतः ।
अर्वाचीनो मघवन्त्सोमपीतय उग्र ऋष्वेभिरा गहि ॥

9. After Vṛtra is struck down as desired the tawny consciousness arouses the home and unites them to understanding through Indra, from beyond.

Turning round he lets Soma drink vigorously and flows to arouse sense activities and support (301)

१०. त्वामिदा ह्यो नरोऽपीप्यन्वज्रिन्भूर्णयः ।
स इन्द्र स्तोमवाहस इह श्रुध्युप स्वसरमा गहि ॥

10. (Indra!) You approach heaven (head) and bestow in men which swells copiously in the vigorous nerves and are guided for drinking.

And Indra praiseworthily conveys them, which is sipped for hearing above, he himself arouses the sense activities bestowing gladness. (302), (813)

D. II.

१. प्रत्यु अदर्श्यायत्यू३च्छन्ती दुहिता दिवः ।
अपो मही वृणुते चक्षुषा तमो ज्योतिष्कृणोति सूनरी ॥

1. It is well-known that the daughter of consciousness (Uṣas) on visiting above unites and nourishes (with her rays), Activity the great chose the sense of sight as desired, the effulgence of consciousness creates gladness in the motley sense activities. (303), (751)

२. इमा उ वां दिविष्टय उस्रा हवन्ते अश्विना ।
अयं वामह्वेऽवसे शचीवसू विशं विशं हि गच्छथः ॥

2. The Aśvins bestowed (vām) Uṣas as oblation within and produced the waking state desired here, through Indra.

Who blesses on invocation with a pleasant path enabling wealth to go to one species of creature after another and arouse (waking state) with might. (304), (753)

३. कुष्ठः को वामश्विना तपानो देवा मर्त्यः ।
घ्नता वामश्मया क्षयमाणोंशुनेत्थमु आद्वन्यथा ॥

3. Who but the lovely Aśvins cultivate (the brain) for mortals to drink ideas?

The Aśvins strike down (Vṛtra) moving into the hill, when the home is depleted, for the motley sense activities to blossom in both (brain and sense organs) and guide them. (305)

४. अयं वां मधुमत्तमः सुतः सोमो दिविष्टिषु ।
तमश्विना पिबतं तिरोअह्न्यं धत्तं रत्नानि दाशुषे ॥

4. The sense perceptions bestow the path as desired by our mind at the wish of Soma for sense activities in the waking state.

He drinks as desired from Aśvins for crossing in the waking state and bestows valuable wealth on the devotees eagerly. (306)

५. आ त्वा सोमस्य गल्दया सदा याचन्नहं ज्या ।
भूर्णिं मृगं न सवनेषु चुक्रुधं क ईशानं न याचिषत् ॥

5. You divide, constantly, what trickles down from Soma from which also we gain sense perception (food).

The sense activities excite the sense organs for Soma juice, for which the angry brain entreats desiring it and rules. (307)

६. अध्वर्यो द्रावया त्वं सोममिन्द्रः पिपासति ।
उपो नूनं युयुजे वृषणा हरी आ च जगाम वृत्रहा ॥

6. You run to us in life-activity, Soma and also Indra protect us in existence.

Now Indra unites separately (yu) with the tawny consciousness for birth of sense activities for us after departure of Vṛtra. (308)

७. अभीषतस्तदा भरेन्द्र ज्यायः कनीयसः ॥
पुरूवसुर्हि मघवन्बभूविथ भरेभरे च हव्यः ।

7. Indra strives victoriously for the sense activities and bestowing them supports them formidably.

Indra arouses wealth abundantly for existence through them and supports them again and again, also their oblations. (309)

८. यदिन्द्र यावतस्त्वमेतावदहमीशीय ।
स्तोतारमिद्दधिषे रदावसो न पापत्वाय रंसिषम् ॥

8. What Indra moves to them for is understanding which the motley sense activities praiseworthily speak out (bestow) in waking and rule us.

The brain praiseworthily bestows curds (sense reactions) which Indra preserves in the nerves (or with which Indra fulfils through the nerves), he moves to protect and bestow to our desires and gladden. (310), (1796)

९. त्वमिन्द्र प्रतूर्तिष्वभि विश्वा असि स्पृधः ।
अशस्तिहा जनिता वृत्रतूरसि त्वं तूर्य तरुष्यतः ॥

9. Indra! You nourish the desires of the sense organs quickly to release and bestow them.

Vṛtra is born powerless, you overcome him, angrily he moves and unites with the fourth state. (311), (1637), (Y.V. 33, 66)

१०. प्र यो रिरिक्ष ओजसा दिवः सदोभ्यस्परि ।
न त्वा विव्याच रज इन्द्र पार्थिवमति विश्वं ववक्षिथ ॥

10. You release nourishment, consciousness constantly goes

around and vigorously releases (the nourishment) to the brain.

Indra! You are also excited through us, the sense organs of terrestrial origin bestow understanding and strengthen it. (312)

D. III.

१. असावि देवं गोऋजीकमन्धो न्यस्मिन्निन्द्रो जनुषेमुवोच ।
बोधामसि त्वा हर्यश्व यज्ञैर्बोधा न स्तोममन्धसो मदेषु ॥

1. Ignorance is won over as desired through the relatives i.e. ideas (devas) bestowed by Indra who guides them to us and tells us men eagerly.

He imparts knowledge to us, consciousness bestows knowledge in life-activity and releases from ignorance through the sense activities praiseworthily. (313)

२. योनिष्ट इन्द्र सदने अकारि तमा नृभिः पुरुहूत प्र याहि ।
असो यथा नोऽविता वृधश्चिद्ददो वसूनि ममदश्च सोमैः ॥

2. At the desire of the source, Indra produces desires in the home in men, the sense activities are abundantly invoked and they move in to arouse.

Like bestowing they favour the growth of mind, Soma also bestows on us wealth (or graciously). (314)

३. अदर्दरुत्समसृजो वि खानि त्वमर्णवान्बद्बधानाँ अरम्णाः ।
महान्तमिन्द्र पर्वतं वि यद्वः सृजद्धारा अव यद्दानवान्हन् ॥

3. (Indra!) You bestow food (sense perceptions), which flow uniformly through the pits and to which you, through consciousness, bind the desires of the brain cells suitably.

The great Indra desires to bestow them from the brain (hill), he flows to support them and bless the desires of the brain cells in waking. (315)

४. सुष्वाणास इन्द्र स्तुमसि त्वा सनिष्यन्तश्चित्तुविनृम्ण वाजम् ।
आ नो भर सुवितं यस्य कोना तना त्मना सह्यामा त्वोताः ॥

4. Indra! You praise and desire to bestow the rays (arrows), you bestow them as gifts within for the desires of the mind mightily and boldly in life-activity.

You support them for prosperity, then you guide the head yourself and the course of the motley sense activities at the same time. (316)

५. जगृह्मा ते दक्षिणमिन्द्र हस्तं वसूयवो वसुपते वसूनाम् ।
विद्मा हि त्वा गोपतिं शूर गोनामस्मभ्यं चित्रं वृषणं रयिं दाः ॥

5. They are born in the home (brain), Indra incites the brain cells to the nerves leading southwards (to sense organs) along the path to wealth graciously (or to the wealth).

He rouses us up to knowledge, as a hero and lord of the cows (sense activities), through the sense perceptions he rains on us a variety of wealth and honours. (317)

६. इन्द्रं नरो नेमधिता हवन्ते यत्पार्या युनजते धियस्ताः ।
शूरो नृषाता श्रवसश्च काम आ गोमति व्रजे भजा त्वं नः ॥

6. Indra satisfies men from the summit (rim) with oblations within, he unites with the sense activities from beyond and satisfies the home.

The hero flows to men during their existence to unite for their desire for knowledge through sense perceptions, you honour them in the enclosure and bind them. (318)

७. वयः सुपर्णा उप सेदुरिन्द्रं प्रियमेधा ऋषयो नाधमानाः ।
अप ध्वान्तमूर्णुहि पूर्धि चक्षुर्मुमुग्ध्या३स्मान्निधयेव बद्धान् ॥

7. Indra speeds up to bestow the golden winged consciousness at a distance, who fondly bestows understanding through the ṛṣis in the home.

Activity runs within in waves to swell and satisfy us, he moves to the bewildered eyes and as if to sip below he binds (steadies) their desires. (319)

८. नाके सुपर्णमुप यत्पतन्तं हृदा वेनन्तो अभ्यचक्षत त्वा ।
हिरण्यपक्षं वरुणस्य दूतं यमस्य योनौ शकुनं भुरण्युम् ॥

8. The golden winged consciousness from heaven above comes down to unite with the brain (heart) desiring to look into it.

The messengers of Varuṇa arouse the wings (brain and sense organs) and gladden them and control us from the source, the sense activities gladden us in existence at propitious time. (320), (1846)

९. ब्रह्म जज्ञानं प्रथमं पुरस्ताद् वि सीमतः सुरुचो वेन आवः ।
स बुध्न्या उपमा अस्य विष्ठाः सतश्च योनिमसतश्च विवः ॥

9. Wisdom is born of knowledge foremost from the east (i.e. sense organs in front of the face), through it our desires are exposed and shine.

And from the depths of heaven hundreds of images like us are released as desirable, the source rides over hundreds of them. (321)

१०. अपूर्व्या पुरुतमान्यस्मै महे वीराय तवसे तुराय ।
विरप्शिने वज्रिणे शन्तमानि वचांस्यस्मै स्थविराय तक्षुः ॥

10. In ancient times you loved to guide abundantly men like us, with great vigour you bestowed them quickly (or willingly).

Through the vigorous nerves you were most bounteous to an abundance of them, you support speech in us, stabilise and control by shaping it. (322)

D. IV.

१. अव द्रप्सो अंशुमतीमतिष्ठदीयानः कृष्णो दशभिः सहस्रैः ।
आवत्तमिन्द्रः शच्या धमन्तमप स्नेहितीर्नृमणा अधत्राः ॥

1. The brain calls bestow understanding through Soma juice as desired by us delivered by the sense organs, they are cultivated and provide protection in a thousand ways.

Indra bestows them by uniting within the home, he is attached to them and runs to bestow them courageously. (323)

२. वृत्रस्य त्वा श्वसथादीषमाणा विश्वे देवा अजहुर्ये सखायः ।
मरुद्भिरिन्द्र सख्यं ते अस्त्वथेमा विश्वाः पृतना जयासि ॥

2. They (the brain cells) envelop and support us, prāṇa at the desire of the home invokes the Aśvins to help the brain cells in existence.

Indra supports ideas (Maruts) to help them, they praiseworthily nourish the sense organs here and win them. (324)

३. विधुं दद्राणं समने बहूनां युवानं सन्तं पलितो जगार ।
देवस्य पश्य काव्यं महित्वाद्या ममार स ह्यः समान ॥

3. Through embracing and agitating dormant ideas the sense activities released the birth of many ideas in the mind (youth) and bestowed them as gifts as desired which they grasped and protected.

Alt. Alone Indra entered (ran to) conflict of life and bestowed many youthful creatures as gifts as desired by the sense activities which released births which they grasped and were protected.

The devas visioned the story of life, now they bestow much on us, they bestow instantly on the home. (325), (1782)

४. त्वं ह त्यत्सप्तभ्यो जायमानोऽशत्रुभ्यो अभवः शत्रुरिन्द्र ।
गूळ्हे द्यावापृथिवी अन्वविन्दो विभुमद्भ्यो भुवनेभ्यो रणं धाः ॥

4. Indra! You have indeed, as is well-known, brought the seven Ṛṣis from the source to the home, made the enemies non-existent, Indra is overthrower.

Secretly he follows the brain and sense organs and is praised, the sense activities pervading all over fearlessly bestow gladness. (326)

५. मेडिं न त्वा वज्रिणं भृष्टिमन्तं पुरुधस्मानं वृषभं स्थिरप्स्नुम् ।
करोष्यर्यस्तरुषीर्दुवस्युरिन्द्र द्युक्षं वृत्रहणं गृणीषे ॥

5. You support me within through the vigorous nerves resoundingly, Indra stabilises the home in many ways (purudha) through sense perceptions (milk-sun) from Activity. (327)

2nd line : You produce eagerly for man quickly and honour him extensively.

You are a celestial being, you strike down Vṛtra as desired by the devotee. (327)

६. प्र वो महे महे वृधे भरध्वं प्रचेतसे प्र सुमतिं कृणुध्वम् ।
विशः पूर्वीः प्र चर चर्षणिप्राः ॥

6. You bestow nourishment greatly, you foster growth greatly, run to support, nourish the mind, nourish us with good understanding and hasten to produce them.

In ancient times you went around the home to nourish and fulfilled diligently. (328), (1793)

७. शुनं हुवेम मघवानमिन्द्रमस्मिन्भरे नृतमं वाजसातौ ।
शृण्वन्तमुग्रमूतये समत्सु घ्नन्तं वृत्राणि सञ्जितं धनानि ॥

7. We invoke prosperity, Indra supports our desire for wealth and man's desires in life-activity continually.

You help powerfully to cook within, at the same time you arouse and strike down Vṛtra, you attach yourself to wealth. (329)

८. उदु ब्रह्माण्यैरत श्रवस्येन्द्रं समर्ये महया वसिष्ठ ।
आ यो विश्वानि श्रवसा ततानोपश्रोता म ईवतो वचांसि ॥

8. You stir up knowledge above, Indra flows to us greatly in our assembly desiring to reside.

He flows to the sense organs, bestows the sense of hearing through the father and supports my speech so greatly. (330)

९. चक्रं यदस्याप्स्वा निषत्तमुतो तदस्मै मध्विच्चच्छद्यात् ।
पृथिव्यामतिषितं यदूधः पयो गोष्वदधा ओषधीषु ॥

9. Who goes around us by himself is Activity who is seated and also bestows sense activities as desired by us instantly.

The sense activities themselves bestow understanding from knowledge (whiteness) arising from sense organs like a cloud and also nourishment. (331)

D. V.

१. त्यमू षु वाजिनं देवजूतं सहोवानं तरुतारं रथानाम् ।
अरिष्टनेमिं पृतनाजमाशुं स्वस्तये तार्क्ष्यमिहा हुवेम ॥

1. You inspire the sense organs through ideas (devas) in life, at the same time you gladden the desires quickly through the sense organs.

From the summit (rim) you nourish through the spokes-like nerves the desires quickly for welfare, if they wane here, we invoke you. (332)

२. त्रातारमिन्द्रमवितारमिन्द्रं हवेहवे सुहवं शूरमिन्द्रम् ।
हुवे नु शक्रं पुरुहूतमिन्द्रमिदं हविर्मघवा वेत्त्विन्द्रः ॥

2. Indra supports to cross over (ignorance), he blesses and gladdens us with oblations after oblations, the valourous Indra.

We now invoke Indra (śakra), he is much invoked here, he bestows wealth through the oblations, Indra knows. (333), (Y.V. 20, 50)

३. यजामह इन्द्रं वज्रदक्षिणं हरीणां रथ्य३विव्रतानाम् ।
प्र श्मश्रुभिर्दोधुवदूर्ध्वधा भुवद्विसेनाभिर्भयमानो वि राधसा ॥

3. Indra gladdens us in life through the vigorous nerves in the south, consciousness honours the sense organs through his vows.

Through his rays (beard) he supports and bestows by agitating the head (ūrdhva), he supports the two troops (to the brain and the sense organs) in existence fearlessly and bestows wealth on the home. (334)

४. सत्राहणं दाधृषिं तुम्रमिन्द्रं महामपारं वृषभं सुवज्रम् ।
हन्ता यो वृत्रं सनितोत वाजं दाता मघानि मघवा सुराधाः ॥

4. He honours life-activity indeed by bestowing the ṛṣis whom Indra gladdens, he gladdens Activity greatly arousing the vigorous nerves.

He strikes down Vṛtra bestows gifts also in life, bestows wealth, Indra bestows ideas (Sura). (335)

५. यो नो वनुष्यन्नभिदाति मर्त उगणा वा मन्यमानस्तुरो वा ।
क्षिधी युधा शवसा वा तमिन्द्राभी ष्याम वृषमणस्त्वोताः ॥

5. Food (sense activities) desires to move eagerly from the source, divide themselves in mortals, also bestow their retinue and bestow speedily on mind from the home.

Indra desires to bestow with might understanding dwelling (to the brain) by uniting with it, with shining desire he moves to us and rains the motley sense activities in the home. (336)

६. यं वृत्रेषु क्षितय स्पर्धमाना यं युक्तेषु तुरयन्तो हवन्ते ।
यं शूरसातौ यमपामुपज्मन्यं विप्रासो वाजयन्ते स इन्द्रः ॥

6. He controls Vṛtra dwelling (in the home) in rivalry, he controls him who is yoked and powerfully guides the oblations.

Valiantly he controls him continually, Activity above controls the mind, inspires and bestows him, Indra guides him in life-activity and bestows him. (337)

७. इन्द्रापर्वता बृहता रथेन वामीरिष आ वहतं सुवीराः ।
वीतं हव्यान्यध्वरेषु देवा वर्धेथां गीर्भिरिडया मदन्ता ॥

7. On the hill Indra bestows much on the sense organs towards our comfort and desires, the good hero conveys them willingly.

He desires (to make) oblations in life-activity, the deva fosters their growth, he supports the oblations of the sense activities on the hill. (338)

८. इन्द्राय गिरो अनिशितसर्गा अपः प्रैरयत्सगरस्य बुध्नात् ।
यो अक्षेणेव चक्रियौ शचीभिर्विष्वक्तस्तम्भ पृथिवीमुत द्याम् ॥

8. Indra moves unrestingly on the hill to the surging Activity whom he incites to nourish our regions (atmosphere) from the depths (of heaven).

He (Activity) wanders around, like the eyes, and with might supports to stabilise the cosmos and also the home through the sense organs. (339)

९. आ त्वा सखायः सख्या ववृत्युस्तिरः पुरू चिदर्णवां जगम्याः ।
पितुर्नपातमा दधीत वेधा अस्मिन्क्षये प्रतरां दीद्यानः ॥

9. You help like a friend, envelop and unite with and bestow to cross (over ignorance), abundant streams (of sense activities) are made to take birth accessible to mind.

The father (Activity) bestows on me knowledge through the sense organs (descendants), he moves to our homes to nourish us through the sense organs to cross. (340)

१०. को अद्य युङ्क्ते धुरि गा ऋतस्य शिमीवतो भामिनो दुर्हृणायून् ।
आसन्नेषामप्सुवाहो मयोभून्य एषां भृत्यामृणधत्स जीवात् ॥

10. What (or who) unites now to set the sense activities in motion and release them?

Ṛta releases them to approach me for knowledge, the door shines to convey and guide what is in need.

Activity who is near eagerly conveys him (Ṛta) leading to gladness and guides him, he supports him to bestow on mortals to live. (341)

BOOK IV : CHAPTER II

D. I.

१. गायन्ति त्वा गायत्रिणोऽर्चन्त्यर्कमर्किणः ।
ब्रह्माणस्त्वा शतक्रत उद्वंशमिव येमिरे ॥

1. Indra ! You guide the sense activities, you honour the three states with them before consciousness (sun) praiseworthily.

You do a hundred acts for knowledge, you support them abova like a crossbeam for our comfort. (342), (1344)

२. इन्द्रं विश्वा अवीवृधन्त्समुद्रव्यचसं गिरः ।
रथीतमं रथीनां वाजानां सत्पतिं पतिम् ॥

2. Indra favours the sense organs, fosters their growth by gladdening them, perceives them all from the brain.

He is fond of the vehicles, he is the charioteer in life, he is the lord of existence and is our lord (or path). (343), (827), (Y.V. 12, 56)

३. इममिन्द्र सुतं पिब ज्येष्ठममर्त्यं मदम् ।
शुक्रस्य त्वाभ्यक्षरन्धारा ऋतस्य सादने ॥

3. Here the mind drinks from Indra, he is the eldest to us mortals and makes us joyous.

He speeds us through consciousness and supports to gladden us through Ṛta in the home (sādana). (344)

४. यदिन्द्र चित्र म इह नास्ति त्वादातमद्रिवः ।
राधस्तन्नो विदद्वस उभयाहस्त्या भर ॥

4. Indra is to us here of varied (help), he bestows on us from the hill.

He guides wealth knowing the home he supports both (brain and sense organs) through the nerves (his hands). (345), (1172)

५. श्रुधी हवं तिरश्च्या इन्द्र यस्त्वा सपर्यति ।
सुवीर्यस्य गोमतो रायस्पूर्धि महाँ असि ॥

5. Indra bestows oblations of understanding through the sense of hearing for which he gives his services to them.

He arouses our vigour through sense activities, he controls us greatly by enabling us to swell with satisfaction. (346), (883)

६. असावि सोम इन्द्र ते शविष्ठ धृष्णवा गहि।
आ त्वा पृणक्त्विन्द्रियं रजः सूर्यो न रश्मिभिः॥

6. Soma bestows through Indra and with might he arouses sense activities afresh boldly.

He nourishes against ignorance and bestows variedly on the sense organs before the rays of consciousness. (347), (1028)

७. एन्द्र याहि हरिभिरुप कण्वस्य सुष्टुतिम्।
दिवो अमुष्य शासतो दिवं यय दिवावसो॥

7. Indra moves to arouse consciousness to support the brain cells above suitably.

Consciousness bestows on us existence eagerly, consciousness moves swiftly, consciousness bestows favours. (348)

८. आ त्वा गिरो रथीरिवास्थुः सुतेषु गिर्वणः।
अभि त्वा समनूषत गावो वत्सं न धेनवः॥

8. You are like a charioteer on the hill abidingly, you are desired on the hill by mind.

At the same time you are eager for him like the cows are towards their calves. (349)

९. एतो न्विन्द्रं स्तवाम शुद्धं शुद्धेन साम्ना।
शुद्धैरुक्थैर्वावृध्वांसं शुद्धैराशीर्वान्ममत्तु॥

9. Indra bestows sense activities mightily praiseworthily on us to purify, they give us pure satisfaction.

Purifyingly and praiseworthily they bestow and support to foster growth, they bless us in purity. (350), (1402)

१०. यो रयिं वो रयिन्तमो यो द्युम्नैर्द्युम्नवत्तमः।
सोमः सुतः स इन्द्र तेऽस्ति स्वधापते मदः॥

10. You bestow wealth, you bestow desire for wealth, new desire for wealth from heaven.

Soma bestows on mind through Indra, he is the lord of sense activities determined by himself. (351)

D. II.

१. प्रत्यस्मै पिपीषते विश्वानि विदुषे भर।
अरङ्गमाय जग्मयेऽपश्चादध्वने नरः॥

1. You nourish me, also falten me and support knowledge through sense organs.

Varied colourful creatures are marvelously born of sense activities through prāṇa and then men enter life-journey. (352), (1440)

२. आ नो वयो वयःशयं महान्तं गह्वरेष्ठां महान्तं पूर्विनेष्ठाम् ।
उग्रं वचो अपावधीः ॥

2. You invigorate the face, and speedily bestow sleep, the great one (Indra) desires sense activities which are desired by the spinal system, the great one desires the ancient ones mightily.

Activity bestows understanding through speech vigorously. (353)

३. आ त्वा रथं यथोतये सुम्नाय वर्तयामसि ।
तुविकूर्मिमृतीषहमिन्द्रं शविष्ठ सत्पतिम् ॥

3. You help the sense organs likewise binding them to the subsisting courses splendidly.

Indra approaches the sense organs in waking at the desire of mortals with might as the path for existence. (354), (1771)

४. स पूर्व्यो महोनां वेनः क्रतुभिरानजे ।
यस्य द्वारा मनुः पिता देवेषु धिय आनजे ॥

4. He bestowed a great many desires in ancient times supporting their births from the face at proper times.

You are the gate (opening) for mind, the father (Activity) gives satisfaction to him through ideas (devas) when (the senses) take birth in the face. (355)

५. यदी वहन्त्याशवो भ्राजमाना रथेष्वा ।
पिबन्तो मदिरं मधु तत्र श्रवांसि कृण्वते ॥

5. Which (the ideas) you convey to the sense organs (śava), what the sense organs desire to bestow shine in the home (brain).

It (the brain) drinks the intoxicating honey (perceptions), there you support the sense of hearing to create understanding. (356)

६. त्यमु वो अप्रहणं गृणीषे शवसस्पतिम् ।
इन्द्रं विश्वासाहं नरं शचिष्ठं विश्ववेदसम् ॥

6. The lord of the sense organs and brain cells is well-known

to strike down (Vṛtra) and bestow nourishment eagerly on the devotee.

Indra bestows on the sense organs of men in waking, desiring to unite with them bestowing all knowledge on the home. (357)

७. दधिक्राव्णो अकारिषं जिष्णोरश्वस्य वाजिनः ।
सुरभि नो मुखा करत्प्र न आयूंषि तारिषत् ॥

7. Curds (sense reactions) are produced from desires, prāṇa wins the desires in the head in life-activity.

The face (i.e. the sense organs) produces them pleasantly from the sense perceptions (nourishment) to cross over (ignorance) as desired in life. (358), (Y.V. 23, 32)

८. पुरां भिन्दुर्युवा कविरमितौजा अजायत ।
इन्द्रो विश्वस्य कर्मणो धर्ता वज्री पुरुष्टुतः ॥

8. In ancient times when the earth (or brain cells were) was young, Agni (the wise) bestowed and established mammoth creatures from the source.

Indra supports the duties of the cosmos (or of sense organs) through the vigorous nerves praiseworthily. (359), (1250)

That mammoth creatures were produced in the early part of evolution was known to this ancient race of devas and asuras who were inhabitants of the Arctic belt, along with some other races, before glaciation. This matter is discussed in the introduction. The ancient people may have come across skeletons of these creatures.

D. III.

१. प्रप्र वस्त्रिष्टुभमिषं वन्दद्वीरायेन्दवे ।
धिया वो मेधसातये पुरन्ध्या विवासति ॥

1. Indra nourishes and fulfils the home by supporting its wishes regarding both (brain cells and sense organs), praiseworthily the hero bestows on the brain cells.

He bestows satisfaction continually through understanding, through residing in the home he lets the home to be sipped. (360)

२. कश्यपस्य स्वर्विदो यावाहुः सयुजाविति ।
ययोर्विश्वमपि व्रतं यज्ञं धीरा निचाय्य ॥

2. The brain cells in the head invoke to see heaven for knowledge, and unite with it to release here.

For which Indra moves to the sense organs as a duty to life activity and the multitude (of cells) constantly. (361)

३. अर्चत प्रार्चत नरः प्रियमेधासो अर्चत ।
अर्चन्तु पुत्रका उत पुरमिद् धृष्ण्वर्चत ॥

3. Men worship, they worship nourishment, they worship willingly for bestowal of understanding.

They honour their progeny (sense organs) also, the brain in the city, who bestows boldly and is worshipped. (362)

४. उक्थमिन्द्राय शंस्यं वर्धनं पुरुनिःषिधे ।
शक्रो यथा सुतेषु नो रारणत्सख्येषु च ॥

4. Indra is praised, praiseworthily he fosters growth, he bestows desires abundantly.

Indra likewise bestows desires on mind, bestows gladness and befriends him also. (363)

५. विश्वानरस्य वस्पतिमनानतस्य शवसः ।
एवैश्च चर्षणीनामूती हुवे रथानाम् ॥

5. The lord of the home (Indra) releases the sense activities to mind and bestows them from the homes of men with might.

At the call of sense organs he helps by speeding them actively. (364)

६. स घा यस्ते दिवो नरो धिया मर्तस्य शमतः ।
ऊती स बृहतो दिवो द्विषो अंहो न तरति ॥

6. And indeed he strives for them in waking and satisfies men, they calm us.

He bestows help greatly in waking, on the desires of both (sense organs and brain cells). He overcomes needs (aṁhasā). (365)

७. विभोष्ट इन्द्र राधसो विभ्वी रातिः शतक्रतो ।
अथा नो विश्वचर्षणे द्युम्नं सुदत्र मंहय ॥

7. Through the desire to shine Indra bestows wealth, through existence he is ready to bestow doing a hundred deeds.

Then he is active with sense organs, he bids farewell to our needs through good gifts from heaven. (366)

८. वयश्चित्ते पतत्रिणो द्विपाच्चतुष्पादर्जुनि ।
उषः प्रारन्नृतूँरनु दिवो अन्तेभ्यस्परि ॥

8. The food for Mind lies along three paths both in bipeds and quadrupeds, the white rays (arjuni).

Oh, Uṣas fulfils now and gladdens men, they go around within in waking. (367)

९. अमी ये देवा स्थन मध्य आ रोचने दिवः ।
कद्व ऋतं कदमृतं का प्रत्ना व आहुतिः ॥

9. The deva mind constantly wears away, sense activities move to it and brighten it in waking.

Prajāpati bestows the desires of both (brain and sense organs) Prajāpati bestows the mortal's desires which were bad in ancient times, he bestows on being invoked. (368)

१०. ऋचं साम यजामहे याभ्यां कर्माणि कृण्वते ।
वि ते सदसि राजतो यज्ञं देवेषु वक्षतः ॥

10. The Sāma Veda hymns are great for worship, they create understanding in the purposeful activities of life.

Through them the assembly (of brain cells) control life-activity, devas (ideas) strengthen it. (369)

D. IV.

१. विश्वाः पृतना अभिभूतरं नरः सजूस्ततक्षुरिन्द्रं जजनुश्च राजसे ।
क्रत्वे वरे स्थेमन्यामुरीमुतोग्रमोजिष्ठं तरसं तरस्विनम् ॥

1. The sense organs nourish and guide men to cross (ignorance) in existence.

Indra works in harmony with the father (Activity) in the home extensively, born to rule since creation.

You produce gifts abidingly to mind extensively and also to the community of brain cells (village) vigorously, all for crossing, Aśvins bestow them. (370)

२. श्रत्ते दधामि प्रथमाय मन्यवेऽहन्यद्दस्युं नर्यं विवेरपः ।
उभे यत्वा रोदसी धावतामनु भ्यसाते शुष्मात्पृथिवी चिदद्रिवः ॥

2. They give faith primarily to mind from the brain cells, which Activity rides on in men in waking for their wants.

He unites with both (brain cells and sense organs), bestows

now understanding from both continually and rushes from the sense organs to bestow on mind from the brain (hill). (371)

३. समेत विश्वा ओजसा पतिं दिवो य एक इद्भूरतिथिर्जनानाम् ।
स पूर्व्यो नूतनमाजिगीषं तं वर्तनीरनु वावृत एक इत् ॥

3. At the same time the motley sense activities bestow vigorously to the sense organs and they move towards the lord consciousness, who is alone in giving existence through the guests (Aditi) in men.

And in ancient times he won our desire for sense activities in a novel way, which subsist now and he is alone to envelop and bestow. (372)

४. इमे त इन्द्र ते वयं पुरुष्टुत ये त्वारभ्य चरामसि प्रभूवसो ।
न हि त्वदन्यो गिर्वणो गिरःसघत्क्षोणीरिव प्रति तद्धर्यं नो वचः ॥

4. Here Indra bestows the motley sense activities on us and controls praiseworthily, he grasps them and goes around nourishing for existence to the home (or in the home of the lord).

There is none other than you desirous of the brain (hill) of the devotee, you are like a king in the assembly which you nourish and support and bestow also from them. (373)

५. चर्षणीधृतं मघवानमुक्थ्या३मिन्द्रं गिरो बृहतीरभ्यनूषत ।
वावृधानं पुरुहूतं सुवृक्तिभिरमर्त्यं जरमाणं दिवेदिवे ॥

5. Indra praiseworthily supports it diligently, Indra is greatly attached to the brain (hill).

He envelops and bestows on the brain cells who invoke him much, supports men to welfare day after day till old age. (374)

६. अच्छा व इन्द्रं मतयः स्वर्युवः सध्रीचीर्विश्वा उशतीरनूषत ।
परि ष्वजन्त जनयो यथा पतिं मर्यं न शुन्ध्युं मघवानमूतये ॥

6. Indra bestows pure understanding quickly from heaven on mind (youth), he is attached to the sense organs eagerly having a common aim.

Desires from beyond are born in men, which protect men properly (yathā), Indra unites with them helping to purify. (375)

७. अभि त्यं मेषं पुरुहूतमृग्मियमिन्द्रं गीर्भिर्मदता वस्वो अर्णवम् ।
यस्य द्यावो न विचरन्ति मानुषं भुजे मंहिष्ठमभि विप्रमर्चत ॥

7. The Aśvins are well-known to invoke Indra to approach the sense organs and support them with sense activities from the brain (hill), the home releases surging streams.

Heaven (head) bestows them which by going around feeds men munificently to honour them and inspire. (376)

८. त्यं सु मेषं महया स्वर्विदं शतं यस्य सुभ्वः साकमीरते ।
अत्यं न वाजं हवनस्यदं रथमिन्द्रं ववृत्यामवसे सुवृक्तिभिः ॥

8. You are well-known to arouse the Aśvins to move to gladden us by acquainting us with heaven, they brought into existence hundreds of creatures together with you and gladdened them.

You are known to bestow oblations from the sense organs on our homes in life, you bestowed them and favoured their subsistence for prosperity. (377)

९. घृतवती भुवनानामभिश्रियोर्वी पृथ्वी मधुदुघे सुपेशसा ।
द्यावापृथिवी वरुणस्य धर्मणा विष्कभिते अजरे भूरिरेतसा ॥

9. Clarified butter bestows on the creatures prosperity extensively, the sweet perceptions from sense activities bestow the forms of creatures.

The sense organs bestow on the head the dharma (nature) of the external world (Varuṇa) which bestows abundant streams (of ideas) unendingly to make the head active. (378), (Y.V. 34, 45)

१०. उभे यदिन्द्र रोदसी आपप्राथोषा इव ।
महान्तं त्वा महीनां सम्राजं चर्षणीनाम् ।
देवी जनित्र्यजीजनद्भद्रा जनित्र्यजीजनत् ।

10. Activity spreads himself out between the brain cells and sense organs as Uṣas does, through Indra.

Indra! You are great, you are diligently active in your great sovereign region.

The devi (Aditi) wins welfare to men from the three states, life-activity of men comes from the birth place. (379), (1090)

११. प्र मन्दिने पितुमदर्चता वचो यः
कृष्णगर्भा निरहन्नृजिश्वना ।
अवस्यवो वृषणं वज्रदक्षिणं
मरुत्वन्तं सख्याय हुवेमहि ॥

11. If the brain is sluggish Indra nourishes mightily by honouring sense activities for drinks (pitu) and rushes them speedily and also bestows on them desiring to dispel the gloom at the source.

He favours the brain cells vigorously through the spirited nerves and satisfies them mightily bestowing ideas (Maruts) within and befriends them, being invoked greatly. (380)

D. V.

१. इन्द्र सुतेषु सोमेषु क्रतुं पुनीष उक्थ्यम् ।
विदे वृधस्य दक्षस्य महाँ हि षः ॥

1. Indra repeatedly produces desires praiseworthily in mind through Soma.

He fosters knowledge and satisfies our desires greatly indeed (381), (746)

२. तमु अभि प्र गायत पुरुहूतं पुरुष्टुतम् ।
इन्द्रं गीर्भिस्तविषमा विवासत ॥

2. You unite greatly with sense activities to nourish, being abundantly invoked and praised.

Indra! You are powerful on the hill (brain) which you ride on for my existence. (382)

३. तं ते मदं गृणीमसि वृषणं पृक्षु सासहिम् ।
उ लोककृत्नुमद्रिवो हरिश्रियम् ॥

3. You desire sense activities for the devotee whom you honour and to whom you rain food to nourish victoriously.

Also you bestow on the hill now to produce perceptions and indeed release prosperity. (383), (880)

४. यत्सोममिन्द्र विष्णवि यद्वा घ त्रित आप्त्ये ।
यद्वा मरुत्सु मन्दसे समिन्दुभि : ॥

4. Indra unites with Soma to be actively bestowing what is suitable for the three states.

What he bestows is ideas (Maruts) who arouse gladness and appease the brain cells. (384)

५. एदु मधोर्मदिन्तरं सिञ्चाध्वर्यो अन्धसः ।
एवा हि वीरस्तवते सदावृधः ॥

5. Behold the crossing of ignorance from the sweet perceptions mightily tingling in life-activity.

They arouse knowledge vigorously in the home and speed up its growth constantly. (385), (1684)

६. एन्दुमिन्द्राय सिञ्चत पिबाति सोम्यं मधु ।
प्र राधांसि चोदयते महित्वना ॥

6. Indra tingles along to the brain cells which drink sense perceptions from Soma.

He supports wealth to nourish, also unites with it above with great desire. (386), (1509)

७. एतो न्विन्द्रं स्तवाम सखायः स्तोम्यं नरम् ।
कृष्टीर्यो विश्वा अभ्यस्त्येक इत् ॥

7. Indra releases the motley sense activities to me praiseworthily, helps quickly both brain cells and sense organs of men and controls.

He cultivates extensively through the sense organs and is alone to strive for them. (387)

८. इन्द्राय साम गायत विप्राय बृहते बृहत् ।
ब्रह्मकृते विपश्चिते पनस्यवे ॥

8. Indra bestows on us by uniting us to sense activities, inspires us greatly and increases them.

He produces knowledge and inspires mind with it admirably from the brain cells. (388), (1025)

९. य एक इद्विदयते वसु मर्ताय दाशुषे ।
ईशानो अप्रतिष्कुत इन्द्रो अङ्ग ॥

9. You move alone to unite with wealth (of sense perceptions) for knowledge and serve mortals eagerly.

You rule us, Indra's limb prāṇa nourishes the sense organs (Kū). (389), (1341)

१०. सखाय आ शिषामहे ब्रह्मेन्द्राय वज्रिणे ।
स्तुष ऊ ष वो नृतमाय धृष्णवे ॥

10. You help to release much desires for knowledge through vigorous nerves, Indra!

You bestow praiseworthily through the sense organs of men marvellously new (ideas) boldly. (390)

BOOK V : CHAPTER I

D. I.

१. गृणे तदिन्द्र ते शव उपमां देवतातये ।
यद्धंसि वृत्रमोजसा शचीपते ॥

1. Indra has bestowed the devotee a body in the image of the father of the devas,

whom he supports by releasing him from Vṛtra vigorously along the path of might. (391)

२. यस्य त्यच्छम्बरं मदे दिवोदासाय रन्धयन् ।
अयं स सोम इन्द्र ते सुतः पिब ॥

2. He is well-known to serve the devotee with sense activities from the pure ākāśa in the waking state to sip and gladden him.

Indra shows mind the path to Soma to drink. (392)

३. एन्द्र नो गधि प्रिय सत्राजिदगोह्य ।
गिरिर्न विश्वतः पृथु पतिर्दिवः ॥

3. Indra wins sense activities in life for him and satisfies him with them.

They spread themselves out from the hill (brain) to the sense organs for them to drink in the waking state. (393), (1247)

It is the sense organs which reveal the objects of the cosmos or external world. They also form the body or cloak for the sense activities. Hence the sense organs are invariably referred to as the body, cosmos or equivalent expressions.

४. य इन्द्र सोमपातमो मदः शविष्ठ चेतति ।
येना हंसि न्या३त्रिणं तमीमहे ॥

4. Indra moves and fulfils Soma's desires through sense activities to animate the sense organs (body) as desired.

He indeed supports them and guides to the three states as greatly desired. (394)

५. तुचे तुनाय तत्सु नो द्राघीय आयुर्जीवसे ।
आदित्यासः समहसः कृणोतन ॥

5. You move to manifest what is needed for which you run

to mind with the knowledge and bestow on him through prāṇa from the Jīva.

Aditi victoriously bestows (the knowledge) to gladden us by producing and guiding. (395)

६. वेत्था हि निर्ऋतीनां वज्रहस्त परिवृजम् ।
अहरहः शुन्ध्युः परिपदामिव ॥

6. Thus they bestow by arousing established procedure (Ṛti) out of the vigorous nerves (hands) going around the enclosure.

They (sense activities) separate themselves in the waking state and unite to purify (the sense organs) and go around as if to protect the home. (396)

७. अपामीवामप स्त्रिधमप सेधत दुर्मतिम् ।
आदित्यासो युयोतना नो अंहसः ॥

7. Activity pushes open (the doors to brain cells), Activity bestows the sense activities (the woman), Activity at a distance is the door to understanding.

Prāṇa bestows Aditi and guides and releases us from distress. (397)

८. पिबा सोममिन्द्र मन्दतु त्वा यं ते सुषाव हर्यश्वाद्रिः ।
सोतुर्बाहुभ्यां सुयतो नार्वा ॥

8. When sluggish Soma drinks from Indra, who controls him, the tawny consciousness bestows him who gushes from the hill,

and conveys Soma juice to both (brain cells and sense organs), arouses them and unites to bestow on men. (398), (927)

D. II.

१. अभ्रातृव्यो अना त्वमनापिरिन्द्र जनुषा सनादसि ।
युधेदापित्वमिच्छसे ॥

1. Indra! You are the brother of mind through our sense organs (face), who (mind) drinks from them from the origin since ancient times.

You desire even to fight for bestowing to you. (399), (1389)

२. यो न इदमिदं पुरा प्र वस्य आनिनाय तमु व स्तुषे ।
सखाय इन्द्रमूतये ॥

2. Indra! You approached our home from the source in ancient times to bestow nourishment on us and to guide them to the sense organs (face) praiseworthily, you help them as a friend. (400)

३. आ गन्ता मा रिषण्यत प्रस्थावानो माप स्थात समन्यवः ।
दृढा चिद्यमयिष्णवः ।।

3. The sense activities flow within me to unite and nourish abidingly desires in me, Activity abidingly bestows on mind from the brain cells.

Prāṇa establishes the mind with new desires. (401)

४. आ याह्ययमिन्दवेऽश्वपते गोपत उर्वरापते ।
सोमं सोमपते पिब ।।

4. They move bestowed by the brain cells, Prāṇa is their path, he (mind) drinks the perceptions, the reservoir (brain) bestows him to drink.

He drinks Soma juice from lord Soma. (402)

५. त्वया ह स्विद्युजा वयं प्रति श्वसन्तं वृषभ ब्रुवीमहि ।
संस्थे जनस्य गोमतः ।।

5. You move indeed to unite with and sweat for us panting within nourishing us, you rain and bestow us (speak to us) greatly and shine.

Indra (rich in cows) stays with men. (403)

६. गावश्चिद्धा समन्यवः सजात्येन मरुतः सबन्धवः ।
रिहते ककुभो मिथः ।।

6. The sense perceptions are bestowed to mind at the same time as to the brain cells, Ideas (Maruts) of the same family are bestowed on their relatives.

They caress the brain summit and establish themselves (or they caress the brain and sense organs and shine by establishing themselves). (404)

७. त्वं न इन्द्रा भर ओजो नृम्णं शतक्रतो विचर्षणे ।
आ वीरं पृतनासहम् ।।

7. Indra! You honour men and support them vigorously doing a hundred deeds diligently.

You are valiant and victorious in fights. (405)

८. अधा ह्यीन्द्र गिर्वण उप त्वा काम ईमहे ससृग्महे ।
उदेव ग्मन्त उदभिः ॥

8. Indra is indeed desirous of the brain (hill) you desire to rule above and bestow sense activities to flow greatly.

You speed them up, they move within to contact (moisten) us. (406), (710)

९. सीदन्तस्ते वयो यथा गोश्रीते मधौ मदिरे विवक्षणे ।
अभि त्वामिन्द्र नोनुमः ॥

9. You bestow on us in the home above, the sense activities are cooked, sense reactions (intoxicating liquor) ride over the pleasant sense activities instantly.

Now they make obeisances to you, Indra! (407)

१०. वयमु त्वामपूर्व्य स्थूरं न कच्चिद्भरन्तोऽवस्यवः ।
वज्रिं चित्रं हवामहे ॥

10. To us you are great (sthūra), whom you support within, you favour the brain cells.

The vigorous nerves perceive and support oblations greatly (or bestow a variety of oblations). (408), (708)

D. III.

१. स्वादोरित्था विषूवतो मधोः पिबन्ति गौर्यः ।
या इन्द्रेण सयावरीर्वृष्णा मदन्ति
शोभथा वस्वीरनु स्वराज्यम् ॥

1. Indra releases sense activities thus on all sides for knowledge of sense perceptions which (the sense activities) and the sense organs (buffaloes) yield to drink.

Indra moves and bestows them on brain cells which release sense perceptions vigorously and splendidly, now he is comfortable in the home in his own region. (409)

२. इत्था हि सोम इन्मदो ब्रह्म चकार वर्धनम् ।
शविष्ठ वज्रिन्नोजसा पृथिव्या निः
शशा अहिमर्चन्ननु स्वराज्यम् ॥

2. Thus Soma arouses sense activities mightily and produces also knowledge and fosters it.

He bestows mightily through the vigorous nerves on sense organs, now he honours the mind below by arousing him in his own region. (410)

३. इन्द्रो मदाय वावृधे शवसे वृत्रहा नृभिः ।
तमिन्महत्स्वाजिषूतिमर्भे हवामहे स वाजेषु प्र नोऽविषत् ।।

3. Indra moves to sense activities to increase them and bestow with might, Vṛtra departs in men.

You desire greatly to help poor (devotees) like us in life, you bestow much oblations in life to nourish and work for it. (411), (1002)

४. इन्द्र तुभ्यमिदद्रिवोऽनुत्तं वज्रिन्वीर्यम् ।
यद्ध त्यं मायिनं मृगं तव त्यन्माययावधीरर्चन्ननु स्वराज्यम् ।।

4. Indra! Both of you approach us on the hill to bestow the best for vigour through the nerves.

Which are well-known to bestow on the sense organs (mṛgam) mightily and marvellously, and bestow understanding marvellously and honour us steadily in your own region. (412)

५. प्रेह्यभीहि धृष्णुहि न ते वज्रो नि यंसते ।
इन्द्र नृम्णं हि ते शवो हनो वृत्रं
जया अपोऽर्चन्ननु स्वराज्यम् ।।

5. To nourish here you arouse the sense activities boldly and support them to move along the vigorous nerves.

Indra honours men with welfare through the sense organs striking down Vṛtra and winning Activity, now you honour us in your own dominion. (413)

६. यदुदीरत आजयो धृष्णवे धीयते धनम् ।
युङ्क्ष्वा मदच्युता हरी कं हनः
कं वसौ दधोऽस्माँ इन्द्र वसौ दधः ।।

6. What he sets in motion above and wins boldly and bestows is understanding by uniting with sense perceptions.

He bestows on the home by uniting with them, the sense perceptions drip and indeed release desires striking down (Vṛtra) desiring to bestow on the home, Indra bestows on us in the home. (414), (1004)

७. अक्षन्नमीमदन्त ह्यव प्रिया अधूषत ।
अस्तोषत स्वभानवो विप्रा नविष्ठया
मती योजा न्विन्द्र ते हरी ॥

7. The eyes honour the sense activities within which arouse them fondly.

The brain (home) by itself bestows the light on them inspiring fresh knowledge as desired, Indra unites with the tawny consciousness and releases it. (415)

८. उपो षु शृणुही गिरो मघवन्मातथा इव ।
कदा नः सूनृतावतः कर इदर्थयास इद्योजा न्विन्द्र ते हरी ॥

8. Above (perceptions) from the sense organs are cooked (prepared) and transformed on the hill and released as wealth as if honouring it.

They arouse knowledge in men which is bound to them producing thus the purport (of the perception), Indra bestows it thus vigorously before the tawny consciousness. (416)

९. चन्द्रमा अप्स्वां३न्तरा सुपर्णो धावते दिवि ।
न वो हिरण्यनेमयः पदं विन्दन्ति
विद्युतो वित्तं मे अस्य रोदसी ॥

9. Activity bestows on mind, the golden winged consciousness, releases it and bestows understanding in waking.

What is bestowed by consciousness is protected in the home by Prāṇa praiseworthily, which adorns us praiseworthily bestowing also knowledge like lightning from both (brain cells and sense organs). (417)

१०. प्रति प्रियतमं रथं वृषणं वसुवाहनम् ।
स्तोता वामश्विनावृषि स्तोमेभिर्भूषति
प्रति माध्वी मम श्रुतं हवम् ॥

10. The sense organs nourish us with desires in kindness, Indra honours us by conveying it as wealth.

The Aśvins praiseworthily bestow it on us, they rain them to adorn us, the sweet perceptions nourish us as oblations of hearing. (418), (1743)

D. IV.

१. आ ते अग्न इधीमहि द्युमन्तं देवाजरम् ।
यद्ध स्या ते पनीयसी समिद्दीदयति
द्यवीषं स्तोतृभ्य आ भर ॥

1. Agni! They kindle us (i.e. oblations of hearing) greatly, then ideas (devas) from heaven are born to gladden us,

which strive to bestow on us the objects of perception (kindling fuel) in compassion (or distributes them), heaven favours us with our desires praiseworthily and supports them. (419), (1022)

२. आग्निं न स्ववृक्तिभिर्होतारं त्वा वृणीमहे ।
शीरं पावकशोचिषं वि वो मदे यज्ञेषु स्तीर्णबर्हिषं विवक्षसे ॥

2. Agni himself supports the yajña preparations, presides over it and gladdens by enveloping it greatly.

He sharpens it, bestows on the head to fulfil and shine, rides on sense activities (perceptions) in life and strengthens the yajña through the nerves spread out. (420)

३. महे नो अद्य बोधयोषो राये दिवित्मती ।
यथा चिन्नो अबोधयः सत्यश्रवसि वाय्ये सुजाते अश्वसूनृते ॥

3. He instructs us greatly now, in understanding, controlling us eagerly in waking.

Likewise he instructs us with ideas which flow and are bound to us as if sewn in existence, prāṇa arouses the men by arousing heaven (or the source.) (421), (1740)

४. भद्रं नो अपि वातय मनो दक्षमुत क्रतुम् ।
अथा ते सख्ये अन्धसो वि वो मदे
रणा गावो न यवसे विवक्षसे ॥

4. He bestows also welfare on the mind now, Ṛta also satisfies him.

They help us to relieve us of ignorance riding on sense activities, the sense perceptions gladden the brain cells through promoting growth. (422)

५. क्रत्वा महाँ अनुष्वधं भीम आ वावृते शवः ।
श्रिय ऋष्व उपाकयोर्नि शिप्री हरिवां
दधे हस्तयोर्वज्रमायसम् ॥

5. He produces great things and now, formidable in the home, he bestows from it to envelop the sense organs.

Prosperity, bestowed extensively above, flows, the sharp rays of consciousness please us by bestowing all, through the vigorous nerves on the home marvellously. (423)

६. स घा तं वृषणं रथमधि तिष्ठाति गोविदम् ।
यः पात्रं हारियोजनं पूर्णमिन्द्रा
चिकेतति योजा न्विन्द्र ते हरी ॥

6. Indra indeed bestows our desires through the sense organs and satisfies us at his wish with knowledge through sense activities.

He hastens to support and fulfil by uniting and conveying, Indra perceives the desires fully and uniting with them bestows before consciousness. (424)

७. अग्निं तं मन्ये यो वसुरस्तं यं यन्ति धेनवः ।
अस्तमर्वन्त आशवोऽस्तं नित्यासो
वाजिन इषं स्तोतृभ्य आ भर ॥

7. Agni desires to move towards mind and control him in the home of Indra and guide the milch-cow to him.

He hastens from the home to the sense organs, he bestows constantly from the home in life and supports desires praiseworthily. (425), (1737)

८. न तमंहो न दुरितं देवासो अष्ट मर्त्यम् ।
सजोषसो यमर्यमा मित्रो नयति वरुणो अति द्विषः ॥

8. Devas (ideas) indeed bestow desires quickly which mortals acquire.

Indra acts in harmony with them and controls the brain (Mitra) and guides largely (ideas of) Varuṇa to both the sense organs and brain cells as desired. (426)

D. V.

१. परि प्र धन्वेन्द्राय सोम स्वादुर्मित्राय पूष्णे भगाय ॥

1. Indra goes around for nourishment and bestows freshly on Soma, he is himself the door to the brain (Mitra), consciousness moves in for prosperity. (427), (1367)

२. पर्यू षु प्र धन्व वाजसातये परि वृत्राणि सक्षणिः ।
द्विषस्तरध्या ऋणया न ईरसे ।।

2. You go around to the sense organs to bestow fresh nourishment in life continually, going around you envelop and support them by bestowing instantly.

You release from the home for the desires of both brain cells and sense organs, you are obliged to move to them, arouse and bestow on them. (428), (1364)

३. पवस्व सोम महान्त्समुद्रः पिता देवानां विश्वाभि धाम ।।

3. The great Soma himself bestows to drink (or protect) and gladdens the father Activity with ideas bestowed from home on the sense organs. (429), (1241)

४. पवस्व सोम महे दक्षायाश्वो न निक्तो वाजी धनाय ।।

4. Soma himself bestows to drink greatly, prāṇa satisfies us in life through the mother with wealth. (430), (1332)

५. इन्दुः पविष्ट चारुर्मदायापामुपस्थे कविर्भगाय ।।

5. Activity bestows on the brain cells to drink perceptions and gladdens them, he is controlled by Agni and consciousness. (431)

६. अनु हि त्वा सुतं सोम मदामसि महे समर्यराज्ये ।
वाजाँ अभि पवमान प्र गाहसे ।।

6. Activity! Now you arouse the mind and bestow on him our perceptions greatly from the region of the assembly.

The sense activities plunge into the home to bestow to drink in life-activity. (432), (1366)

७. क ई व्यक्ता नरः सनीडा रुद्रस्य मर्या अथा स्वश्वाः ।।

7. The brain (head) manifests in men by bestowing gifts of oblations, then prāṇa himself moves to men through the nerves (for manifestation). (433)

८. अग्ने तमद्याश्वं न स्तोमैः क्रतुं न भद्रं हृदिस्पृशम् ।
ऋध्यामा त ओहैः ।।

8. Agni desires now prāṇa to produce welfare by contacting the brain, he is the path to transform to prosperity. (434), (1777), (Y.V. 15, 44)

९. आविमर्या आ वाजं वाजिनो अग्मं देवस्य सवितुः सवम् ।
स्वर्गां अर्वन्तो जयत ।।

9. The Aśvins move into men in life, they come mightily in life, they stimulate ideas and bestow them.

They hasten from heaven and are victorious. (435)

१०. पवस्व सोम द्युम्नी सुधारो महाँ अवीनामनुपूर्व्यः ।।

10. Soma himself bestows from heaven (head) to drink to support well, the great one blesses us now as in olden times. (436)

BOOK V : CHAPTER II

D. I.

१. विश्वतोदावन्विश्वतो न आ भर यं त्वा शविष्ठमीमहे ॥

1. Indra! You bestow on the sense organs desiring knowledge for the brain (home) and so you support and control them with might against being depleted (i.e. the brain). (437)

२. एष ब्रह्मा य ऋत्विय इन्द्रो नाम श्रुतो गृणे ॥

2. You seek knowledge for the worshipper, Indra honours us by enabling us to hear songs (sāmans) (or Tradition sings of you by the name of Indra). (438), (1768)

३. ब्रह्माण इन्द्रं महयन्तो अर्कैरवर्धयन्नहये हन्तवा उ ॥

3. Indra guides Soma greatly praiseworthily favouring him who bestows within to sip in waking state. (439)

४. अनवस्ते रथमश्वाय तक्षुस्त्वष्टा वज्रं पुरुहूत द्युमन्तम् ॥

4. Prāṇa moves to the home from sense organs with new (knowledge) sense of touch, Tvaṣṭā (carves) by letting it gain from the vigorous nerves, the brain within invokes them much. (440)

५. शं पदं मघं रयीषिणो न काममव्रतो हिनोति न स्पृशद्रयिम् ॥

5. Streams of desires toil for steps for wealth, our vows on desires arouse the motley sense perceptions to caress us with wealth. (441)

६. सदा गावः शुचयो विश्वधायसः सदा सेवा अरेपसः ॥

6. The sense activities bestow constantly which shine, they strive to bestow from the sense organs which are constantly brightened (stained) by ideas (devas). (442)

७. आ याहि वनसा सह गावः सचन्त वर्तनिं यदूधभिः ॥

7. They (ideas) move, arouse and bestow desires together with sense perceptions (activities), unite with them (for the to subsist which are like the clouds. (443)

८. उप प्रक्षे मधुमति क्षियन्तः पुष्येम रयिं धीमहे त इन्द्र ॥

8. Above they (the ideas) nouriṣh the brain (home) with understanding, with sense perceptions, Indra nourishes us with much knowledge through the wealth (of perceptions). (444)

९. अर्चन्त्यर्कं मरुतः स्वर्का आ स्तोभति श्रुतो युवा स इन्द्रः ॥

9. Knowledge honours ideas (Maruts) with much praise, Mind itself praises ideas for hearing released by Indra. (445)

१०. प्र व इन्द्राय वृत्रहन्तमाय विप्राय गाथं गायत यं जुजोषते ॥

10. Indra moves to strike down Vṛtra (interia) to bestow nourishment,

which inspires the devotee, the sense activities unite with him, control and work in harmony. (446)

D. II.

१. अचेत्यग्निश्चिकितिर्हव्यवाड् न सुमद्रथः ॥

1. Agni instructs mind by establishing oblations in him by arousing sense activities and sense organs. (447)

२. अग्ने त्वं नो अन्तम उत त्राता शिवो भुवो वरूथ्यः ॥

2. Agni! You are very intimate with us and also support and help us beneficently in existence. (448), (1107)

३. भगो न चित्रो अग्निर्महोनां दधाति रत्नम् ॥

3. Agni bestows much valuable wealth of variety through consciousness. (449)

४. विश्वस्य प्र स्तोभ पुरो वा सन्यदि वेह नूनम् ॥

4. He nourishes the brain (city) praiseworthily through the sense organs which he now conveys and bestows them as gifts. (450)

५. उषा अप स्वसुष्टमः सं वर्तयति वर्तनिं सुजातता ॥

5. Activity aptly and eagerly sets up everything, in activity along proper courses, the father arouses births. (451)

६. इमा नु कं भुवना सीषधेमेन्द्रश्च विश्वे च देवाः ॥

6. Indra bestows the desires of the creatures on the brain in the home and also of the sense organs through ideas. (452), (1110), (Y.V. 25, 46)

७. वि स्रुतयो यथा पथा इन्द्र त्वद्यन्तु रातयः ॥

7. Indra is ready to bestow and guide along the path (desired by Activity) the sense of hearing. (453), (1770)

८. अया वाजं देवहितं सनेम मदेम शतहिमाः सुवीराः ॥

8. The hero (Indra) moves into life-activity to bestow welfare here for us to rejoice in life during a hundred winters. (454)

९. ऊर्जा मित्रो वरुणः पिन्वतेडाः पीवरीमिषं कृणुही न इन्द्र ॥

9. Indra bestows oblations (of ideas) of Varuṇa (external world) abundantly on the brain (Mitra) as nourishment, he opens its eyes and releases exuberantly to create transformations (455)

१०. इन्द्रो विश्वस्य राजति ॥

10. Indra controls the sense organs. (456)

D. III.

१. त्रिकद्रुकेषु महिषो यवाशिरं
तुविशुष्मस्तृम्पत्सोममपिबद्विष्णुना सुतं यथावशम् ।
स ईं ममाद महि कर्म कर्तवे महामुरुं सैनं
सश्चद्देवो देवं सत्य इन्दुः सत्यमिन्द्रम् ॥

1. The rays (missiles of sense activities) run to the desires of the three states through the nerves to gladden through the brain cells in the head.

They gush powerfully to satisfy Soma who by drinking them works for the needs of mind according to his pleasure.

And they gladden us mightily by creating purposeful activities through the armies of sense objects.

Ideas (devas) unite with the deva (Soma) for the existence of brain cells. Indra controls existence. (457), (1486)

२. अयं सहस्रमानवो दृशः कवीनां मतिर्ज्योतिर्विधर्म ।
ब्रध्नः समीचीरुषसः समैरयदरेपसः
सचेतसः स्वसरे मन्युमन्तश्चिता गोः ॥

2. Agni bestows a thousand paths to look for on the brain (home) for understanding through the effulgence of conscious-

ness, according to dharma. Uṣas (Dawn) turns towards the brain and streams her rays without blemish.

She unites with the motley sense activities by bestowing her rays within, with which the mind also unites. (458)

३. एन्द्र याह्युप नः परावतो नायमच्छा
विदथानीव सत्पतिरस्ता राजेव सत्पतिः ।
हवामहे त्वा प्रयस्वन्तः सुतेष्वा पुत्रासो न
पितरं वाजसातये मंहिष्ठं वाजसातये ॥

3. Indra binds the closely united understanding (knowledge) from heaven above and guides it (to mind) nearby.

The lord of existence controlling, like a king, directs and guides and bestows the path to existence.

You strive to bestow much oblations within to nourish the desires of the mind bestowing as to a son mightily.

The father gladdens continually in life by munificent bestowals of births (of ideas). (459)

४. तमिन्द्रं जोहवीमि मघवानमुग्रं
सत्रा दधानमप्रतिष्कुतं श्रवांसि भूरिः ।
मंहिष्ठो गीर्भिरा च यज्ञियो ववर्त
राये नो विश्वा सुपथा कृणोतु वज्री ॥

4. Indra desires to initiate (birth) transformations for which he approaches wealth to bestow powerfully in life and bestows it on the brain cells as nourishment to create and help the sense of hearing abundantly.

He supports the hill with munificent (wealth) and also fosters life-activity by bestowals. He controls the sense organs and produces for the motley sense activities good paths to them along the vigorous nerves. (460)

५. अस्तु श्रौषट् पुरो अग्निं धिया दध आ नु
त्यच्छर्धो दिव्यं वृणीमह इन्द्रवायू वृणीमहे ।
यद्ध क्राणा विवस्वते नाभा सन्दाय नव्यसे ।
अध प्र नूनमुप यन्ति धीतयो देवाँ अच्छा न धीतयः ॥

5. The home (brain) exclaims its satisfaction whom Agni satisfies by moving to it and bestowing now.

It is well-known that half the ideas nearly envelop us to gladden Indra and the nerves who choose from them, who willingly ride on knowledge from the source and bestow gifts newly to sip.

Now the devas guide him above to knowledge by nourishing him, they amount to pure knowledge. (461)

६. प्र वो महे मतयो यन्तु विष्णवे
मरुत्वते गिरिजा एवयामरुत् ।
प्र शर्धाय प्र यज्यवे सुखादये
तवसे भन्दविष्टये धुनिव्रताय शवसे ॥

6. Ideas (Maruts) bestow nourishment greatly, guide and work afresh for knowledge which takes birth in the hill and hasten in their paths resoundingly.

They nourish boldly, they nourish the brain cells in life-activity urging them to devour vigorously.

They (ideas) praise their (brain) cells, desires and rush with might as their duty. (462)

७. अया रुचा हरिण्या पुनानो विश्वा द्वेषांसि
तरति सयुग्वभिः सूरो न सयुग्वभिः ।
धारा पृष्ठस्य रोचते पुनानो अरुषो हरिः ।
विश्वा यद्रूपा परियास्यृक्वभिः सप्तास्येभिरृक्वभिः ॥

7. The sense activities shine on the paths to the sense organs repeatedly to support the desires of both brain and mind.

The sense activities bestow by uniting for the crossing over, the hero Indra bestows them by uniting to cross over (ignorance).

The tawny consciousness repeatedly shines and supports our prosperity.

Whatever forms of objects of the world go around in us devotees, they are those supported by Activity in the devotee. (463), (1590)

८. अभि त्यं देवं सवितारमोण्योः कविक्रतु-
मर्चामि सत्यसवं रत्नधामभि प्रियं मतिम् ।
ऊर्ध्वा यस्यामतिर्भा अदिद्युतत्सवीमनि
हिरण्यपाणिरमिमीत सुक्रतुः कृपा स्वः ॥

8. It is well-known that Savitā gladdens and guides through Agni producing ideas. He honours us with Soma juice in existence. He bestows valuable wealth for knowledge lovingly.

He strives for knowledge to shine in the head and vivifies (Savīmani) by uniting with duality (objects).

His golden hands gladden us here by doing good to us in compassion himself. (464)

९. अग्नि होतारं मन्ये दास्वन्तं वसोः सूनुं
सहसो जातवेदसं विप्रं न जातवेदसम् ।
य ऊर्ध्वया स्वध्वरो देवो देवाच्या कृपा
घृतस्य विभ्राष्टिमनु शुक्रशोचिष आजुह्वानस्य सर्पिषः ॥

9. Agni presides over Mind and gladdens, he bestows himself to the home which sprout up.

He bestows all knowledge from the source with might and inspires the devotee from source.

He (deva), himself moves to the head in life-activity and honours ideas (devas).

Now clarified butter without a frying pan shines and flows to us from his tongues (sense activities). (465), (1813)

१०. तव त्यन्नर्यं नृतोऽप इन्द्र प्रथमं पूर्व्यं दिवि प्रवाच्यं कृतम् ।
यो देवस्य शवसा प्रारिणा असु रिणन्नपः ।
भुवो विश्वमभ्यदेवमोजसा विदेदूर्जं शतक्रतुर्विदेदिषम् ॥

10. It is well-known that you (Agni) dance about in men and that Indra's activity was predominant in ancient days and that consciousness made the announcement of object and ideas.

That deva (consciousness) with his might released the vital sense activities released by Activity and fulfilled us. He bestows the vigour and devas (ideas) on the sense organs and bestows the nourishment on knowledge and Indra of a hundred deeds gives us the desire for knowledge. (466)

Pāvamāna (Fickle Mind) Kāṇḍa

D. IV.

१. उच्चा ते जातमन्धसो दिवि सद्भूम्या ददे ।
उग्रं शर्म महि श्रवः ॥

1. From above (heaven) they (the jīvas) were born in ignorance, consciousness released homes to them on earth.

He bestows much cooked up ideas and protects us powerfully, (467), (672), (Y.V. 26, 16)

२. स्वादिष्ठया मदिष्ठया पवस्व सोम धारया ।
इन्द्राय पातवे सुतः ॥

2. Soma supports the mind (son) by bestowing him the sweet perceptions to drink as desired for knowledge as desired.

Indra fulfils the mind through them. (468), (689)

३. वृषा पवस्व धारया मरुत्वते च मत्सरः ।
विश्वा दधान ओजसा ॥

3. (Soma) bestows (rains) streams (of sense activities) on us to drink, ideas (Maruts) also flow to us for knowledge.

The sense organs bestow on the brain cells vigorously. (469), (803)

४. यस्ते मदो वरेण्यस्तेना पवस्वान्धसा ।
देवावीरघशंसहा ॥

4. The sense activities (perceptions) strive excellently, they bestow on us to drink and relieves us of ignorance.

Devas (ideas) dependent on them (sense activities) bless us praiseworthily. (Or at the vigour of the deva Soma) indeed (ignorance) departs praiseworthily. (470), (815)

५. तिस्रो वाच उदीरते गावो मिमन्ति धेनवः ।
हरिरेति कनिक्रदत् ॥

5. They (sense activities) bestow on the three states (brain, mind and sense organs), also set (the brain), above in activity, the sense perceptions approach us within like a milch-cow.

The tawny consciousness bestows on (releases) the motley sense activities resoundingly. (471)

६. इन्द्रायेन्दो मरुत्वते पवस्व मधुमत्तमः ।
अर्कस्य योनिमासदम् ।।

6. Indra moves to the brain cells and bestows ideas (Maruts) on the sweet sense activities desired by us, to drink for the sake of our knowledge.

The source bestows it on us praiseworthily. (472), (1076)

७. असाव्यंशुर्मदायाप्सु दक्षो गिरिष्ठाः ।
श्येनो न योनिमासदत् ।।

7. Activity bestows on us Soma juice (aṁśu) from (through) sense activities and satisfies on the hill as desired.

He watches our home from the source like a hawk. (473), (1008)

८. पवस्व दक्षसाधनो देवेभ्यः पीतये हरे ।
मरुद्भ्यो वायवे मदः ।।

8. The tawny consciousness secures (sâdhana) and bestows on the home devas (ideas) which it drinks and bestows them on us to drink.

The sense activities bestow the ideas (Maruts) fearlessly on the brain cells. (474), (919)

९. परि स्वानो गिरिष्ठाः पवित्रे सोमो अक्षरत् ।
मदेषु सर्वधा असि ।।

9. Soma goes around pantingly on the hill as desired and beneficently gladdens the home.

The rays (missiles) of sense activities bestow all. (475), (1093)

१०. परि प्रिया दिवः कविर्वयांसि नप्त्योर्हितः ।
स्वानैर्याति कविक्रतुः ।।

10. Consciousness goes around lovingly, whom Agni (wise) supports us with and who bestows welfare on the sense organs (dependents).

Agni pantingly moves to them to produce sense perceptions. (476). (935)

D. V.

१. प्र सोमासो मदच्युतः श्रवसे नो मघोनाम् ।
सुता विदथे अक्रमुः ।।

1. Soma bestows sense activities which drip and nourish, he cooks them in the home for wealth.

He directs them to mind in due course. (477), (769)

२. प्र सोमासो विपश्चितोऽपो नयन्त ऊर्मयः ।
वनानि महिषा इव ।।

2. Soma releases nourishment and inspires mind with them, Activity guides them within in waves,

like buffaloes in the forest. (478), (764)

३. पवस्वेन्दो वृषा सुतः कृधी नो यशसो जने ।
विश्वा अप द्विषो जहि ।।

3. (Soma) himself bestows (sense perceptions) on the brain cells to drink, creates knowledge excellently in men.

Activity arouses desires in both brain and mind to be born through the sense organs. (479), (778)

४. वृषा ह्यसि भानुना द्युमन्तं त्वा हवामहे ।
पवमान स्वर्दृशम् ।।

4. Consciousness rains his rays from heaven to the head within which releases much oblations,

to the fickle Mind to look up to heaven. (480), (784)

५. इन्दुः पविष्ट चेतनः प्रियः कवीनां मतिः ।
सृजदश्वं रथीरिव ।।

5. The brain cells bestow what the mind desires to drink, Agni (the wise) lets understanding,

flow through prāṇa as if he were the Vehicle. (481)

६. असृक्षत प्र वाजिनो गव्या सोमासो अश्वया ।
शुक्रासो वीरयाशवः ।।

6. Nourishment flows into the home in life from sense perceptions bestowed by Soma through prāṇa.

Streams from the sense organs approach the home released by consciousness. (482), (1034)

७. पवस्व देव आयुषगिन्द्रं गच्छतु ते मदः ।
वायुमा रोह धर्मणा ॥

7. Sense activities themselves flow through prāṇa (life) which bestow to drink, they flow from Indra joyously.

Nerves bestow them here in accordance with dharma. (483), (1235)

८. पवमानो अजीजनद्दिवश्चित्रं न तन्यतुम् ।
ज्योतिर्वैश्वानरं बृहत् ॥

8. The fickle Mind wins for men in waking state diverse ideas from sense perceptions which guide it. (484), (889)

९. परि स्वानास इन्दवो मदाय बर्हणा गिरा ।
मधो अर्षन्ति धारया ॥

9. Sense activities move powerfully (barhaṇā) on the hill, and going around bestow on brain cells themselves.

Wealth flows within in streams. (485), (1122)

१०. परि प्रासिष्यदत्कविः सिन्धोरूर्मावधि श्रितः ।
कारुं बिभ्रत्पुरुस्पृहम् ॥

10. Agni goes around and fulfils by bestowing our desires through waves of Sindhu and bestows satisfaction by cooking them.

The devotee, without any delusion, is abundantly eager for them. (486)

BOOK VI: CHAPTER I

D. I

१. उषो षु जातमप्तुरं गोभिर्भङ्गं परिष्कृतम् ।
इन्दुं देवा अयासिषुः ॥

1. Activity readily separates the sense activities to go around and produce from the sense organs for births above (in the brain).

The deva (Activity) indefatigably bestows his missiles (rays) on the brain cells. (487), (762), (1335)

२. पुनानो अक्रमीदभि विश्वा मृधो विचर्षणिः ।
शुम्भन्ति विप्रं धीतिभिः ॥

2. He bestows repeatedly at proper times on the sense organs, unwearied and diligently active.

He inspires beneficence within with understanding. (488), (924)

३. आविशन्कलशं सुतो विश्वा अर्षन्नभि श्रियः ।
इन्दुरिन्द्राय धीयते ॥

3. From the sense organs (the perceptions) flow to the brain in the head to be cooked quickly (to be released) to Mind.

Indra unites with the brain cells for understanding. (489)

४. असर्जि रथ्यो यथा पवित्रे चम्वोः सुतः ।
कार्ष्मन्वाजी न्यक्रमीत् ॥

4. The (perceptions) from the sense organs surge to the brain, likewise they are bestowed to Mind beneficently to sip.

They cultivate the mind in life-activity guiding him properly. (490)

५. प्र यद्गावो न भूर्णयस्त्वेषा आयासो अक्रमुः ।
घ्नन्तः कृष्णामप त्वचम् ॥

5. What the sense perceptions nourish are the impetuous desires, indefatigably and properly.

Activity strikes down ignorance by being sipped. (491), (892)

६. अपघ्नन्पवसे मृधः क्रतुवित्सोम मत्सरः ।
नुदस्वादेवयुं जनम् ॥

6. Activity strikes down ignorance unweariedly in the home and protects it, Soma produces knowledge which flows to us,
which he himself pushes to the devotees among men. (492)

७. अया पवस्व धारया यया सूर्यमरोचयः ।
हिन्वानो मानुषीरपः ॥

7. As consciousness ascends in me he hastens to bestow on us the paths to protect ourselves and supports it.
He arouses Activity afresh in men. (493), (1216)

८. स पवस्व य आविथेन्द्रं वृत्राय हन्तवे ।
वव्रिवांसं महीरपः ॥

8. Indra moves to bestow on us drinks himself to manifest for which he strikes down Vṛtra (inertia).
Remaining concealed in the body he gladdens and comforts us through Activity. (494)

९. अया वीती परि स्रव यस्त इन्दो मदेष्वा ।
अवाहन्नवतीर्नव ॥

9. Desiring the paths (or fortune-wealth) he flows around and strives to bestow the desires of the brain cells through sense perceptions.
He conveys new ideas to knowledge (or he conveys newer and newer ideas). (495), (1210)

१०. परि द्युक्षं सनद्रयिं भरद्वाजं नो अन्धसा ।
स्वानो अर्ष पवित्र आ ॥

10. He goes around heaven for the sake of home to bestow wealth as gift, to support life and to release us from ignorance, pantingly he flows from the summit to support or he flows beneficently. (496)

We may note that it is the devas who carry on all activities in us and gather knowledge and impart it to the brain at first. From the brain knowledge is transferred to mind also, which is retained by mind so that there is a duplicate record. Man is then Mind receiving knowledge from the devas. At death the record of the brain is destroyed and what the mind holds is carried forward to an after-life for rebirth.

What then is the jīva? The jīva is the creator individualized.

He is the witness or consciousness, remaining unchanged, attached to successive minds or men in successive lives. (496)

D. II.

१. अचिक्रदद्वृषा हरिर्महान्मित्रो न दर्शतः ।
सं सूर्येण दिद्युते ॥

1. When the great tawny consciousness visits the brain (Mitra) he releases a variety of ideas to it.

All these from the mighty consciousness are like lightning flashes. (497), (1042)

२. आ ते दक्षं मयोभुवं वह्निमद्या वृणीमहे ।
पान्तमा पुरुस्पृहम् ॥

2. They satisfy us in existence and convey rejoicings by enveloping us greatly.

They fulfil us within and are abundantly desired. (498), (1137)

३. अध्वर्यो अद्रिभिः सुतं सोमं पवित्र आ नय ।
पुनाहीन्द्राय पातवे ॥

3. In life-activity Soma guides mind from the hill (brain) beneficially.

Indra bestows on him (Soma) the path repeatedly. (499), (1225), (Y.V., 20, 30)

४. तरत्स मन्दी धावति धारा सुतस्यान्धसः ।
तरत्स मन्दी धावति ॥

4. He bestows to cross (ignorance), gladdens, jumps across (or bestows knowledge) to support Mind in releasing from ignorance.

He bestows for us to cross, by bestowing knowledge. (500), (1057)

५. आ पवस्व सहस्रिणं रयिं सोम सुवीर्यम् ।
अस्मे श्रवांसि धारय ॥

5. Soma himself bestows thousands of items of wealth to absorb (drink) arousing vigour.

He supports by cooking and bestowing streams of them. (501)

६. अनु प्रत्नास आयवः पदं नवीयो अक्रमुः ।
रुचे जनन्त सूर्यम् ॥

6. Now he bestows nourishment and guides it to the brain cells, the home drinks freshly properly.

Consciousness shines on them in men. (502)

७. अर्षा सोम द्युमत्तमोऽभि द्रोणानि रोरुवत् ।
सीदन्योनौ वनेष्वा ॥

7. Soma flows from heaven as we desire, to bestow on the brain (pot) resoundingly.

From the source he bestows a forest of desires on the home (brain). (503), (994)

८. वृषा सोम द्युमाँ असि वृषा देव वृषव्रतः ।
वृषा धर्माणि दध्रिषे ॥

8. Soma rains (his bounties) on us from heaven, rains ideas and works as his duty (vow).

He rains and bestows them on the ṛṣis as his duty (dharma) (504), (781)

९. इषे पवस्व धारया मृज्यमानो मनीषिभिः ।
इन्दो रुचाभि गा इहि ॥

9. He himself bestows desires to be imbibed (drunk) and supports and cleanses in the homes of men.

The sense activities arouse them from the brain cells to shine. (505), (841)

१०. मन्द्रया सोम धारया वृषा पवस्व देवयुः ।
अव्या वारेभिरस्मयुः ॥

10. Soma supports them pleasantly, he rains them himself to the devotee and protects.

The Aśvins support the wealth attached to him. (506)

११. अया सोम सुकृत्यया महान्त्सन्नभ्यवर्धथाः ।
मन्दान इद्वृषायसे ॥

11. Soma hastens to arouse and produce wealth (ayā), the great one bestows sense perceptions to foster its growth.

He strives to shower them on the brain cells and mind. (507)

१२. अयं विचर्षणिर्हितः पवमानः स चेतति ।
हिन्वान आप्यं बृहत् ॥

12. He is active about wealth for welfare of the fickle mind, bestows and manifests him.

Activity arouses and controls desires in him greatly. (508)

१३. प्र न इन्दो महे तु न ऊर्मि न बिभ्रदर्षसि ।
अभि देवाँ अयास्यः ॥

13. He nourishes the brain cells greatly in powerful (tu) waves and flows vehemently.

He moves to devas (ideas) for our sake. (509)

१४. अपघ्नन्पवते मृधोऽप सोमो अराव्णः ।
गच्छन्निन्द्रस्य निष्कृतम् ॥

14. Activity strikes down (intertia) to protect knowledge in fights, Soma bestows desires through Activity.

He (Soma) goes to meet Indra at the appointed place. (510), (1213)

D. III.

१. पुनानः सोम धारयापो वसानो अर्षसि ।
आ रत्नधा योनिमृतस्य सीदस्युत्सो देवो हिरण्ययः ॥

1. Activity repeatedly supports Soma by flowing into the home.

He bestows valuable wealth on mortals from the source, as soon as the golden consciousness rises he unites to release our wants through ideas (devas). (511), (675)

२. परीतो षिञ्चता सुतं सोमो य उत्तमं हविः ।
दधन्वाँ यो नर्यो अप्स्वा३न्तरा सुषाव सोममद्रिभिः ॥

2. Soma goes around and sprinkles to mind the best oblations.

Soma bestows new gifts himself to men through Activity within who releases them eagerly on the hill. (512), (1313)

३. आ सोम स्वानो अद्रिभिस्तिरो वाराण्यव्यया ।
जनो न पुरि चम्वोर्विशद्धरिः सदो वनेषु दध्रिषे ॥

3. Soma pantingly crosses over on the hill to the Aśvins who guide the gifts.

He bestows extensively on the home (brain) for people to sip from the home and supports constantly the missiles of sense activities by bestowing desires. (513), (1689)

४. प्र सोम देववीतये सिन्धुर्न पिप्ये अर्णसा ।
अंशोः पयसा मदिरो न जागृविरच्छा कोशं मधुश्चुतम् ।

4. Soma nourishes Sindhu with ideas (devas) desired by her who drinks waves of them.

He bestows Soma juice to drink, the intoxicating drink drips from the sweet perceptions nearby in the head in the waking state. (514), (767)

५. सोम उ ष्वाणः सोतृभिरधि ष्णुभिरवीनाम् ।
अश्वयेव हरिता याति धारया मन्द्रया याति धारया ॥

5. Soma is eager for desires for pressing Soma juice for both (brain and mind) and satisfies their desires by supporting and blessing them.

Prāṇa hastens to convey along the path and supports them, he moves to them pleasantly and supports them. (515), (997)

६. तवाहं सोम रारण सख्य इन्दो दिवेदिवे ।
पुरूणि बभ्रो नि चरन्ति मामव परिधीँरति ताँ इहि ॥

6. Soma! You bestow rejoicing on us, Indra helps you in the waking state daily.

The tawny consciousness goes around here below abundantly, favours us, gladdens by going around and arousing knowledge. (516), (922)

७. मृज्यमानः सुहस्त्या समुद्रे वाचमिन्वसि ।
रयिं पिशङ्गं बहुलं पुरुस्पृहं पवमानाभ्यर्षसि ॥

7. He puts the home in order arousing the nerves (hands) and gladdens by bestowing mightily on speech and binding them to it.

You let flow to the fickle mind various kinds of wealth abundantly with great eagerness. (517), (1079)

८. अभि सोमास आयवः पवन्ते मद्यं मदम् ।
समुद्रस्याधि विष्टपे मनीषिणो मत्सरासो मदच्युतः ॥

8. Soma bestows on the brain cells to drink the sweet perceptions joyously.

He gladdens us by satisfying from above, he flows in us men and bestows sense perceptions to drip. (518), (856)

९. पुनानः सोम जागृविरव्या वारैः परि प्रियः ।
त्वं विप्रो अभवोऽङ्गिरस्तम मध्वा यज्ञं मिमिक्ष णः ॥

9. Soma bestows wealth on us repeatedly in waking by going around lovingly.

You inspire the sense organs most desired by Aṅgiras (sense activities) by bestowing sense activities to approach and mingle with them in life-activity. (519)

१०. इन्द्राय पवते मदः सोमो मरुत्वते सुतः ।
सहस्रधारो अत्यव्यमर्षति तमी मृजन्त्यायवः ॥

10. Indra moves to protect knowledge from the sense perceptions, Soma bestows ideas (Maruts) on mind.

Prāṇa lets thousands of streams of them to flow which adorn the longing brain cells. (520)

११. पवस्व वाजसातमोऽभि विश्वानि वार्या ।
त्वं समुद्रः प्रथमे विधर्मं देवेभ्यः सोम मत्सरः ॥

11. He bestows desires continually in life himself for sense organs to drink for the sake of wealth.

He bestows on us gladness primarily in accordance with his dharma (duty), he hurries ideas (devas) to flow to us. (521)

१२. पवमाना असृक्षत पवित्रमति धारया ।
मरुत्वन्तो मत्सरा इन्द्रिया हया मेधामभि प्रयांसि च ॥

12. Understanding flows beneficially from the home to the fickle mind in streams.

Ideas (Maruts) bestow on it within by flowing to our sense organs and move to nourish knowledge and also support it. (522)

D. IV.

१. प्र तु द्रव परि कोशं नि षीद नृभिः पुनानो अभि वाजमर्ष ।
अश्वं न त्वा वाजिनं मर्जयन्तोऽच्छा बर्हो रशनाभिर्नयन्ति ॥

1. Maruts (or Soma)! You run to bestow going around and staying in men, then you flow in life-activity repeatedly.

Prāṇa wins you for mortals in life from the nearby nerves and guides and supports your essence. (523), (677)

२. प्र काव्यमुशनेव ब्रुवाणो देवो देवानां जनिमा विवक्ति ।
महिव्रतः शुचिबन्धुः पावकः पदा वराहो अभ्येति रेभन् ।।

2. Maruts (or Soma)! You nourish poems (wisdom), eagerly bestow ideas on speech, you vivify that we are from the deva source and have great duties (vows), related to shining ones bestow on the brain for fulfilment of (the descendant) man in the line of boar (animal) i.e. by bestowing speech (bana) on the motley sense activities. (524), (1116)

३. तिस्रो वाच ईरयति प्र वह्निर्ऋतस्य धीतिं ब्रह्मणो मनीषाम् ।
गावो यन्ति गोपतिं पृच्छमानाः सोमं यन्ति मतयो वावशानाः ।।

3. Soma! You bestow on the three (brain, sense organs and mind) and also unite with them for their comfort, nourish them, Ṛta conveys and satisfies men with knowledge.

The lord of men (Indra) guides the sense activities to mingle with the brain (home). You guide Soma to us and bestow him on our home (brain.) (525). (859)

४. अस्य प्रेषा हेमना पूयमानो देवो देवेभिः समपृक्त रसम् ।
सुतः पवित्रं पर्येति रेभन् मितेव सद्म पशुमन्ति होता ।।

4. Soma! You nourish our desires i.e. of our mind letting ideas (devas) swell in our homes, the devas mingle as equals with their essences (content).

The motley sense perceptions go around to mind beneficently and resoundingly and establish themselves immediately presiding over the mind. (526), (1399)

५. सोमः पवते जनिता मतीनां जनिता दिवो जनिता पृथिव्याः ।
जनिताग्नेर्जनिता सूर्यस्य जनितेन्द्रस्य जनितोत विष्णोः ।।

5. Soma protects understanding born of thoughts (perceptions), born in waking, born through sense organs,

born through Agni, revealed by consciousness, released by Indra, originating from Viṣṇu above. (527), (943)

६. अभि त्रिपृष्ठं वृषणं वयोधामङ्गोषिणमवावशन्त वाणीः ।
वना वसानो वरुणो न सिन्धुर्वि रत्नधा दयते वार्याणि ।।

6. Indra (bull) bestows strength on the three states foremost through his limb (prāṇa) who eagerly favours their desires from the home.

Sindhu bestows the desires for Varuṇa (external world) of the brain (home) in the form of valuable wealth distributing them in the enclosure. (528), (1408)

७. अक्रांत्समुद्रः प्रथमे विधर्मं जनयन् प्रजा भुवनस्य गोपाः ।
वृषा पवित्रे अधि सानो अव्ये बृहत्सोमो वावृधे स्वानो अद्रिः ।।

7. The first step in producing creatures (subjects) taken by the protector of the creatures in accordance with dharma was in the ocean waters.

The Aśvins from beyond the summit showered their blessings graciously in the form of the great Soma who pantingly bestowed growth on the hill. (529), (1253)

Creation is said to have commenced in the ocean waters and it was initiated by the Aśvins who alone were competent to pass from one level of activity to another. They sent Soma the sustainer of Activity to initiate creative activity.

८. कनिक्रन्ति हरिरा सृज्यमानः सीदन्वनस्य जठरे पुनानः ।
नृभिर्यतः कृणुते निर्णिजं गामतो मतिं जनयत स्वधाभिः ।।

8. Consciousness being invoked by the brain (home) flows in and bestows repeatedly on the desires of the brain cells (jaṭhare) in the home.

He unites with and supports men, creates knowledge (understanding) in us from the sense perceptions with his bright robe (nirṇija), he unites with men of his own will. (530)

९. एष स्य ते मधुमाँ इन्द्र सोमो वृषा वृष्णः परि पवित्रे अक्षाः ।
सहस्रदाः शतदा भूरिदावा शश्वत्तमं बर्हिरा वाज्यस्थात् ।।

9. The sense perceptions flow to us through Indra, Soma showers them on us powerfully by going round the home beneficently.

There are thousands of burning demands, and hundreds of bestowals, abundant demands (conflagrations), constant desires which the nerves satisfy by releasing in life-activity abidingly. (531)

The demands of the cell organisms and the several organs of the body constantly are mentioned here. These are all being attended to automatically within the system without our knowledge.

१०. पवस्व सोम मधुमाँ ऋतावापो वसानो अधि सानो अव्ये ।
अव द्रोणानि घृतवन्ति रोह मदिन्तमो मत्सर इन्द्रपानः ॥

10. Soma bestows sense perceptions on us himself, Ṛta bestows Activity, the Aśvins from beyond the summit bestow them on the brain (home).

They favour the brain with clarified butter bestowed within by desires ascending to the sense activities and flowing to us, which Indra binds (retains) for fulfilment. (532)

D. V.

१. प्र सेनानीः शूरो अग्ने रथानां गव्यन्नेति हर्षते अस्य सेना ।
भद्रान् कृण्वन्निन्द्रहवांत्सखिभ्य आ सोमो वस्त्रा रभसानि दत्ते ॥

1. The heroic Agni arouses and guides his troops of sense activities to nourish the sense organs, the missiles (rays) flow to us in troops.

Indra helps the oblations producing desire in us for welfare, Soma bestows vehemently (rabhasa) on the brain cells (Vastra—woven like a garment). (533)

२. प्र ते धारा मधुमतीरसृग्रन्वारं यत्पूतो अत्येष्यव्यम् ।
पवमान पवसे धाम गोनां जनयंत्सूर्यमपिन्वो अर्कैः ॥

2. The streams of sense perceptions nourish understanding and bestow it, which flowed earlier towards the wealth, which swelled after release by Prāṇa at the desire of the Aśvins, with which it (understanding) united.

The sense perceptions bestow on the fickle mind to drink from the home, Consciousness controls men (or from the source) and we drink freshly praiseworthily. (534)

३. प्र गायताभ्यर्चाम देवांत्सोमं हिनोत महते धनाय ।
स्वादुः पवतामति वारमव्यमा सीदतु कलशं देव इन्दुः ॥

3. I worship sense activities to nourish me by uniting, they bestow here ideas which arouse the motley sense activities to much wealth.

The palatable (perceptions) are drunk by our understanding, the Aśvins bestow wealth on the deva brain cells in the head.

Alt. Understanding drinks the palatable perceptions, the Aśvins bestow wealth for understanding in the home which urge devas to toil for the brain cells. (535)

४. प्र हिन्वानो जनिता रोदस्यो रथो न वाजं सनिषन्नयासीत् ।
इन्द्रं गच्छन्नायुधा संशिशानो विश्वा वसु हस्तयोरादधानः ॥

4. Nourishment arouses desires in brain and sense organs (heaven and earth) through the sense organs in life-activity, the desires are bestowed as gifts on the brain.

Indra goes to fight for food (sense perceptions) (Or Indra goes to unite with anna to bestow) and bestows bounteously on the sense organs graciously through his hands (nerves). (536)

५. तक्षद्यदी मनसो वेनतो वाग् ज्येष्ठस्य धर्मं द्युक्षोरनीके ।
आदीमायन्वरमा वावशाना जुष्टं पतिं कलशे गाव इन्दुम् ॥

5. Indra (the elder) in accordance with his dharma (duty) bestows from heaven the desires of the mind for speech in the home before (or below) him.

In ancient times the lord bestowed on my brain a marvellous gift, an acceptable one, through the sense activities whom he urged to release to the brain cells. (537)

६. साकमुक्षो मर्जयन्त स्वसारो दश धीरस्य धीतयो धनुत्रीः ।
हरिः पर्यद्रवज्जाः सूर्यस्य द्रोणं ननक्षे अत्यो न वाजी ॥

6. (Indra) together (with sense activities) won for the mortals to go strong from their own essential nature, three means of protection (armour), praiseworthy of a lasting nature (eyes, ears and speech) towards understanding.

The tawny consciousness going around drips births (by revealing.

Soma flows from the head and approaches prāṇa in life-activity. (538), (1418)

७. अधि यदस्मिन्वाजिनीव शुभः स्पर्धन्ते धियः सूरे न विशः ।
अपो वृणानः पवते कवीयान्व्रजं न पशुवर्धनाय मन्म ॥

7. What is bestowed in life leading to welfare gives satisfaction, the Soma juice competes in the home to give satisfaction.

Activity envelops understanding and binds it to us, to drink (or/and protects) in the enclosure of Agni (poet), the sense activities (paśu) fosters growth of and guides our mind. (539)

८. इन्दुर्वाजी पवते गोन्योघा इन्द्रे सोमः सह इन्वन्मदाय ।
हन्ति रक्षो बाधते पर्यराति वरिवस्कृण्वन्वृजनस्य राजा ॥

8. Indra guides and bestows sense activities on the brain cells in life-activity to preserve knowledge, and together with Soma bestows mighty desires through the sense activities.

He strikes down (enemies) to protect us from being hurt, goes around ready to bestow, creates freedom for the desires to rule us in our enclosure. (540), (1019)

९. अया पवा पवस्वैना वसूनि माँश्चत्व इन्दो सरसि प्र धन्व ।
ब्रध्नश्चिद्यस्य वातो न जूतिं पुरुमेधाश्चित्तकवे नरं धात् ॥

9. Indra (Vasu) bestows us and protects the paths, then he bestows us for drinking, you bestow Soma juice, also you flow to the brain cells to bestow fresh nourishment.

The ruddy consciousness inspires them (brain cells) with understanding, Agni bestows abundant understanding on the mind of man. (541), (1104)

१०. महत्तत्सोमो महिषश्चकारापाँ यद्गर्भोऽवृणीत देवान् ।
अदधादिन्द्रे पवमान ओजोऽजनयत्सूर्ये ज्योतिरिन्दुः ॥

10. Soma gladdens him (mind), fulfils the sense organs (buffalo) from the brain (prison), Activities envelop what is born of them with devas (ideas).

Then Indra bestows on the fickle mind powerfully, consciousness unites with men's brain cells with his effulgent rays. (542), (1255)

११. असर्जि वक्वा रथ्ये यथाजौ धिया मनोता प्रथमा मनीषा ।
दश स्वसारो अधि सानो अव्ये मृजन्ति वह्निं सदनेष्वच्छ ॥

11. Speech surges bestowed by sense organs, likewise the Aśvins satisfy the mind of man also.

The Aśvins protect it with their resources from beyond the summit, smoothen (the path) within, convey it and bestow it near the home (brain) as desired. (543)

१२. अपामिवेदूर्मयस्तर्तुराणाः प्र मनीषा ईरते सोममच्छ ॥
नमस्यन्तीरुप च यन्ति सं चाच विशन्त्युशतीरुशन्तम् ॥

12. Activity approaches and bestows (for speech), prāṇa beholds the extensive (gift) and nourishes men with it speedily, Soma induces it which is close-by.

He honours it (speech) within above, also guides all also to the home eagerly and then longs to browse. (544)

BOOK VI : CHAPTER II

D. I.

१. पुरोजिती वो अन्धसः सुताय मानयित्नवे ।
अप श्वानं श्नथिष्टन सखायो दीर्घजिह्व्यम् ॥

1. Soma! You won the home and bestowed on it (ideas) to release Mind from ignorance, thus bestowing (mā) new (ideas) and distributing them.

Activity swells and honours and pierces (śnatha) wishes through the long tongues (of sense activities) and controls them. (545), (697)

२. अयं पूषा रयिर्भगः सोमः पुनानो अर्षति ।
पतिर्विश्वस्य भूमनो व्यख्यद्रोदसी उभे ॥

2. Consciousness protects eagerly the path to wealth and thus Soma flows in repeatedly.

The lord gives existence to mind from our home (brain), he is known to run to us above for the wants of both (brain and mind). (546), (818)

३. सुतासो मधुमत्तमाः सोमा इन्द्राय मन्दिनः ।
पवित्रवन्तो अक्षरन् देवान् गच्छन्तु वो मदाः ॥

3. Soma bestows on mind sense perceptions and desires to us through Indra and gladdens us mightily.

He bestows devas (ideas) beneficially within the home to gladden and they come to bestow sense perceptions. (547), (872)

४. सोमाः पवन्त इन्दवोऽस्मभ्यं गातुवित्तमाः ।
मित्राः स्वाना अरेपसः स्वाध्यः स्वर्विदः ॥

4. Soma bestows on the brain cells to drink who bestow on us devotees knowledge desired.

The panting (agitated) brain (Mitra) is unblemished and repeats to itself the knowledge from heaven. (548), (1101)

५. अभी नो वाजसातमं रयिमर्ष शतस्पृहम् ।
इन्दो सहस्रभर्णसं तुविद्युम्नं विभासहम् ॥

5. To bestow desires in life-activity, wealth flows in to us hundreds of times eagerly.

It associates with the brain cells thousands of times, through the mighty heaven he becomes clear indeed. (549), (1238)

६. अभी नवन्ते अद्रुहः प्रियमिन्द्रस्य काम्यम् ।
वत्सं न पूर्वं आयुनि जातं रिहन्ति मातरः ॥

6. Indra controls our desires fondly to establish new ones within.

The mind (child) is born from the previous life whom the mother (sense activities) caresses and bestows. (550)

७. आ हर्यताय धृष्णवे धनुष्टन्वन्ति पौंस्यम् ।
शुक्रा वि यन्त्यसुराय निर्णिजे विपामग्रे महीयुवः ॥

7. He moves boldly with new ones (wealth) desired by the mind eagerly, and bestows to fatten him; consciousness is well-known to arouse and control (mind) through his guidance, whom he previously inspires (with perceptions) from the sense organs (mahī). (551)

८. परि त्यं हर्यतं हरिं बभ्रुं पुनन्ति वारेण ।
यो देवान्विश्वां इत्परि मदेन सह गच्छति ॥

8. It is well-known that the tawny consciousness eagerly sends his rays repeatedly in the enclosure.

That deva goes around to the sense organs together with sense activities. (552), (1329), (1681)

९. प्र सुन्वानायान्धसो मर्तो न वष्ट तद्वचः ।
अप श्वानमराधसं हता मखं न भृगवः ॥

9. He arouses mortals, nourishes afresh and guides releasing from ignorance and newly gaining speech.

Pantingly Activity supports indeed the wealth from the sense activity vigorously. (553), (774), (1386)

D. II.

१. अभि प्रियाणि पवते चनोहितो नामानि यह्वो अधि येषु वर्धते ।
आ सूर्यस्य बृहतो बृहन्नधि रथं विष्वञ्चमरुहद्विचक्षणः ॥

1. Consciousness lovingly protects understanding and

gladdens us with welfare, he is invoked by the home from beyond, his rays promote growth.

Consciousness envelops indeed the home, the sense organs pray (bṛha) for it from beyond; he ascends, looks at the home and sips it. (554)

२. अचोदसो नो धन्वन्त्विन्दवः प्र स्वानासो बृहद्देवेषु हरयः ।
वि चिदश्नाना इषयो अरातयोऽर्यो नः सन्तु सनिषन्तु नो धियः ॥

2. He honours and bestows the wealth desired above praiseworthily, he is associated with ideas himself greatly and conveys them.

You bestow on us a variety of desires through the mind. You bestow gifts on men. You bestow on us the desires and satisfy us. (555)

३. एष प्र कोशे मधुमाँ अचिक्रवदिन्द्रस्य वज्रो वपुषो वपुष्टमः ।
अभ्यृ३तस्य सुदुघा घृतश्चुतो वाश्रा अर्षन्ति पयसा च धेनवः ॥

3. The sense perceptions flow in the head to nourish, Indra perceives and causes the bestowal through the nerves marvellously which release to fatten.

He arouses and bestows the milk (perceptions) on Ṛta, clarified butter drips from the sense perceptions and flows in the brain along with the latter. (556)

४. प्रो अयासीदिन्दुरिन्द्रस्य निष्कृतं सखा सख्युर्न प्र मिनाति सङ्गिरम् ।
मर्य इव युवतिभिः समर्षति सोमः कलशे शतयामना पथा ॥

4. Indra fulfils the brain cells in the home with nourishment, meeting the mind at the appointed place he helps it extensively by approaching him.

Like a youth going to meet his beloved Soma flows evenly in the brain (pot) and along a hundred paths to Mind, (557), (1152)

५. धर्ता दिवः पवते कृत्व्यो रसो दक्षो देवानामनुमाद्यो नृभिः ।
हरिः सृजानो अत्यो न सत्वभिर्वृथा पाजांसि कृणुषे नदीष्वा ॥

5. Consciousness supports us by protecting understanding, produces the essence and satisfies, men hail the devas.

Consciousness flows from the source and supports prāṇa to bestow existence at his will, supports life-activity, releases eagerly the desires bestowed resoundingly (nada). (558), (1228)

६. वृषा मतीनां पवते विचक्षणः सोमो अह्नां प्रतरीतोषसां दिवः ।
प्राणा सिन्धूनां कलशाँ अचिक्रददिन्द्रस्य हार्दिमाविशन्मनीषिभिः ॥

6. Soma showers understanding, he protects understanding, is discerning, great and nourishes to cross over (ignorance) eagerly in waking.

Prāṇa perceives Sindhu in the head, produced and bestowed by Indra on the brain in the home of man. (559), (821)

७. त्रिरस्मै सप्त धेनवो दुदुह्रिरे सत्यामाशिरं परमे व्योमनि ॥
चत्वार्यन्या भुवनानि निर्णिजे चारूणि चक्रे यदृतैरवर्धत ॥

7. The three states of our are served by the seven rays (of Activity) for our comfort and they bestow on us from the remote ākāśa (space).

They are led from the fourth state to the creatures at the appointed places, they go around gladdening us, they are constant, bestow and promote our growth. (560), (1423)

८. इन्द्राय सोम सुषुतः परि स्रवापामीवा भवतु रक्षसः सह ।
मा ते रसस्य मत्सत द्वयाविनो द्रविणस्वन्त इह सन्त्विन्दवः ॥

8. Soma urges Indra (or vice versa) towards mind to go around, they flow together and approach and bestow, protecting existence.

They bestow the essences in our existence, they move towards both (brain and sense organs) mightily, bestow wealth here, within and bestow gifts on the brain cells. (561)

९. असावि सोमो अरुषो वृषा हरी राजेव दस्मो अभि गा अचिक्रदत् ।
पुनानो वारमत्येष्यव्ययं श्येनो न योनिं घृतवन्तमासदत् ॥

9. The tawny consciousness showers his ruddy rays through Soma at his seat and like a king he perceives the sense activities and bestows his rays that they may produce.

Prāṇa goes to them repeatedly and abidingly in the enclosure, watching like a hawk at the source he releases clarified butter within our homes. (562), (1316)

१०. प्र देवमच्छा मधुमन्त इन्दवोऽसिष्यदन्त गाव आ न धेनवः ।
बर्हिषदो वचनावन्त ऊधभिः परिस्रुतमुस्रिया निर्णिजं धिरे ॥

10. The devas nearby nourish the sense activities and bestow the brain cells, the sense perceptions bestow our desires within like a milch-cow.

They bestow on the home through the nerves and gladden us from within, existing like a rain-cloud, Indra (bull) meets them at the appointed place and satisfies us. (563)

११. अञ्जते व्यञ्जते समञ्जते क्रतुं रिहन्ति मध्वाभ्यञ्जते ।
सिन्धोरुच्छ्वासे पतयन्तमुक्षणं हिरण्यपावाः पशुमप्सु गृभ्णते ॥

11. They (ideas) ornament us, they ornament as clusters, they caress us within and produce (gifts) for us, they are an adornment to sense activities.

They shine in the home with Sindhu guide, protect and foster growth, consciousness releases them to fulfil.

Activity holds the sense activities (paśu). (564), (1614)

१२. पवित्रं ते विततं ब्रह्मणस्पते प्रभुर्गात्राणि पर्येषि विश्वतः ।
अतप्ततनूर्न तदामो अश्नुते शृतास इद्वहन्तः सं तदाशत ॥

12. They (the ideas) are to a great extent beneficial to Soma (Brahmaṇaspati—lord of knowledge), limb of Agni-Savitā, goes around as desired by the sense organs.

They warm (agitate) us up delicately they (arrive) uncooked and are cooked up on the hill and thus they are conveyed; all of them are food for us. (565), (875)

D. III.

१. इन्द्रमच्छ सुता इमे वृषणं यन्तु हरयः ।
श्रुष्टे जातास इन्दवः स्वर्विदः ॥

1. Indra who is near mind here guides him powerfully by conveying (ideas) to him.

He produces from the source and bestows the knowledge of heaven on the brain cells. (566), (694)

२. प्र धन्वा सोम जागृविरिन्द्रायेन्दो परि स्रव ।
द्युमन्तं शुष्ममा भर स्वर्विदम् ॥

2. Soma bestows new nourishment in waking and bestows them on the brain cells through Indra by going around.

From heaven he rushes within to us to support us in knowing heaven. (567)

३. सखाय आ नि षीदत पुनानाय प्र गायत ।
शिशुं न यज्ञैः परि भूषत श्रिये ॥

3. He moves as a friend in the home repeatedly and nourishes by uniting with sense activities.

He goes around to mind in life that he may adorn us in prosperity. (568), (1157)

४. तं वः सखायो मदाय पुनानमभि गायत ।
शिशुं न हव्यैः स्वदयन्त गूर्तिभिः ॥

4. (Soma) bestows desires as a friend of sense activities and repeatedly unites with them.

He himself distributes oblations within to the mind of man. (569), (1098)

५. प्राणा शिशुर्महीनां हिन्वन्नृतस्य दीधितिम् ।
विश्वा परि प्रिया भुवदध द्विता ॥

5. Prāṇa arouses mind greatly and Ṛta bestows on him satisfaction.

He goes around to the sense organs lovingly and bestows (their gifts) in existence on both (brain and mind). (570), (1013)

६. पवस्व देववीतय इन्दो धाराभिरोजसा ।
आ कलशं मधुमांत्सोम नः सदः ॥

6. He favours ideas and bestows them himself on the brain cells to drink and supports their streams vigorously.

Soma binds the sense percepts to the brain (pot) constantly. (571), (1326)

७. सोमः पुनान ऊर्मिणाव्यं वारं वि धावति ।
अग्रे वाचः पवमानः कनिक्रदत् ॥

7. Soma repeatedly comes in waves to the enclosure and divides them.

Earlier the sense activities produce and bestow speech on mind (572), (940)

८. प्र पुनानाय वेधसे सोमाय वच उच्यते ।
भृतिं न भरा मतिभिर्जुजोषते ॥

8. Soma moves repeatedly to nourish the speech of the devotee by uniting above.

He supports it to uphold understanding victoriously marching in step with it. (573).

९. गोमन्न इन्दो अश्ववत्सुतः सुदक्ष धनिव ।
शुचिं च वर्णमधि गोषु धारय ॥

9. The sense perceptions are food to the brain cells, Prāṇa satisfies the mind with understanding, like wealth. They shine, also they satisfy us in a variety of ways; sense activities support them with their rays. (574), (1611)

१०. अस्मभ्यं त्वा वसुविदमभि वाणीरनूषत ।
गोभिष्टे वर्णमभि वासयामसि ॥

10. You are beneficial to us with Knowledge and you are attached to desires.

You are fond of the variety of sense activities and bind their paths to the home. (575)

११. पवते हर्यतो हरिरति ह्वरांसि रंह्या ।
अभ्यर्ष स्तोतृभ्यो वीरवद्यशः ॥

11. Consciousness eagerly protects understanding and bestows it, supports the spinal cord to sip and gladdens.

He flows fearlessly and praiseworthily like a hero, revealing himself excellently. (576)

१२. परि कोशं मधुश्चुतं सोमः पुनानो अर्षति ।
अभि वाणीर्ऋषीणां सप्ता नूषत ॥

12. Soma goes around the head dripping sense perceptions (honey) and flows repeatedly.

The ṛṣis honour you for desires to whom they are attached. (577)

D. IV.

१. पवस्व मधुमत्तम इन्द्राय सोम क्रतुवित्तमो मदः ।
महि द्युक्षतमो मदः ॥

1. Soma himself bestows and protects sense perceptions and our desires through Indra, produces knowledge and desires through sense activities (or joyously).

The sense activities are mightily celestial desires. (578), (692)

२. अभि द्युम्नं बृहद्यश इषस्पते दीदिहि देव देवयुम् ॥
वि कोशं मध्यमं युव ॥

2. Soma, the lord of desires, from heaven honours us greatly

and excellently and shines; he arouses the devotees and bestows ideas (devas).

He controls mind with sense perceptions through the head. (579), (1011)

३. आ सोता परि षिञ्चताश्वं न स्तोममप्तुरं रजस्तुरम् ।
वनप्रक्षमुदप्रुतम् ॥

3. Prāṇa goes around sprinkling Soma juice praiseworthily from Activity readily from the mighty sky (rajas).

Desires nourish the home and rejoicings spring from them. (580), (1394)

४. एतमु त्यं मदच्युतं सहस्रधारं वृषभं दिवोदुहम् ।
विश्वा वसूनि बिभ्रतम् ॥

4. The motley sense activities are also controlled, the sense activities drip; Indra lets thousands of streams of milk (perceptions) in the waking state.

He bestows them on the home beneficially without confusion. (581)

५. स सुन्वे यो वसूनां यो रायामानेता य इडानाम् ।
सोमो यः सुक्षितीनाम् ॥

5. Indra (Vasu) bestows Soma juice and like a king he leads us to oblations.

Soma hastens to arouse the home. (582), (1096)

६. त्वं ह्या३ङ्ग दैव्यं पवमान जनिमानि द्युमत्तमः ।
अमृतत्वाय घोषयन् ॥

6. You (Indra) are a limb of heaven, the fickle mind is divine; he takes birth in the home out of desires from or to heaven.

He moves and bestows on mortals and shouts out. (583), (938)

७. एष स्य धारया सुतोऽव्या वारेभिः पवते मदिन्तमः ।
क्रीडन्नूर्मिरपामिव ॥

7. Streams (of perceptions) flow to our mind from the Aśvins in the enclosure which protect understanding and gladden our desires.

Activity approaches and bestows on men and plays with them. (584)

८. य उस्रिया अपि या अन्तरश्मनि निर्गा अकृन्तदोजसा ।
अभि व्रजं तत्निषे गव्यमश्व्यं वर्मीव धृष्णवा रुज ।
ओ३म् वर्मीव धृष्णवा रुज ॥

8. Indra (bull) moves about, also he moves within on the hill, guides sense activities, produces vigorously and bestows.

He boldly bestows the sense activities in the enclosure and guides them as desired for our food which like an armour shatters (enemy missiles).

The sense activities like an armour shatters (enemy missiles). (585)

Āraṇya Kāṇḍa

BOOK VI: CHAPTER III

D. I.

१. इन्द्र ज्येष्ठं न आ भर ओजिष्ठं पुपुरि श्रवः।
यद्दिधृक्षेम वज्रहस्त रोदसी उभे सुशिप्र पप्राः॥

1. The eldest (Indra) swells into the city (brain) to cook and bestow and to support it vigorously,

which induces to convey safety through the vigorous hands (nerves) to both (brain and mind or sense organs) arousing nourishment and fulfilling to heart's content (cheekful). (586)

२. इन्द्रो राजा जगतश्चर्षणीनामधिक्षमा विश्वरूपं यदस्य।
ततो ददाति दाशुषे वसूनि चोदद्राध उपस्तुतं चिदर्वाक्॥

2. Indra is a king, he is diligently active in the world and satisfies us patiently (or bestows from beyond on the home) which releases forms of objects to us through the sense organs.

He bestows wealth successfully on the dependent devotee's mind. (587)

३. यस्येदमा रजोयुजस्तुजे जने वनं स्वः।
इन्द्रस्य रन्त्यं बृहत्॥

3. Indra strives here to unite with brain cells (raja—dust, pollen) and bestow, himself, to stimulate desires in men.

Indra gladdens and controls us greatly. (588)

४. उदुत्तमं वरुण पाशमस्मदवाधमं वि मध्यमं श्रथाय।
अथादित्य व्रते वयं तवानागसो अदितये स्याम॥

4. Above (in the head) Varuṇa (external world) who is bound to us (as if by a cord) favours our homes with the best (gifts) through the sense activities which control and loosen (ideas from objects).

Then Aditi has a duty to us, she releases through the spinal cord to us who are in want (aditi). (589)

५. त्वया वयं पवमानेन सोम भरे कृतं वि चिनुयाम शश्वत्।
तन्नो मित्रो वरुणो मामहन्तामदितिः सिन्धुः पृथिवी उत द्यौः॥

5. Aditi moves, bestows and controls the fickle mind mightily. Soma supports her producing desires along the separate paths constantly.

(Mitra's) longings through (ideas) of Varuṇa as food, she agitates the sense organs also the head (heaven) and binds them. (590)

६. इमं वृषणं कृणुतैकमिन्माम् ॥

6. Here Indra produces mightily all alone. (591)

७. स न इन्द्राय यज्यवे वरुणाय मरुद्भ्यः ।
वरिवोवित्परिस्रव ॥

7. Indra bestows gifts on the brain cells in life of ideas of the external world (Varuṇa).

The knowledge moves around freely. (592), (673), (Y.V. 26, 17)

८. एना विश्वान्यर्य आ द्युम्नानि मानुषाणाम् ।
सिषासन्तो वनामहे ॥

8. Then from the head (heaven) he moves to the sense organs of men.

And he willingly bestows much desires as gifts. (593), (674), (Y.V. 26.18)

९. अहमस्मि प्रथमजा ऋतस्य पूर्वं देवेभ्यो अमृतस्य नाम ।
यो मा ददाति स इदेवमावदहमन्नमन्नमदन्तमद्मि ॥

9. My "Self" was born foremost (in ancient times) prior to Ṛta, among devas honoured as immortal.

They bestowed on me and speeded me here telling me that mind will honour me and that my food will be sense activities and that they will approach me within. (594)

D. II.

१. त्वमेतदधारयः कृष्णासु रोहिणीषु च ।
परुष्णीषु रुशत्पयः ॥

1. They bestow on me streams of sense activities; they arouse the coming into existence of the missiles and cultivate the brain.

The variegated missiles (sense activities) browse and hasten to protect us. (595)

२. अरूरुचदुषसः पृश्निरग्रिय उक्षा मिमेति भुवनेषु वाजयुः ।
मायाविनो ममिरे अस्य मायया नृचक्षसः पितरो गर्भमादधुः ॥

2. Uṣas at first bestowed a variety of creatures, approached us (creatures) and strengthened the motley sense perceptions in the devotees on earth.

They favoured us mightily and marvellously for our comfort, they hastened to bestow on us; the father looked at mortals and bestowed rejoicings from the source to arouse us. (596), (877)

३. इन्द्र इद्धर्योः सचा सम्मिश्ल आ वचोयुजा ।
इन्द्रो वज्री हिरण्ययः ॥

3. Indra supports us here by uniting with us, he mingles with all for yoking them to speech.

Indra arouses the (relevant) nerves and gladdens us by hastening them. (597), (797)

४. इन्द्र वाजेषु नोऽव सहस्रप्रधनेषु च ।
उग्र उग्राभिरूतिभिः ॥

4. Indra favours us in life-activity nourishing us with thousands of items of wealth (of speech) also.

He is powerful and helps us powerfully. (598), (798)

५. प्रथश्च यस्य सप्रथश्च नामानुष्टुभस्य हविषो हविर्यत् ।
धातुर्द्युतानात्सवितुश्च विष्णो रथन्तरमा जभारा वसिष्ठः ॥

5. It (speech) spreads out, it is extensive, and gladdens, bestows praises as oblations and unites with them as desired.

It bestows readily like lightning, it stimulates musical notes also, it is a worker (Viṣṇu) within the sense organ, is released through the mouth, desires to live in it. (599)

६. नियुत्वान्वायवा गह्ययं शुक्रो अयामि ते ।
गन्तासि सुन्वतो गृहम् ॥

6. The brain cells bestow myriads of new sounds (speech) which they control to illumine and to which they are related.

It (speech) is bound to sense activity within the home of the devotee. (600)

७. यज्जायथा अपूर्व्यं मघवन्वृत्रहत्याय ।
तत्पृथिवीमप्रथयस्तदस्तभ्ना उतो दिवम् ।।

7. It (speech) was born in life-activity in ancient days after Indra had struck down inertia (Vṛtra).

He spreads it through our sense organ (or in our world) and strove to establish it also, in waking state. (601)

D. III.

१. मयि वर्चो अथो यशोऽथो यज्ञस्य यत्पयः ।
परमेष्ठी प्रजापतिर्दिवि द्यामिव दृंहतु ।।

1. Prāṇa bestows and honours us, then he is famous, then he unites with our life-activity and speeds up protection.

The supreme lord, the lord of the subjects approaches us in waking state and bestows (all gifts) and establishes them. (602)

२. सं ते पयांसि समु यन्तु वाजाः सं वृष्ण्यान्यभिमातिषाहः ।
आप्यायमानो अमृताय सोम दिवि श्रवांस्युत्तमानि धिष्व ।।

2. He supports us to partake (drink) of them all, he guides us to all of them in life, he rains them all and guides us against hostility victoriously.

Activity moves to the home, Soma moves to the mortals in waking state, cooks and bestows on us the best and gladdens us himself. (603)

३. त्वमिमा ओषधीः सोम विश्वास्त्वमपो अजनयस्त्वं गाः ।
त्वमाततनोरुर्वा३न्तरिक्षं त्वं ज्योतिषा वि तमो ववर्थ ।।

3. Soma approaches and bestows nourishment on the home praiseworthily and strives for sense activities born of Activity.

He bestows and guides extensively to the reservoir (brain), he wins the desires of the mind through the motley sense perceptions which let desires to subsist through bestowals. (604)

४. अग्निमीळे पुरोहितं यज्ञस्य देवमृत्विजम् ।
होतारं रत्नधातमम् ।।

4. Agni arouses desires in the city through oblations in life-activity of ideas to the devotees.

As the presiding deva he gladdens us by bestowing valuable wealth as desired. (605)

५. ते मन्वत प्रथमं नाम गोनां त्रिः सप्त परमं नाम जानन् ।
ता जानतीरभ्यनूषत क्षा आविर्भुवन्नरुणीर्यशसा गावः ॥

5. He bestows primarily on mind, the sense activities honour the three states, the seven-fold Activity from the source honours us supremely.

He is attached to the home and so grabs it. The Aśvins bestow the sense activities on the creatures and consciousness bestows splendour on them. (606)

६. समन्या यन्त्युपयन्त्यन्याः समानमूर्वं नद्यस्पृणन्ति ।
तमू शुचिं शुचयो दीदिवांसमपान्नपातमुप यन्त्यापः ॥

6. (Activity) moves to mind to bestow and guide it eagerly, he guides others to him, he bestows equally on all extensively and strives to nourish them resoundingly within.

He is flaming and illuminates.

Consciousness sheds his rays on Activity and supports him and guides him to the sense organs (descendants), from above he guides Activity. (607)

७. आ प्रागाद्भद्रा युवतिरह्नः केतूंत्समीर्त्सति ।
अभूद्भद्रा निवेशनी विश्वस्य जगतो रात्री ॥

7. Sense activities bestow for the welfare of the mind to cross (ignorance) in waking and fulfil; they arouse desires in him at the same time for (or in existence).

You enter to guide and bestow welfare in existence. You bestow on our home and release them to the three states to animate them. (608)

८. प्रक्षस्य वृष्णो अरुषस्य नू महः प्र नो वचो विदथा जातवेदसे ।
वैश्वानराय मतिर्नव्यसे शुचिः सोम इव पवते चारुरग्नये ॥

8. Indra (bull) nourishes our home, the ruddy Consciousness now gladdens us, he nourishes speech and directs it to cause the birth of Knowledge to release.

Activity strives for fresh understanding and glows and bestows to protect knowledge gladdening us like Agni. (609)

९. विश्वे देवा मम शृण्वन्तु यज्ञमुभे रोदसी अपां नपाच्च मन्म ॥
मा वो वचांसि परिचक्ष्याणि वोचं सुम्नेष्विद्वो अन्तमा मदेम ॥

9. He bestows on the brain cells looking new (ideas) within

in life-activity, to both brain and sense organs also for the sake of mind.

He bestows and supports my speech, he goes around and looks up the sense organs, bestows knowledge excellently through speech, which is intimate with sense activities here. (610)

१०. यशो मा द्यावापृथिवी यशो मेन्द्रबृहस्पती ।
यशो भगस्य विन्दतु यशो मा प्रतिमुच्यताम् ।
यशसा३स्याः संसदोऽहं प्रवदिता स्याम् ॥

10. My brain and sense organs are excellent; Indra and Soma (Bṛhaspati) are splendorous; Consciousness is splendorous and is praised; he nourishes me excellently to release me (from ignorance). He bestows on me excellently; constantly I hover about him as his object (second).

The creator or Prajāpati reveals all ideas of objects presented before him just as the sun reveals all gross objects. Consciousness in human beings is the universal being individualised and is the "Self" in man. Thus while revealing objects or ideas the universal being reveals himself to every being as consciousness. So, no other efforts are needed to realise him than to see him in every created object. The mind then sees both his revealed and concealed forms simultaneously. (611)

११. इन्द्रस्य नु वीर्याणि प्रवोचं यानि चकार प्रथमानि वज्री ।
अहन्नहिमन्वपस्ततर्द प्र वक्षणा अभिनत्पर्वतानाम् ॥

11. Indra now vigorously nourishes our speech through the sense organ (vehicle) and also the brain (prison) primarily through his vigorous nerves.

Activity distributes the nourishment to mind by dispersing it in the spinal cord (ahi) in waking state (ahan), and lets him grow through the sense perceptions from the hill. (612)

१२. अग्निरस्मि जन्मना जातवेदा घृतं मे चक्षुरमृतं म आसन् ।
त्रिधातुरर्को रजसो विमानोऽजस्रं ज्योतिर्हविरस्मि सर्वम् ॥

12. Agni lets knowledge be born in me in my life and has bestowed on me the sense of sight from the immortals source for the sake of clarified butter.

He rules the three constituents (dhātu) of our being through the brain (home), the effulgent consciousness bestows on me everything and blesses me. (613)

१३. पात्यग्निर्विपो अग्रं पदं वेः पाति यह्वश्चरणं सूर्यस्य ।
पाति नाभा सप्तशीर्षाणमग्निः पाति देवानामुपमादमृष्वः ॥

13. Agni is well-known to inspire us before bestowing on us (sense activities) to drink at home and fulfilling; he fulfils by invoking consciousness and gladdening us.

Agni fulfils by bestowing on our head from the source through the seven-fold Activity; he fulfils mortals himself and gladdens through ideas from above. (614)

D. IV.

१. भ्राजन्त्यग्ने समिधान दीदिवो जिह्वा चरत्यन्तरासनि ।
स त्वं नो अग्ने पयसा वसुविद्रयिं वर्चो दृशेऽदाः ॥

1. Agni shines when he is kindled with objects of perception (fuel sticks) and beams down in the waking state, with his tongues (sense activities) going around within bestowing.

And you bestow sense perceptions and wealth of knowledge through Indra (Vasu) and you have bestowed the splendorous sense of sight. (615)

२. वसन्त इन्नु रन्त्यो ग्रीष्म इन्नु रन्त्यः ।
वर्षाण्यनु शरदो हेमन्तः शिशिर इन्नु रन्त्यः ॥

2. (Agni!) The spring season (of life-creation) is mightily praised; you gladden us (the creatures) mightily in the summer season (of life-creation); you gladden us in the rainy season which is praised; in the autumn, winter and dewy seasons (of life-creation) you gladden us mightily and are praised. (616)

३. सहस्रशीर्षाः पुरुषः सहस्राक्षः सहस्रपात् ।
स भूमिं सर्वतो वृत्वात्यतिष्ठद्दशाङ्गुलम् ॥

3. The puruṣa (creator) has a thousand heads, has a thousand eyes and a thousand flights of fancy.

He envelops the entire world (universe) and transcends it and looks upon it as at a finger (dṛśāṅgulam). (617), (Y.V. 31, 1)

Thousand heads etc. really mean here myriads. Then "pāt" is translated as feet by some. Then the expression "dṛśāṅgulam" is rendered as "daśāṅgulam".

४. त्रिपादूर्ध्व उदैत्पुरुषः पादोऽस्येहाभवत्पुनः ।
तथा विष्वङ व्यक्रामदशनानशने अभि ॥

4. Three parts of the puruṣa are above and beyond glittering (not perceivable); we are at his feet here taking repeated existences.

Truly the cosmos is his manifestation, rejoicing (or bestowing on us) animate and inanimate objects. (618), (Y.V. 31, 4)

५. पुरुष एवेदं सर्वं यद्भूतं यच्च भाव्यम् ।
पादोऽस्य सर्वा भूतानि त्रिपादस्यामृतं दिवि ।।

5. All this here is the puruṣa, all that exists and also all that may come into existence; he bestows and fulfils all creatures (or all creatures like us are at his feet); three parts of him are in the immortal heaven (divi). (619), (Y.V. 31, 2)

६. तावानस्य महिमा ततो ज्यायाँश्च पूरुषः ।
उतामृतत्वस्येशानो यदन्नेनातिरोहति ।।

6. He desires us much; the puruṣa supports us also with Activity from the source.

Also he rules us from his immortal home through the sense activities (anna) which transform us to cross over (ignorance). (620)

७. ततो विराडजायत विराजो अधि पूरुषः ।
स जातो अत्यरिच्यत पश्चाद्भूमिमथो पुरः ।।

7. The cosmos is born of Activity who is united to it; the puruṣa controls it from beyond.

It is well-known that he bestows births and then releases them and unites with them; then he created the worlds; then the brain (city), (621), (Y.V. 31, 5)

Here, the order of creation is mentioned. The puruṣa creates the creatures first in the subtle world as ideas. They take birth in the material world and the puruṣa unites with them as sense activities. Then the worlds are formed from the floating matter in the form of ideas which are created earlier. Then the brain cells and creatures are manifested. The percepts of the creatures proceeding from the creator as ideas give the form to the external world which is at first a mass of material particles. So the world clothes the ideas of the creator.

Our scriptures and philosophers and saints look down upon the world as unreal or illusion. The world's true form is no doubt as ideas bereft of activity. It does not act but is acted upon. That does not make it unreal. The world is the alternate form of the creator and is as real as he is. For, it is the creator who is both the subject and object at alternate moments.

८. मन्ये वां द्यावापृथिवी सुभोजसौ
ये अप्रथेथाममितमभि योजनम् ।
द्यावापृथिवी भवतं स्योने ते नो मुञ्चतमंहसः ॥

8. The brain and sense organs (heaven and earth) bestow on mind to consume; the sense activities spread out to them and establish themselves by uniting with them.

The brain and sense organs are desired in existence; they bestow pleasantly and abundantly through the nerves (reed grass). (622)

९. हरी त इन्द्र श्मश्रूण्युतो ते हरितौ हरि ।
तं त्वा स्तुवन्ति कवयः पुरुषासो वनर्गवः ॥

9. The rays (beard) of the tawny consciousness unites with Indra who conveys them through the nerves (dūrvā grass).

They bestow within praiseworthily, the puruṣa bestows desires through the sense activities on our head (brain). (623)

१०. यद्वर्चो हिरण्यस्य यद्वा वर्चो गवामुत ।
सत्यस्य ब्रह्मणो वर्चस्तेन मा संसृजामसि ॥

10. What is excellent about consciousness and what is splendid about sense activities also,

is the existence arising from them; all their splendours flow to us. (624)

११. सहस्तन्न इन्द्र दद्ध्योज ईशे ह्यस्य महतो विरप्शिन् ।
क्रतुं न नृम्णं स्थविरं च वाजं वृत्रेषु शत्रून्त्सहना कृधी नः ॥

11. Indra guides them with might and bestows them on us vigorously; he rules our head with mighty exuberance.

He supports now manly stout creatures, also creates understanding by striking down Vṛtra, the enemy with might in life activity. (625)

१२. सहर्षभाः सहवत्सा उदेत विश्वा रूपाणी बिभ्रतीर्द्व्यूध्नीः ।
उरुः पृथुरयं वो अस्तु लोक इमा आपः सुप्रपाणा इह स्त ॥

12. Above, the motley sense activities flow with might for the

forms of objects to appear through the sense organs without confusion as a cloud and released to the mind.

The streams of sense activities released by Activity in our world spread themselves out extensively arousing nourishment for drinking here. (626)

D. V.

१. अग्न आयूंषि पवसे आसुवोर्जमिषं च नः ।
आरे बाधस्व दुच्छुनाम् ॥

1. Agni ! You protect our lives from the home, you arouse and open our eyes to the nourishment and gladden us.

Against any calamity you bestow (remedy) yourself through the spokeslike nerves. (627), (1464), (1518)

२. विभ्राड् बृहत्पिबतु सोम्यं मध्वायुर्दधद्यज्ञपतावविह्रुतम् ।
वातजूतो यो अभिरक्षति त्मना प्रजाः पिपर्ति बहुधा वि राजति ॥

2. Soma drinks much without flurry, bestows sense perceptions (activities) in life for the course of life-activity without crookedness.

He agitates the nerves to protect the subjects himself, also bestows from beyond greatly by virtue of ruling them. (628), (1453)

३. चित्रं देवानामुदगादनीकं चक्षुर्मित्रस्य वरुणस्याग्नेः ।
आप्रा द्यावापृथिवी अन्तरिक्षं सूर्य आत्मा जगतस्तस्थुषश्च ॥

3. Agni, from above visualised before him a variety of creatures in the waters through ideas from the brain (Mitra) and external world (Varuṇa).

He fulfilled the brain, sense organs and mind (heaven, earth and antarikṣa) of the animate creatures eagerly and abidingly, by himself and through consciousness. (629)

४. आयं गौः पृश्निरक्रमीदसदन्मातरं पुरः ।
पितरं च प्रयन्त्स्वः ॥

4. The nourishing earth revolves in the reverse direction (west to east) along the path of the speckled stars to the home of its mother (antarikṣa),

and its father (Sun) too who himself guides and fulfils. (630), (1376), (Y. V. 3, 6)

५. अन्तश्चरति रोचनास्य प्राणादपानती ।
व्यख्यन्महिषो दिवम् ॥

5. He goes around within (the expanse) going up and coming down like prāṇa and apāna, which shine within us,

manifesting himself like a buffalo before the Sun (or a great desire for the Sun), (631), (1377), (Y. V. 3, 8)

६. त्रिंशद्धाम विराजति वाक्पतङ्गाय धीयते ।
प्रति वस्तोरह द्युभिः ॥

6. The flight of speech united to understanding is governed by thirty steps of activity in the home (brain).

They nourish it extensively here from heaven (head). (632), (1378)

The activities preceding the emergence of speech are as follows: —

(1) Agni rouses up sense activity; (2) The Aśvins seize it, (3) Aśvins transfer it to sense of touch; (4) Touch transfers it to brain cells; (5) Brain cells transfer it to nerves of vocal cord, (6) Brain induces prāṇa; (7) Prāṇa arouses breath through the nerves; (8) Prāṇa arouses the nerves of the tongue; (9) Prāṇa arouses vulva; (10) Prāṇa arouses mind; (11) Ideas flow from brain to mind; (12) New ideas flow from heaven; (13) Prāṇa arouses the lungs and abdominal muscles.

Every transfer from subtle plane to gross or vice versa is carried out by the Aśvins reckoned as two steps of activity. In this manner thirty steps of activity are gone through before speech emerges.

७. अप त्ये तायवो यथा नक्षत्रा यन्त्यक्तुभिः ।
सूराय विश्वचक्षसे ॥

7. It is well-known that the sense activities protect the brain cells; the brain cells likewise guide their rays.

They perceive the sense organs like heroes and bestow on them. (633)

८. अदृश्रन्नस्य केतवो वि रश्मयो जनाँ अनु ।
भ्राजन्तो अग्नयो यथा ॥

8. The sense activities (anna) perceive and bestow through their rays on men now.

They shine within; Agni shines likewise. (634)

९. तरणिर्विश्वदर्शतो ज्योतिष्कृदसि सूर्य ।
विश्वमाभासि रोचनम् ॥

9. They visit the sense organs for crossing over (ignorance); consciousness produces and bestows them through his rays.

The sense organs bestow the appearances of object which shine. (635)

१०. प्रत्यङ् देवानां विशः प्रत्यङ्ङुदेषि मानुषान् ।
प्रत्यङ् विश्वं स्वर्दृशे ॥

10. Every organ is the home of the devas (ideas); every organ is desired above in men.

Heaven perceives every limb through sense organs. (636)

११. येना पावक चक्षसा भुरण्यन्तं जनाँ अनु ॥
त्वं वरुण पश्यसि ॥

11. The sense activities bestow on the head and fulfil and now they look at the agitated state within and bestow on them.

They look at the external world. (637), (Y. V. 33, 32)

१२. उद्द्यामेषि रजः पृथ्वहा मिमानो अक्तुभिः ।
पश्यञ्जन्मानि सूर्य ॥

12. The Aśvins in compassion convey from the atmosphere above (in the head) and spread the rays (of perceptions) approaching the home.

Consciousness from the source looks at the home to reveal them. (638)

१३. अयुक्त सप्त शुन्ध्युवः सूरो रथस्य नप्त्यः ।
ताभिर्याति स्वयुक्तिभिः ॥

13. The seven-pronged Activity detaches itself to clarify the mind (youth) and the hero accordingly hastens to the sense organs (descendants).

He moves to them to support and yokes himself to them. (639)

१४. सप्त त्वा हरितो रथे वहन्ति देव सूर्य ।
शोचिष्केशं विचक्षण ॥

14. Activity ? You convey the tawny consciousness to the sense organs; the deva consciousness,

illumines the desires perceived in the home coming from the nerves (hair). (640)

MAHĀNĀMNYĀRCIKA

१. (१) विदा मघवन् विदा गातुमनुशंसिषो दिशः ।
(२) शिक्षा शचीनां पते । पूर्वीणां पुरूवसो ॥

1. Indra (Maghavan) knows (all); he knows now the desires of the devotee, praises the desires and directs them.

The lord of might instructs, in the ancient paths profusely in the home. (641)

२. आभिष्ट्वमभिष्टिभिः । (३) स्वाऽ३र्न्नांशुः ।
प्रचेतन प्रचेतये—(४)—न्द्र द्यु म्नाय न इषे ॥

2. He bestows (vomits) for the desires victoriously himself in surges quickly.

He nourishes manifestation and he nourishes the mind, from heaven the desires from the sense organs. (642)

३. एवा हि शक्रो । (५) राये वाजाय वज्रिवः ।
शविष्ठ वज्रिन्नृञ्जसे । मंहिष्ठ वज्रिन्नृञ्जसे ।
आ याहि पिब मत्स्व ॥

3. Indra (Śakra) arouses and speeds up (life-activity); he is the king in life-activity and bestows through the vigorous nervers.

He strives with might through the nerves; he strives praiseworthily (to bestow) through his vigorous nerves.

He moves himself to arouse us to drink. (643)

४. (१) विदा राये सुवीर्यं भुवो वाजानां पतिर्वशाँ अनु ।
(१) मंहिष्ठ वज्रिन्नृञ्जसे । यः शविष्ठः शूराणाम् ॥

4. He controls knowledge and arouses vigour; he is now the lord of life-activity at home.

He strives praiseworthily to release it through the vigorous nerves.

He hurries it with might, as a hero. (644)

५. यो मंहिष्ठो मघोनाम । (३) अंजुर्न्न शोचिः ।
चिकित्वो अभि नो नय । (४) इन्द्रो विदे नमुस्तुहि ॥

5. Indra is munificent with the mighty Soma juice which shines brightly.

He bestows it for our knowledge and to guide us. Indra arouses and praises the desire for knowledge. (645)

६. ईशे हि शक्रस् । (५) तमूतये हवामहे जेतारमपराजितम् ।
स नः स्वर्षदति द्विषः । (६) ऋतुश्छन्द ऋतं बृहत् ।।

6. Indra (Śakra) rules to arouse us and bestow. He desires to help with much oblations, which he wins to gladden us and which he wins from yonder world.

He bestows as gifts on the home from heaven to the desires of both brain and mind; the great Ṛta (also) produces them and gladdens us. (646)

७. (१) इन्द्रं धनस्य सातये हवामहे जेतारमपराजितम् ।
(२) स नः स्वर्षदति द्विषः । स नः स्वर्षदति द्विषः ।।

7. Indra bestows on us wealth continually with much oblations won to gladden us and which he wins from beyond.

He bestows the gifts on the home from heaven for the desires of both brain and mind. He bestows the desires of both brain and mind through the home. (647)

८. पूर्वस्य यत्ते अद्रिवों—(३)—ऽशुर्मदाय ।
सुम्न आ धेहि नो वसो । (४) पूर्तिः शविष्ठ शस्यते ।
वशी हि शक्रो । (५) नूनं तन्नव्यं संन्यसे ।।

8. In ancient times he united with the sense activities quickly on the hill (brain).

He bestowed wealth on the home by arousing it; he satisfied the desires of the brain cells for sense organs. Indra arouses the brain. Now the Aśvins guide nourishment to all of them and bestow. (648)

९. प्रभो जनस्य वृत्रहन् त्समर्येषु ब्रवावहै ।
(६) शूरो यो गोषु गच्छति सखा सुशेवो अद्वयुः ।।

9. The lord strikes down Vṛtra for the sake of men; he conveys the rays (missiles of sense activities) to the assembly and delivers (announces) them.

Heroically he goes to the help of sense activities and to serve both brain and mind by uniting with them. (649)

Pañca purīṣapadāni

१०. एवाह्योऽ३ऽ३ऽ३ वा । एवा ह्यग्ने । एवाहीन्द्र ।
एवा हि पूषन् । एवा हि देवाः ॥

10. Speed up now. Agni ! Speed up bestowals. Indra ! Speed up. Consciousness arouses us and speeds up; the devas arouse us and speed up. (650)

Part I — Summary

1) Mantras on Agni (1-114)	—114
2) Mantras on Indra (115-466)	—352
3) Mantras on Mind (467-585)	—119
4) Mantras on Forest of ideas (586-640)	—55
5) Mahānāmnyārcika (641-650)	—10
Total	650

INDRA

Although Agni, Aśvins, Consciousness, Soma Activity are devas from heaven and superior to Indra, yet Indra is given more prominence and many more mantras are devoted to him than to the others. It is because he is the one moving between heaven and earth i.e. between the brain and the sense organs and also because he feeds man or mind with all the knowledge imparted by the devas to cross over ignorance.

The devas impart everything to the brain which is transferred to mind by Indra. Indra again is incharge of all the functions of the body which he discharges through the nervous system.

Life-activity depends on the association of ideas and matter or inertia which retains everything within itself. This inertia has to be overcome every time knowledge has to be prised out of it. This is carried out by Indra.

Indra may be considered to have risen out of matter and ascended to heaven by dint of his ability. This is what the purāṇas say.

PART II

UTTARA ĀRCIKA

BOOK I : CHAPTER I

D. I.

१. उपास्मै गायता नरः पवमानायेन्दवे ।
अभि देवाँ इयक्षते ।।

1. Sense activities unite with us men above (head) and the brain cells bestow them on the fickle mind,

and hurries to him ideas (devas). (651), (763) (Y. V. 33, 62)

२. अभि ते मधुना पयोऽथर्वाणो अशिश्रयुः ।
देवं देवाय देवयु ।।

2. They (the brain cells) drink the sweet sense activities, then their desires are sharpened and cooked,

with ideas, ideas move into the devotee. (652)

३. स नः पवस्व शं गवे शं जनाय शमर्वते ।
शं राजन्नोषधीभ्यः ।।

3. The sense activities themselves toil and bestow gifts to protect, they hasten to satisfy men by toiling.

They toil to control food (sense perceptions) which nourish understanding. (653)

D. II.

१. दविद्युतत्या रुचा परिष्टोभन्त्या कृपा ।
सोमाः शुक्रा गवाशिरः ।।

1. They (the sense activities) are well-known to bestow like lightning, desiring (rucā) to create liking in both brain and sense organs (or mind) for the yonder world and fulfil.

Soma bestows the sense activities in the head to illumine it. (654)

२. हिन्वानो हेतृभिर्हित आ वाजं वाज्यक्रमीत् ।
सीदन्तो वनुषो यथा ।।

2. Being the cause of desires he arouses them and supports in life-activity; this is the way of life-activity.

Desires move eagerly in the home. (655)

३. ऋधक्सोम स्वस्तये संजग्मानो दिवा कवे ।
पवस्व सूर्यो दृशे ।

3. Soma bestows in the head (kave) for prosperity to all movable creatures on the brain in waking.

Consciousness perceives and bestows protection himself. (656)

D. III.

१. पवमानस्य ते कवे वाजिन्त्सर्गा असृक्षत ।
अर्वन्तो न श्रवस्यवः ।।

1. They surge and flow in the home in life-activity and bestow on our fickle mind from the brain (head).

Hearing from him (mind) they bestow from the brain cells. (657)

२. अच्छा कोशं मधुश्चुतमसृग्रं वारे अव्यये ।
अवावशन्त धीतयः ।।

2. The sense perceptions nearby in the head drip and flow in the community (of brain cells) as wealth from the Aśvins.

They are bestowed to reside within for the sake of understanding. (658)

३. अच्छा समुद्रमिन्दवोऽस्तं गावो न धेनवः ।
अग्मन्नृतस्य योनिमा ।

3. They bestow on the brain cells nearby and gladden them in the home like the cows do to the calves.

The source bestows the sense perceptions on our mind. (659)

D. IV.

१. अग्न आ याहि वीतये गृणानो हव्यदातये ।
नि होता सत्सि बर्हिषि ।।

1. Agni moves in to arouse desires in the singers and bestow oblations.

He presides below and binds us to existence through the motley sense activities. (660)

२. तं त्वा समिद्भिरङ्गिरो घृतेन वर्धयामसि ।
बृहच्छोचा यविष्ठ्य ॥

2. You support them with sense objects (fuel sticks) and you foster the growth of clarified butter through the sense activities (Aṅgiras),

which are much accustomed to incite the brain cells. (661), (Y. V. 3, 3)

३. स नः पृथु श्रवाय्यमच्छा देव विवाससि ।
बृहदग्ने सुवीर्यम् ॥

3. The gifts (sense activities) spread out, praiseworthily; the devas nearby ride on them, bestow and bind (or ride on) the brain cells.

Agni arouses much vigour. (662)

D. V.

१. आ नो मित्रावरुणा घृतैर्गव्यूतिमुक्षतम् ।
मध्वा रजांसि सुक्रतू ॥

1. The sense activities help to increase the desire of the brain (Mitra) for the external world (Varuṇa) for clarified butter.

They support varied perceptions which do good. (663), (220)

२. उरुशंसा नमोवृधा मह्ना दक्षस्य राजथः ।
द्राघिष्ठाभिः शुचिव्रता ॥

2. They (the sense activities) are extensively praised; they honour and foster growth in us; they control and satisfy us and are honoured (mahnā).

They run to bestow our desires with bright duties (vows). (664)

३. गृणाना जमदग्निना योनावृतस्य सीदतम् ।
पातं सोममृतावृधा ॥

3. Agni causes the birth of sense activities in the devotees; they come from the source and envelop us in the home as desired.

Soma fulfils the desires and fosters their growth in mortals. (665)

D. VI.

१. आ याहि सुषुमा हि त इन्द्र सोमं पिबा इमम् ।
एदं बर्हिः सदो मम ॥

1. Indra moves and arouses our minds to do good by drinking from Soma here.
Behold the motley sense activities always in us. (666), (191)

२. आ त्वा ब्रह्मयुजा हरी वहतामिन्द्र केशिना ।
उप ब्रह्माणि नः शृणु ॥

2. Indra unites with knowledge, indeed to release it before the long haired consciousness by conveying it.
Above knowledge is cooked and bound (naḥ). (667)

३. ब्रह्माणस्त्वा युजा वयं सोमपामिन्द्र सोमिनः ।
सुतावन्तो हवामहे ॥

3. You unite with knowledge for us and fulfil through Soma; Soma is mighty (or is bound),
to bestow on mind within much oblations. (668)

D. VII.

१. इन्द्राग्नी आ गतं सुतं गीर्भिर्नभो वरेण्यम् ।
अस्य पातं धियेषिता ॥

1. Indra and Agni come to support mind from the hill (brain), from heaven (sky) excellently,
whose desires they satisfy and protect. (669), (Y. V. 7, 31)

२. इन्द्राग्नी जरितुः सचा यज्ञो जिगाति चेतनः ।
अया पातमिमं सुतम् ॥

2. Indra and Agni unite with the devotee in life-activity to win sense activities for mind.
They guard the paths to mind here. (670)

३. इन्द्रमग्निं कविच्छदा यज्ञस्य जूत्या वृणे ।
ता सोमस्येह तृम्पताम् ॥

3. Indra and Agni bestow what is desired by the brain (head) in life; they are well-known to envelop and inspire it.
They satisfy through Soma here as desired. (671)

D. VIII.

१. उच्चा ते जातमन्धसो दिवि सद्भूम्या ददे ।
उग्रं शर्म महि श्रवः ॥

1. They bestow above (to the brain) from the source to release from ignorance in the waking state by bestowing on the home from the sense organs.

They cook much and bestow powerful protection. (672), (467), (Y. V. 26, 16)

२. स न इन्द्राय यज्यवे वरुणाय मरुद्भ्यः ।
वरिवोवित्परि स्रव ॥

2. Indra bestows as gifts ideas (Maruts) of Varuṇa on the brain cells in life-activity,

who flow around in freedom acquainting us. (673), (592), (Y. V. 26, 17)

३. एना विश्वान्यर्य आ द्युम्नानि मानुषाणाम् ।
सिषासन्तो वनामहे ॥

3. Then they bestow on the home of man; they are the wealth of men.

They bestow desires as gifts from the great forest (Varuṇa). (674), (593), (Y. V. 26, 18)

D. IX.

१. पुनानः सोम धारयापो वसानो अर्षसि ।
आ रत्नधा योनिमृतस्य सीदस्युत्सो देवो हिरण्ययः ॥

1. Activity supports Soma repeatedly, who flows to the brain (fat).

He bestows valuable wealth on the mortals from the source; he bestows also devas (ideas) on us in languid state and hastens to arouse gladness. (675), (511)

२. दुहान ऊधर्दिव्यं मधु प्रियं प्रत्नं सधस्थमासदत् ।
आपृच्छ्यं धरुणं वाज्यर्षसि नृभिर्धौतो विचक्षणः ॥

2. The sense perceptions (honey) fondly bestow on the ancient assembly (of the brain cells) in the home; the divine milk separates to be consumed.

They flow in life-activity for supporting and controlling it;

they support men by cleansing (objects) and making them visible (i.e. illumine (objects). (676)

D. X.

१. प्र तु द्रव परि कोशं नि षीद नृभिः पुनानो अभि वाजमर्ष ।
अश्वं न त्वा वाजिनं मर्जयन्तोऽच्छा बर्हो रशनाभिर्नयन्ति ॥

1. They (sense activities) run around the brain (head) to nourish and so they flow in life-activity repeatedly to the home languishing men below.

Prāṇa! You win much within for mortals in the mighty life-activity and you support by guiding (the motley sense activities, near you) as if roped to you. (677), (523)

२. स्वायुधः पवते देव इन्दुरशस्तिहा वृजना रक्षमाणः ।
पिता देवानां जनिता सुदक्षो विष्टम्भो दिवो धरुणः पृथिव्याः ॥

2. Prāṇa! You unite with the brain cells, which are helpless, yourself and bestow ideas to protect understanding which envelops men to protect them.

The father is born among devas who arouses and satisfies by supporting (Viṣṭambho) in waking; he supports and binds sense organs to us. (678)

३. ऋषिर्विप्रः पुरएता जनानामृभुर्धीर उशना काव्येन ।
स चिद्विवेद निहितं यदासामपीच्यां३ गुह्यं नाम गोनाम् ॥

3. The sense activities inspire the ṛṣi (sage) with a variety (of ideas) born in the city (brain) which the Ṛbhus (central nervous system) stabilise eagerly to amount to a mighty poem (composition).

They bestow on the mind below welfare through knowledge; they serve secretly; the sense organs are honoured and controlled by the sense activities. (679)

D. XI.

१. अभि त्वा शूर नोनुमोऽदुग्धा इव धेनवः ।
ईशानमस्य जगतः स्वर्दृशमीशानमिन्द्र तस्थुषः ॥

1. The sense activities valiantly bestow what is wanting like the milch-cow yielding milk.

They rule the animated creatures like us; Indra rules us for heaven to look at us; he is abidingly eager for it. (680), (233), (Y. V. 27, 35)

२. न त्वावां अन्यो दिव्यो न पार्थिवो न जातो न जनिष्यते ।
अश्वायन्तो मघवन्निन्द्र वाजिनो गव्यन्तस्त्वा हवामहे ।।

2. None other than you, either divine or terrestrial, existing or to come in the future, bestows like you.

The bounteous Indra guides prāṇa in life-activity, who guides the sense activities mightily to bestow much oblations. (681)

D. XII.

१. कया नश्चित्र आ भुवदूती सदावृधः सखा ।
कया शचिष्ठया वृता ।।

1. Indra! You help to increase constantly the messengers who bestow in existence, who move to the head that it may achieve a variety (of ideas).

They willingly envelop the head by moving to it with might. (682), (169), (Y. V. 27, 39)

२. कस्त्वा सत्यो मदानां मंहिष्ठो मत्सदन्धसः ।
दृढा चिदारुजे वसु ।।

2. The sense activities bestow praiseworthily on the brain (head) in existence, munificently and release me from ignorance in the home.

Indra (Vasu) indeed perceives and shatters it and establishes us. (683), (Y. V. 27, 40)

३. अभी षु णः सखीनामविता जरितृणाम् ।
शतं भवास्यूतये ।।

3. He binds the missiles (iṣu) to his friend mind and blesses him in the devotee.

He helps us in hundreds of things in existence. (684), (Y. V. 27, 41)

D. XIII.

१. तं वो दस्ममृतीषहं वसोर्मन्दानमन्धसः ।
अभि वत्सं न स्वसरेषु धेनव इन्द्रं गीर्भिर्नवामहे ।।

1. He (Indra) desires to bestow the wishes on mortals marvellously in waking state.

Indra bestows a gift on mind by dispelling his ignorance.

Indra bestows streams of missiles (of sense-activities) on mind himself and supports him afresh from the brain (hill). (685), (236), (Y. V. 26, 11)

२. द्युक्षं सुदानुं तविषीभिरावृतं गिरिं न पुरुभोजसम् ।
क्षुमन्तं वाजं शतिनं सहस्रिणं मक्षू गोमन्तमीमहे ॥

2. He arouses the brain cells (dānu) in the home from heaven and supports them powerfully enveloping their desires on the hill with abundant food.

The food within, in life-activity, releases the birth of hundreds of mighty (ideas), nay even thousands of them quickly by the sense perceptions approaching within greatly. (686)

D. XIV.

१. तरोभिर्वो विदद्वसुमिन्द्रं सबाध ऊतये ।
बृहद्‌गायन्तः सुतसोमे अध्वरे हुवे भरं न कारिणम् ।

1. Indra bestows them to support the crossing (of ignorance) through knowledge graciously (or through wealth of knowledge) and helps by bestowing towards trouble.

He guides the sense activities much within; the mind invokes Soma in life for support from the mighty head (prison). (687)

२. न यं दुध्रा वरन्ते न स्थिरा मुरो मदेषु शिप्रमन्धसः ।
य आदृत्या शशमानाय सुन्वते दाता जरित्र उक्थ्यम् ॥

2. He, the impetuous (dudhrā) guides gifts within and stabilises them with extensive missiles of sense activities to release the cheekful of ignorance in one.

It is well-known that he considers about mind by moving to the home of the devotee and bestowing on him who praises him. (688)

D. XV.

१. स्वादिष्ठया मदिष्ठया पवस्व सोम धारया ।
इन्द्राय पातवे सुतः ॥

1. Soma himself supports by moving to the sweet perceptions desiring understanding and releases them for drinking.

Indra moves and bestows on mind and fulfils. (689), (468)

२. रक्षोहा विश्वचर्षणिरभि योनिमयोहते ।
द्रोणे सधस्थमासवत् ॥

2. He protects him (mind) by modifications through the sense organs with whom he is busy to effect the transformations from the source through prāṇa.

He bestows on the languishing assembly (of brain cells) in the head. (690), (Y. V. 26, 26)

३. वरिवोधातमो भुवो मंहिष्ठो वृत्रहन्तमः ।
पर्षि राधो मघोनाम् ॥

3. The desires are bestowed full freedom in existence, munificently, after Vṛtra is struck down as desired.

They are satisfied on succeeding in obtaining gifts. (691)

D. XVI.

१. पवस्व मधुमत्तम इन्द्राय सोम क्रतुवित्तमो मदः ।
महि द्युक्षतमो मदः ॥

1. Indra himself bestows on Soma sense perceptions and his desires to drink, who produces the knowledge desired joyously.

He (Soma) produces much desires in the home from the sense activities from heaven. (692), (578)

२. यस्य ते पीत्वा वृषभो वृषायतेऽस्य पीत्वा स्वर्विदः ।
स सुप्रकेतो अभ्यक्रमीदिषोऽच्छा वाजं नैतशः ॥

2. Indra (bull)! You strive to swell towards him (Soma), shower (sense activities) to unite with, who overflows to us to know about heaven.

He bestows to arouse and nourish our desires in due course through the motley sense activities near him in life-activity. (693)

D. XVII.

१. इन्द्रमच्छ सुता इमे वृषणं यन्तु हरयः ।
श्रुष्टे जातास इन्दवः स्वर्विदः ॥

1. Indra showers (his gifts) on mind near him and conveys them to him speedily to guide him.

He produces from the source and bestows them on the brain cells for knowledge of heaven. (694), (566)

२. अयं भराय सानसिरिन्द्राय पवते सुतः ।
सोमो जैत्रस्य चेतति यथा विदे ॥

2. He moves to support the path victoriously of understanding and protect it for mind.

Soma likewise acquaints the mind of the devotee. (695)

२. अस्येदिन्द्रो मदेष्वा ग्राभं गृभ्णाति सानसिम् ।
वज्रं च वृषणं भरत्समप्सुजित् ॥

3. Indra bestows on us sense activities as desired by seizing us in the waking state and speaking to us victoriously.

He showers them through the vigorous nerves. Activity supports him at the same time whom he wins and arouses. (696)

D. XVIII.

१. पुरोजिती वो अन्धसः सुताय मादयित्नवे ।
अप श्वानं श्नथिष्टन सखायो दीर्घजिह्वयम् ।

1. He overcomes the brain (city) and releases it from ignorance; he moves to Mind and gladdens it thus afresh.

Activity swells and honours by piercing and helps with his long tongues (rays). (697), (545)

२. यो धारया पावकया परिप्रस्यन्दते सुतः ।
इन्दुरश्वो न कृत्व्यः ॥

2. They support by bestowing on the brain to drink; they go around and trickle down (prasyanda) to Mind.

Prāṇa bestows them on the brain cells and produces them for us. (698)

३. तं दुरोषमभी नरः सोमं विश्वाच्या धिया ।
यज्ञाय सन्त्वद्रयः ॥

3. Soma desires men to consume them and eagerly satisfies us by moving to the sense organs.

He bestows on us streams of them as gifts in life. (699)

D. XIX.

१. अभि प्रियाणि पवते चनोहितो नामानि यह्वो अधि येषु वर्धते ॥
आ सूर्यस्य बृहतो बृहन्नधि रथं विष्वञ्चमरुहद्विचक्षणः ।

1. Fondly Soma protects understanding to gladden us with welfare; he hails the home from beyond and fosters the growth of the rays (of sense activities) by moving to the home.

Consciousness increases them greatly from beyond the sense organs; he ascends above the sense organs and perceives them instantly. (700)

२. ऋतस्य जिह्वा पवते मधु प्रियं वक्ता पतिर्धियो अस्या अदाभ्यः ।
दधाति पुत्रः पित्रोरपीच्यां३ नाम तृतीयमधि रोचनं दिवः ॥

2. Ṛta bestows on us lovingly the sweet perceptions (honey) to drink from the tongues (of sense activities) which he imparts (vaktā); the lord satisfies us inviolably.

He bestows on our children (sense organs); also supports them extensively secretly; consciousness from beyond the three states honours us and shines. (701)

३. अव द्युतानः कलशाँ अचिक्रदन्नृभिर्येमाणः कोश आ हिरण्यये ।
अभी ऋतस्य दोहना अनूषताधि त्रिपृष्ठ उषसो वि राजसि ॥

3. Heaven blesses the brain (pot) through the nerves (threads); the golden consciousness hastens to the head, perceives and resoundingly supports men by controlling and binding them.

Ṛta is attached to the sense perceptions (milk) and satisfies the three states foremost which Uṣas rules over. (702)

D. XX.

१. यज्ञायज्ञा वो अग्नये गिरागिरा च दक्षसे ।
प्रप्र वयममृतं जातवेदसं प्रियं मित्रं न शंसिषम् ॥

1. Agni bestows on us satisfaction in life after life to man after man.

He nourishes and fulfils us mortals (or from the immortal source) for all knowledge to be born to us; fondly he praises the desires of the brain (Mitra). (703), (35), (Y. V. 27, 42)

२. ऊर्जो नपातं स हिनायमस्मयुर्दाशेम हव्यदातये ।
भुवद्वाजेष्वविता भुवद्वृध उत त्राता तनूनाम् ॥

2. He bestows nourishment on the sense organs (descendants); he arouses and guides and does service being attached to us and bestows oblations.

He bestows on us desires in life activity for existence, fosters the growth of existence and also supports them delicately. (704), (Y. V. 27, 44)

D. XXI.

१. एह्यू षु ब्रवाणि तेऽग्न इत्थेतरा गिरः ।
एभिर्वर्धास इन्दुभिः ॥

1. Behold Agni proclaiming to the sense organs and thus bestowing the motley sense activities from the hill.

They support the growth and bestow on the brain cells. (705), (7)

२. यत्र क्व च ते मनो दक्षं दधस उत्तरम् ।
तत्र योनिं कृणवसे ॥

2. There they satisfy Mind wherever he is and bestow his wants mightily.

They are supported from the source for producing for the brain (home). (706)

३. न हि ते पूर्तमक्षिपद्भुवन्नेमानां पते ।
अथा दुवो वनवसे ॥

3. Welfare swells as desired (by the mind) through the rays (fingers of the sense activities) which bestow on the home of the creatures, the lord (Indra).

Then he releases them to be consumed as desired in the home. (707)

D. XXII.

१. वयमु त्वामपूर्व्य स्थूरं न कच्चिद्भरन्तोऽवस्यवः ।
वज्रिं चित्रं हवामहे ॥

1. To us you are incomparably great (sthūra). What he supports within are the brain cells whom he blesses,

and bestows a great variety of oblations. (708), (408)

२. उप त्वा कर्मन्नूतये स नो युवोग्रश्चक्राम यो धृषत् ।
त्वामिध्यवितारं ववृमहे सखाय इन्द्र सानसिम् ॥

2. Above you help our purposeful activities; you bestow gifts on the mind boldly; earlier prāṇa goes around us.

You approach us and favour us for crossing by sipping

(perceptions); you envelop us and bestow to help us victoriously. (709)

D. XXIII.

१. अधा हीन्द्र गिर्वण उप त्वा काम ईमहे ससृग्महे ।
उदेव ग्मन्त उदभिः ॥

1. Indra! You are a lover of the hill; above you bestow much desires to flow greatly.

You hasten above the sense activities to flow within to the fluids (brain). (710), (406)

२. वार्ण त्वा यव्याभिर्वर्धन्ति शूर ब्रह्माणि ।
वावृध्वांसं चिदद्रिवो दिवेदिवे ॥

2. You support the brain cells to utter sounds and promote the growth of knowledge heroically.

You run to us to envelop and bestow for growth day after day. (711)

३. युञ्जन्ति हरी इषिरस्य गाथयोरौ रथ उरुयुगे वचोयुजा ।
इन्द्रवाहा स्वर्विदा ॥

3. The tawny consciousness unites with our desires; he unites the sense organs extensively to the devotee and unites speech to him.

Indra conveys knowledge from heaven. (712)

BOOK I: CHAPTER II

D. I.

१. पान्तमा वो अन्धस इन्द्रमभि प्र गायत ।
विश्वासाहं शतक्रतुं मंहिष्ठं चर्षणीनाम् ।।

1. Indra! You fulfil our desires within by bestowals; you release us from ignorance and you unite with sense activities to nourish us.

I have faith in you, doer of a hundred deeds; you are munificent and diligently active. (713), (155)

२. पुरुहूतं पुरुष्टुतं गाथान्यां३ सनश्रुतम् ।
इन्द्र इति ब्रवीतन ।।

2. You are abundantly invoked, praised by devotees, bestow gifts on hearing.

So it is said of Indra, for guiding us. (714)

३. इन्द्र इन्नो महोनां दाता वाजानां नृतुः ।
महाँ अभिज्ञ्वा यमत् ।।

3. Indra is mighty, bestows much on men in life.
He is great and controls us to bestow knowledge. (715)

D. II.

१. प्र व इन्द्राय मादनं हर्यश्वाय गायत ।
सखायः सोमपाव्ने ।।

1. Indra moves and bestows nourishment, unites with sense activities to bestow wealth and moves to consciousness.
He helps Soma in fulfilling our desires. (716), (156)

२. शंसेदुक्थं सुदानव उत द्युक्षं यथा नरः ।
चकृमा सत्यराधसे ।।

2. Behold him being praised verbally (ukhtam) for arousing and bestowing gifts from heaven on the brain (home), likewise on men (i.e. Mind).

Also he produces and bestows on us wealth for existence. (717)

३. त्वं न इन्द्र वाजयुस्त्वं गव्युः शतक्रतो ।
त्वं हिरण्ययुर्वसो ॥

3. Indra! You are vigorous (Vājayu) in uniting with sense activities praiseworthily, doer of a hundred deeds.

You unite with the golden consciousness in the home. (718)

D. III.

१. वयमु त्वा तदिदर्था इन्द्र त्वायन्तः सखायः ।
कण्वा उक्थेभिर्जरन्ते ॥

1. Indra! You bestow on us what is here our wealth (aim). You move within to guide us and help us.

You bestow on the brain cells praiseworthily and support them to the end of old age. (719)

२. न घेमन्यदा पपन वज्रिन्नपसो नविष्टौ ।
तवेदु स्तोमंश्चिकेत ॥

2. You do not strike at mind; you bestow him admirably to drink through the vigorous nerves and are active about new desires.

Praiseworthily you behold the desires. (720)

३. इच्छन्ति देवाः सुन्वन्तं न स्वप्नाय स्पृहयन्ति ।
यन्ति प्रमादमतन्द्राः ।

3. The devotees desire ideas within (or you desire ideas in devotees); you yourself guide them to Activity; you guide them eagerly).

You guide them unweariedly to nourish and gladden us. (721)

D. IV.

१. इन्द्राय मद्वने सुतं परि ष्टोमन्तु नो गिरः ।
अर्कमर्चन्तु कारवः ॥

1. Indra moves towards sense perceptions desired by mind; goes around the brain praiseworthily.

You honour consciousness within who releases them within the head (prison). (722)

२. यस्मिन्विश्वा अधि श्रियो रणन्ति सप्त संसदः ।
इन्द्रं सुते हवामहे ॥

2. You strive mightily with sense organs for us from beyond and the seven-pronged Activity praiseworthily bestows on us prosperity through them and gladdens us.

Indra bestows much oblations on Mind. (723)

३. त्रिकद्रुकेषु चेतनं देवासो यज्ञमत्नत ।
तमिद्वर्धन्तु नो गिरः ॥

3. The missiles (of sense activities) manifest from all the three regions; our lady bestows ideas in life.

They foster the growth of the brain on the hill. (724)

D. V.

१. अयं त इन्द्र सोमो निपूतो अधि बर्हिषि ।
एहीमस्य द्रवा पिब ॥

1. Indra who controls Soma swells from down below to him for the motley sense activities from beyond.

They flow to us here to drink. (725), (159)

२. शाचिगो शाचिपूजनायं रणाय ते सुतः ।
आखण्डल प्र हूयसे ॥

2. The sense activities perceive and bestow; the sense activities perceive and swell towards men to control and move to gladden mind,

who invokes Indra (destroyer) to bestow nourishment. (726)

३. यस्ते शृङ्गवृषो णपात्प्रणपात्कुण्डपाय्यः ।
न्यस्मिन् दध्र आ मनः ॥

3. He strives to rain from the hill to nourish the sense organs (descendants); the head (pot) excretes quickly to the sense organs.

They guide us and give support to mind. (727)

D. VI.

१. आ तू न इन्द्र क्षुमन्तं चित्रं ग्राभं सं गृभाय ।
महाहस्ती दक्षिणेन ॥

1. Indra! You grab the nutrition of various sorts within; you grab all

with your great hands what comes from the south.

The nutrition comprises all the nervous impulses, blood and breath. (728)

२. विद्मा हि त्वा तुविकूर्मिं तुविदेष्णं तुवीमघम् ।
तुविमात्रमवोभिः ॥

2. You acquaint us with them and arouse us; you approach the sense organs much; you honour and bestow their desires much; you are much bountiful.

You bestow much to support and bless them. (729)

३. न हि त्वा शूर देवा न मर्तासो दित्सन्तम् ।
भीमं न गां वारयन्ते ॥

3. None, whether deva or mortal, bestows like your heroic self; bestows gifts as desired.

You are formidable and guide the sense activities within the enclosure. (730)

D. VII.

१. अभि त्वा वृषभा सुते सुतं सृजामि पीतये ।
तृम्पा व्यश्नुही मदम् ॥

1. Indra! You shower Soma juice on your friend mind which flows to him to drink

to satisfaction on our hill; the sense perceptions modify him. (731)

२. मा त्वा मूरा अविष्यवो मोपहस्वान आ दभन् ।
मा कीं ब्रह्मद्विषं वनः ॥

2. Indra! Do not be impetuous in working for the brain cells; do not laugh at the desires above nor cause injury.

The head over desires to be active about knowledge. (732)

३. इह त्वा गोपरीणसं महे मन्दन्तु राधसे ।
सरो गौरो यथा पिब ॥

3. Here you associate with sense activities and go around much with them for wealth when dull within (or to gladden within).

And you release them (for the sense organs) to drink like bulls. (733)

D. VIII.

१. इदं वसो सुतमन्धः पिबा सुपूर्णमुदरम् ।
अनाभयिन्नरिमा ते ॥

1. Here the mind shines bright after drinking up ignorance well, bellyful. Here wealth (Vasu) drinks up the ignorance of mind arousing full delight and gladness.

The host (of wealth) is released to us from the source. (734), (124)

२. नृभिर्धौतः सुतो अश्नैरव्या वारैः परिपूतः ॥
अश्वो न निक्तो नदीषु ॥

2. The Aśvins go around the enclosure and swell towards the mind of man to cleanse it from the hill for his comfort.

Prāṇa releases the rays of sense activities to flow resoundingly. (735)

३. तं ते यवं यथा गोभिः स्वादुमकर्म श्रीणन्तः ।
इन्द्र त्वास्मिन्त्सधमादे ॥

3. They (the Aśvins) desire the brain cells, likewise the sense activities; the sense activities cook the pleasant duties within.

Indra himself is our comrade (in this). (736)

D. IX.

१. इदं ह्यन्वोजसा सुतं राधानां पते ।
पिबा त्वा३स्य गिर्वणः ॥

1. The lord of wealth bestows now vigorously freshly on Mind.

He drinks them from the hill with desire. (737)

२. यस्ते अनु स्वधामसत्सुते नि यच्छ तन्वम् ।
स त्वा ममत्तु सोम्य ॥

2. He (Soma) now by himself bestows on us existence through mind whom he controls below by bestowing him.

Soma bestows existence on us powerfully. (738)

३. प्र ते अश्नोतु कुक्ष्योः प्रेन्द्र ब्रह्मणा शिरः ।
प्र बाहू शूर राधसा ॥

3. From the hill he (Soma) nourishes the sense organs and

home through the motley sense activities; Indra nourishes our head through Soma (brahmaṇā).

The hero conveys the nourishment as wealth. (739)

D. X.

१. आ त्वेता नि षीदतेन्द्रमभि प्र गायत ।
सखाय स्तोमवाहसः ॥

1. Soma! You reside below with the motley sense activities; Indra unites you to them for nourishment.

As friend he conveys them praiseworthily and bestows on him. (740), (164)

२. पुरूतमं पुरूणामीशानं वार्याणाम् ।
इन्द्रं सोमे सचा सुते ॥

2. Abundant desires rule us often in the enclosure.
Indra unites Soma to Mind. (741)

३. स घा नो योग आ भुवत्स राये स पुरन्ध्या ॥
गमद्वाजेभिरा स नः ॥

3. Indeed he unites with him to bestow existence on mind; he controls and bestows on the city (brain) in compassion.

In our life-activity he supports us with gifts. (742)

D. XI.

१. योगेयोगे तवस्तरं वाजेवाजे हवामहे ।
सखाय इन्द्रमूतये ।

1. Indra! You gladden the home every time you unite with it and you bestow great oblations in life after life.

You move as a friend and help us. (743), (163), (Y. V. 11, 14)

२. अनु प्रत्नस्यौकसो हुवे तुविप्रतिं नरम् ।
यं ते पूर्वं पिता हुवे ॥

2. Now you bestow nourishment and guide us alone when invoked; you nourish men powerfully.

The ancient father controls him (Indra) when invoked. (744)

३. आ घा गमद्यदि श्रवत्सहस्रिणीभिरूतिभिः ।
वाजेभिरुप नो हवम् ॥

3. You help us with thousands of things indeed which come to us and flow (or which cook understanding).

You support the oblations in life, above. (745)

D. XII.

१. इन्द्र सुतेषु सोमेषु क्रतुं पुनीष उक्थ्यम् ।
विदे वृधस्य दक्षस्य महाँ हि षः ॥

1. Indra produces the missiles of sense activities to Soma repeatedly as he desires, praiseworthily for the sake of mind.

He increases our knowledge and satisfies us greatly indeed, as desired. (746), (381)

२. स प्रथमे व्योमनि देवानां सदने वृधः ॥
सुपारः सुश्रवस्तमः समप्सुजित् ॥

2. He bestows ideas (devas) primarily from ākāśa (heaven) to foster growth of the brain (home).

He arouses it and fulfils by bestowing; he hears our desires well and at the same time wins Activity. (747)

३. तमु हुवे वाजसातय इन्द्रं भराय शुष्मिणम् ।
भवा नः सुम्ने अन्तमः सखा वृधे ॥

3. Indra! You are invoked continually in life-activity to support us by gushing mightily to us.

You bind us to wealth in existence as an intimate friend and foster our growth. (748)

D. XIII.

१. एना वो अग्निं नमसोर्जो नपातमा हुवे ।
प्रियं चेतिष्ठमरतिं स्वध्वरं विश्वस्य दूतममृतम् ॥

1. Then Agni bestows on us nourishment which makes obeisances to him and is invoked by the sense organs.

Lovingly he gladdens our mind, whom he likes, with sweet wealth (perceptions) from the sense organs through the messengers (ideas) from the immortal home. (749), (45), (Y. V. 15, 32)

२. स योजते अरुषा विश्वभोजसा स दुद्रवत्स्वाहुतः ।
सुब्रह्मा यज्ञः सुशमी वसूनां देवं राधो जनानाम् ॥

2. The ruddy consciousness unites with them and releases

what comes from the sense organs for consumption, which flow and offer by themselves to be consumed. (Y. V. 15, 33)

Indra toils well for ideas (devas) to arouse knowledge in life-activity for the prosperity of the people. (750), (Y. V. 15, 34)

D. XIV.

१. प्रत्यु अदर्श्यायत्यू३च्छन्ती दुहिता दिवः ।
अपो मही वृणुते चक्षुषा तमो ज्योतिष्कृणोति सूनरी ॥

1. The daughter of consciousness (Uṣas) is well-known to visit (the head) above and unite with it to bestow.

Activity envelops us greatly and looks up eagerly at the desires; consciousness produces the motley sense perceptions to gladden us. (751), (303)

२. उदुस्रियाः सृजते सूर्यः सचा उद्यन्नक्षत्रमर्चिवत् ।
तवेदुषो व्युषि सूर्यस्य च सं भक्तेन गमेमहि ॥

2. Above, Indra (bull) flows to consciousness, unites above with the brain-cells (stars) to guide them, and honours them with understanding.

He beholds Uṣas eagerly for us, also consciousness in men who all come to him with great devotion. (752)

D. XV.

१. इमा उ वां दिविष्टय उस्रा हवन्ते अश्विना ।
अयं वामह्वेऽवसे शचीवसू विशंविशं हि गच्छथः ॥

1. Here, Indra indeed bestows the oblations from the Aśvins within at the desire of heaven (or consciousness).

He bestows the paths on us on being invoked, bestows favours, he goes to home after home (man after man) with might graciously. (753), (304)

२. युवं चित्रं ददथुर्भोजनं नरा चोदेथां सूनृतावते ।
अर्वाग्रथं समनसा नि यच्छतं पिबतं सोम्यं मधु ॥

2. He bestows on mind a variety of foods for consumption; the sense activities above make people joyous through knowledge.

He runs to connect manas (mind) to sense perceptions to drink from Soma who controls them and bestows. (754)

D. XVI.

१. अस्य प्रत्नामनु द्युतं शुक्रं दुदुह्रे अह्रयः ।
पयः सहस्रसामृषिम् ॥

1. Consciousness bestows milk (perceptions) straight, as desired by heaven, as of old.

We drink thousands of them bestowed by the Ṛṣis. (755), (Y. V. 3, 16)

२. अयं सूर्यं इवोपदृगयं सरांसि धावति ।
सप्त प्रवत आ दिवम् ॥

2. Consciousness respects the paths of the sense activities in the home, supports their flow and bestows knowledge.

The seven-pronged Activity nourishes understanding in the waking state. (756)

३. अयं विश्वानि तिष्ठति पुनानो भुवनोपरि ।
सोमो देवो न सूर्यः ॥

3. Soma repeatedly follows the path to the sense organs of creatures at his wish.

Soma throws light on ideas, like Sūrya. (757)

D. XVII.

१. एष प्रत्नेन जन्मना देवो देवेभ्यः सुतः ।
हरिः पवित्रे अर्षति ॥

1. In ancient times Soma sought ideas in life-activity (or vice versa); he aroused and hastened them.

Indeed he released them to flow beneficially. (758), (1264)

२. एष प्रत्नेन मन्मना देवो देवेभ्यस्परि ।
कविर्विप्रेण वावृधे ॥

2. In ancient times mind sought ideas from the brain (home); the devas went around to him.

Agni (the wise) inspired him mightily and bestowed growth on him. (759)

३. दुहानः प्रत्नमित्पयः पवित्रे परि षिच्यसे ।
क्रन्दं देवाँ अजीजनः ॥

3. In ancient times sense perceptions beneficially went around

and sprinkled on him to drink and hastened to establish him.

The ideas won men resoundingly. (760)

D. XVIII.

१. उप शिक्षापतस्थुषो भियसमा धेहि शत्रवे ।
पवमान विदा रयिम् ॥

1. Above Uṣas instructs us in the abiding paths and arouses and bestows fearlessness of enemies.

He bestows knowledge on mind through wealth. (761)

२. उपो षु जातमप्तुरं गोभिर्भङ्गं परिष्कृतम् ।
इन्दुं देवा अयासिषुः ॥

2. Above Activity willingly sub-divides the sense activities who go around to the sense organs and produce the birth of sense perceptions above (in the brain cells).

The deva is indefatigable with the brain cells offering sense perceptions. (762), (467), (1335)

३. उपास्मै गायता नरः पवमानायेन्दवे ।
अभि देवाँ इयक्षते ॥

3. Above the sense activities unite with us men, which the brain cells bestow on the fickle mind,

on his longings for ideas. (763), (651), (Y. V. 33, 62)

D. XIX.

१. प्र सोमासो विपश्चितोऽपो नयन्त ऊर्मयः ।
वनानि महिषा इव ॥

1. Soma bestows nourishment to inspire mind. Activity guides the waves to him,

like guiding the buffaloes in a forest. (764), (478)

२. अभि द्रोणानि बभ्रवः शुक्रा ऋतस्य धारया ।
वाजं गोमन्तमक्षरन् ॥

2. The tawny consciousness bestows his rays on the head, which support Ṛta in bright light.

In life activity the sense activities are imperishable within (or the sense activities flow in the home to gladden us). (765)

३. सुता इन्द्राय वायवे वरुणाय मरुद्भ्यः ।
सोमा अर्षन्तु विष्णवे ॥

3. Indra bestows from the brain cells ideas of the external world (Varuṇa) on mind.

Soma flows within to work for new (ideas). (766)

D. XX.

१. प्र सोम देववीतये सिन्धुर्न पिप्ये अर्णसा ।
अंशोः पयसा मदिरो न जागृविरच्छा कोशं मधुश्चुतम् ।

1. Soma nourishes sense activities (Sindhu) by bestowing waves of ideas (devas) which they desire and drink.

He bestows Soma juice to drink; the spiritous liquor drips from the sweet sense perceptions near the head in waking state. (767), (514)

२. आ हर्यतो अर्जुनो अत्के अव्यत प्रियः सूनुर्न मर्ज्यः ।
तमीं हिन्वन्त्यपसो यथा रथं नदीष्वा गभस्त्योः ॥

2. The Aśvins fondly win for the mind (son) of mortals, desired a mantle (armour) (atka) of knowledge (whiteness).

They arouse desires as longed for and give a helping hand like a charioteer, bestowing the desires resoundingly. (768)

D. XXI.

१. प्र सोमासो मदच्युतः श्रवसे नो मघोनाम् ।
सुता विदथे अक्रमुः ॥

1. Soma releases nourishment munificently to drip from sense activities which he cooks at home,

and directs them to mind in due course. (769), (477)

२. आदीं हंसो यथा गणं विश्वस्यावीवशन्मतिम् ।
अत्यो न गोभिरज्यते ॥

2. In ancient times retinues of ideas blessed the sense organs watching over like a swan and the brain with understanding.

Prāṇa supported the sense organs united to Aśvins. (770)

३. आदीं त्रितस्य योषणो हरिं हिन्वन्त्यद्रिभिः ।
इन्दुमिन्द्राय पीतये ॥

3. In ancient times the sense activities indeed released to the three states and aroused desires on the hill for them.

Indra bestows on them through the brain cells to drink. (771)

D. XXII.

१. अया पवस्व देवयु रेभन्पवित्रं पर्येषि विश्वतः ।
मधोर्धारा असृक्षत ॥

1. The sense activities bestow to the paths to the home for drinking by the devotee beneficially and resoundingly.

They flow to the home in copious streams. (772)

२. पवते हर्यतो हरिरति ह्वरांसि रंह्या ।
अभ्यर्ष स्तोतृभ्यो वीरवद्यशः ॥

2. They protect understanding eagerly; indeed they release it and gladden us, by hastening through the spinal cord.

They flow fearlessly and praiseworthily to be deemed heroic and excellent. (773)

३. प्र सुन्वानायान्धसो मर्तो न वष्ट तद्वचः ।
अप श्वानमराधसं हता मखं न भृगवः ॥

3. They nourish the devotees and guide them against ignorance; mortals have newly gained speech from them.

Activity honours prāṇa for (bestowing) wealth; indeed he supports sense activities vigorously and bestows. (774)

BOOK II : CHAPTER I

D. I.

१. पवस्व वाचो अग्रियः सोम चित्राभिरूतिभिः ।
अभि विश्वानि काव्या ।।

1. Soma himself bestowed on us speech first to drink from and supports it in a variety of ways,
desired by the brain (home) to compose poems. (775)

२. त्वं समुद्रिया अपोऽग्रियो वाच ईरयन् ।
पवस्व विश्वचर्षणे ।।

2. Activity flows and gladdens you, before stirring up speech he himself actively bestows on the sense organ to drink from. (776)

३. तुभ्येमा भुवना कवे महिम्ने सोम तस्थिरे ।
तुभ्यं धावन्ति धेनवः ।।

3. Activity! You bestow much in the head of creatures; Soma establishes them for comfort.
You run within to convey the libations of milk (speech). (777)

D. II.

१. पवस्वेन्दो वृषा सुतः कृधी नो यशसो जने ।
विश्वा अप द्विषो जहि ।।

1. Activity! You bestow on the brain cells yourself to drink and rain on mind to create satisfaction and fame on men.
Activity arouses desires through the sense organs in both brain and mind. (778), (479)

२. यस्य ते सख्ये वयं सासह्याम पृतन्यतः ।
तवेन्दो द्युम्न उत्तमे ।।

2. You help them and bestow them on us and immediately unite and guide them to nourish.
You are the best from heaven for the brain cells. (779)

३. या ते भीमान्यायुधा तिग्मानि सन्ति धूर्वणे ।
रक्षा समस्य नो निदः ।।

3. You move to them formidably, guide, unite and bestow on them passionately, bestow gifts and agitate with desires.
You protect us all and do not blame us. (780)

D. III.

१. वृषा सोम द्युमाँ असि वृषा देव वृषव्रतः ।
वृषा धर्माणि दध्रिषे ॥

1. Soma rains to us from heaven; he rains ideas; he envelops us following the same law (or he rains his duties).
He rains dharma (codes of behaviour) and he bestows on the Ṛṣis (Activity). (781), (504)

२. वृष्णस्ते वृष्ण्यं शवो वृषा वनं वृषा सुतः ।
स त्वं वृषन्वृषेदसि ॥

2. He works in the home; he envelops and guides the sense organs; he rains desires; he rains them to the mind.
And Indra (Vṛiṣan) rains to Soma. (782)

३. अश्वो न चक्रदो वृषा सं गा इन्दो समर्वतः ।
वि नो राये दुरो वृधि ॥

3. Prāṇa goes around and bestows them, rains all sense activities and runs to the brain cells at the same time.
He opens the door to growth through controlling them. (783)

D. IV.

१. वृषा ह्यसि भानुना द्युमन्तं त्वा हवामहे ।
पवमान स्वर्दृशम् ॥

1. Consciousness rains his rays from heaven and fixes (ideas) he illumines the great oblations within the head.
The fickle mind (is enabled to) see heaven. (784), (480)

२. यदद्भिः परिषिच्यसे मर्मृज्यमान आयुभिः ।
द्रोणे सधस्थमश्नुषे ॥

2. What you (consciousness) strive to sprinkle (from the heavenly) waters to cleanse the homes of mortals is life to them, for which the assembly on the hill in the head is eager. (785)

३. आ पवस्व सुवीर्यं मन्दमानः स्वायुध ।
इहो ष्विन्दवा गहि ॥

3. When the brain (home) is sluggish you arouse vigour by yourself uniting with it bestowing for drinking.

You praiseworthily bestow sense activities to arouse (the brain). (786)

D. V.

१. पवमानस्य ते वयं पवित्रमभ्युन्दतः ।
सखित्वमा वृणीमहे ॥

1. They (the sense activities) bestow on our mind and control him beneficially by uniting and giving what he lacks.

They are our friends and envelop us greatly. (787)

२. ये ते पवित्रमूर्मयोऽभिक्षरन्ति धारया ।
तेभिर्नः सोम मृडय ॥

2. They stream in waves beneficially; flow within to support us.

Soma binds them to us in compassion. (788)

३. स नः पुनान आ भर रयिं वीरवतीमिषम् ।
ईशानः सोम विश्वतः ॥

3. They bestow gifts repeatedly and support us with wealth and open our eyes to understanding vigorously.

Soma rules over understanding in the home. (789)

D. VI.

१. अग्निं दूतं वृणीमहे होतारं विश्ववेदसम् ।
अस्य यज्ञस्य सुक्रतुम् ॥

1. Agni chooses his messengers greatly who preside and gladden us by bestowing all knowledge on the brain (home).

They do good to us in our lives. (790)

२. अग्निमग्निं हवीमभिः सदा हवन्त विश्पतिम् ।
हव्यवाहं पुरुप्रियम् ॥

2. Flaming ardour (agni) is Agni's oblation; the lord of the home indeed bestows it within.

It bestows oblations in waking with abundant love. (791)

३. अग्ने देवाँ इहा वह जज्ञानो वृक्तबर्हिषे ।
असि होता न ईड्यः ॥

3. Agni conveys ideas to us here for the birth of knowledge on the spread-out nerves (sacred grass).
He presides over the oblations. (792)

D. VII.

१. मित्रं वयं हवामहे वरुणं सोमपीतये ।
या जाता पूतदक्षसा ॥

1. Soma swells over to us with great oblations from the external world (Varuṇa) to the brain (Mitra).
They swell to us from the source and give satisfaction. (793)

२. ऋतेन यावृतावृधावृतस्य ज्योतिषस्पती ।
ता मित्रावरुणा हुवे ॥

2. Ṛta moves and envelops and causes to increase them; the lord of effulgence envelops them.
Mitra and Varuṇa invoke them. (794)

३. वरुणः प्राविता भुवन्मित्रो विश्वाभिरूतिभिः ।
करतां नः सुराधसः ॥

3. Varuṇa fulfils the brain (Mitra) with knowledge in creatures; he supports the sense organs and helps.
They produce longings and are bound up with wealth. (795), (Y.V. 33, 46)

D. VIII.

१. इन्द्रमिद्गाथिनो बृहदिन्द्रमर्केभिरर्किणः ।
इन्द्रं वाणीरनूषत ॥

1. Indra approaches the devotee to bestow; Indra is greatly supported by consciousness praiseworthily.
Indra is greatly attached to Sarasvatī. (796), (198)

२. इन्द्र इद्धर्योः सचा सम्मिश्ल आ वचोयुजा ।
इन्द्रो वज्री हिरण्ययः ॥

2. Indra only supports us, bestows also, mingles with all and unites for speech.
Indra hastens to arouse gladness through the vigorous nerves. (797), (597)

३. इन्द्र वाजेषु नोऽव सहस्त्रप्रधनेषु च ।
उग्र उग्राभिरूतिभिः ॥

3. Indra bestows what is born of the sense organs and blesses us with thousands of items of nourishment and also wealth.

He is powerful and helps powerfully. (798), (598)

४. इन्द्रो दीर्घाय चक्षस आ सूर्यं रोहयद्दिवि ।
वि गोभिरद्रिमैरयत् ॥

4. Indra looks on us long and steadily and bestows as long as consciousness is ascending in waking state.

Through supporting sense activities on the hill, he unites us to comfort. (799)

D. IX.

१. इन्द्रे अग्ना नमो बृहत्सुवृक्तिमेरयामहे ।
धिया धेना अवस्यवः ॥

1. Indra honours Agni much, who arouses the flow of much desires through the nerves.

He satisfies the brain cells by favouring them with much milk (perceptions). (800)

२. ता हि शश्वन्त ईडत इत्था विप्रास ऊतये ।
सबाधो वाजसातये ॥

2. He arouses them constantly and is praised; thus he inspires and bestows, and helps.

And he bestows to win over being troubled constantly. (801)

३. ता वां गीर्भिर्विपन्युवः प्रयस्वन्तो हवामहे ।
मेधसाता सनिष्यवः ॥

3. He bestows much to support the brain (hill) to inspire the mind; he strives to nourish him within with much oblations.

He bestows understanding and gifts through the brain cells. (802)

D. X.

१. वृषा पवस्व धारया मरुत्वते च मत्सरः ।
विश्वा दधान ओजसा ॥

1. He bestows on us much himself to drink and supports ideas for understanding also to flow to us.

He bestows on the brain cells from the sense organs vigorously. (803), (469)

२. तं त्वा धर्तारमोण्यो३: पवमान स्वर्दृशम् ।
हिन्वे वाजेषु वाजिनम् ।।

2. You desire to support and gladden with what is in want and let mind look at heaven.

You arouse and bestow the missiles (of sense activities) and honour life-activity. (804)

३. अया चित्तो विपानया हरिः पवस्व धारया ।
युजं वाजेषु चोदय ।।

3. The tawny consciousness inspires the mind with the path and guides and he himself bestows on him to drink the streams (of perceptions).

He unites with the missiles in life-activity as soon as he rises. (805)

D. XI.

१. वृषा शोणो अभिकनिक्रदद्गा नदयन्नेषि पृथिवीमुत द्याम् ।
इन्द्रस्येव वग्नुरा शृण्व आजौ प्रचोदयन्नर्षसि वाचमेमाम् ।।

1. The tawny consciousness sheds his rays resoundingly to bestow on us milk (sense perceptions) and distributes them between the sense organs and also the head (brain).

Indra hastens to release speech praiseworthily; the Aśvins cook and bestow it above to nourish, and guide its flow and release it also here. (806)

२. रसाय्यः पयसा पिन्वमान ईरयन्नेषि मधुमन्तमंशुम् ।
पवमान सन्तनिमेषि कृण्वन्निन्द्राय सोम परिषिच्यमानः ।।

2. The essence of (speech) hastens in its path and the juice flows abundantly from the home as desired from the sense activity within as Soma juice.

The Aśvins bestow it as gift on the fickle mind in whom Indra creates the desire and Soma sprinkles it. (807)

३. एवा पवस्व मदिरो मदायोदग्राभस्य नमयन्वधस्नुम् ।
परि वर्णं भरमाणो रुशन्तं गव्युर्नो अर्ष परि सोम सिक्तः ।।

3. Soma himself hastens to bestow the spiritous liquor from the sense activity which he grabs above, honours and overcomes it now for us.

The varied activities go around supporting the home which is browing within; the sense activities flow around in waves as Soma's effusions. (808)

D. XII.

१. त्वामिद्धि हवामहे सातौ वाजस्य कारवः ।
त्वां वृत्रेष्विन्द्र सत्पतिं नरस्त्वां काष्ठास्वर्वतः ॥

1. He (Soma) bestows great oblations on the brain continually in life-activity and releases them in the enclosure.

You envelop and support (the brain) mightily; Indra the lord of existence bestows his (Soma's) gifts on men from heaven to our homes as understanding. (809), (234), (Y.V. 27, 37)

२. स त्वं नश्चित्र वज्रहस्त धृष्णुया मह स्तवानो अद्रिवः ।
गामश्वं रथ्यमिन्द्र सं किर सत्रा वाजं न जिग्युषे ॥

2. You bestow a variety (of ideas) to be achieved through the vigorous nerves (hands) and move boldly to gladden by bestowing desires praiseworthily.

Prāṇa scatters all my sense activities from the sense organs of Indra and supports them in life, he wins the sense-activities eagerly. (810), (Y.V. 27, 38)

D. XIII.

१. अभि प्र वः सुराधसमिन्द्रमर्च यथा विदे ।
यो जरितृभ्यो मघवा पुरूवसुः सहस्रेणेव शिक्षति ॥

1. Indra arouses the wealth (of perceptions) and honours it as enjoined in order to nourish.

Indra (Maghavā) is abundantly beneficent to the devotee bestowing a thousand ideas and instructing him. (811), (235)

२. शतानीकेव प्र जिगाति धृष्णुया हन्ति वृत्राणि दाशुषे ।
गिरेरिव प्र रसा अस्य पिन्विरे दत्राणि पुरुभोजसः ॥

2. Indra moves to strike down Vṛtra in order to serve eagerly by winning from sense activities boldly hundreds of kinds of nourishment and guide them quickly to the head.

He bestows and releases the nourishment on the hill; their essence bestows abundant comfort on us; he supports abundantly their consumption victoriously. (812)

D. XIV.

१. त्वमिद्धा ह्यो नरोऽपीप्यन्वज्रिन् भूर्णयः ।
स इन्द्र स्तोमवाहस इह श्रुध्युप स्वसरमा गहि ॥

1. You approach men and bestow on them from heaven which swell through the impetuous nerves to be drunk.

And Indra praiseworthily conveys them here and bestows; he cooks them above to be sipped and himself arouses and bestows sense perceptions to gladden us. (813), (302)

२. मत्स्वा सुशिप्रिन्हरिवस्तमीमहे त्वया भूषन्ति वेधसः ।
तव श्रवांस्युपमान्युक्थ्य सुतेष्विन्द्र गिर्वणः ॥

2. He arouses us himself to sharpen (the appetite) for nourishment mightily; you produce the desire for consciousness in the home who adorns the devotee.

He supports the cooking above in the home praiseworthily; Indra, lover of the hill, bestows the desires of the mind. (814)

D. XV.

१. यस्ते मदो वरेण्यस्तेना पवस्वान्धसा ।
देवावीरघशंसहा ॥

1. You strive for him (mind) for sense perceptions excellently; you bestow yourself for him to drink and release him from ignorance.

You willingly favour him praiseworthily. (815), (470)

२. जघ्निर्वृत्रममित्रियं सस्निर्वाजं दिवेदिवे ।
गोषातिरश्वसा असि ॥

2. On Vṛtra being struck down, births take place in my mind for comfort, and thus in the brain cells day after day in life-activity.

Prāṇa bestows the sense perceptions. (816)

३. सम्मिश्लो अरुषो भुवः सूपस्थाभिर्न धेनुभिः ।
सीदं छ्येनो न योनिमा ॥

3. The ruddy consciousness mixes with all in existence; he supports the cooking of the sense perceptions.

From his seat he bestows on us the images of all (ideas) from the source. (817)

All objects of the outer world (Varuṇa) are indeed ideas of heaven with form and substance. These objects are the subject-matter of sense perceptions which are revealed as such to the brain and mind by consciousness.

D. XVI.

१. अयं पूषा रयिर्भगः सोमः पुनानो अर्षति ।
पतिर्विश्वस्य भूमनो व्यख्यद्रोदसी उभे ॥

1. Consciousness eagerly protects the paths to wealth; Soma repeatedly flows for them.

The lord runs to bestow and manifest abundantly (bhūmana) through our sense organs in both brain and mind. (818), (546)

२. समु प्रिया अनूषत गावो मदाय घृष्वयः ।
सोमासः कृण्वते पथः पवमानास इन्दवः ॥

2. All are fondly attached to sense activities and they move to bestow on us (their gifts) joyously and boldly.

Soma produces understanding and bestows them on mind along the path from the brain cells. (819)

३. य ओजिष्ठस्तमा भर पवमान श्रवाय्यम् ।
यः पञ्च चर्षणीरभि रयिं येन वनामहे ॥

3. He moves to support desires of the mind praiseworthily and vigorously.

He hastens the five sense activities diligently towards (acquiring) wealth which is greatly desired. (820)

The sense activities only establish contact between heaven and the external world which furnishes the matter for sense perceptions which are conveyed via one of the sense organs and nerves to the brain to be revealed by consciousness.

D. XVII.

१. वृषा मतीनां पवते विचक्षणः सोमो अह्नां प्रतरीतोषसां दिवः ।
प्राणा सिन्धूनां कलशां अचिक्रददिन्द्रस्य हार्द्यािवशन्मनीषिभिः ॥

1. Soma showers understanding on us and he protects or bestows on us to drink diligently; Soma nourishes us with them in waking state to cross (ignorance) which consciousness gives eagerly.

Sindhu fulfils him resoundingly in the head through Indra who bestows her on the brain in men's homes. (821), (559)

२. मनीषिभिः पवते पूर्व्यः कविर्नृभिर्यतः परि कोशां असिष्यदत् ।
त्रितस्य नाम जनयन्मधु क्षरन्निन्द्रस्य वायुं सख्याय वर्धयन् ॥

2. Men preserve ancient knowledge (tradition). Agni supports men by uniting with them by going around the brain and bestowing its desires.

The sense perceptions from the source flow around honouring the three states. Indra and the nerves help in fostering their growth. (822)

३. अयं पुनान उषसो अरोचयदयं सिन्धुभ्यो अभवदु लोककृत् ।
अयं त्रिः सप्त दुदुहान आशिरं सोमो हृदे पवते चारु मत्सरः ॥

3. Uṣas releases the paths to Sindhu repeatedly as soon as she ascends, for Sindhu to create existence to the world.

The paths are three (to the brain, sense organs and mind). Activity bestows the sense perceptions to be consumed by the brain (head); the brain drinks (protects) understanding which gladdens by flowing to us. (823)

The world comes into existence only when the sense activities passing via the sense organs appraise the objects of the world.

D. XVIII.

१. एवा ह्यसि वीरयुरेवा शूर उत स्थिरः ।
एवा ते राध्यं मनः ॥

1. Uṣas or Indra hasten them (sense activities) from heaven, bestows them extensively like a hero and stabilises them also heroically.

They are speeded up to control mind successfully. (824), (232)

२. एवा रातिस्तुविमघ विश्वेभिर्धायि धातृभिः ।
अधा चिदिन्द्र नः सचा ॥

2. They speed up ready to bestow wealth abundantly; they support the sense organs to bestow; they are establishers.

Then Indra binds them by uniting. (825)

३. मो षु ब्रह्मेव तन्द्रयुर्भुवो वाजानां पते ।
मत्स्वा सुतस्य गोमतः ॥

3. The sense organs hasten to bestow knowledge; when they are weary the lord of life-activity (Indra) unites with them.

Indra (rich in cattle) arouses them himself for me. (826)

D. XIX.

१. इन्द्रं विश्वा अवीवृधंत्समुद्रव्यचसं गिरः ।
रथीतमं रथीनां वाजानां सत्पतिं पतिम् ॥

1. Indra favours the sense organs, bestows growth through them and gladdens, perceiving them all from the brain.

He desires to control them and he is the conveyor in life; he is the lord of existence and the path here. (827), (343), (Y.V.12, 56)

२. सख्ये त इन्द्र वाजिनो मा भेम शवसस्पते ।
त्वामभि प्र नोनुमो जेतारमपराजितम् ॥

2. Indra is a helper (friend) in life, bestows formidably, the lord of might.

He bestows the kind of nourishment in need, the unconquerable (aparājita) wins for crossing (ignorance) and gladdens. (828)

३. पूर्वीरिन्द्रस्य रातयो न वि दस्यंत्यूतयः ।
यदा वाजस्य गोमत स्तोतृभ्यो मंहते मघम् ॥

3. Indra bestows since ancient days; he is ready to bestow new (ideas); he controls our wants and helps us.

In life he is rich in sense activities which he praiseworthily bestows as gifts for wealth. (829)

BOOK II: CHAPTER II

D. I.

१. एते असृग्रमिन्दवस्तिरः पवित्रमाशवः ।
विश्वान्यभि सौभगा ॥

1. The motley sense activities flow first to the brain cells to bestow for their comfort at home graciously bestow food.
They guide them to welfare through the sense organs. (830)

२. विघ्नन्तो दुरिता पुरु सुगा तोकाय वाजिनः ।
त्मना कृण्वन्तो अर्वतः ॥

2. They pierce the brain cells and release abundantly for consumption; the sense activities arouse the sense organs in life.
They themselves hasten to produce and bestow within. (831)

३. कृण्वन्तो वरिवो गवेऽभ्यर्षन्ति सुष्टुतिम् ।
इडामस्मभ्यं संयतम् ॥

3. The sense activities produce new things in freedom and flow within suitably.
Oblations to us are continuous. (832)

D. II.

१. राजा मेधाभिरीयते पवमानो मनावधि ।
अन्तरिक्षेण यातवे ॥

1. They (the sense activities) control understanding and support their uniting with mind and bestow satisfaction to the home.
They move towards the mind. (833)

२. आ नः सोम सहो जुवो रूपं न वर्चसे भर ।
सुष्वाणो देववीतये ॥

2. They are tied to us and release victoriously; they incite and bestow new forms and support them.
Desires rush wishing ideas (or devas). (834)

३. आ न इन्दो शतग्विनं गवां पोषं स्वश्व्यम् ।
वहा भगत्तिमूतये ॥

3. The sense activities sharpen the brain cells mightily; they fulfil eagerly with their own steeds (rays).

Consciousness helps them to convey. (835)

D. III.

१. तं त्वा नृम्णानि बिभ्रतं सधस्थेषु महो दिवः ।
चारुं सुकृत्ययेमहे ॥

1. Sense activities! You desire courageously to go around in the assembly greatly in the waking state.

You gladden us, hasten to do us great good. (836)

२. संवृक्तधृष्णुमुक्थ्यं महामहिव्रतं मदम् ।
शतं पुरो रुरुक्षणिम् ॥

2. The sense activities with great vows (duties) all envelop the head very praiseworthily.

The Aśvins (ruru) bestow desires on the (brains) in a moment. (837)

३. अतस्त्वा रयिरभ्ययद्राजानं सुक्रतो दिवः ।
सुपर्णो अव्यथी भरत् ॥

3. Then you seize wealth which you honour and control to do us good in the waking state.

The golden winged consciousness supports them undaunted. (838)

४. अधा हिन्वान इन्द्रियं ज्यायो महित्वमानशे ।
अभिष्टिकृद्विचर्षणिः ॥

4. Then you arouse desires for the sense organs and you let me achieve much through them victoriously.

You are very diligent to produce what is desired by us. (839)

५. विश्वस्मा इ स्वर्दृशे साधारणं रजस्तुरम् ।
गोपामृतस्य विर्भरत् ॥

5. Our sense organs are sighted upon by heaven which is common to all, by which they are quickly excited.

The protector of men vigorously protects men. (840)

D. IV.

१. इषे पवस्व धारया मृज्यमानो मनीषिभिः ।
इन्दो रुचाभि गा इहि ॥

1. The sense activities themselves bestow desires to drink and support them, which adorn the homes of men.

The brain cells shine to arouse sense activities to come. (841), (505)

२. पुनानो वरिवस्कृध्यूर्जं जनाय गिर्वणः ।
हरे सृजान आशिरम् ॥

2. Heaven (Space) repeatedly creates nourishment to the desires of the brain (hill) of men.

The tawny consciousness flows from the source to the head. (842)

३. पुनानो देववीतय इन्द्रस्य याहि निष्कृतम् ।
द्युतानो वाजिभिर्हितः ॥

3. They desire ideas (devas) repeatedly; Indra moves to the appointed place to arouse them.

Heaven guides them to the nerves to support life in welfare. (843)

D. V.

१. अग्निनाग्निः समिध्यते कविर्गृहपतिर्युवा ।
हव्यवाड्जुह्वास्यः ॥

1. Fire is derived from Agni and fuel sticks (sense objects) unite with fire (Agni). Agni crosses the home for the mind to drink.

Oblations are bestowed through the tongues (flames) to us. (844)

२. यस्त्वामग्ने हविष्पतिर्दूतं देव सपर्यति ।
तस्य स्म प्राविता भव ॥

2. Agni! You strive for the lord of oblations (Activity) to serve as messenger to ideas (devas).

They are to us fulfillers of understanding in existence. (845)

३. यो अग्निं देववीतये हविष्माँ आविवासति ।
तस्मै पावक मृडय ॥

3. Agni is desirous of ideas as oblations for us which he gives through residing with us.

He fulfils by bestowing them on the head in compassion. (846)

D. VI.

१. मित्रं हुवे पूतदक्षं वरुणं च रिशादसम् ॥
धियं घृताचीं साधन्ता ॥

1. At the call of the brain (Mitra), the external world, Varuṇa and also ideas (Maruts) swell to him to satisfy.

They satisfy and enable clarified butter also to be formed. (847), (Y.V. 33, 57)

२. ऋतेन मित्रावरुणावृतावृधावृतस्पृशा ।
क्रतुं बृहन्तमाशाथे ॥

2. Ṛta envelops Mitra and Varuṇa, fosters their growth and nourishes by contacting them,

inspires great desires within. (848)

३. कवी नो मित्रावरुणा तुविजाता उरुक्षया ।
दक्षं दधाते अपसम् ॥

3. Agni (the wise) from the mighty source meets Mitra and Varuṇa extensively in their dwelling places.

He works diligently and bestows satisfaction. (849)

D. VII.

१. इन्द्रेण सं हि दृक्षसे संजग्मानो अबिभ्युषा ।
मन्दू समानवर्चसा ॥

1. Indra arouses all, considers about the home and bestows on the homes of all mobile creatures eagerly without fear,

and gladdens the home by bestowing vigour. (850)

२. आदह स्वधामनु पुनर्गर्भत्वमेरिरे ।
दधाना नाम यज्ञियम् ॥

2. And now he bestows indeed by himself and pushes me again in a fresh birth and releases me resoundingly for my comfort.

He bestows on the brain cells what is named this life-activity. (851)

३. वीडु चिदारुजत्नुभिर्गुहा चिदिन्द्र वह्निभिः ।
अविन्द उस्रिया अनु ॥

3. Indra establishes the mind resoundingly by supporting births (of ideas) secretly; he conveys them to him.

Indra now makes himself known. (852)

From the previous three mantras we learn a few things. We have learnt from the previous mantras that the universal powers carry on all the subtle activities from the unseen world of heaven and impart them all as ideas to the brain cells which preserve them, including all the knowledge of the external world and the desires arising therefrom. The brain is made to pass on all this information to the mind so that during life we have a duplicate record of our current life experiences. At death the brain is buried or burnt away. There remains only the mind which is uprooted from its present abode by Indra who supports it secretly to a new existence and establishes it, when it becomes acquainted with Indra again.

The main purpose of the mind is accordingly for continued human existence and activity. The remnants of previous life's experience, acquire a new body derived from a fresh pair of parents and a new environment, physical and mental and they are yoked together to enter on a new life-course.

We learn also a fantastic new idea which contradicts all that we have been so far taught by all our looks on philosophy and spiritual wisdom. We are taught by them that man is responsible for all his doings and that God is a mute witness. Contrary to all that this Veda tells us that desires and ideas for such desires all flow from heaven and the universal devas distribute them among men as they may determine, unless desired by the mind from earlier experiences. The devas deal mainly with the brain and only secondarily with the mind. As seen from the foregoing mantras, the mind has no initiative about which we vaunt much, attributing all achievements in life to it. This Veda emphatically declares that God is not only the chief actor of all that takes place in the world and the creatures but he also witnesses them through man only and not directly. Man or mind is just a witness of the creator's activities and is the link for successive lives.

D. VIII.

१. ता हुवे ययोरिदं पप्ने विश्वं पुरा कृतम् ।
इन्द्राग्नी न मर्धतः ॥

1. He (Mind) invokes, the sense activities (drinks) hasten to release to him admirably producing what is desired by the city (brain) through the sense organs (viśvam).

Indra and Agni bestow all that on mortals. (853)

२. उग्रा विघनिना मृध इन्द्राग्नी हवामहे ।
ता नो मृडात ईदृशे ॥

2. Formidable Indra and Agni without being wearied of striking down (Vṛtra) they bestow great oblations.

They look on us with compassion through the nerves. (854)

३. हथो वृत्राण्यार्या हथो दासानि सत्पती ।
हथो विश्वा अप द्विषः ॥

3. They strike down (Vṛtra) for man (ārya); the lord of existence Indra strikes down by way of services.

Activity strikes down for the sake of wishes of both brain and mind for sense organs. (855)

D. IX.

१. अभि सोमास आयवः पवन्ते मद्यं मदम् ।
समुद्रस्याधि विष्टपे मनीषिणो मत्सरासो मदच्युतः ॥

1. Soma bestows on the brain cells; he bestows sense perceptions which he controls joyously within to drink.

And he gladdens and satisfies the three worlds of men and he flows to them to let sense activities (perceptions) to drip. (856), (518)

२. तरत्समुद्रं पवमान ऊर्मिणा राजा देव ऋतं बृहत् ॥
अर्षा मित्रस्य वरुणस्य धर्मणा प्र हिन्वान ऋतं बृहत् ॥

2. He bestows in waves on mind to cross over ignorance and to bestow joy; he releases the birth of the great deva Ṛta.

He flows to Mitra and Varuṇa as his duty to arouse desires through the great Ṛta. (857)

३. नृभिर्येमाणो हर्यतो विचक्षणो राजा देवः समुद्रयः ॥

3. He supports men through the home (brain) as wished for diligently and releases the birth of ideas and gladdens them. (858)

D. X.

१. तिस्रो वाच ईरयति प्र वह्निर्ऋतस्य धीतिं ब्रह्मणो मनीषाम् ।
गावो यन्ति गोपतिं पृच्छमानाः सोमं यन्ति मतयो वावशानाः ॥

1. The three states set speech in activity and nourish (i.e. brain, body and sense organs); Ṛta conveys understanding to it; the mind desires knowledge.

The lord of men (Indra) guides the sense activities, looks for (enquires for) Soma and guides the understanding bestowed by him in the home. (859), (525)

२. सोमं गावो धेनवो वावशानाः सोमं विप्रा मतिभिः पृच्छमानाः ।
सोमः सुत ऋच्यते पूयमानः सोमे अर्कास्त्रिष्टुभः सं नवन्ते ॥

2. Soma bestows libations of milk (sense perceptions) from sense activities in the home; Soma inspires us with knowledge seeking for the home.

Soma swells from the home and honours mind, Soma releases to the three states all anew through the sense activities (Stri) before consciousness. (860)

३. एवा नः सोम परिषिच्यमान आ पवस्व पूयमानः स्वस्ति ।
इन्द्रमा विश बृहता मदेन वर्धया वाचं जनया पुरंधिम् ॥

3. Soma speeds them up and binds them by sprinkling; he swells in the home and bestows to drink himself for welfare.

Indra bestows on the home great quantities of sense activities, fosters them, bestows them to sip by the people and satisfies the home. (861)

D. XI.

१. यद्द्याव इन्द्र ते शतं शतं भूमीरुत स्युः ।
न त्वा वज्रिन्त्सहस्रं सूर्या अनु न जातमष्ट रोदसी ॥

1. Those to whom Indra moves and bestows he destroys in hundreds in creatures to whom they are sewn (as it were), (i.e. brain cells). And now you move along the vigorous nerves to arouse thousands (of brain cells) to achieve (new creatures) from the source with heaven and earth (brain and sense organs). (862), (278)

Existing creatures are destroyed to some extent for new species (of a more developed type) to be ushered on the world scene.

२. आ पप्राथ महिना वृष्ण्या वृषन्विश्वा शविष्ठ शवसा ।
अस्माँ अव मघवन् गोमति व्रजे वज्रिं चित्राभिरुतिभिः ।।

2. In the beginnings (of creation) he rained many new creatures and nourished them; he rained them sense organs as desired by the body with might.

Indra favoured us with knowledge through sense activities in the enclosure and helped us in a variety of ways through the vigorous nerves. (863)

D. XII.

१. वयं घ त्वा सुतावन्त आपो न वृक्तबर्हिषः ।
पवित्रस्य प्रस्रवणेषु वृत्रहन्परि स्तोतार आसते ।।

1. (Indra!) You bestow on mind and control him; Activity bestows on him through the nerves spread out.

The rays (missiles) flow beneficially and nourish; on Vṛtra being struck down they go around praiseworthily to him and bestow existence. (864), (261)

२. स्वरन्ति त्वा सुते नरो वसो निरेक उक्थिनः ।।
कदा सुतं तृषाण ओक आ गमदिन्द्र स्वब्दीव वंसगः ।।

2. Indra! You gladden the mind of man yourself; you are alone spoken about down below for wealth (Vasu).

The mind is always thirsty; Indra comes from the head (pot) to him.

The bull (Indra) bestows by raining on him. (865)

३. कण्वेभिर्धृष्णवा धृषद्वाजं दर्षि सहस्रिणम् ।
पिशङ्गरूपं मघवन्विचर्षणे मक्षू गोमन्तमीमहे ।।

3. He bestows on the brain cells and supports them; he flows boldly in life-activity to bestow thousands of mighty (gifts).

He is diligently active about a variety of forms of creatures quickly through the sense activities which are greatly desired. (866)

D. XIII.

१. तरणिरित्सिषासति वाजं पुरंध्या युजा ।
आ व इन्द्रं पुरुहूतं नमे गिरा नेमिं तष्टेव सुद्रुवम् ।।

1. He releases to cross (ignorance) and bestows existence as desired; in life-activity he swells and unites and gladdens by letting to sip.

Indra much invoked bestows and is honoured on the hill; he hastens to arouse the summit (nemi of the brain) to bestow as he pleases. (867), (238)

२. न दुष्टुतिर्द्रविणोदेषु शस्यते न स्रेधन्तं रयिर्नशत् ।
सुशक्तिरिन्मघवं तुभ्यं मावते देष्णं यत्पार्ये दिवि ॥

2. The sense activities cross over eagerly above to unite with and bestow wealth (of perceptions) on the brain cells which do not commit an error to achieve them.

Indra (Maghavan) releases to the best of his ability [or he bestows wealth (magha) to the best of his ability]; both of you bestow understanding to me as desired by uniting with the yonder world in waking state. (868)

D. XIV.

१. तिस्रो वाच उदीरते गावो मिमन्ति धेनवः ।
हरिरेति कनिक्रदत् ॥

1. Above, all the three states are aroused for speech; the sense activity approaches us within to bestow milk (speech).

Consciousness releases the motley sense activity resoundingly. (869)

२. अभि ब्रह्मीरनूषत यह्वीर्ऋतस्य मातरः ।
मर्जयन्तीर्दिवः शिशुम् ॥

2. For speech to be attached to knowledge Ṛta hastens to release mother.

Mortals win it in the waking state of Mind. (870)

३. रायः समुद्रांश्चतुरोऽस्मभ्यं सोम विश्वतः ।
आ पवस्व सहस्रिणः ॥

3. Soma rules us and gladdens extensively, remaining hidden, through the sense organs.

He bestows thousands of mighty (ideas) to drink. (871)

D. XV.

१. सुतासो मधुमत्तमाः सोमा इन्द्राय मन्दिनः ।
पवित्रवन्तो अक्षरं देवान्गच्छन्तु वो मदाः ॥

1. Soma bestows on mind sense perceptions and desires and gladdens mightily through Indra.

Ideas (devas) come flowing in beneficially and bestow through sense activities. (872), (547)

> २. इन्दुरिन्द्राय पवत इति देवासो अब्रुवन् ।
> वाचस्पतिर्मखस्यते विश्वस्येशान ओजसः ॥

2. Indra moves to brain cells to bestow knowledge to drink; ideas are released for this, it is said.

The lord of speech unites vigorously with sense organs whom he rules vigorously. (873)

> ३. सहस्रधारः पवते समुद्रो वाचमीङ्खयः ।
> सोमस्पती रयीणां सखेन्द्रस्य दिवेदिवे ॥

3. Thousands of supports protect knowledge which is ocean-like which is shaken up by speech.

Soma protects it through wealth (of sense perceptions); Indra helps it day after day. (874)

D. XVI.

> १. पवित्रं ते विततं ब्रह्मणस्पते प्रभुर्गात्राणि पर्येषि विश्वतः ।
> अतप्ततनूर्न तदामो अश्नुते शृतास इद्वहन्तः सं तदाशत ॥

1. The limbs of the lord Soma (Brahmaṇaspati) go around the sense organs willingly; they are beneficial to a great extent.

Their paths are delicate; they are cooked on the hill in the home and conveyed within; all of them serve us. (alt) He warms up (cooks) delicately. (875), (565)

What (sense activities) are uncooked on the hill, after cooking he conveys them and serves all.

> २. तपोष्पवित्रं विततं दिवस्पदेऽर्चन्तो अस्य तन्तवो व्यस्थिरन् ।
> अवन्त्यस्य पवितारमाशवो दिवः पृष्ठमधि रोहन्ति तेजसा ॥

2. He fulfils us eagerly and beneficially to a large extent in the path of the waking state; he honours us, guides and bestows to fix up permanently.

He favours us and bestows the desire to cross and protects us in waking state; he satisfies us foremost, bestows for changes through the radiances. (876)

३. अरूरुचदुषसः पृश्निरग्रिय उक्षा मिमेति भुवनेषु वाजयुः ।
मायाविनो ममिरे अस्य मायया नृचक्षसः पितरो गर्भमा दधुः ॥

3. The Aśvins (ruru) also bestowed a variety of creatures at first on Uṣas to reveal; the motley sense activities approached the creatures to foster their growth swiftly (vājayu).

They bless us marvellously for our comfort by approaching us; they look up men and bestow marvellously on us; the father bestows on us from the source to arouse us. (877), (596)

D. XVII.

१. प्र मंहिष्ठाय गायत ऋताव्ने बृहते शुक्रशोचिषे ।
उपस्तुतासो अग्नये ।

1. The sense activities unite and nourish munificently; Ṛta bestows them desires; consciousness lights up the desires.

Praises are released to Agni. (878)

२. आ वंसते मघवा वीरवद्यशः समिद्धो द्युम्न्याहुतः ।
कुविन्नो अस्य सुमतिर्भवीयस्यच्छा वाजेभिरागमत् ॥

2. Indra bestows existence vigorously acclaiming splendour; he guides and offers fuel sticks (objects of perception) to heaven.

He bestows mightily on our sense organs; he arouses understanding in existence which he commands; he comes to us to support life-activity. (879)

D. XVIII.

१. तं ते मदं गृणीमसि वृषणं पृक्षु सासहिम् ।
उ लोककृत्नुमद्रिवो हरिश्रियम् ॥

1. The devotee desires sense activities for it; Indra nourishes them with food victoriously.

Consciousness produces prosperity on the hill for the worlds. (880), (383)

२. येन ज्योतींष्यायवे मनवे च विवेदिथ ।
मन्दानो अस्य बर्हिषो वि राजसि ॥

2. Consciousness rides on them (sense activities) and bestows them on the brain cells and mind.

He rules the mind from the brain cells through the nerves. (881)

३. तद्द्या चित्त उक्थिनोऽनु ष्टुवन्ति पूर्वथा ।
वृषपत्नीरपो जया दिवेदिवे ॥

3. That (consciousness) now reveals (acclaims) mind, praises and bestows as of old.

Activity showers on the path and guides it to gain day after day. (882)

D. XIX.

१. श्रुधी हवं तिरश्च्या इन्द्र यस्त्वा सपर्यति ।
सुवीर्यस्य गोमतो रायस्पूर्धि महाँ असि ॥

1. Indra! You strive to serve by uniting with the sense of hearing as oblation for understanding to cross over (ignorance).

You arouse vigour in us through sense activities which swell to satisfy; you are great. (883), (346)

२. यस्त इन्द्र नवीयसीं गिरं मन्द्रामजीजनत् ।
चिकित्विन्मनसं धियं प्रत्नामृतस्य पिप्युषीम् ॥

2. Indra strives; he strives afresh for speech (gira); he wins it pleasantly for us men.

He instructs mind by bestowing all mightily, satisfies and controls and also gives him eagerly to drink old (ideas) of mortals. (884)

३. तुम ष्टवाम यं गिर इन्द्रमुक्थानि वावृधुः ।
पुरूण्यस्य पौंस्या सिषासन्तो वनामहे ॥

3. You bestow eagerly on us; control us on the hill; you bestow praiseworthily for our growth (or by enveloping and arousing).

You strive abundantly for prosperity; you bestow eagerly great desires. (885)

BOOK III: CHAPTER I

D. I.

१. प्र त आश्विनीः पवमान धेनवो दिव्या असृग्रन्पयसा धरीमणि ।
प्रान्तरिक्षात्स्थाविरीस्ते असृक्षत ये त्वा मृजन्त्यृषिषाण वेधसः ॥

1. The Aśvins nourish the fickle mind bestowing milk (sense perceptions) divine which flows first to be drunk and gives support like to a jewel.

They fulfil within releasing him of old (Sthavira) ideas which flow in the home; you push away the old desires of the devotee and cleanse him. (886)

२. उभयतः पवमानस्य रश्मयो ध्रुवस्य सतः परि यन्ति केतवः ।
यदी पवित्रे अधि मृज्यते हरिः सत्ता नि योनौ कलशेषु सीदति ॥

2. The rays (of sense activities) from both brain cells and sense organs unite with the fickle mind for abiding existence; they go around guiding desires,

which graciously satisfy; the tawny consciousness puts them in order; in existence the rays (missiles) from the source reside in the head (pot). (887)

३. विश्वा धामानि विश्वचक्ष ऋभ्वसः प्रभोष्टे सतः परि यन्ति केतवः ।
व्यानशी पवसे सोम धर्मणा पतिर्विश्वस्य भुवनस्य राजसि ॥

3. The sense organs bestow on the home, the sense organs perceive the spinal nerves (Ṛbhus) and bestow on them which nourish as desired in existence and shine; they go around guiding the desires.

Soma nourishes from the home through them which are pervasive; the lord Indra of the sense organs of the creatures rules them in accordance with established rules (dharma). (888)

The Ṛbhus comprising the central spinal cord and the two long nerves at its sides are considered as terrestial in origin and are said to have reached heaven (head) first, after Indra.

D. II.

१. पवमानो अजीजनद्दिवश्चित्रं न तन्यतुम् ।
ज्योतिर्वैश्वानरं बृहत् ॥

1. The fickle mind wins a variety of ideas for man in waking. state whom the sense activities unite with and guide.

They are the light of Activity (cosmic man). (889), (484)

२. पवमान रसस्तव मदो राजन्नदुच्छुनः ।
वि वारमव्यमर्षति ॥

2. The fickle mind is the essence of sense perceptions; it is a demon to control.

It flows abidingly through gifts. (890)

३. पवमानस्य ते रसो दक्षो वि राजति द्युमान् ।
ज्योतिर्विश्वं स्वर्दृशे ॥

3. The fickle mind is their essence and satisfies us; he is controlled by heaven through the home.

Through the light of the cosmos i.e. consciousness it looks at heaven. (891)

D. III.

१. प्र यद्गावो न भूर्णयस्त्वेषा अयासो अक्रमुः ।
घ्नन्तः कृष्णामप त्वचम् ॥

1. The sense perceptions nourish it; it is agitated by desires; it is indefatigable in its manner (krama).

Activity cultivates it with wealth within; it sips the wealth. (892), (491)

२. सुवितस्य वनामहेति सेतुं दुराव्यम् ।
साह्याम दस्युमव्रतम् ॥

2. For his prosperity much desires from beyond are dammed (stored) for consumption which control him like a king.

The sense activities aid the steps (course) for his needs. (893)

३. शृण्वे वृष्टेरिव स्वनः पवमानस्य शुष्मिणः ।
चरन्ति विद्युतो दिवि ॥

3. They cook and bestow like rains resoundingly and they gush to mind mightily.

They go around like lightning in waking. (894)

४. आ पवस्व महीमिषं गोमदिन्दो हिरण्यवत् ।
अश्ववत्सोम वीरवत् ।

4. The sense activities open the eyes of the brain cells greatly themselves and bestow for drinking which the golden consciousness releases to them.

Soma bestows to them vigorously through prāṇa. (895)

५. पवस्व विश्वचर्षण आ मही रोदसी पृण ।
उषाः सूर्यो न रश्मिभिः ॥

5. He (Soma) is diligent with the sense organs and bestows them himself to drink and greatly nourishes heaven and earth (brain and sense organs).

He is eager for the rays of consciousness. (896)

६. परि णः शर्मयन्त्या धारया सोम विश्वतः ।
सरा रसेव विष्टपम् ॥

6. Soma! You protect and guide and support the sense organs, go around and bind them,

and stream along all over like the juices. (897)

D. IV.

१. आशुरर्ष बृहन्मते परि प्रियेण धाम्ना ।
यत्रा देवा इति ब्रुवन् ॥

1. He flows quickly, goes around bestowing (bṛhan) understanding fondly in the home.

There the ideas speak thus (as understanding). (898)

२. परिष्कृण्वन्ननिष्कृतं जनाय यातयन्निषः ।
वृष्टिं दिवः परि स्रव ॥

2. He produces desires from beyond and bestows them to sense activities (anna) at appointed places and guides the desires along the paths to men,

which flow around prominently in waking. (899)

३. अयं स यो दिवस्परि रघुयामा पवित्र आ ।
सिन्धोरूर्मा व्यक्षरत् ॥

3. He bestows the paths on them to go around in waking; they run in their courses beneficially.

The waves of Sindhu flow to us. (900)

४. सुत एति पवित्र आ त्विषिं दधान ओजसा ।
विचक्षाणो विरोचयन् ॥

4. The motley perceptions graciously bestow on the mind from the head vehemently and vigorously.

They perceive instantly and illuminate objects. (901)

५. आविवासन्परावतो अथो अर्वावतः सुतः ।
इन्द्राय सिच्यते मधु ।।

5. Riding in yonder world they bestow gifts of understanding and hasten to mind.

Indra moves, unites and discharges sense perceptions. (902)

६. समीचीना अनूषत हरिं हिन्वन्त्यद्रिभिः ।
इन्दुमिन्द्राय पीतये ।

6. Consciousness turns on to us and gets attached to us; he is known to stir up the desires on the hill.

Indra moves to the brain cells for them to drink. (903)

D. V.

१. हिन्वन्ति सूरमुस्रयः स्वसारो जामयस्पतिम् ।
महामिन्दुं महीयुवः ।।

1. The heroic Indra (bull) from his own resources arouses and bestows within, the lord of his progeny prāṇa.

He bestows by uniting with the sense organs (mahī) to the great brain cells. (904)

२. पवमान रुचारुचा देव देवेभ्यः सुतः ।
विश्वा वसून्या विश ।।

2. The fickle mind has ideas which shine or do not; the devas (ideas) arouse them.

Indra guides the home to the sense organs. (905)

३. आ पवमान सुष्टुतिं वृष्टिं देवेभ्यो दुवः ।
इषे पवस्व संयतम् ।।

3. The fickle mind is competent for the rain of ideas (devas) bestowed for his consumption.

Desires bestow themselves continuously to drink. (906)

D. VI.

१. जनस्य गोपा अजनिष्ट जागृविरग्निः सुदक्षः सुविताय नव्यसे ।
घृतप्रतीको बृहता दिविस्पृशा द्युमद्वि भाति भरतेभ्यः शुचिः ।।

1. The protector of men is desired by men; Agni satisfies them well in waking state; he strives afresh for our prosperity.

He nourishes us with clarified butter in the head, greatly in waking state by caressing us; he shines with sense activities from heaven; he supports them glowingly. (907), (Y. V. 15, 27)

२. त्वामग्ने अङ्गिरसो गुहा हितमन्वविन्दं च्छिश्रियाणं वनेवने ।
स जायसे मथ्यमानः सहो महत्त्वामाहुः सहसस्पुत्रमङ्गिरः ।।

2. Agni! You are an Aṅgirasa; you are known to bestow what is good on mind; you desire the prosperity of his forest of desires.

You bestow from the source; you churn the home; at the same time you make great offerings; the Aṅgiras are the sons of might. (908), (Y. V. 15, 28)

३. यज्ञस्य केतुं प्रथमं पुरोहितमग्निं नरस्त्रिषधस्थे समिन्धते ।
इन्द्रेण देवैः सरथं स बर्हिषि सीदन्नि होता यजथाय सुक्रतुः ।।

3. Desires are predominant in life-activity; Agni presides over them; he bestows and supports men's desires abidingly with sense objects (fuel sticks).

Indra goes in the same chariot as the devas; is seated over the nerves to preside below; he does good in life-activity. (909)

D. VII.

१. अयं वां मित्रावरुणया सुतः सोम ऋतावृधा ।
ममेदिह श्रुतं हवम् ।।

1. Śoma bestows the paths to Mitra and Varuṇa on mind; Ṛta fosters their growth.

We have here the oblations from hearing. (910), (Y. V. 7, 9)

२. राजानावनभिद्रुहा ध्रुवे सदस्युत्तमे ।
सहस्रस्थूण आशाते ।।

2. He releases desires from the source and establishes them firmly to be abiding in the home as most important.

He is the pillar for thousands of desires. (911)

३. ता सम्राजा घृतासुती आदित्या दानुनस्पती ।
सचेते अनवह्वरम् ।।

3. He is the sovereign lord of clarified butter for the mind; Aditi is the lord of brain cells.

He unites with the motley sense activities for new gifts. (912)

D. VIII.

१. इन्द्रो दधीचो अस्थभिर्वृत्राण्यप्रतिष्कुतः ।
जघान नवतीर्नव ॥

1. Indra abidingly supports clarified butter and counteracts Vṛtra (inertia).

He strikes him down to cross over to newer and newer creatures. (913)

२. इच्छन्नश्वस्य यच्छिरः पर्वतेष्वपश्रितम् ।
तद्विदच्छर्यणावति ॥

2. Prāṇa desires to control us for a long time cooking the desires on the hill; he scatters them.

He goes around knowledge to acquaint us with. (914)

३. अत्राह गोरमन्वत नाम त्वष्टुरपीच्यम् ।
इत्था चन्द्रमसो गृहे ॥

3. Indeed he who support sense activities to gladden us with knowledge is named Tvaṣṭṛ who remains concealed.

Thus the home bestows on mind. (915)

D. IX.

१. इयं वामस्य मन्मन इन्द्राग्नी पूर्व्यस्तुतिः ।
अभ्राद्वृष्टिरिवाजनि ॥

1. This pleasant mind in the home was praised (instituted) in ancient times by Indra and Agni.

The sky (heaven) bestowed him; the rains (of gifts) released him to life-activity. (916)

२. शृणुतं जरितुर्हवमिन्द्राग्नी वनतं गिरः ।
ईशाना पिप्यतं धियः ॥

2. Indra-Agni cook desires (or as desired) as oblations for the devotee and bestow them on sense activities on the hill.

They rule them for the devotee to drink as desired to satisfaction. (917)

३. मा पापत्वाय नो नरेन्द्राग्नी माभिशस्तये ।
मा नो रीरधतं निदे ॥

3. Let not man sin against Indra-Agni; let them not curse us.

Release (gifts) to the home; we are your subjects in the home, as desired by us. (918)

D. X.

१. पवस्व दक्षसाधनो देवेभ्यः पीतये हरे ।
मरुद्भ्यो वायवे मदः ॥

1. The devas succeed in satisfying us by themselves bestowing to drink and they swell over to the tawny consciousness.

Ideas (Maruts) are bestowed on the brain cells through sense activities. (919), (474)

२. सं देवैः शोभते वृषा कविर्योनावधि प्रियः ।
पवमानो अदाभ्यः ॥

2. All devas are beautiful; Agni rains them from the source in kindness to satisfy us.

The fickle mind is indestructible. (920)

३. पवमान धिया हितो३ऽभि योनिं कनिक्रदत् ।
धर्मणा वायुमारुहः ॥

3. The fickle mind satisfies us with welfare, imploring piteously to the source.

He ascends to the sense activities through the nerves. (921)

D. XI.

१. तवाहं सोम रारण सख्य इन्दो दिवेदिवे ।
पुरूणि बभ्रो नि चरन्ति मामव परिधीं रति ताँ इहि ॥

1. Soma bestows and gladdens him (mind) in waking; the brain cells help him day after day.

The tawny consciousness goes around abundantly; blesses us in the enclosure; gives us enjoyment as desired here. (922), (516)

२. तवाहं नक्तमुत सोम ते दिवा दुहानो बभ्र ऊधनि ।
घृणा तपन्तमति सूर्यं परःशकुना इव पप्तिम ॥

2. He (consciousness) carries away ignorance; also Soma, milk (sense perceptions) from the sky nourishes us in waking.

Knowledge warms up the devotee within; consciousness from beyond, like a good omen, protects it as lord. (923)

D. XII.

१. पुनानो अक्रमीदभि विश्वा मृधो विचर्षणिः ।
शुम्भन्ति विप्रं धीतिभिः ॥

1. Consciousness repeatedly and with diligence proceeds to the sense organs without weariness.

He adorns us within and inspires us with understanding. (924), (488)

२. आ योनिमरुणो रुहद्गमदिन्द्रो वृषा सुतम् ।
ध्रुवे सदसि सीदतु ॥

2. Consciousness from the source rises up as Indra comes and rains to mind.

He is abidingly bound to the home and resides in it. (925)

३. नू नो रयिं महामिन्दोऽस्मभ्यं सोम विश्वतः ।
आ पवस्व सहस्रिणम् ॥

3. Now Soma bestows wealth from our sense organs on the great brain cells.

He bestows thousands of mighty things (ideas) himself to drink. (926)

D. XIII.

१. पिबा सोममिन्द्र मदन्तु त्वा यं ते सुषाव हर्यश्वाद्रिः ।
सोतुर्बाहुभ्यां सुयतो नार्वा ॥

1. Soma! You drink sense activities through Indra; you control them and bestow them eagerly before consciousness (Haryaśva) on the hill.

With Soma juice in your hands you arouse men to unite with them and bestow them. (927), (398)

२. यस्ते मदो युज्यश्चारुरस्ति येन वृत्राणि हर्यश्व हंसि ।
स त्वामिन्द्र प्रभूवसो ममत्तु ॥

2. You strive for sense perceptions for them to unite with and gladden them, and you envelop them; consciousness indeed supports.

You bestow them on Indra to nourish us and bestow existence on us. (928)

३. बोधा सु मे मघवन्वाचमेमां यां ते वसिष्ठो अर्चति प्रशस्तिम् ।
इमा ब्रह्म सधमादे जुषस्व ॥

3. (Soma!) You arouse us to understanding; Indra (Maghavan) who is the path here for speech desires to reside, whom you honour and praise.

Here Knowledge as a comrade himself rejoices us. (929)

D. XIV.

१. विश्वाः पृतना अभिभूतरं नरः सजूस्ततक्षुरिन्द्रं जजनुश्च राजसे ।
क्रत्वे वरे स्थेमन्यामुरीमुतोग्रमोजिष्ठं तरसं तरस्विनम् ॥

1. The sense organs are ancient and are for crossing over to existence for men; nourishment (sense activities) from Activity attach themselves to Indra who, born with creation controls and bestows them.

They produce gifts abidingly for mind extensively, also for the brain (village) vigorously, all for crossing over (ignorance); Aśvins are the ferry. (930)

२. नेमिं नमन्ति चक्षसा मेषं विप्रा अभिस्वरे ।
सुदीतयो वो अद्रुहोऽपि कर्णे तरस्विनः समृक्वभिः ॥

2. The Aśvins honour the summit (rim of the brain), look on and bestow on it and inspire it towards heaven.

They arouse and bestow without hurting for hearing (ears) for crossing over or to singing (speech) whatever it be. (931)

३. समु रेभासो अस्वरन्निन्द्रं सोमस्य पीतये ।
स्वः पतिर्यदी वृधे धृतव्रतो ह्योजसा समूतिभिः ॥

3. They are all released resoundingly from heaven by Indra; they drink from Soma (or drink Soma juice).

The lord himself fosters their growth because of the duty (vow) for clarified butter; he helps them all vigorously from heaven. (932)

D. XV.

१. यो राजा चर्षणीनां याता रथेभिरध्रिगुः ।
विश्वासां तरुता पृतनानां ज्येष्ठं यो वृत्रहा गृणे ॥

1. Indra busily controls them; supports the paths to the sense organs irresistably.

Indra (the eldest) makes Vṛtra (inertia) abandon the devotee in the fights swiftly and confidently. (933)

२. इन्द्रं तं शुम्भ पुरुहन्मन्नवसे यस्य द्विता विधर्तरि ।
हस्तेन वज्रः प्रति धायि दर्शतो महां देवो न सूर्यः ॥

2. Indra desires our welfare; he destroys abundantly thinking of releasing new ones (ideas, creatures); he releases by supporting his second (prāṇa).

He nourishes by his vigorous hands (nerves); he bestows; ideas (devas) visit the great one, are bound to him by associating with him extensively. (934)

D. XVI.

१. परि प्रिया दिवः कविर्वयांसि नप्त्योर्हितः ।
स्वानैर्याति कविक्रतुः ॥

1. He goes around in kindness in waking for Agni (wise one) to support us and for extensive welfare to sense organs (descendants).

Pantingly he wends his course to Agni for inspiration (Kratu). (935)

२. स सूनुर्मातरा शुचिर्जातो जाते अरोचयत् ।
महान्मही ऋतावृधा ॥

2. The mother releases to mind (Son) flaming down from the source; then ascends up to the source.

The great one fosters the growth through the sense organs (mahī) through Ṛta. (936)

३. प्रप्र क्षयाय पन्यसे जनाय जुष्टो अद्रुहः ।
वीत्यर्ष पनिष्टये ॥

3. She strives admirably for men in the home (or if loss is suffered) to nourish and fulfil, for eager births (of ideas) without hurting.

She flows with vigour admirably willingly. (937)

D. XVII.

१. त्वं ह्या३ङ्ग दैव्यं पवमान जनिमानि द्युमत्तमः ।
अमृतत्वाय घोषयन् ॥

1. (Indra!) You are a limb of heaven, divine; you bestow to the home to drink; you bestow to those down below from the source; our desires are heavenly.

You move to mortals (move from the immortal source), guide and proclaim. (938), (583)

२. येना नवग्वा दध्यङ्ङपोर्णुते येन विप्रास आपिरे ।
देवानां सुम्ने अमृतस्य चारुणो येन श्रवांस्याशत ॥

2. The curds (sense reactions) are an appendage of the nine-fold activity (rays) (namely 7 of Activity plus two of Aśvins); they arise from the surging waves of Activity; they bestow inspiration and release as associates.

The devas who are splendorous to mortals and gladden them, desire to support the cooking and bestowing. (939)

D. XVIII.

१. सोमः पुनान ऊर्मिणाव्यं वारं वि धावति ।
अग्रे वाचः पवमानः कनिक्रदत् ॥

1. Soma in waves repeatedly bestows on us gifts through which he gives us understanding,

at first through speech, bestowing and protecting it in the home resoundingly, (940), (572)

२. धीभिर्मृजन्ति वाजिनं वने क्रीडन्तमत्यविम् ।
अभि त्रिपृष्ठं मतयः समस्वरन् ॥

2. He supports Knowledge; cleanses them in life-activity through desires; sports with prāṇa within to favour us.

He hastens to our three states foremost and gladdens them equally himself. (941)

३. असर्जि कलशां अभि मीढ्वांत्सप्तिर्न वाजयुः ।
पुनानो वाचं जनयन्नसिष्यदत् ॥

3. He surges towards the brain (head) and races to bestow rewards through the seven-aspected activity.

He guides the birth of speech repeatedly and bestows our desires. (942)

It is said here that Soma, a heavenly being guides speech through the brain. It is not the mind which guides it. It is only a witness to the speech and of course it imbibes all that is said.

Mind plays its part only in disembling which the brain cannot and will not do. It is on this basis that lie detectors are made use of.

D. XIX.

१. सोमः पवते जनिता मतीनां जनिता दिवो जनिता पृथिव्याः ।
जनिताग्नेर्जनिता सूर्यस्य जनितेन्द्रस्य जनितोत विष्णोः ॥

1. Soma protects understanding born in men; understanding takes birth in waking state; it is born of the sense organs or from the world.

It takes birth from Agni; revealed by consciousness through Indra, it arises also from Viṣṇu. (943), (527)

२. ब्रह्मा देवानां पदवीः कवीनामृषिर्विप्राणां महिषो मृगाणाम् ।
श्येनो गृध्राणां स्वधितिर्वनानां सोमः पवित्रमत्येति रेभन् ॥

2. Knowledge is the path of ideas (devas); Agni (poet) inspires it through the ṛṣis and gladdens our desires through the sense organs (mṛga).

Soma smells like a vulture himself and satisfies our desires graciously through the motley sense perceptions resoundingly. (944)

३. प्रावीविपद्वाच ऊर्मिं न सिन्धुर्गिर स्तोमान्पवमानो मनीषाः ।
अन्तः पश्यन्वृजनेमावराण्या तिष्ठति वृषभो गोषु जानन् ॥

3. Sindhu skilfully (prāvī) scatters speech in waves from the brain (hill) which the mind desires and praises the home.

Indra (bull) perceives it in the enclosure and bestows it excellently at his wish through sense activities from the source. (945)

D. XX.

१. अग्निं वो वृधन्तमध्वराणां पुरूतमम् ।
अच्छा नप्त्रे सहस्वते ॥

1. Agni bestows abundant desires in life-activity within and fosters their growth.

And overcomes the sense organs nearby for Knowledge. (946), (21)

२. अयं यथा न आभुवत्त्वष्टा रूपेव तक्ष्या ।
अस्य क्रत्वा यशस्वतः ॥

2. He (Agni) creates the paths (for Knowledge) as Tvaṣṭṛ (sense of touch) carved out forms of creatures.

He creates and bestows understanding on us splendidly. (947)

३. अयं विश्वा अभि श्रियोऽग्निर्देवेषु पत्यते ।
आ वाजैरुप नो गमत् ॥

3. The path (for Knowledge) is the sense organs; Agni unites with the path of the devas for prosperity.

He comes to us from above for the sake of life-activity. (948)

D. XXI.

१. इममिन्द्र सुतं पिब ज्येष्ठममर्त्यं मदम् ।
शुक्रस्य त्वाभ्यक्षरन्धारा ऋतस्य सादने ॥

1. Here, the mind drinks sense perceptions from Indra who is the eldest to us mortals.

Consciousness (śukra) runs to support him; Ṛta releases the gifts. (949)

२. न किष्ट्वद्रथीतरो हरी यदिन्द्र यच्छसे ।
न किष्ट्वानु मज्मना न किः स्वश्व आनशे ॥

2. The charioteer Indra, at the desire of the brain expressed to him, crosses over to the tawny consciousness, through whom he controls and bestows.

Alt. On the brain (head) expressing its desire for the sense organs (vehicles) the tawny consciousness crosses over, whom Indra controls, and bestows.

And now, in his greatness he himself arouses the brain and lets him achieve through Prāṇa. (950)

३. इन्द्राय नूनमर्चतोक्थानि च ब्रवीतन ।
सुता अमत्सुरिन्दवो ज्येष्ठं नमस्यता सहः ॥

3. And now Indra is honoured and praised and also he announces to guide.

He the eldest (Indra) arouses the mind, and bestows to him from the brain cells; he honours him and unites him victoriously. (951)

D. XXII.

१. इन्द्र जुषस्व प्र वहा याहि शूर हरिह ।
पिबा सुतस्य मतिर्न मधोश्चकानश्चारुर्मदाय ॥

1. Indra himself rejoices to convey nourishment; heroically he moves and indeed arouses the tawny consciousness or he moves, arouses it (nourishment) and conveys it here.

The mind drinks it for understanding; the sweet sense perceptions also satisfy him and please him to rejoice. (952)

२. इन्द्र जठरं नव्यं न पृणस्व मधोर्दिवो न ।
अस्य सुतस्य स्वा३र्नोप त्वा मदाः सुवाचो अस्थुः ॥

2. Indra nourishes the brain cells afresh himself with wealth in waking state.

He himself abidingly arouses our mind to the good speech (gifts) of sense perceptions in waves from above. (953)

३. इन्द्रस्तुराषाण्मित्रो न जघान वृत्रं यतिर्न ।
बिभेद वलं भृगुर्न ससाहे शत्रून्मदे सोमस्य ॥

3. Indra strikes down Vṛtra (inertia) and overcomes him to bestow gifts (Sau) on the brain (Mitra) for him to cross over ignorance.

Without differentiation he supports the brain cells (vala) through the sense organs (gu) and overcomes the enemies of sense activities for the sake of Soma. (954)

BOOK III: CHAPTER II

D. I.

१. गोवित्पवस्व वसुविद्धिरण्यविद्रेतोधा इन्दो भुवनेष्वर्पितः ।
त्वं सुवीरो असि सोम विश्ववित्तं त्वा नर उप गिरेम आसते ॥

1. The father of heaven lets streams of rays to the brain cells himself to acquaint them with sense activities to drink and gladden them with knowledge of wealth (Vasu).

Soma! You are acquainted with the sense organs and so you arouse them vigorously and bestow them on the brain (hill) of man above. (955)

२. त्वं नृचक्षा असि सोम विश्वतः पवमान वृषभ ता वि धावसि ।
स नः पवस्व वसुमद्धिरण्यवद्वयं स्याम भुवनेषु जीवसे ॥

2. Soma! You look at man; you make the brain (home) known to the fickle mind through Indra (bull) who resides to bestow him.

You bestow on him wealth (vasu) yourself as gifts to drink and support and satisfy both the brain cells and sense organs, through sense activities, of the creatures during their life-time. (956)

३. ईशान इमा भुवनानि ईयसे युजान इन्दो हरितः सुपर्ण्यः ।
तास्ते क्षरन्तु मधुमद्घृतं पयस्तव व्रते सोम तिष्ठन्तु कृष्टयः ॥

3. Here you rule the creatures; you strive to unite the brain cells to the source and convey the golden-winged consciousness to them.

Sweet sense perceptions and clarified butter flow into their home which they drink; Soma as per his vow (duty) cultivates them as he desires. (957)

D. II.

१. पवमानस्य विश्ववित्प्र ते सर्गा असृक्षत ।
सूर्यस्येव न रश्मयः ॥

1. Our mind is acquainted with the sense organs; they flow to him from the brain (home) in surges, and nourish him,

as consciousness does with his rays. (958)

२. केतुं कृण्वं दिवस्परि विश्वा रूपाभ्यर्षसि ।
समुद्रः सोम पिन्वसे ॥

2. Soma produces desires and bestows; he goes around in waking state to sense organs and flows to forms of objects.

Soma bestows joy profusely. (959)

३. जज्ञानो वाचमिष्यसि पवमान विधर्मणि ।
क्रन्दं देवो न सूर्यः ॥

3. The mind desires speech in accordance with dharma, as Knowledge is derived (born) through it.

Ideas (devas) produce it in the home like consciousness. (960)

D. III.

१. प्र सोमासो अधन्विषुः पवमानास इन्दवः ।
श्रीणाना अप्सु वृञ्जते ॥

1. Soma bestows nourishment by releasing wealth through the missiles (of sense activities); the brain cells bestow them on the fickle mind.

Activity cooks the sense activities arouses (the mind) bestows and pleases it. (961)

२. अभि गावो अधन्विषुरापो न प्रवता यतीः ।
पुनाना इन्द्रमाशत ॥

2. Activity bestows wealth through the rays (missiles) of sense activities which move to him (mind) and nourishes him with Knowledge.

Indra bestows on him hundreds of items repeatedly. (962)

३. प्र पवमान धन्वसि सोमेन्द्राय मादनः ।
नृभिर्यतो वि नीयसे ॥

3. You bestow wealth to nourish the mind and bind him to it; Soma bestows wealth through Indra.

Through striving to guide, you support men by uniting with them. (963)

४. इन्दो यदद्रिभिः सुतः पवित्रं परिदीयसे ।
अरमिन्द्रस्य धाम्ने ॥

4. He who is nourished by the brain cells on the hill is mind, which the enclosure strives for beneficially.

He is gladdened in Indra's home. (964)

५. त्वं सोम नृमादनः पवस्व चर्षणीधृतिः ।
सस्निर्यो अनुमाद्यः ॥

5. Soma! You bestow wealth on man; you consider actively and bestow drinks yorself.

You are hailed by the brain cells (sasa) below. (965)

६. पवस्व वृत्रहन्तम उक्थेभिरनुमाद्यः ।
शुचिः पावको अद्भुतः ॥

6. You strike down Vṛtra (inertia) as desired and yourself bestow to drink; you support praiseworthily those who hail, speedily.

You are glowing, purifying and wonderful. (966)

७. शुचिः पावक उच्यते सोमः सुतः स मधुमान् ।
देवावीरघशंसहा ॥

7. Soma! Flaming and purifying, you are accustomed to unite with mind and bestow sweet perceptions from the home.

The vigour of the deva is indeed praised. (967)

D. IV.

१. प्र कविर्देववीतयेऽव्या वारेभिरव्यत ।
साह्वान्विश्वा अभि स्पृधः ॥

1. Soma! Agni nourishes you with ideas desired by you; the Aśvins support you with wealth abidingly.

At the call of the sense organs you release; you gain (spṛ) from them and bestow. (968)

२. स हि ष्मा जरितृभ्य आ वाजं गोमन्तमिन्वति ।
पवमानः सहस्रिणम् ॥

2. In the same manner you bestow the desires of the devotee; in life-activity you bestow understanding mightily through sense perceptions within.

You bestow mightily in thousands on the brain (home) to drink. (969)

३. परि विश्वानि चेतसा मृज्यसे पवसे मती ।
स नः सोम श्रवो विदः ॥

3. You go around the sense organs and bestow on mind, you strive to put him in order through understanding from the home to drink.

Soma bestows gifts, cooks and bestows Knowledge. (970)

४. अभ्यर्ष बृहद्यशो मघवद्भ्यो ध्रुवं रयिम् ।
इषं स्तोतृभ्य आ भरः ॥

4. Indra flows fearlessly to bestow wealth abidingly with great splendour.

He supports our desires praiseworthily. (971)

५. त्वं राजेव सुव्रतो गिरः सोमाविवेशिथ ।
पुनानो वह्ने अद्भुत ॥

5. Indra! You are like a king with good duties (vows) on the hill; through you Soma enters.

You convey him repeatedly wonderfully. (972)

६. स वह्निरप्सु दुष्टरो मृज्यमानो गभस्त्योः ।
सोमश्चमूषु सीदति ॥

6. And you convey Activity to arouse and release warmly for consumption; you put the home in order with your hands (nerves).

Soma sips the sense organs from the home. (973)

७. क्रीडुर्मखो न मंहयुः पवित्रं सोम गच्छसि ।
दधत्स्तोत्रे सुवीर्यम् ॥

7. To sport with extensively and vigorously Soma goes to honour beneficent prāṇa,

who bestows praiseworthily arousing vigour in him.

Alt. Soma sports with extensively and vigorously, bestows abundantly (maṁha) by uniting, comes to us beneficially.

He bestows arousing vigour praiseworthily. (974)

D. V.

१. यवंयवं नो अन्धसा पुष्टंपुष्टं परि स्रव ।
विश्वा च सोम सौभगा ॥

1. He releases ignorance from cell after cell by going behind everyone of them and flows around to them.

He (Soma) bestows welfare on the home also. (975)

२. इन्दो यथा तव स्तवो यथा ते जातमन्धसः ।
नि बर्हिषि प्रिये सदः ॥

2. The brain cells are praised like Soma; they are likewise born from the source and release ignorance.

They are seated on the nerves below willingly. (976)

३. उत नो गोविदश्ववित्पवस्व सोमान्धसा ।
मक्षूतमेभिरहभिः ॥

3. To know the sense activities he is acquainted by prāṇa and he himself bestows them to drink also; Soma releases ignorance from us.

He removes (separates) distress quickly. (977)

४. यो जिनाति न जीयते हन्ति शत्रुमभीत्य ।
स पवस्व सहस्रजित् ॥

4. He is an overcomer; he unites to win; strikes down foes causing fear.

He wins thousands (of ideas) and himself bestows them to drink. (978)

D. VI.

१. यास्ते धारा मधुश्चुतोऽसृग्रमिन्द ऊतये ।
ताभिः पवित्रमासदः ॥

1. He (Soma) moves into the home to support the sweet perceptions to drip; flows first to the brain cells to help.

He bestows on them beneficially in the home. (979)

२. सो अर्षेन्द्राय पीतये तिरो वाराण्यव्यया ।
सीदन्नृतस्य योनिमा ॥

2. Soma! You flow to Indra to bestow; you cross over into the enclosure to the Aśvins to drink (sense activities).

You dwell or rest at the source of men to bestow (maa). (980)

३. त्वं सोम परि स्रव स्वादिष्ठो अङ्गिरोभ्यः ।
वरिवोविद्घृतं पयः ॥

3. Soma! You flow around; the Aṅgiras bestow of their own accord.

They bestow in freedom Knowledge to drink. (981)

D. VII.

१. तव श्रियो वर्ष्यस्येव विद्युतोऽग्नेश्चिकित्र उषसामिवेतयः ।
यदोषधीरभिसृष्टो वनानि च परि स्वयं चिनुषे अन्नमासनि ॥

1. Soma! You rain prosperity with lightning like speed; Agni supports knowingly; Uṣas approaches the devotee.

What you produce eagerly and lastingly are desires; also you go round yourself to control perceptions (cin) eagerly and bestow sense activities as gift. (982)

२. वातोपजूत इषितो वशाँ अनु तृषु यदन्ना वेविषद्वितिष्ठसे ।
आ ते यतन्ते रथ्यो३यथा पृथक् शर्धांस्यग्ने अजरस्य धक्षतः ॥

2. And now you urge desires through the nerves above; (satisfy the sense activities (anna) by bestowing to work on both (the brain cells and sense organs) and bestow on them as desired.

They unite with the sense organs (vehicles) within separately (severally); Agni satisfies them boldly ever fresh. (983)

३. मेधाकारं विदथस्य प्रसाधनमग्निं होतारं परिभूतरं मतिम् ।
त्वामर्भस्य हविषः समानमित्त्वां महो वृणते नान्यं त्वत् ॥

3. Agni commands and obtains nourishment for the sake of understanding, presides and gladdens us; goes around to cross over (ignorance) in existence through understanding.

He bestows oblations on insignificant men like us; he approaches us as an equal; the sense activities envelop us greatly (or you choose us greatly); there is no one like you. (984)

D. VIII.

१. पुरूरुणा चिद्ध्यस्त्यवो नूनं वां वरुण ।
मित्र वंसि वां सुमतिम् ॥

1. The mind resoundingly sips abundantly from the brain cells now that Varuṇa (outer world) has bestowed.

The brain (Mitra) bestows and supports the bestowal of understanding to us. (985)

२. ता वां सम्यगद्रुह्वाणेषमश्याम धाम च ।
वयं वां मित्रा स्याम ॥

2. He together with sense activities hastens to us on call at our desire, also to the home.

The brain (Mitra) bestows on us them. (986)

३. पातं नो मित्रा पायुभिरुत त्रायेथां सुत्रात्रा ।
साह्याम दस्यूं तनूभिः ॥

3. The brain (Mitra) fulfils our desires; supports our drinking both (sense activities and perceptions); supports the motley sense activities; supports the connecting thread (Indra).

He assists us in our wants delicately. (987)

D. IX.

१. उत्तिष्ठन्नोजसा सह पीत्वा शिप्रे अवेपयः ।
सोममिन्द्र चमू सुतम् ॥

1. Soma at his wish bestows nourishment (food) also and drinks together with us; inspires us in mouthfuls speedily.

The mind caresses (sips) Soma through Indra. (988)

२. अनु त्वा रोदसी उभे स्पर्धमानमददेताम् ।
इन्द्र यद्दस्युहाभवः ॥

2. Now you bestow on both brain and sense organs rivalling (for gifts) the motley sense activities and honouring them release.

Indra infers their wants in existence. (989)

३. वाचमष्टापदीमहं नवस्रक्तिमृतावृधम् ।
इन्द्रात्परितन्वं ममे ॥

3. Speech is gained in 8 steps in waking state; it grows from nine corners of mortals.

Indra goes around to them; guides and bestows speech. (990)

The organs instrumental in producing speech are: (1) brain; (2) nerves; (3) mouth (roof); (4) tongue; (5) lips; (6) teeth; (7) lungs; (8) larynx; (9) throat. Eight steps of activities take place from among them.

D. X.

१. इन्द्राग्नी युवामिमे३ऽभि स्तोमा अनूषत ।
पिबतं शम्भुवा सुतम् ॥

1. Indra-Agni approach our mind to whom he is praiseworthily attached.

The mind toils to drink the desires bestowed by them in existence. (991)

२. या वां सन्ति पुरुस्पृहो नियुतो दाशुषे नरा ।
इन्द्राग्नी ताभिरा गतम् ॥

2. Indra-Agni move to bestow on us abundant gifts eagerly and serve myriads (of brain cells) of men.

Indra-Agni have come here to support them. (992)

३. ताभिरा गच्छतं नरोपेदं सवनं सुतम् ।
इन्द्राग्नी सोमपीतये ॥

3. They have come to support men's desires from above and the desires of mind.

Soma swells over to Indra Agni. (993)

D. XI.

१. अर्षा सोम द्युमत्तमोऽभि द्रोणानि रोरुवत् ।
सीदन्योनौ वनेष्वा ॥

1. Soma flows from heaven for our desires and to release understanding in the brain (head) resoundingly.

From his seat in the source he bestows desires as we wish. (994), (503)

२. अप्सा इन्द्राय वायवे वरुणाय मरुद्भ्यः ।
सोमा अर्षन्तु विष्णवे ॥

2. Activity bestows ideas (Maruts) of the outer world and he releases them through the nerves.

Soma flows within to work freshly. (995)

३. इषं तोकाय नो दधदस्मभ्यं सोम विश्वतः ।
आ पवस्व सहस्रिणम् ॥

3. Soma moves towards the wishes of the sense organs (descendants) and bestows on us knowledge (through them) in the home.

He bestows for drinking thousands of mighty (ideas). (996)

D. XII.

१. सोम उ ष्वाणः सोतृभिरधि ष्णुभिरवीनाम् ।
अश्वयेव हरिता याति धारया मन्द्रया याति धारया ।।

1. Soma is eager after desires; he supports Soma pressing in the brain which he supports and blesses.

Like a horse he conveys it, supports the path and streams along pleasantly. (997), (515)

२. अनूपे गोमान् गोभिरक्षाः सोमो दुग्धाभिरक्षाः ।
समुद्रं न संवरणान्यग्मन्मन्दी मदाय तोशते ।।

2. Soma now bestows sense activities above; supports them in the home; supports sense perceptions in the home.

And he gladdens us, guides sense activities in the enclosure to mind and gladdens and satisfies him. (998)

D. XIII.

१. यत्सोम चित्रमुक्थ्यं दिव्यं पार्थिवं वसु ।
तन्नः पुनान आ भर ।।

1. Soma unites praiseworthily a variety of ideas with terrestial objects for wealth.

He supports food (sense perceptions) repeatedly. (999)

२. वृषा पुनान आयूंषि स्तनयन्नधि बर्हिषि ।
हरिः सन्योनिमासदः ।।

2. He showers them repeatedly in life from his bosom, guides them and satisfies through the nerves.

The tawny consciousness from our source bestows gifts on the home. (1000)

३. युवं हि स्थः स्वःपती इन्द्रश्च सोम गोपती ।
ईशाना पिप्यतं धियः ।।

3. He himself arouses mind abidingly as his lord; Indra also is the lord of sense activities with Soma.

They rule them; also let them be drunk as desired and satisfy. (1001)

D. XIV.

१. इन्द्रो मदाय वावृधे शवसे वृत्रहा नृभिः ।
तमिन्महत्स्वाजिषूतिमर्भे हवामहे स वाजेषु प्र नोऽविषत् ।।

1. Indra bestows on us joyously and fosters growth with might; Vṛtra flees from men.

He wins much mighty desires himself helping poor us with great oblations and nourishes us with sense activities in life and works. (1002), (411)

२. असि हि वीर सेन्योऽसि भूरि पराददिः ।
असि दभ्रस्य चिद्वृधो यजमानाय शिक्षसि सुन्वते भूरि ते वसु ॥

2. He is vigorous in arousing us; he bestows abundant troops (of ideas) from beyond.

You foster the growth of the mind of insignificant men like us; as master you teach the devotees like us and bestow abundant wealth. (1003)

३. यदुदीरत आजयो धृष्णवे धीयते धनम् ।
युङ्क्षवा मदच्युता हरी कं हनः कं वसौ दधोऽस्मां इन्द्र वसौ दधः ॥

3. You win what you aroused water and courageously united with wealth (sense perceptions) for understanding.

You unite with the home to bestow sense perceptions to drip; you indeed release desires (Kam) and indeed from heaven, bestow wealth; Indra has bestowed on us a home. (1004), (414)

D. XV.

१. स्वादोरित्था विषूवतो मधोः पिबन्ति गौर्यः ।
या इन्द्रेण सयावरीर्वृष्णा मदन्ति शोभथा वस्वीरनु स्वराज्यम् ॥

1. The sweet perceptions are released thus; the sweet perceptions work for (or servants of) understanding by drinking in from sense organs (buffalo).

Indra moves and bestows them on the brain cells extensively and vigorously; the perceptions grace the home and now he seeks his own region. (1005)

२. ता अस्य पृशनायुवः सोमं श्रीणन्ति पृश्नयः ।
प्रिया इन्द्रस्य धेनवो वज्रं हिन्वन्ति सायकं वस्वीरनु स्वराज्यम् ॥

2. Now Soma cooks them variously and caresses the mind with them.

Indra bestows the sense perceptions with love through the vigorous nerves, arouses (the cells) within to unyoke as desired, in the home and now he seeks his own region. (1006)

३. ता अस्य नमसा सहः सपर्यन्ति प्रचेतसः ।
व्रतान्यस्य सश्चिरे पुरूणि पूर्वचित्तये वस्वीरनु स्वाराज्यम् ।।

3. He honours us and at the same time bestows nourishment on the mind.

It is his long-standing duty (vow) to the brain cells; he swells over to the mind and bestows abundantly from the home and now he seeks his own region. (1007)

D. XVI.

१. असाव्यंशुर्मदायाप्सु दक्षो गिरिष्ठाः ।
श्युनो न योनिमासदत् ।।

1. (Indra) bestows on us sense activities from Activity quickly and satisfies the desires of the brain (hill).

He watches our home like a hawk from the source. (1008), (473)

२. शुभ्रमन्धो देववातमप्सु धौतं नृभि सुतम् ।
स्वदन्ति गावः पयोभिः ।।

2. Activity cleans up ignorance with knowledge through ideas and the nerves and purifies the minds of men.

The (cells) within drink sweet perceptions from the sense activities. (1009)

३. आदीमश्व न हेतारमशूशुभन्नमृताय ।
मधो रसं सधमादे ।

3. In ancient times prāṇa was not the cause of delighting (the manifestations), (plants), the sense activities from the immortal world swelled to them for welfare.

The sense perception touch was the comrade of the sap. (1010)

The plant world in the beginnings of creation is here referred to. The sense perceptions, primarily the sense of differentiation and the sense of touch from heaven maintained the plant world in conjunction with the sap from the world of matter i.e. earth, water, air and sun. Prāṇa is associated only with mobile life.

D. XVII.

१. अभि द्युम्नं बृहद्यश इषस्पते दिदीहि देव देवयुम् ।
वि कोशं मध्यमं युव ।।

1. The lord of desires, Soma, bestows and shines through his ideas to the devotees to bestow wealth excellently,

through the brain (head) on mind with sense perceptions controlled by him. (1011), (579)

२. आ वच्यस्व सुदक्ष चम्वोः सुतो विशां वह्निर्न विश्पतिः ।
वृष्टिं दिवः पवस्व रीतिमपो जिन्वन् गविष्टये धियः ॥

2. The lord of the home himself moves towards speech to arouse satisfaction in the mind by sipping from the home.

He rains it in waking state; he himself bestows it to be drunk, what Activity has released, which he willingly wins from sense activities as desired and satisfies. (1012)

D. XVIII.

१. प्राणा शिशुर्महीनां हिन्वन्नृतस्य दीधितिम् ।
विश्वा परि प्रिया भुवदध द्विता ॥

1. Prāṇa arouses the mind's desires greatly bestowing satisfaction on men.

He goes around the sense organs in kindness bestowing them on both brain and mind of creatures. (1013), (570)

२. उप त्रितस्य पाष्यो३रभक्त यद्गुहा पदम् ।
यज्ञस्य सप्त धामभिरध प्रियम् ॥

2. Above he seizes the bonds of the three states to which he bestows to drink.

He supports the seven-pronged Activity in the home to bestow in life-activity. (1014)

३. त्रीणि त्रितस्य धारया पृष्ठेष्वैरयद्रयिम् ।
मिमीते अस्य योजना वि सुक्रतुः ॥

3. He himself arouses three streams of wealth (of perceptions) and moves to the three states foremost to support.

He approaches to establish them by uniting for doing good. (1015).

D. XIX.

१. पवस्व वाजसातये पवित्रे धारया सुतः ।
इन्द्राय सोम विष्णवे देवेभ्यो मधुमत्तरः ॥

1. Indra himself continually bestows to drink beneficially and moves to support mind.

Indra is active with Soma for fresh ideas of sweet perceptions to release to us. (1016)

२. त्वां रिहन्ति धीतयो हरिं पवित्रे अद्रुहः ।
वत्सं जातं न मातरः पवमान विधर्मणि ॥

2. The tawny consciousness caresses them within graciously for understanding without hurting.

The mother bestows on mind from the sources; she bestows them from the home to drink according to dharma (established rules). (1017)

३. त्वं द्यां च महिव्रत पृथिवीं चाति जभ्रिषे ।
प्रति द्रापिममुञ्चथाः पवमान महित्वना ॥

3. Consciousness! You are divine, also with much duties (vows) to the sense organs (earth) for whom you grasp the ṛṣis (sense activities).

You run to nourish them and also to release them to us; you bestow them on the home to drink with much desires. (1018)

D. XX.

१. इन्दुर्वाजी पवते गोन्योघा इन्द्रे सोमः सह इन्वन्मदाय ।
हन्ति रक्षो बाधते पर्यरातिं वरिवस्कृण्वन्वृजनस्य राजा ॥

1. The brain cells drink (protect) understanding in life-activity; the sense activities bestow freshly; Indra and Soma together bestow mighty desires.

They strike down troubles to protect us; go around ready to bestow with freedom to produce desires in the enclosure to control us. (1019), (540)

२. अध धारया मध्वा पृचानस्तिरो रोम पवते अद्रिदुग्धः ।
इन्दुरिन्द्रस्य सख्यं जुषाणो देवो देवस्य मत्सरो मदाय ॥

2. Then they bestow streams of sense perceptions, nourish and gladden us to cross (ignorance); the sense activities release knowledge to drink on the hill through sense perceptions.

Indra helps the brain cells joyously with ideas; the devas (ideas) flow to us with sense activities. (1020)

३. अभि व्रतानि पवते पुनानो देवो देवान्त्स्वेन रसेन पृञ्चन् ।
इन्दुर्धर्माण्यृतुथा वसानो दश क्षिपो अव्यत सानो अव्ये ॥

3. To protect understanding ideas have repeated duties (vows); the devas themselves are with mighty essences to nourish and gladden us.

Ṛta bestows protection (armour) at the summit (of the brain) on the brain cells through the rays (fingers) of sense activities in accordance with his duty; the Aśvins bestow on him abidingly. (1021)

D. XXI.

१. आ ते अग्न इधीमहि द्युमन्तं देवाजरम् ।
यद्ध स्या ते पनीयसी समिद्दीदयति द्यवीषं स्तोतृभ्य आ भर ॥

1. Agni! the unaging ideas (devas) within us from heaven are the items of much knowledge.

They bestow on us admirably objects of perception (fuel-sticks) in compassion; they favour our desires from heaven and support us praiseworthily. (1022), (419)

२. आ ते अग्न ऋचा हविः शुक्रस्य ज्योतिषस्पते ।
सुश्चन्द्र दस्म विश्पते हव्यवाट्तुभ्यंहूयत इषं स्तोतृभ्य आ भर ॥

2. Agni! They (the ideas) are oblations to hymns; they brighten us; they are lords of illuminating light.

They arouse mind who is in want; they are lords in the home; are oblations in the enclosure; you are both invoked to support our desires praiseworthily. (1023)

३. ओभे सुश्चन्द्र विश्पते दर्वी श्रीणीष आसनि ।
उतो न उत्पुपूर्या उक्थेषु शवसस्पत इषं स्तोतृभ्य आ भर ॥

3. You both arouse the mind; the lord of the home cooks desires in the hood of the spinal cord (to bestow) as gifts.

They swell and warm us up (illuminate) praiseworthily along the path of might and support our desires praiseworthily. (1024), (Y.V.15, 43)

D. XXII.

१. इन्द्राय साम गायत विप्राय बृहते बृहत् ।
ब्रह्मकृते विपश्चिते पनस्यवे ॥

1. Indra bestows on us sense activities to unite with us to inspire us greatly and bestow,

knowledge by producing it and also for the mind to drink admirably from the brain cells. (1025), (388)

२. त्वमिन्द्राभिभूरसि त्वं सूर्यमरोचयः ।
विश्वकर्मा विश्वदेवो महाँ असि ॥

2. Indra! You bestow existence and bind us to it; you cause consciousness to rise up in us.

You produce the sense organs to us; you are a cosmic deva and you are great. (1026)

३. विभ्राजं ज्योतिषा स्व३रगच्छो रोचनं दिवः ।
देवास्त इन्द्र सख्याय येमिरे ॥

3. Through the effulgent light of consciousness you bestow sense activities nearby yourself, on the rise of waking state or consciousness.

Indra! You help ideas which approach and bestow on us. (1027)

D. XXIII.

१. असावि सोम इन्द्र ते शविष्ठ धृष्णवा गहि ।
आ त्वा पृणक्त्विन्द्रियं रजः सूर्यो न रश्मिभिः ॥

1. Soma! You bestow through Indra, who boldly and with might arouses sense activities afresh.

You bestow on and nourish the sense organs against ignorance; the rays of consciousness agitate them. (1028), (347)

२. आ तिष्ठ वृत्रहन्रथं युक्ता ते ब्रह्मणा हरी ।
अर्वाचीनं सु ते मनो ग्रावा कृणोतु वग्नुना ॥

2. At your wish you strike down Vṛtra; unite with sense organs which amount to knowledge and which you release.

You turn round to arouse mind from the hill; the motley sense activities now produce speech. (1029)

३. इन्द्रमिद्धरी वहतोऽप्रतिधृष्टशवसम् ।
ऋषीणां सुष्टुतीरुप यज्ञं च मानुषाणाम् ॥

3. Indra supports the brain (fat) and conveys nourishment to him boldly and with might.

The ṛṣis above are competent for life-activity and also for men. (1030), (Y.V. 8, 35)

BOOK IV : Chapter I

D. I.

१. ज्योतिर्यज्ञस्य पवते मधु प्रियं पिता देवानां जनिता विभूवसुः ।
दधाति रत्नं स्वधयोरपीच्यं मदिन्तमो मत्सर इन्द्रियो रसः ॥

1. In life-activity the effulgent consciousness protects understanding from the sweet perceptions in kindness and also from ideas from the source (arising) for them, through whom wealth comes into existence.

He bestows wealth of his own self abundantly remaining concealed; the sense perceptions with mighty desires, being the essence of sense organs, flow to us. (1031)

२. अभिक्रन्दन्कलशं वाज्यर्षति पतिर्दिवः शतधारो विचक्षणः ।
हरिर्मित्रस्य सदनेषु सीदति मर्मृजानोऽविभिः सिन्धुभिर्वृषा ॥

2. The lord (Indra) flows to the head resoundingly in life-activity in waking state and perceives in an instant hundreds of streams.

The tawny consciousness bestows on the brain in the home the missiles (of sense activities) to mortals to polish and bless and supports the rains of Sindhu. (1032)

३. अग्रे सिन्धूनां पवमानो अर्षस्यग्रे वाचो अग्रियो गोषु गच्छसि ।
अग्रे वाजस्य भजसे महद्धनं स्वायुधः सोतृभिः सोम सूयसे ॥

3. At first Sindhu bestows on the home to drink; Speech flows from her at first; sense activities flow to it (home) earlier.

We worship life-activity first which bestows great wealth by itself by uniting; Soma strives to arouse the devotees. (1033)

D. II.

१. असृक्षत प्र वाजिनो गव्या सोमासो अश्वया ।
शुक्रासो वीरयाशवः ॥

1. In life-activity nourishment flows to the home, Soma releases sense activities through prāṇa.

The streams approach the sense-organs eagerly and shine. (1034), (482)

२. शुम्भमाना ऋतायुभिर्मृज्यमाना गभस्त्योः ।
पवन्ते वारे अव्यये ॥

2. Ṛta unites with and supports the home to cleanse (or polish) through the hands (nerves) for the welfare of the home.

The Aśvins bestow for drinking wealth (of sense perceptions). (1035)

३. ते विश्वा दाशुषे वसु सोमा दिव्यानि पार्थिवा ।
पवन्तामान्तरिक्ष्या ॥

3. They (Aśvins and Ṛta) serve the sense organs eagerly. Soma arouses devas towards the sense organs (terrestrial organs) and bestows them. (1036)

D. III.

१. पवस्व देववीरति पवित्रं सोम रंह्या ।
इन्द्रमिन्दो वृषा विश ॥

1. The devas (ideas) themselves bestow to drink, bless and gladden.

Soma flows beneficently; Indra rains them (ideas) to the brain cells in the home. (1037)

२. आ वच्यस्व महि प्सरो वृषेन्दो द्युम्नवत्तमः ।
आ योनिं धर्णसिः सदः ॥

2. The brain cells themselves rain much speech in (or for) enjoyment (psara) from heaven, as desired for understanding.

The source supports and binds it (understanding) to the home. (1038)

३. अधुक्षत प्रियं मधु धारा सुतस्य वेधसः ।
अपो वसिष्ट सुक्रतुः ॥

3. Activity agitates the home in kindness and supports the sense perceptions for the mind of the devotee.

Activity desires to dwell here to do good. (1039)

४. महान्तं त्वा महीरन्वापो अर्षन्ति सिन्धवः ।
यद्गोभिर्वासयिष्यसे ॥

4. Activity! You are great within (or gladden from within); you bestow much to gladden, bestowing Sindhu to flow within.

What the sense activities strive to support in the home are desires. (1040)

५. समुद्रो अप्सु मामृजे विष्टम्भो धरुणो दिवः ।
सोमः पवित्रे अस्मयुः ॥

5. Activity is an ocean (or bestows gladness); he arouses mortals to bestow births (of ideas) to support (viṣṭambho), waking state or consciousness supports him.

Soma beneficially unites with us. (1041)

६. अचिक्रदद्वृषा हरिर्महान्मित्रो न दर्शतः ।
सं सूर्येण दिद्युते ॥

6. The great tawny consciousness rains a variety (of gifts) through his rays to the brain (Mitra) at his visits.

Everything from consciousness flashes forth mightily. (1042), (497)

७. गिरस्त इन्द्व ओजसा मर्मृज्यन्ते अपस्युवः ।
याभिर्मदाय शुम्भसे ॥

7. Activity bestows vigorously on the brain cells in their home on the hill; he guides them in mortals to the mind to polish him.

They (brain cells) support him joyously and bestow welfare. (1043)

८. तं त्वा मदाय घृष्वय उ लोककृत्नुमीमहे ।
तव प्रशस्तये महे ॥

8. Activity! You desire the sense activities to move boldly to us to produce the world for great changes (mī) praiseworthily.

You are greatly praised for it. (1044)

९. गोषा इन्दो नृषा अस्यश्वसा वाजसा उत ।
आत्मा यज्ञस्य पूर्व्यः ॥

9. Prāṇa bestows us sense activities eagerly on the brain cells of men, releasing them in life.

The Self (ātmā) is prior to life-activity. (1045)

१०. अस्मभ्यमिन्दविन्द्रियं मधोः पवस्व धारया ।
पर्जन्यो वृष्टिमाँ इव ।

10. The brain cells discharge to the sense organs in us sense

activities; they themselves bestow them to drink and support them.

They rain like a cloud burst. (1046)

D. IV.

१. सना च सोम जेषि च पवमान महि श्रवः ।
अथा नो वस्यसस्कृधि ॥

1. From of old even, Soma won desires and cooked and conveyed them greatly to the fickle mind.

Then the brain cells in the home created satisfaction. (1047)

२. सना ज्योतिः सना स्व३र्विश्वा च सोम सौभगा ।
अथा नो वस्यसस्कृधि ॥

2. Consciousness is from ancient times; Heaven is ancient; the sense organs too which bestows us welfare.

Then the brain cells in the home create satisfaction. (1048)

३. सना दक्षमुत क्रतुमप सोम मृधो जहि ।
अथा नो वस्यसस्कृधि ॥

3. Activity satisfied us as from old times with his power; Soma bestowed births arousing mortals.

Then the brain cells in the home create satisfaction. (1049)

४. पवीतारः पुनीतन सोममिन्द्राय पातवे ।
अथा नो वस्यसस्कृधि ॥

4. Soma crosses the rim (of the brain) repeatedly to guide Indra who moves to fulfil him.

Then the brain cells in the home satisfy us. (1050)

५. त्वं सूर्ये न आ भज तव क्रत्वा तवोतिभिः ।
अथा नो वस्यसस्कृधि ॥

5. Consciousness! You are worshipped. You bestow by revealing; you help us.

Then the brain cells satisfy us. (1051)

६. तव क्रत्वा तवोतिभिर्ज्योक्पश्येम सूर्यम् ।
अथा नो वस्यसस्कृधि ॥

6. Consciousness! You have been seen since a long time; you bestow by revealing and you help us.

Then the brain cells satisfy us. (1052)

७. अभ्यर्ष स्वायुध सोम द्विबर्हसं रयिम् ।
अथा नो वस्यसस्कृधि ॥

7. Soma flows to unite and bestow himself; he bestows (barha) all wealth on brain and mind.

Then the brain cells satisfy us. (1053)

८. अभ्यर्षानपच्युतो वाजिन्त्समत्सु सासहिः ।
अथा नो वस्यसस्कृधि ॥

8. Activity flows to us to let drip all (ideas) in life-activity victoriously by arousing us.

Then the brain cells in the home satisfy us. (1054)

९. त्वां यज्ञैरवीवृधन्पवमान विधर्मणि ।
अथा नो वस्यसस्कृधि ॥

9. Activity! You favour life-activity; foster growth of the fickle mind according to dharma.

Then the brain cells in the home satisfy us. (1055)

१०. रयिं नश्चित्रमश्विनमिन्दो विश्वायुमा भर ।
अथा नो वस्यसस्कृधि ॥

10. The brain cells achieve a variety of wealth from the Aśvins who unite with sense organs and bestow to support us.

Then the brain cells in the home satisfy us. (1056)

D. V.

१. तरत्स मन्दी धावति धारा सुतस्यान्धसः ।
तरत्स मन्दी धावति ॥

1. Understanding bestows for crossing over and gives joy and supports mind against ignorance by bestowing.

Understanding bestows for crossing over and gives gladness. (1057)

२. उस्रा वेद वसूनां मर्तस्य देव्यवसः ।
तरत्स मन्दी धावति ॥

2. Indra knows the devas from their homes as wealth to mortals.

Understanding bestows for crossing over and gives joy. (1058)

३. ध्वस्रयोः पुरुषन्त्योरा सहस्राणि दद्महे ।
तरत्स मन्दी धावति ॥

3. If wealth (or streams of sense activities) decays the puruṣa bestows on you (Indra) greatly through the Aśvins (ura).

Understanding bestows for crossing over and gives joy. (1059)

४. आ ययोस्त्रिंशतं तना सहस्राणि च दद्महे ।
तरत्स मन्दी धावति ॥

4. He (the puruṣa) hastens to the sense activities to guide hundreds of times and even thousands of times by bestowing on her greatly.

Understanding bestows for crossing over and gives joy. (1060)

D. VI.

१. एते सोमा असृक्षत गृणानाः शवसे महे ।
मदिन्तमस्य धारया ॥

1. Soma flows to the motley sense activities in the home of the devotee greatly with might.

He supports our desires mightily through sense activities. (1061)

२. अभि गव्यानि वीतये नृम्णा पुनानो अर्षसि ।
सनद्वाजः परि स्रव ॥

2. He repeatedly flows to the sense activities with manly vigour desiring them.

He flows around in life bestowing gifts. (1062)

३. उत नो गोमतीरिषो विश्वा अर्ष परिष्टुभः ।
गृणानो जमदग्निना ॥

3. Also desiring knowledge through sense activities he flows to the sense organs praiseworthily.

The sense activities are born in the devotee from Agni. (1063)

D. VII.

१. इमं स्तोममर्हते जातवेदसे रथमिव सं महेमा मनीषया ।
भद्रा हि नः प्रमतिरस्य संसद्यग्ने सख्ये मा रिषामा वयं तव ॥

1. Here they flow praiseworthily for the birth and bestowal of knowledge by approaching the sense organs; they bestow all to gladden men.

They arouse and bind the understanding which nourishes our welfare; Agni helps all these at once; do not hurt us; we belong to you. (1064), (66)

२. भरामेध्मं कृणवामा हवींषि ते चितयन्तः पर्वणापर्वणा वयम् ।
जीवातवे प्रतरां साधया धियोऽग्ने सख्ये मा रिषामा वयं तव ॥

2. Agni! You support us in the home; you produce and bestow oblations on us; they are bestowed from time to time to the mind within us.

You enable the jiva to cross (ignorance) by nourishing and satisfy him; help us; do not hurt us; we belong to you. (1065)

३. शकेम त्वा समिधं साधया धियस्त्वे देवा हविरदन्त्याहुतम् ।
त्वमादित्यां आ वह तान्ह्यु३श्मस्यग्ने सख्ये मा रिषामा वयं तव ॥

3. Agni! You help us by approaching the home and bestowing; you enable to satisfy us by offering ideas (devas) through the channels (nerves) as oblations.

You convey Aditi through the nerves on call, to reach us, help us; do not hurt us; we belong to you. (1066)

D. VIII.

१. प्रति वां सूर उदिते मित्रं गृणीषे वरुणम् ।
अर्यमणं रिशादसम् ॥

1. On rising you nourish us by arousing the brain (Mitra) of the devotee and bestowing his desires for Varuṇa.

We, men, honour the Maruts (ideas). (1067)

२. राया हिरण्यया मतिरियमवृकाय शवसे ।
इयं विप्रा मेधसातये ।

2. The king, golden consciousness, moves to release knowledge by enveloping the body (sense organs), with might.

Here he inspires understanding continually. (1068)

३. ते स्याम देव वरुण ते मित्र सूरिभिः सह ।
इषं स्वश्च धीमहि ॥

3. The deva Varuṇa is ignorant (in darkness); the brain (Mitra) is wise (lord) at the same time.

Desiring also to undərstand him greatly himself. (1069)

D. IX.

१. भिन्धि विश्वा अप द्विषः परि बाधो जही मृधः ।
वसु स्पार्हं तदा भर ॥

1. The sense organs are divided; Activity goes around to the desires of both (brain and sense organs); troubles depart in his fights.

He supports by bestowing on them for wealth eagerly. (1070), (134)

२. यस्य ते विश्वमानुषग्भूरेर्दत्तस्य वेदति ।
वसु स्पार्हं तदा भर ॥

2. You bestow existence on the sense organs of men through sense activities and knowledge on us through them.

You support wealth eagerly through them. (1071)

३. यद्वीडाविन्द्र यत्स्थिरे यत्पर्शाने पराभृतम् ।
वसु स्पार्हं तदा भर ॥

3. Indra bestows them to consolidate; he stabilises them; unites with the brain cells (cavities) supporting them from beyond.

He supports wealth eagerly for them. (1072), (207)

D. X.

१. यज्ञस्य हि स्थ ऋत्विजा सस्नी वाजेषु कर्मसु ।
इन्द्राग्नी तस्य बोधतम् ॥

1. He arouses life-activity abidingly in the devotee; guides the brain cells to the sense activities in life arousing them to activity.

Indra-Agni bestow knowledge on them as desired. (1073)

२. तोशासा रथयावाना वृत्रहणापराजिता ।
इन्द्राग्नी तस्य बोधतम् ॥

2. He smites down Vṛtra (inertia) to win from beyond the desires for the sense organs to bestow satisfaction.

Indra-Agni bestow knowledge through them. (1074)

३. इदं वां मदिरं मध्वधुक्षन्नद्रिभिर्नरः ।
इन्द्राग्नी तस्य बोधतम् ॥

3. Here they bestow Soma juice (spirituous liquor) releasing sense activities in the home and arousing and supporting the brain (hill) of men.

Indra-Agni bestow knowledge through them. (1075)

D. XI.

१. इन्द्रायेन्दो मरुत्वते पवस्व मधुमत्तमः ।
अर्कस्य योनिमासदम् ॥

1. Indra moves to the brain cells with ideas (Maruts) for understanding and himself bestows sense perceptions and our desires to drink.

Consciousness from the source bestows on our home. (1076) (472)

२. तं त्वा विप्रा वचोविदः परिष्कृण्वन्ति धर्णसिम् ।
सं त्वा मृजन्त्यायवः ॥

2. You desire to inspire speech from knowledge; you create desires from beyond within and support binding them.

You are well-known to polish them all in the brain cells. (1077)

३. रसं ते मित्रो अर्यमा पिबन्तु वरुणः कवे ।
पवमानस्य मरुतः ॥

3. They (the brain cells) drink (ideas) of Varuṇa from Agni (the wise) (or drink the story of Varuṇa) and bestow their essence on men.

Maruts (ideas) bestow to our home to drink (or protect). (1078)

D. XII.

१. मृज्यमानः सुहस्त्या समुद्रे वाचमिन्वसि ।
रयिं पिशङ्गं बहुलं पुरुस्पृहं पवमानाभ्यर्षसि ॥

1. Indra! You win from mortal's homes the mighty speech by arousing the nerves and gladden them.

You let flow to the fickle mind a variety of wealth in large quantities with great eagerness. (1079), (517)

२. पुनानो वारे पवमानो अव्यये वृषो अचिक्रदद्वने ।
देवानां सोम पवमान निष्कृतं गोभिरञ्जानो अर्षसि ॥

2. You rain wealth on the fickle mind repeatedly by observing him, producing and bestowing for his desires.

You bestow ideas (devas) on our mind, meeting the sense activities at appointed places and supporting their flow from the source. (1080)

D. XIII.

१. एतमु त्यं दश क्षिपो मृजन्ति सिन्धुमातरम् ।
समादित्येभिरख्यत ॥

1. The rays (fingers) of the motley sense activities win from within protection (daśa) for mortals and the mother Sindhu gladdens us.

All of Aditi are known to support by uniting. (1081)

२. समिन्द्रेणोत वायुना सुत एति पवित्र आ ।
सं सूर्यस्य रश्मिभिः ॥

2. The motley sense activities together with Indra bestow on mind by uniting, beneficially.

They are like the sun's rays. (1082)

३. स नो भगाय वायवे पूष्णे पवस्व मधुमान् ।
चारुर्मित्रे वरुणे च ॥

3. Consciousness bestows gifts on the brain cells for prosperity and bestows sweet perceptions on the home to drink, of itself;

and gladdens Mitra (brain) and Varuṇa also. (1083)

D. XIV.

१. रेवतीर्नः सधमाद इन्द्रे सन्तु तुविवाजाः ।
क्षुमन्तो याभिर्मदेम ॥

1. Indra binds us abundantly to his comrades (sense activities) and bestows gifts vehemently in life.

The sense perceptions support us within as nourishment. (1084)

२. आ घ त्वावान् त्मना युक्तः स्तोतृभ्यो धृष्णवीयानः ।
ऋणोरक्षं न चक्र्योः ॥

2. Indeed you desire to unite yourself and praiseworthily and boldly bless us through the sense organs (yāna).

You are obliged to protect us by going around. (1085)

३. आ यद् दुवः शतक्रतवा कामं जरितॄणाम् ।
ऋणोरक्षं न शचीभिः ॥

3. What the doer of hundred deeds (Indra) bestows for consumption is desires to the devotees.

He is obliged to protect us with might. (1086)

[Here is again a reference to arctic phenomena.]

D. XV.

१. सुरूपकृत्नुमूतये सुदुघामिव गोदुहे ।
जुहूमसि द्यविद्यवि ॥

1. You help to arouse and produce forms of objects praiseworthily; you set up the milking process and approaching us bestow the milk from sense activities.

You bless us with knowledge from heaven through their tongues (rays). (1087)

२. उप नः सवना गहि सोमस्य सोमपाः पिब ।
गोदा इद्रेवतो मदः ॥

2. Above you bind the Soma juice arousing sense activities; Soma bestows on us Soma juice to drink and fulfils.

The sense activities bestow thus wealth joyously. (1088)

३. अथा ते अन्तमानां विद्याम सुमतीनाम् ।
मा नो अति ख्य आ गहि ॥

3. Then they are the paths for knowledge within arousing understanding.

They are known well in the home as being aroused by sense activities. (1089)

D. XVI.

१. उभे यदिन्द्र रोदसी आपप्राथोषा इव ।
महान्तं त्वा महीनां सम्राजं चर्षणीनाम् ।
देवी जनित्र्यजीजनद् भद्रा जनित्र्यजीजनत् ॥

1. Indra reaches both the brain and sense organs eagerly as his primary duty.

He is great within; he looks after a great sovereign region.

The devi (Aditi) from the source wins the three worlds for men's welfare and wins life-activity for them from the source. (1090), (379)

२. दीर्घं ह्यङ्कुशं यथा शक्तिं बिभर्षि मन्तुमः ।
पूर्वेण मघवन्पदा वयामजो यथा यमः ।
देवी जनित्र्यजीजनद्भद्रा जनित्र्यजीजनत् ॥

2. Prāṇa gives us counsel according to his ability through the long nerves like the Kuśa grass through supporting and binding us.

In former times the Aśvins controlled the creatures in the place of Indra (Maghavan) in the same manner. The devī from the source wins the three worlds for men's welfare and wins life-activity for them from the source. (1091)

The long nerves referred to are the afferent and efferent nerves, as we call them now. At a time only one of them is operative and their function is to arouse the brain cells to receive the sense perceptions.

Then it is said that the Aśvins performed the role of Indra. That was at a time when a nervous system had not come into existence.

३. अव स्म दुर्हृणायतो मर्त्तस्य तनुहि स्थिरम् ।
अधस्पदं तमीं कृधि यो अस्माँ अभिदासति ।
देवी जनित्र्यजीजनद्भद्रा जनित्र्यजीजनत् ॥

3. Bless the mortals without being worth; arouse us delicately and steady us.

Produce satisfaction in us from being in the row state of ignorance (tamī); move to serve us.

The devī from the source wins the three worlds for men's welfare and wins life-activity for them from the source. (1092)

D. XVII.

१. परि स्वानो गिरिष्ठाः पवित्रे सोमो अक्षरत् ।
मदेषु सर्वधा असि ।

1. Soma goes around pantingly desirous of the brain (hill) and flows in the home to please.

You bestow on him all the missiles of sense activities. (1093), (475)

२. त्वं विप्रस्त्वं कविर्मधु प्र जातमन्धसः ।
मदेषु सर्वधा असि ॥

2. You inspire us praiseworthily; Agni nourishes us with sense perceptions (honey) from the source to release us from ignorance.

You bestow all the missiles of sense activities. (1094)

३. त्वे विश्वे सजोषसो देवासः पीतिमाशत ।
मदेषु सर्वधा असि ॥

3. You unite with sense organs eagerly; bestow on them ideas which overflow from them as food.

You bestow all the missiles of sense activities. (1095)

D. XVIII.

१. स सुन्वे यो वसूनां यो रायामानेता य इडानाम् ।
सोमो यः सुक्षितीनाम् ॥

1. The sense activities which control the brain (home) bestow oblations of wealth through Indra on the devotees.

Soma arouses the home and speeds up bestowal. (1096), (582)

२. यस्य त इन्द्रः पिबाद्यस्य मरुतो यस्य वार्यमणा भगः ।
आ येन मित्रावरुणा करामह एन्द्रमवसे महे ॥

2. Indra strives for them; they strive to drink ideas (Maruts); consciousness controls their wealth.

They produce great ideas of Varuṇa in Mitra (brain); bestow and gladden it; Indra favours them much. (1097)

D. XIX.

१. तं वः सखायो मदाय पुनानमभि गायत ।
शिशुं न हव्यैः स्वदयन्त गूर्तिभिः ॥

1. Indra moves to help to convey the desires of sense activities to unite with joyously.

He himself guides oblations and bestows on mind praiseworthily. (1098), (569)

२. सं वत्स इव मातृभिरिन्दुर्हिन्वानो अज्यते ।
देवावीर्मदो मतिभिः परिष्कृतः ॥

2. The mother supports the brain cells as if they were children and arouses desires in them for clarified butter.

Ideas (devas) favour sense activities for understanding and produce the desires of heaven. (1099)

३. अयं दक्षाय साधनोऽयं शर्धाय वीतये ।
अयं देवेभ्यो मधुमत्तरः सुतः ॥

3. Indra! You bestow the path on the home; bestow wealth; you desire prosperity (ayam) boldly.

Devas (ideas) are the paths to sense perceptions which they bestow on our mind. (1100)

D. XX.

१. सोमाः पवन्त इन्दवोऽस्मभ्यं गातुवित्तमाः ।
मित्राः स्वाना अरेपसः स्वाध्यः स्वर्विदः ॥

1. Soma bestows on the brain cells within to drink and desires knowledge to us devotees.

He himself bestows on the brain pure knowledge from heaven to sip. (1101), (548)

२. ते पूतासो विपश्चितः सोमासो दध्याशिरः ।
सूरासो न दर्शतासो जिगत्नवो ध्रुवा घृते ॥

2. He swells towards it to bestow; inspires mind; Soma moves to the head to bestow curds (sense reactions).

The hero bestows on visiting (or sighting) him; he wins new (ideas) from sense activities abidingly for clarified butter. (1102)

३. सुष्वाणासो व्यद्रिभिश्चिताना गोरधि त्वचि ।
इषमस्मभ्यमभितः समस्वरन्वसुविदः ॥

3. He bestows desires which gush to us; which the spinal cord (snake) bestows on mind and satisfies.

He establishes the desires in us, and himself gladdens all with the wealth of knowledge. (1103)

D. XXI.

१. अया पवा पवस्वैना वसूनि मांश्चत्व इन्दो सरसि प्र धन्व ।
ब्रध्नश्चिद्यस्य वातो न जूतिं पुरुमेधाश्चित्तकवे नरं धात् ॥

1. Then Indra bestows the path to protect; himself bestows

to drink; you bestow also Soma juice on the brain cells, which flows and binds sense activities to bestow newly.

Consciousness strives to inspire (agitate) mind through the nerves; Agni (the wise) bestows abundant understanding on the minds of men. (1104), (541)

२. उत न एना पवमा पवस्वाधि श्रुते श्रवाय्यस्य तीर्थे।
षष्टिं सहस्रा नैगुतो वसूनि वृक्षं न पक्वं धूनवद्रणाय॥

2. Then he nourishes (fulfils) the branches i.e. sense organs; he himself bestows them for drinking and satisfies; he strives for us to hear the guidance of traditional knowledge.

He bestows thousands of desires through the sense organs graciously, envelops them and cooks them patiently and arouses fresh gladness. (1105)

३. महीमे अस्य वृष नाम शूषे मांश्चत्वे वा पृशने वा वधत्रे।
अस्वापयन्निगुतः स्नेहयच्चापामित्रां अपाचितो अचेतः॥

3. He rains on us from the sense organs (mahī) and honours us; he bestows Soma juice resoundingly; bestows the motley sense activities; bestows protection from injury.

He guides us in sleep through the sense organs below; Activity is a friend of Prāṇa also, who fulfils to digest; Activity manifests mind. (1106)

D. XXII.

१. अग्ने त्वं नो अन्तम उत त्राता शिवो भुवो वरूथ्यः॥

1. Agni! You are intimate with us; also support us in welfare in existence and help us. (1107), (448)

२. वसुरग्निर्वसुश्रवा अच्छा नक्षि द्युमत्तमो रयिं दाः॥

2. Gracious Agni listens to Indra nearby, approaches from heaven to our desires and bestows wealth. (1108), (Y. V. 3, 25)

३. तं त्वा शोचिष्ठ दीदिवः सुम्नाय नूनमीमहे सखिभ्यः॥

3. He arouses our desires to flame up brightly in waking state and moves to them excellently; now he honours us greatly and helps. (1109), (Y. V. 3, 26)

D. XXIII.

१. इमा नु कं भुवना सीषधेमेन्द्रश्च विश्वे च देवाः ॥

1. Here the desires of creatures are praised; he bestows desires and bestows ideas on Indra and the sense organs. (1110), (Y. V. 25, 46)

२. यज्ञं च नस्तन्वं च प्रजां चादित्यैरिन्द्रः सह सीषधातु ॥

2. Agni associates with life-activity, which he guides by bestowing; also men through Aditi and Indra together who release desires and bestow them. (1111), (Y. V. 25, 46)

३. आदित्यैरिन्द्रः सगणो मरुद्भिरस्मभ्यं भेषजा करत् ॥

3. Aditi, Indra and his attendants support ideas (Maruts) in us and produce the birth of nourishment. (1112), (Y. V. 25, 46)

D. XXIV.

१. प्र वोऽर्चोप ।

प्र व इन्द्राय वृत्रहन्तमाय विप्राय गाथं गायत यं जुजोषते ।

1. Indra bestows nourishment and honours us.

Indra hovers about and strikes down Vṛtra, inspires the devotee, unites with sense activities and controls and is devoted to them. (1113)

२. अर्चन्त्यर्कं मरुतः स्वर्का आ स्तोभति श्रुतो युवा स इन्द्रः ॥

2. He honours Maruts (ideas) praiseworthily; he praises consciousness himself.

Indra listens to mind and bestows on him. (1114)

३. उप प्रक्षे मधुमति क्षियन्तः पुष्येम रयिं धीमहे त इन्द्र ॥

3. Above he nourishes the home with sweet perceptions and understanding; he bestows prosperity within the home; he bestows much wealth i.e. Indra. (1115)

BOOK IV: CHAPTER II

D. I.

१. प्र काव्यमुशनेव ब्रुवाणो देवो देवानां जनिमा विवक्ति ।
महिव्रतः शुचिबन्धुः पावकः पदा वराहो अभ्येति रेभन् ।।

1. As if narrating eagerly a story (poem), the devas tell us that we (men) were born among the devas.

With great duties (vows) and related to the flaming (devas), along the path of the animal world purified by Prajāpati (or in the head) to be sung (or manifested) by the motley sense activities. (1116), (524)

The Veda is in conformity with modern concept that man has been evolved out of lower forms of life and in fact from cell organisms as stated in mantras 210, 315, 610 etc. mentioned in the introduction. But this is only half the story as science does not explain what gave rise to cell organs. So the Veda goes on to explain that man originated among the devas or ideas with the motley sense activities, ignorant of the external world of today which did not exist then. Then the creator suppressed one sense activity after another, commencing with speech then with hearing sight etc. reaching touch only to arrive at the level of plant world. When this two was suppressed it gave rise to the world of energy or radiations enveloping the world of ideas. These radiations quietened down to lower and lower forms of energy congealing to the state matter, deprived of voluntary activity, what we call inertia, enveloped by an inner world of energy and an external one of ideas. The seven suppressed ideas begin to burst their bonds, as it does in the highest periodic elements like Radium, Uranium etc. giving rise to life phenomenon in water as a highly controlled chain reaction. Thus, in creative activity there is at first a descent from intelligence to inertia or matter, rather quick and then a slow or measured ascent of the combination of both as life-process or manifestation.

२. प्र हंसासस्तृपला वग्नुमच्छामादस्तं वृषगणा अयासुः ।
अङ्गोषिणं पवमानं सखायो दुर्मर्षं वाणं प्र वदन्ति साकम् ।।

2. Indra's retinue (ideas) indefatigably seize my brain cells

and bestow nourishment to satisfaction by calling to the nearby sense activities in the home.

Agni desires mightily to help the mind letting desires flow through the doors (sense organs or mortals) to nourish him and announce themselves to him together. (1117)

३. स योजत उरुगायस्य जूतिं वृथा क्रीडन्तं मिमते न गावः ।
परीणसं कृणुते तिग्मशृङ्गो दिवा हरिर्ददृशे नक्तमृज्रः ॥

3. The sense perceptions extensively unite with him to bestow and inspire him at their pleasure and sport with him by approaching him with understanding (knowledge) bestowed by sense activities.

The sense activities go around to associate (with sense organs) passionately from the hill (brain) in waking state; consciousness bestows his visit and wipes away ignorance. (1118)

४. प्र स्वानासो रथा इवार्वन्तो न श्रवस्यवः ।
सोमासो राये अक्रमुः ॥

4. As if heard from the brain cells the sense perceptions by themselves hasten to nourish them from the sense organs with whom they are associated.

Soma who controls them, bestows them properly. (1119)

५. हिन्वानासो रथा इव दधन्विरे गभस्त्योः ।
भरासः कारिणामिव ।

5. As if to associate with the sense organs to arouse and bestow, Soma bestows wealth for his (minds), comfort through the hands (nerves).

He supports him by producing mightily and bestows him by approaching. (1120)

६. राजानो न प्रशस्तिभिः सोमासो गोभिरञ्जते ।
यज्ञो न सप्त धातृभिः ॥

6. (Soma) is praised as the king of knowledge; he bestows and supports sense activities to adorn us.

In life-activity he supports the seven-pronged Activity (Vaiśvānara). (1121)

७. परि स्वानास इन्दवो मदाय बर्हणा गिरा ।
मधो अर्षन्ति धारया ॥

7. He himself goes around to associate and bestow joyously on the brain cells on the hill powerfully (barhaṇā).

You move to the sense perceptions (activities) to support them. (1122), (485)

८. आपानासो विवस्वतो जिन्वन्त उषसो भगम् ।
सूरा अण्वं वि तन्वते ॥

8. He associates with Activity and rides on him to win knowledge eagerly through consciousness.

He arouses, guides and bestows them as new knowledge.

Alt. Activity gains (full) consciousness from Uṣas and rides on understanding by associating with him (consciousness).

He arouses, guides and bestows as new knowledge (on men). (1123)

Uṣas or the feeble light of the morning sun is just adequate to illumine lower creatures but the full light of consciousness is necessary for illumining the minds of men, which Activity (Soma) gains for him.

९. अप द्वारा मतीनां प्रत्ना ऋण्वन्ति कारवः ।
वृष्णो हरस आयवः ॥

9. Activity is the door to knowledge and in ancient times it was obliged to be confined within the prison (body) and bestow it (i.e. it remained latent in creatures).

It rained, conveyed and bestowed on the brain cells. (1124)

१०. समीचीनास आशत होतारः सप्तजानयः ।
पदमेकस्य पिप्रतः ॥

10. The seven ṛṣis turned their activities together towards (the earth) and bestowed hundreds of creatures and presided over and guided seven-pronged men who took birth,

all of the same type (gait) and also nourished them. (1125)

११. नाभा नाभिं न आ ददे चक्षुषा सूर्यं दृशे ।
कवेरपत्यमा दुहे ॥

11. Without itself shining at the source it (Activity) bestowed the sense of sight to look at the sun.

Agni is well-known to have given us the sense perceptions to drink. (1126)

१२. अभि प्रियं दिवस्पदमध्वर्युभिर्गुहा हितम् ।
सूरः पश्यति चक्षसा ॥

12. The sense activities unite with both (brain cells and sense organs) in kindness to support them in the waking state for our welfare.

Like heroes they bestow sight to look at. (1127)

D. II.

१. असृग्रमिन्दवः पथा धर्मन्नृतस्य सुश्रियः ।
विदाना अस्य योजना ॥

1. They (the sense activities) flow first to the brain cells along established paths arousing prosperity,

through yoking us to their gifts. (1128)

२. प्र धारा मधो अग्रियो महीरपो वि गाहते ।
हविर्हविःषु वन्द्यः ॥

2. Activity first plunges (gāha) amidst the sense organs (mahī) to support sense perceptions for nourishment.

The missiles invoke oblations to be praised. (1129)

३. प्र युजा वाचो अग्रियो वृषो अचिक्रदद्वने ।
सद्माभि सत्यो अध्वरः ॥

3. Agni builds up (ci) and bestows desires resoundingly and unites with speech to nourish it.

He is known to bestow it immediately in life-activity. (1130)

४. परि यत्काव्या कविर्नृम्णा पुनानो अर्षति ।
स्वर्वाजी सिषासति ॥

4. The wise (Agni) manfully flows repeatedly and goes around uniting in our poems (compositions).

He bestows our desires in life-activity in existence from heaven. (1131)

५. पवमानो अभि स्पृधो विशो राजेव सीदति ।
यदीमृण्वन्ति वेधसः ॥

5. The fickle mind is seated like a king to emulate with the brain (home),

who is here obliged to bestow (to mind) within, the devotee. (1132)

It is here seen clearly that mind gets all information at second hand, i.e. from the brain and it has no direct access to any of it. As stated under mantra 841, the main purpose of the mind is to continue in subsequent existences, what the brain cannot do. Its purpose is also to cultivate desires.

६. अव्या वारे परि प्रियो हरिर्वनेषु सीदति ।
रेभो वनुष्यते मती ॥

6. The Aśvins go around with gifts (or the enclosure) in kindness; the tawny consciousness lies in wait for the desires of sense activities.

He unites eagerly with their desires for understanding resoundingly. (1133)

७. स वायुमिन्द्रमश्विना साकं मदेन गच्छति ।
रणा यो अस्य धर्मणा ॥

7. Indra and the Aśvins go together to the mighty sense activities through the nerves to release them.

They bestow on us gladness in accordance with dharma. (1134)

८. आ मित्रे वरुणे भगे मधोः पवन्त ऊर्मयः ।
विदाना अस्य शक्मभिः ॥

8. Consciousness releases waves of sense activities from Varuṇa (external world) to the brain within to drink,
for us to gain (Vidānā) according to capacity. (1135)

९. अस्मभ्यं रोदसी रयिं मध्वो वाजस्य सातये ।
श्रवो वसूनि सञ्जितम् ॥

9. The sense activities release wealth continuously in us to both brain cells and sense organs (heaven and earth) in life-activity.

Indra (Vasu) heeds them and attaches himself to them desirably. (1136)

१०. आ ते दक्षं मयोभुवं वह्निमद्या वृणीमहे ।
पान्तमा पुरुस्पृहम् ॥

10. The exhilarating sense perceptions envelop us greatly conveying us much gladness and satisfy us.

They fulfil our desires abundantly with eagerness. (1137), (498)

११. आ मन्द्रमा वरेण्यमा विप्रमा मनीषिणम् ।
पान्तमा पुरुस्पृहम् ॥

11. They bestow (mā) pleasantly; they bestow excellently; they bestow to inspire us men mightily.

They fulfil by bestowing within abundantly with eagerness. (1138)

१२. आ रयिमा सुचेतुनमा सुक्रतो तनूष्वा ।
पान्तमा पुरुस्पृहम ॥

12. They bestow wealth; they arouse mind to what it lacks and bestow; they release desires eagerly and produce good to him.

They fulfil our desires abundantly and eagerly. (1139)

D. III.

१. मूर्धानं दिवो अरतिं पृथिव्या वैश्वानरमृत आ जातमग्निम् ।
कविं सम्राजमतिथिं जनानामासन्नः पात्रं जनयन्त देवाः ॥

1. Vaiśvānara (Activity) born of Agni attends to (arati) the sense organs of mortals from the head (brain) in waking state.

Men are competent to be near Agni as guests in his sovereign region; the devas guide men. (1140), (67), (Y. V. 7, 34, 33, 8)

२. त्वां विश्वे अमृत जायमानं शिशुं न देवा अभि सं नवन्ते ।
तव क्रतुभिरमृतत्वमायन् वैश्वानर यत्पित्रोरदीदेः ॥

2. Activity! You flow from the source to the home and the sense organs of mortals and bestow all devas (ideas) on the mind within.

You support the might (power) of mortals; you are wonderful; you unite with the sense organs of man and also support them extensively and shine. (1141)

३. नाभिं यज्ञानां सदनं रयीणां महामाहावमभि सं नवन्त ।
वैश्वानरं रथ्यमध्वराणां यज्ञस्य केतुं जनयन्त देवाः ॥

3. In life-activity, you bestow a great amount of wealth from the source at the cells (hāva) of all and bestow on them.

The sense activities in life-activity of men bestow gifts on the sense organs from the home and desires to guide deva (ideas) on men. (1142)

D. IV.

१. प्र वो मित्राय गायत वरुणाय विपा गिरा ।
महिक्षत्रावृतं बृहत् ॥

1. The sense activities unite with the external world (Varuṇa) and scatter them on the hill to bestow nourishment on the brain (Mitra).

They envelop its desires greatly and support it from the home. (1143)

२. सम्राजा या घृतयोनि मित्रश्चोभा वरुणश्च ।
देवा देवेषु प्रशस्ता ॥

2. The sense activities come from the source to both Varuṇa and Mitra, the sovereign region (of Agni) for clarified butter.

These devas praise ideas (devas). (1144)

३. ता नः शक्तं पार्थिवस्य महो रायो दिव्यस्य ।
महि वां क्षत्रं देवेषु ॥

3. The devas (ideas) are bound to matter to be able (śakta) to control it.

The devas bestow on us great power (strength). (1145)

D. V.

१. इन्द्रा याहि चित्रभानो सुता इमे त्वायवः ।
अण्वीभिस्तना पूतासः ॥

1. Indra moves here from the brain cells to arouse various appearances (perception) in mind.

The rays (fingers) (of perceptions) swell from the breast (of heaven) to him to bestow. (1146), (Y. V. 20, 87)

२. इन्द्रा याहि धियेषितो विप्रजूतः सुतावतः ।
उप ब्रह्माणि वाघतः ॥

2. Indra desires to arouse satisfaction, as desired by Agni, by inspiring the mind with understanding,

above for the knowledge of the devotee. (1147), (Y. V. 20, 88)

३. इन्द्रा याहि तूतुजान उप ब्रह्माणि हरिवः ।
सुते दधिष्व नश्चनः ॥

3. Indra moves to arouse and stimulate powerfully knowledge from the source above for consciousness to release.

He himself bestows on mind, for him to achieve and be glad (1148), (Y. V. 20, 89)

D. VI.

१. तमीडिष्व यो अर्चिषा वना विश्वा परिष्वजत् ।
कृष्णा कृणोति जिह्वया ।।

1. We desire oblations to be bestowed by honouring sense objects (vanā—fire sticks) of the world (viśva) from sense activities) going around themselves and winning them.

The motley sense activities cultivate (the brain) with their rays (tongues). (1149)

२. य इद्ध आविवासति सुम्नमिन्द्रस्य मर्त्यः ।
द्युम्नाय सुतरा अपः ।।

2. Indra resides with us to incite mortals benevolently.
Activity then moves to bestow to mind excellently. (1150)

३. ता नो वाजवतीरिष आशून् पिपृतमर्वतः ।
एन्द्रमग्निं च वोढवे ।।

3. Activity hastens to him and envelops him also to bestow quickly understanding desired from life activity, through the nerves.

Indra and Agni too convey and bestow him. (1151)

D. VII.

१. प्रो अयासीदिन्दुरिन्द्रस्य निष्कृतं सखा सख्युर्न प्र मिनाति सङ्गिरम् ।
मर्य इव युवतिभिः समर्षति सोमः कलशे शतयामना पथा ।।

1. Indra indefatigably helps the brain cells to meet nourishment at appointed places; he also helps the sense activities (nāti) extensively to approach and meet them to nourish.

Like a lover going to meet his beloved, Soma flows at the same time to the head along a hundred paths to the home brain. (1152), (557)

२. प्र वो धियो मन्द्रयुवो विपन्युवः पनस्युवः संवरणेष्वक्रमुः ।
हरिं क्रीडन्तमभ्यनूषत स्तुभोऽभि धेनवः पयसेदशिश्रयुः ।।

2. Soma bestows nourishment pleasantly on mind and satisfies him by scattering it to the admirable youth from the enclosure and bestowing his desires in due course (or properly).

He conveys them to sport with him within and attach himself praiseworthily, for him to have recourse to the sharp sense perceptions (payȧsa) from the milch-cow. (1153)

३. आ नः सोम संयतं पिप्युषीमिषमिन्दो पवस्व पवमान ऊर्मिणा ।
या नो दोहते त्रिरहन्नसश्चुषी क्षुमद्वाजवन्मधुमत्सुवीर्यम् ॥

3. Soma now unites with all in front (face) and opens the eyes of the brain cells to drink them eagerly; he himself bestows on the fickle mind in waves to drink.

The sense activities (milk) from the three sense organs carry their food (anna) separately and eagerly to devote to the brain cells; the food from the sense perceptions in life-activity bestow sweetness and arouse our vigour. (1154)

D. VIII.

१. न किष्टं कर्मणा नशद्यश्चकार सदावृधम् ।
इन्द्रं न यज्ञैर्विश्वगूर्तमृभ्वसमधृष्टं धृष्णुमोजसा ॥

1. Our desires for activities with a purpose do not die out in the head, nor the activities connected with the sense organs; they grow constantly.

Indra praises the sense organs in life-activity; our Ṛbhus (the three spinal nerves) are equally courageous and bestow vigour boldly. (1155), (243)

२. अषाढमुग्रं पृतनासु सासहिं यस्मिन्महीरुरुज्रयः ।
सं धेनवो जायमाने अनोनवुर्द्यावः क्षामीरनोनवुः ॥

2. Indra the unconquerable is terrible in fights; he arouses and bestows with might sense organs (mahī) from the sky (jra) to animal bodies (ruru) (or through the Aśvins).

They are all bestowed in the home from the source by the sense activities (milch-cow) bestowing from the extensive source; they established them in the home and gladdened us with the new ones. (1156)

The sense organs spiringing from the material body, from activities latent in them from formation of matter, are responses to the sense activities.

D. IX.

१. सखाय आ नि षीदत पुनानाय प्रगायत ।
शिशुं नः यज्ञैः परि भूषत श्रिये ॥

1. Indra repeatedly helps the brain (home) to nourish through sense activities which unite with it.

He goes around to mind in life and adorns it to prosperity (1157). (568)

२. समी वत्सं न मातृभिः सृजता गयसाधनम् ।
देवाव्यं३मदमभि द्विशवसम् ॥

2. The mind encounters the mother who flows to him; the sense activities strive for wealth.

We are joyous with the two devas of might. (1158)

३. पुनाता दक्षसाधनं यथा शर्धाय वीतये ।
यथा मित्राय वरुणाय शन्तमम् ॥

3. They repeatedly satisfy us by bestowing wealth; they desire it boldly likewise (us).

Likewise, the brain (Mitra) desires Varuṇa. (1159)

D. X.

१. प्र वाज्यक्षाः सहस्रधारस्तिरः पवित्रं वि वारमव्यम् ।

1. In life the brain (home) is dependent on thousands of streams of nourishment bestowed beneficently through the gifts of the Aśvins. (1160)

२. स वाज्यक्षाः सहस्ररेता अद्भिर्मृजानो गोभिः श्रीणानः ॥

2. The sense activities in life bestow thousands of streams from the ocean of the source on the brain and binds them by cooking. (1161)

३. प्र सोम याहीन्द्रस्य कुक्षा नृभिर्येमानो अद्रिभिः सुतः ॥

3. Indra indeed moves to Soma to nourish the sense organs from the brain; the mind of man is supported by the home on the hill. (1162)

D. XI.

१. ये सोमासः परावति ये अर्वावति सुन्विरे ।
ये वादः शर्यणावति ॥

1. Soma hastens to the devotee, for his comfort, with knowledge from beyond and bestows.

Knowledge is shot out like arrows through speech. (1163)

२. य आर्जीकेषु कृत्वसु ये मध्ये पस्त्यानाम् ।
ये वा जनेषु पञ्चसु ॥

2. He produces them in the head (Soma vessel); Indra moves the sense activities to the sense organs (yānā) dependent on nourishment.

They are bestowed among men as five missiles. (1164)

३. ते नो वृष्टिं दिवस्परि पवन्तामा सुवीर्यम् ।
स्वाना देवास इन्दवः ॥

3. They go around in waking state and rain their rays; they bestow nourishment within and arouse and bestow vigour.

Devas (ideas) bestow by themselves on brain cells. (1165)

D. XII.

१. आ ते वत्सो मनो यमत्परमाच्चित्सधस्थात् ।
अग्ने त्वां कामये गिरा ॥

1. They (ideas) bestow knowledge on mind; from beyond they control the mind in the assembly.

Agni! You are the beloved of the brain. (1166), (8), (Y.V. 12, 115)

२. पुरुत्रा हि सदृङ्ङसि विशो विश्वा अनु प्रभुः ।
समत्सु त्वा हवामहे ॥

2. You arouse and establish the home in many directions; you direct the limbs now to the sense organs and nourish them for existence.

At the same time you arouse great oblations. (1167)

३. समत्स्वग्निमवसे वाजयन्तो हवामहे ॥
वाजेषु चित्रराधसम् ॥

3. Agni! You bless all yourself guiding great many oblations in life-activity.

The missiles (of sense activities) in life are (sources for) a variety of wealth. (1168)

D. XIII.

१. त्वं न इन्द्रा भर ओजो नृम्णं शतक्रतो विचर्षणे ।
आ वीरं पृतनासहम् ॥

1. (Agni!) You support Indra powerfully who, as one of hundred deeds, is diligently active.

He is victorious in fights with vigour. (1169)

२. त्वं हि नः पिता वसो त्वं माता शतक्रतो बभूविथ ।
अधा ते सुम्नमीमहे ॥

2. You arouse the father (Activity) and bind him to Indra; you produce a hundred things through the mother for knowledge in existence.

Then they arouse great reverence in us. (1170)

३. त्वां शुष्मिन्पुरुहूत वाजयन्तमुप ब्रुवे सहस्कृत ।
स नो रास्व सुवीर्यम् ॥

3. You are invoked when (activity) dries up to guide life-activity from above and to produce with might and tell us.

You yourself arouse and bestow vigour as gift. (1171)

D. XIV.

१. यदिन्द्र चित्र म इह नास्ति त्वादातमद्रिवः ।
राधस्तन्नो विदद्वस उभयाहस्त्या भर ॥

1. Indra! What is there which is not given by you on the hill in great variety, for which I am dependent on you.

You guide the wealth in the home with knowledge and support both (the brain cells and sense organs) through your hands (nerves). (1172), (345)

२. यन्मन्यसे वरेण्यमिन्द्र द्युक्षं तदा भर ।
विद्याम तस्य ते वयमकूपारस्य दावनः ॥

2. Indra! You strive to guide the mind excellently through heaven and the home.

You know his course; you bestow his desires from beyond through our sense organs. (1173)

३. यत्ते दिक्षु प्रराध्यं मनो अस्ति श्रुतं बृहत् ।
तेन दृढा चिदद्रिव आ वाजं दर्षि सातये ॥

3. Indra! You listen to him (mind) much; unite him to nourishment with success by bestowing and control him.

You bestow on him from the hill and stabilise him indeed by flowing to him continuously to bestow. (1174)

BOOK V : CHAPTER I

D. I.

१. शिशुं जज्ञानं हर्यतं मृजन्ति शुम्भन्ति विप्रं मरुतो गणेन ।
कविर्गीर्भिः काव्येना कविः सन्त्सोमः पवित्रमत्येति रेभन् ॥

1. Retinues of ideas inspire and convey knowledge to Mind; their birth refines and adorns it.

Soma bestows as gifts the songs of the poet and the poems of the singer with which our motley sense activities beneficently resound. (1175)

२. ऋषिमना य ऋषिकृत्स्वर्षाः सहस्रनीथः पदवीः कवीनाम् ।
तृतीयं धाम महिषः सिषासन्त्सोमो विराजमनु राजतिष्टुप् ॥

2. The ṛṣis (sense activities) move to the mind, the ṛṣis flow by themselves and produce a thousand paths (guidances) from the leader Agni (poet).

Soma bestows as gifts the desires of the three homes and gladdens the desires and controls them; now he rules them above as desired by him. (1176)

३. चमूषच्छ्येनः शकुनो विभृत्वा गोविन्दुर्द्रप्स आयुधानि बिभ्रत् ।
अपामूर्मिं सचमानः समुद्रं तुरीयं धाम महिषो विवक्ति ॥

3. They (the homes) sip eagerly what is nearby at propitious moments, bestowed without rivalry (confusion), the sense activities bestow extensive knowledge on the brain cells during life without delusion.

Waves of activity unite with the home (brain) and gladden the three homes (brain, sense organs and mind), who express satisfaction of their desires. (1177)

D. II.

१. एते सोमा अभि प्रियमिन्द्रस्य काममक्षरन् ।
वर्धन्तो अस्य वीर्यम् ॥

1. Indra out of his love lets the motley sense activities from Soma flow to us as desired by us,

which increase our vigorous activity from within. (1178)

२. पुनानासश्चमूषदो गच्छन्तो वायुमश्विना ।
ते नो धत्त सुवीर्यम् ॥

2. The Aśvins repeatedly go along the nerves from the brain cells (Saśa) to the sense organs (ūṣa) to bestow for them to sip.

They arouse us and bestow vigour. (1179)

३. इन्द्रस्य सोम राधसे पुनानो हार्दि चोदय ।
देवानां योनिमासदम् ॥

3. Indra causes the wealth from Soma to appear repeatedly in the brain (heart).

The devas bestow on our homes from the source. (1180)

४. मृजन्ति त्वा दश क्षिपो हिन्वन्ति सप्त धीतयः ।
अनु विप्रा अमादिषुः ॥

4. (Indra!) You win for mortals an armour through the rays (fingers) of sense activities and arouse understanding in them through the seven-pronged Activity.

Now it is Agni (the wise) who gladdens us with the missiles (rays). (1181)

५. देवेभ्यस्त्वा मदाय कं सृजानमति मेष्यः ।
सं गोभिर्वासयामसि ॥

5. Devas move to us from you to gladden; understanding flows to the head from the source through the Aśvins.

All that is supported by the sense activities in the home. (1182)

६. पुनानः कलशेष्वा वस्त्राण्यरुषो हरिः ।
परि गव्यान्यव्यत ॥

6 The desires of the brain (head) are repeatedly bestowed; the ruddy consciousness guides the garment-like brain.

The Aśvins go round and guide the sense activities to it. (1183)

७. मघोन आ पवस्व नो जहि विश्वा अप द्विषः ।
इन्दो सखायमा विश ॥

7. Activity arouses the sense organs from which spring by themselves bounteous streams for both (the brain and mind) for bestowal and drinking.

He is a friend of the brain cells whom he controls in the home. (1184)

८. नृचक्षसं त्वा वयमिन्द्रपीत स्वर्विदम् ।
भक्षीमहि प्रजामिषम् ॥

8. Indra swells towards men, perceives all, bestows and controls our desires to know heaven.

He opens the eyes of his subjects to consume much (sense perceptions). (1185)

९. वृष्टिं दिवः परि स्रव द्युम्नं पृथिव्या अधि ।
सहो नः सोम पृत्सु धाः ॥

9. He goes around rains (sense activities) in the waking state to satisfy the sense organs from heaven beyond.

At the same time, Soma bestows to nourish what is lacking, by arousing. (1186)

D. III.

१. सोमः पुनानो अर्षति सहस्रधारो अत्यविः ।
वायोरिन्द्रस्य निष्कृतम् ॥

1. Soma flows repeatedly in thousands of streams favoured by prāṇa,

to meet Indra at appointed places through the nerves. (1187)

२. पवमानमवस्यवो विप्रमभि प्र गायत ।
सुष्वाणं देववीतये ॥

2. The brain cells bless the fickle mind and the sense activities unite with them to inspire them.

They desire ideas eagerly to bestow desires. (1188)

३. पवन्ते वाजसातये सोमाः सहस्रपाजसः ।
गृणाना देववीतये ॥

3. Soma bestows continually to drink in life-activity; cooks and bestows thousands of ideas,

on the devotee who desires ideas. (1189)

४. उत नो वाजसातये पवस्व बृहतीरिषः ।
द्युमदिन्दो सुवीर्यम् ॥

4. He himself bestows a great many desires to drink, in life-activity continually,

from heaven to the brain cells to arouse vigour. (1190)

५. अत्या हियाना न हेतृभिरसृग्रं वाजसातये ।
वि वारमव्यमाशवः ॥

5. Prāṇa arouses the sense organs and supports them continually as the prime cause of life-activity,

through the brain (enclosure) by the Aśvins who bestow the food for it. (1191)

६. ते नः सहस्रिणं रयिं पवन्तामा सुवीर्यम् ।
स्वाना देवास इन्दवः ॥

6. They bind it with thousands of items of mighty wealth which they bestow to drink for arousing vigour,

releasing ideas (devas) to the panting (agitated) brain cells. (1192)

७. वाश्रा अर्षन्तीन्दवोऽभि वत्सं न मातरः ।
दधन्विरे गभस्त्योः ॥

7. The mother (sense activities) flow to the brain cells to bestow like to the lowing calves (by the cow).

They bestow on them wealth through the nerves for our comfort. (1193)

८. जुष्ट इन्द्राय मत्सरः पवमानः कनिक्रदत् ।
विश्वा अप द्विषो जहि ॥

8. Indra moves and flows to us resoundingly for births desired by the fickle mind.

Activity arouses the desires of both (brain and mind) for births arising from sense organs. (1194)

९. अपघ्नन्तो अराव्णः पवमानाः स्वर्दृशः ।
योनावृतस्य सीदत ॥

9. Activity is wealth within; bestows us desires for it; lets the fickle mind view heaven.

It envelops us from the source (i.e. our home). (1195)

D. IV.

१. सोमा असृग्रमिन्दवः सुता ऋतस्य धारया ।
इन्द्राय मधुमत्तमाः ॥

1. Soma bestows first on the brain cells; Ṛta arouses and supports them (in continuation).

Indra moves towards sense perceptions which we desire. (1196).

२. अभि विप्रा अनूषत गावो वत्सं न धेनवः ।
इन्द्रं सोमस्य पीतये ॥

2. The sense activities are attached to Agni (poet) like the calves to the milch-cow.

Indra swells over to Soma. (1197)

३. मदच्युत्क्षेति सादने सिन्धोरूर्मा विपश्चित् ।
सोमो गौरी अधि श्रितः ॥

3. The motley sense activities joyously drip in the home and settle down; the waves of Sindhu stir up the mind.

Soma releases sense activities from beyond after acquiring it. (1198)

४. दिवो नाभा विचक्षणोऽव्या वारे महीयते ।
सोमो यः सुक्रतुः कविः ॥

4. Consciousness from the centre (of existence) perceives (all) instantaneously; the Aśvins unite much with it for the sake of wealth (or in the enclosure).

Soma hastens to arouse and produce through Agni (poet) (or to do good through Agni). (1199)

५. यः सोमः कलशेष्वा अन्तः पवित्र आहितः ।
तमिन्दुः परि षस्वजे ॥

5. Soma hastens to bestow the desires of the brain (pot); he is gracious within for our welfare.

He himself gives rise (birth) to the desires of beyond in the brain cells which wish for them. (1200)

६. प्र वाजमिन्दुरिष्यति समुद्रस्याधि विष्टपि ।
जिन्वन्कोशं मधुश्चुतम् ॥

6. He unites with brain cells willingly to nourish speech, and also bestows as desired from the ocean beyond.

He wins the desires of the brain and lets them drip as sweet perceptions. (1201)

७. नित्यस्तोत्रो वनस्पतिर्धेनामन्तः सबर्दुघाम् ।
हिन्वानो मानुषा युजा ॥

7. The lord of desires (Soma) is praised daily for readily yielding sense perceptions (milk) through the milch-cow (sense activities) within.

He eagerly gives rise to desires in the home to unite with. (1202)

८. आ पवमान धारया रयिं सहस्रवर्चसम् ।
अस्मे इन्दो स्वाभुवम ॥

8. He supports the fickle mind with a thousand excellent items of wealth.

He himself bestows existence on our brain cells. (1203)

९. अभि प्रिया दिवः कविर्विप्रः स धारया सुतः ।
सोमो हिन्वे परावति ॥

9. Agni (poet) inspires the mind fondly to support him in the waking state.

Soma arouses him to new knowledge from beyond. (1204)

D. V.

१. उत्ते शुष्मास ईरते सिन्धोरूर्मेरिव स्वनः ।
वाणस्य चोदया पविम् ॥

1. If mind dries up, (Soma) arouses waves of Sindhu releasing like flashes of thunder.

Then desires spring up in us from the rim of the brain. (1205)

२. प्रसवे त उदीरते तिस्रो वाचो मखस्युवः ।
यदव्य एषि सानवि ॥

2. They (the desires) give birth above to agitation of the three states and bestow also vigorously on mind.

Whom the Aśvins also seek for gifts. (1206)

३. अव्या वारैः परि प्रियं हरिं हिन्वन्त्यद्रिभिः ।
पवमानं मधुश्चुतम् ॥

3. The Aśvins go around the enclosure (with gifts) in fondness; consciousness is well-known to arouse desires in the brain (hill).

Then sweet perceptions drip to mind. (1207)

४. आ पवस्व मदिन्तम पवित्रं धारया कवे ।
अर्कस्य योनिमासदम् ॥

4. Agni himself bestows on us the understanding desired to drink, beneficently supporting us.

Praiseworthily from the source of my home, (or consciousness releases it to my home). (1208)

५. स पवस्व मदिन्तम गोभिरञ्जानो अक्तुभिः ।
एन्द्रस्य जठरं विश ॥

5. And Indra himself bestows the understanding desired by supporting the sense activities which anoint us, against ignorance,

in the home of the brain cells through Indra. (1209)

D. VI.

१. अया वीती परि स्रव यस्त इन्दो मदेष्वा ।
अवाहन्नवतीर्नव ॥

1. Indra goes around the paths desiring to strive to bestow the desires of brain cells for sense activities.

He conveys food for new knowledge.

Alt. He conveys (the sense activities) to cross over to newer and newer species of creatures. (1210), (495)

The desire for change to a new species arises in the existing species and registered in their minds. The inadequacies and grievances felt by them over a long time and in concert are responded to by the creator devising some improvement and ushering in a new creature in the world.

२. पुरः सद्य इत्थाधिये दिवोदासाय शंबरम् ।
अध त्यं तुर्वशं यदुम् ॥

2. The city (brain) is given satisfaction thus immediately; consciousness bestows excellent services from heaven (ambara).

Then it is well-known that he crosses over to the home where the sense activities are. (1211)

३. परि णो अश्वमश्वविद्गोमदिन्दो हिरण्यवत् ।
क्षरा सहस्रिणीरिषः ॥

3. Prāṇa now goes around; Prāṇa knows the sense activities;

the tawny consciousness releases the sense activities to the brain cells.

He releases thousands of desires in the home. (1212)

D. VII.

१. अपघ्नन्पवते मृधोऽप सोमो अराव्णः ।
गच्छन्निन्द्रस्य निष्कृतम् ॥

1. Activity strikes down (ignorance) to protect understanding; Soma bestows Activity on mortals and releases desires,

for which he goes to meet Indra at the appointed place. (1213), (510)

२. महो नो राय आ भर पवमान जही मृधः ।
रास्वेन्दो वीरवद्यशः ॥

2. Activity is a great controller; he supports the fickle mind to forsake weariness.

He bestows vigour on brain cells himself indicating his excellence. (1214)

३. न त्वा शतं च न ह्रुतो राधो दित्सन्तमा मिनन् ।
यत्पुनानो मखस्यसे ॥

3. Activity! You do not destroy nor are you a stumbling block to prosperity; you approach us through the mother and bestow the desired gifts.

Repeatedly you strive to unite with us vigorously. (1215)

D. VIII.

१. अया पवस्व धारया यया सूर्यमरोचयः ।
हिन्वानो मानुषीरपः ॥

1. Consciousness on rising hastens to support the paths himself to protect.

He arouses desires in men through Activity. (1216), (493)

२. अयुक्त सूर एतशं पवमानो मनावधि ।
अन्तरिक्षेण यातवे ॥

2. He unites to arouse and release the motley sense activities to toil for the fickle mind in the home and bestow satisfaction.

He releases the paths to mind. (1217)

३. उत त्या हरितो रथे सूरो अयुक्त यातवे ।
इन्दुरिन्द्र इति ब्रुवन् ॥

3. Also it is well-known that the tawny consciousness unites and releases the paths to the sense organs.
from the brain cells for Indra, so it is said. (1218)

D. IX.

१. अग्निं वो देवमग्निभिः सजोषा यजिष्ठं दूतमध्वरे कृणुध्वम् ।
यो मर्त्येषु निध्रुविर्ऋतावा तपुर्मूर्धा घृतान्नः पावकः ॥

1. Agni bestows ideas (deva); Agni unites with them eagerly desiring life-activity; these messengers (ideas) run to create the Soma Yajña (life-activity).

These missiles (ideas) constantly move in bestowed by Ṛta; they warm up the brain with clarified butter from sense perceptions and purify it. (1219)

२. प्रोथदश्वो न यवसेऽविष्यन्यदा महः संवरणाद्व्यस्थात् ।
आदस्य वातो अनु वाति शोचिरध स्म ते व्रजनं कृष्णमस्ति ॥

2. Prāṇa a match for anyone (protha) guides them (ideas) in the home, whose desires he bestows and guides and gladdens them in the enclosure abidingly.

He bestows them now on the nerves accustomed to release them to us; they cultivate the enclosure (brain). (1220) (Y.V 15, 62)

३. उद्यस्य ते नवजातस्य वृष्णोऽग्ने चरन्त्यजरा इधानाः ।
अच्छा द्यामरुषो धूम एषि सं दूतो अग्न ईयसे हि देवान् ॥

3. Agni! these new ideas from the source plough us and change us; they go around the brain cells ever fresh.

The ruddy consciousness is near to our heaven and arouses us to all the messengers who strive to arouse us and bestow desires. (1221)

D. X.

१. तमिन्द्रं वाजयामसि महे वृत्राय हन्तवे ।
स वृषा वृषभो भुवत् ॥

1. Indra loves life-activity; he moves much to Vṛtra (inertia) to strike him down.

And Indra (bull) rains knowledge in existence. (1222)

२. इन्द्रः स दामने कृत ओजिष्ठः स बले हितः ।
द्युम्नी श्लोकी स सोम्यः ॥

2. Indra bestows on the home; produces vigorously releasing welfare to the brain cells.

He bestows from heaven praiseworthily through Soma. (1223)

३. गिरा वज्रो न सम्भृतः सबलो अनपच्युतः ।
ववक्ष उग्रो अस्तृतः ॥

3. He supports all on the hill through the nerves; he bestows on the brain cells by uniting with and cooking the sense organs.

He bestows to grow strong; he is unconquerable. (1224)

D. XI.

१. अध्वर्यो अद्रिभिः सुतं सोमं पवित्र आ नय ।
पुनाहीन्द्राय पातवे ॥

1. Presiding on the hill (brain) in life-activity, Soma guides the mind beneficently.

Indra bestows on him the path repeatedly. (1225), (499), (Y. V. 20, 30)

२. तव त्य इन्दो अन्धसो देवा मधोर्व्याशत ।
पवमानस्य मरुतः ॥

2. Soma! You are well-known to release brain cells from ignorance, through ideas.

Sense perceptions are our food. (1226)

३. दिवः पीयूषमुत्तमं सोममिन्द्राय वज्रिणे ।
सुनोता मधुमत्तमम् ॥

3. Consciousness swells over the brain to best advantage releasing Indra to the nerves,

which guide well the sense perception desired by us. (1227)

D. XII.

१. धर्ता दिवः पवते कृत्व्यो रसो दक्षो देवानामनुमाद्यो नृभिः ।
हरिः सृजानो अत्यो न सत्वभिर्वृथा पाजांसि कृणुषे नदीष्वा ॥

1. Consciousness supports us; protects understanding pro-

duces its essence for us; men hail devas (ideas) (or the deva) to satisfy them.

Consciousness flows from the source; prāṇa supports existence at his pleasure, supports the cooking of ideas and produces them eagerly and bestow desires resoundingly. (1228), (558)

२. शूरो न धत्त आयुधा गभस्त्योः स्व३ः सिषासन्रथिरो गविष्टिषु ।
इन्द्रस्य शुष्ममीरयन्नपस्युभिरिन्दुर्हिन्वानो अज्यते मनीषिभिः ॥

2. Valiantly he (consciousness) bestows on us life; bestows it himself through his rays (hands); releases the sense organs and bestows them eagerly as his gifts as desired by the sense activities.

If the streams of sense perceptions (food) wane, Indra gushes to us, arouses desires in both brain cells and sense organs and is victorious for men. (1229)

३. इन्द्रस्य सोम पवमान ऊर्मिणा तविष्यमाणो जठरेष्वा विश ।
प्र नः पिन्व विद्युदभ्रेव रोदसी धिया नो वाजाँ उप माहि शश्वतः ॥

3. Indra bestows on our mind waves (of sense activities perceptions); bestow from the brain cells in the home courageously and controls.

He nourishes profusely and binds them, lightning-like in poor men like us; satisfies both brain cells and sense organs and in life-activity above arouses and bestows constantly. (1230)

D. XIII.

१. यदिन्द्र प्रागपागुदङ्न्यग्वा हूयसे नृभिः ।
सिमा पुरू नृषूतो अस्यानवेऽसि प्रशर्ध तुर्वशे ॥

1. On being invoked by men, what Indra does is to fulfil through Activity; he guides the sense activities to sense organs,

with which we are bound up; the mind is new to us; the brain (home) nourishes it boldly. (1231), (279)

२. यद्वा रुमे रुशमे श्यावके कृप इन्द्र मादयसे सचा ।
कण्वासस्त्वा स्तोमेभिर्ब्रह्मवाहस इन्द्रा यच्छन्त्या गहि ॥

2. What is bestowed on me resoundingly I browse upon at night; Indra strives to unite and bestow on me (my needs) in compassion.

You support the brain cells praiseworthily during sleep; convey and bestow knowledge; you are well-known to control and arouse sense activities. (1232)

D. XIV.

१. उभयं शृणवच्च न इन्द्रो अर्वागिदं वचः ।
सत्राच्या मघवान्त्सोमपीतये धिया शविष्ठ आ गमत् ।।

1. Indra controls both brain cells and sense organs and cooks afresh also; hastens here to bestow also, (new creatures).

He moves to life-activity (Satra) and swells over to Soma for his satisfaction for which he comes with might. (1233)

२. तं हि स्वराजं वृषभं तमोजसा धिषणे निष्टतक्षतुः ।
उतोपमानां प्रथमो नि षीदसि सोमकामं हि ते मनः ।।

2. Indra desires to arouse and control himself; desires to bestow powerfully on the head (Soma vessel) and fashion (carve) new creatures dependent on him,

for which he is the foremost deva also above in the home; Soma's desire is the welfare of the mind. (1234)

D. XV.

१. पवस्व देव आयुषगिन्द्रं गच्छतु ते मदः ।
वायुमा रोह धर्मणा ।।

1. Indra goes to the sense activities himself to bestow on the deva prāṇa (life) to protect (creatures),

who (prāṇa) ascends up the nerves as established (dharma). (1235), (483)

२. पवमान नि तोशसे रयिं सोम श्रवाय्यम् ।
इन्दो समुद्रमा विश ।।

2. Soma bestows satisfaction on mind praiseworthily with wealth (of sense perceptions).

He bestows gladness on the brain cells in our homes. (1236)

३. अपघ्नन्पवसे मृधः [क्रतुवित्सोम मत्सरः ।
नुदस्वादेवयुं जनम्] ।।

3. Activity strikes down weariness in the home and protects; Soma produces the knowledge which flows to us.

Now he bestows the wants of men by uniting with devas (ideas). (1237)

D. XVI.

१. अभी नो वाजसातमं [रयिमर्ष शतस्पृहम् ।
इन्दो सहस्रभर्णसं तुविद्युम्नं विभासहम्] ॥

1. To bestow desires in life-activity [wealth flows in a hundred (streams) eagerly,

to the brain cells to support them in a thousand ways to be associated mightily and excellently without glamour in the waking state]. (1238), (549)

२. वयं ते अस्य राधसो वसोर्वसो पुरुस्पृहः ।
नि नेदिष्ठतमा इषः स्याम सम्ने ते अध्रिगो ॥

2. They bestow on us wealth and control one man (home) after another with abundant eagerness.

Our immediate wishes are desires closest to us, all of which are from the motley sense activities which are irresistible. (1239)

३. परि स्य स्वानो अक्षरदिन्दुरव्ये मदच्युतः ।
धारा य ऊर्ध्वो अध्वरे भ्राजा न याति गव्ययुः ॥

3. The Aśvins go around us by themselves and flow to the brain cells to let sense perceptions drip.

They move to the head to bestow and give support in life-activity and unite with sense activities to brighten its path. (1240)

D. XVII.

१. पवस्व सोम महान्त्समुद्रः पिता देवानां विश्वाभि धाम ॥

1. Soma himself bestows on us to drink; the great one gladdens our father (Activity).

Devas (ideas) bestow on the sense organs from the home. (1241), (429)

२. शुक्रः पवस्व देवेभ्यः सोम दिवे पृथिव्यै शं च प्रजाभ्यः ॥

2. Devas (ideas) themselves bestow to drink and brighten us; Soma toils for the sense organs of the subjects. (1242)

३. दिवो धर्तासि शुक्रः पीयूषः सत्ये विधर्मन्वाजी पवस्व ॥

3. Consciousness swells over to the brain and supports it in waking (brightness); he himself bestows to protect life-activity in existence in accordance with dharma. (1243)

D. XVIII

१. प्रेष्ठं वो अतिथिं स्तुषे मित्रमिव प्रियम् ।
अग्ने रथं न वेद्यम् ॥

1. The guests (ideas) praiseworthily bestow nourishment as desired with the kindness like that of a friend.

Agni controls knowledge through the sense organs. (1244), (5)

२. कविमिव प्रशंस्यं यं देवास इति द्विता ।
नि मर्त्येष्वादधुः ॥

2. He controls ideas (devas) like a poet praiseworthily and bestows thus on both brain cells and sense organs.

He himself bestows the desires of mortals. (1245)

३. त्वं यविष्ठ दाशुषो नॄँः पाहि शृणुही गिरः ।
रक्षा तोकमुत त्मना ॥

3. Agni! Being fond of the brain cells you give services to men eagerly; you crush (creatures) surprisingly on the hill to arouse (new ones) and fulfil.

You yourself protect the offspring. (1246), (Y. V. 13, 52)

D. XIX.

१. एन्द्र नो गधि प्रिय सत्राजिदगोह्य ।
गिरिर्न विश्वतः पृथुः पतिर्दिवः ॥

1. Indra satisfies the sense activities in kindness and wins life-activity (Soma yajña) for the sense activities from heaven.

He spreads them out to the sense organs from the brain (hill) and protects them in the waking state. (1247), (393)

२. अभि हि सत्य सोमपा उभे बभूथ रोदसी ।
इन्द्रासि सुन्वतो वृधः पतिर्दिवः ॥

2. To rouse up both the brain cells and sense organs to existence, Soma bestows on them for welfare.

Indra binds them to the devotee to foster growth and protects him in the waking state. (1248)

३. त्वं हि शश्वतीनामिन्द्र दर्ता पुरामसि ।
हन्ता दस्योर्मनोर्वृधः पतिर्दिवः ॥

3. Indra arouses and supports Soma constantly in the city (brain).

Indeed he fosters the growth of mind's wants within, in the path of the waking state. (1249)

D. XX.

१. पुरां भिन्दुर्युवा कविरमितौजा अजायत ।
इन्द्रो विश्वस्य कर्मणो धर्ता वज्री पुरुष्टुतः ॥

1. In ancient times when the brain cells (earth) were (was) young, Agni (poet) established odd creatures from the source.

Indra supported the duties of the body (sense organs) through the nerves praiseworthily. (1250), (359)

These odd creatures are the mammoths of olden times. We see that before the mind was well developed the body grew to great bulks. The trees grow to much greater bulk.

२. त्वं बलस्य गोमतोऽपावरद्रिवो बिलम् ।
त्वां देवा अबिभ्युषस्तुज्यमानास आविषुः ॥

2. Rich in sense activities, you bestowed gifts from activity on the hill on the brain cells compulsorily.

Fearlessly you won devas (ideas) eagerly and praiseworthily and bestowed them in the home in various directions. (1251)

३. इन्द्रमीशानमोजसाभि स्तोमैरनूषत ।
सहस्रं यस्य रातय उत वा सन्ति भूयसीः ॥

3. Indra rules vigorously and bestows to be attached to us praiseworthily.

He bestowed thousands (of creatures) and bestowed on them also gifts to bind them to existence. (1252)

BOOK V: CHAPTER II

D. I.

१. अक्रान्त्समुद्रः प्रथमे विधर्मन् जनयन्प्रजा भुवनस्य गोपाः ।
वृषा पवित्रे अधि सानो अव्ये बृहत्सोमो वावृधे स्वानो अद्रिः ॥

1. The first step taken by the protector of the creaturers, in accordance with dharma, for the birth of subjects (creatures) and their guidance, was in the ocean waters.

The Aśvins rained on Soma beneficently from beyond the summit to foster growth to Soma greatly who himself bestowed (on brain cells) on the hill for the growth. (1253), (529)

The first step taken during creation is said to be in accordance with established rules (dharma). That means the rules for creation were already laid down in heaven or world of ideas by the creator. What we witness on earth is truly manifestation of ideas which are clothed in form and substance on earth. No sort of activity is possible without prior thought and planning and the creative process is no exception to it. We have already explained under mantra 1116 how the foundation was laid in the plane of ideas for the state of manifestation. Manifestation is a reversal of the earlier process of creation or blossoming out.

Since manifestation is a combined activity of the subtle and gross i.e. ideas and matter or inertia, the ideas had to descend to the level of matter before combining them to life process.

Water was found to be the ideal source for making a start with cell life as it has dissolved substances furnishing the materials for cells in easily accessible form. Secondly the latent heat of water furnished the energy requirement for the building up process.

The Aśvins who are the direct vehicles of the creator always mediate between him and his objective world. Further they assist in passing form one level of activity to another, such as from higher to lower or vice versa.

Then the Aśvins are said to have rained to Soma and what he rained was Activity or Vaiśvānara. These two devas, Activity and Soma, always go together. They are related as action and reaction.

२. मत्सि वायुमिष्टये राधसे नो मत्सि मित्रावरुणा पूयमानः ।
मत्सि शर्धो मारुतं मत्सि देवान्मत्सि द्यावापृथिवी देव सोम ॥

2. I am willingly bound to the nervous system which releases wealth to me; I am willingly bound to the brain (Mitra) and the external world (Varuṇa) who swells over to the home.

I am bound to the bold ideas (Maruts); I am bound to the Devas (Indra, Soma etc.), to the head and sense organs (heaven and earth) which the devas release to me. (1254)

३. महत्तत्सोमो महिषश्चकारापां यद्गर्भोऽवृणीत देवान् ।
अदधादिन्द्रे पवमान ओजोऽजनयत्सूर्ये ज्योतिरिन्दुः ॥

3. Great is he who releases, and gladdens me with desires, and also a body (prison) i.e. Activity who envelops us from the source and guides ideas.

Indra bestows food on the fickle mind and strength; the effulgence of consciousness from the source unites with brain cells (to reveal them). (1255), (542)

D. II.

१. एष देवो अमर्त्यः पर्णवीरिव दीयते ।
अभि द्रोणान्यासदम् ॥

1. Ideas (devas) like leaves or feathers seek mortals vigorously to unite with them and bestow,

and to guide the brain in the head. (1256)

Ideas float all over space enveloping everything contained within it. They are in various forms i.e. everything is some form of idea namely radiations, light, heat, sound air, water, earth. Ideas are the building blocks of the creatures and the universe. The creator is the source of all ideas and they are all his objective counterparts, he being the universal subject.

२. एष विप्रैरभिष्टुतोऽपो देवो वि गाहते ।
दधद्रत्नानि दाशुषे ॥

2. Wise men willingly seek ideas; also activity plunges into them,

and bestow valuable gifts to the devotees. (1257)

Activity establishes only the connection between the universal subject and the objects of the world and it is the accompanying ideas which give the content of the established connection.

३. एष विश्वानि वार्या शूरो यन्निव सत्वभिः ।
पवमानः सिषासति ॥

3. The brave seek the wealth of the sense organs which give existence to us as if guiding us.

They bestow existence on mind as desired. (1258)

४. एष देवो रथर्यति पवमानो दिशस्यति ।
आविष्कृणोति वग्वनुम् ॥

4. Ideas seek to unite with sense organs and these unite with mind to give it direction.

The sense activities then manifest them by bestowing speech praiseworthily. (1259)

After the brain has received sense perceptions through the sense organs, these are passed on to and unite with mind. These ideas are manifested through speech. These are called revelations which is how the Vedas rose and not directly from god's mouth. But our mouths are all god's mouths.

५. एष देवो विपन्युभिः पवमान ऋतायुभिः ।
हरिर्वाजाय मृज्यते ॥

5. Ideas seek to inspire and guide both the brain cells and sense organs; Ṛta unites mind with them.

The tawny consciousness wins them for mortals in life by revealing them. (1260)

६. एष देवो विपा कृतोऽति ह्वरांसि धावति ।
पवमानो अदाभ्यः ॥

6. The ideas seek to create and inspire through the motley sense activities; the spinal cord supports them and releases understanding,

to the fickle mind inviolably. (1261)

७. एष दिवं वि धावति तिरो रजांसि धारया ।
पवमानः कनिक्रदत् ॥

7. Consciousness flows to divide knowledge and supports their distinctive colours

in the mind resoundingly. (1262)

८. एष दिवं व्यासरत्तिरो रजांस्यस्तृतः ।
पवमानः स्वध्वरः ॥

8. Consciousness seeks to cross over and envelop us; prāṇa supports it pleasantly
with sweet gifts to the fickle mind. (1263)

९. एष प्रत्नेन जन्मना देवो देवेभ्यः सुतः ।
हरिः पवित्रे अर्षति ॥

9. Ancient creatures (life-courses) sought ideas, and ideas hastened to mind.

The tawny consciousness flows to the rim of the brain for the three states (or to support). (1264)

१०. एष उ स्य पुरुव्रतो जज्ञानो जनयन्निषः ।
धारया पवते सुतः ॥

10. Abundant duties (vows) seek and call us for the birth of knowledge to guide men's desires.

They move to support mind to drink knowledge. (1265)

D. III.

१. एष धिया यात्यण्व्या शूरो रथेभिराशुभिः ।
गच्छन्निन्द्रस्य निष्कृतम् ॥

1. The hero (knowledge) is supported by sense organs quickly seeking to give satisfaction along new paths,
for which Indra goes to appointed places. (1266)

२. एष पुरू धियायते बृहते देवतातये ।
यत्रामृतास आशत ॥

2. Abundant satisfaction flows by uniting with the great father of the Devas, Savitā.

There food (sense activities) are released to mortals. (1267)

३. एतं मृजन्ति मर्ज्यमुप द्रोणेष्वायवः ।
प्रचक्राणं महीरिषः ॥

3. The motley sense activities win (gifts) for mortals; mortals win the desires of the brain cells in the head above.

They go around nourishing (the cells) with desires for sense organs (mahī). (1268)

४. एष हितो वि नीयतेऽन्तः शुन्ध्यावता पथा ।
यदी तुञ्जन्ति भूर्णयः ॥

4. They seek our welfare through guidance within, along the path of purified knowledge,
which stimulates guidance in existence. (1269)

५. एष रुक्मिभिरीयते वाजी शुभ्रेभिरंशुभिः ।
पतिः सिन्धूनां भवन् ॥

5. The golden consciousness flows to support life by uniting with it and supporting Soma juice with his radiance.
He protects Sindhu in the home. (1270)

६. एष शृङ्गाणि दोधुवच्छिशीते यूथ्यो३ वृषा ।
नम्णा दधान ओजसा ॥

6. Consciousness seeks the brain (hill) to agitate the slumbering brain cells and bestow by speaking to the multitude, the rains his rays,
bestowing courageously and vigorously. (1271)

७. एष वसू नि पिब्दनः परुषा ययिवाँ अति ।
अव शादेषु गच्छति ॥

7. The puruṣa hastens to us from beyond seeking beneficently to tread upon us.
He comes along the nerves (śâda, grass) to favour. (1272)

८. एतमु त्यं दश क्षिपो हरिं हिन्वन्ति यातवे ।
स्वायुधं मदिन्तमम् ॥

8. It is well-known that the motley sense activities bind and protect with their rays (fingers).
Consciousness arouses them and bestows their paths.
He unites with the home himself and gladdens us mightily as desired. (1273)

D. IV.

१. एष उ स्य वृषा रथोऽव्या वारेभिरव्यत ।
गच्छन्वाजं सहस्रिणम् ॥

1. The Aśvins flow at our cell to support the gifts through the sense organs abidingly,
comes to life-activity for a thousand mighty things. (1274)

२. एतं त्रितस्य योषणो हरिं हिन्वन्त्यद्रिभिः ।
इन्दुमिन्द्राय पीतये ॥

2. Our prāṇa (Trita) moves to the motley sense activities eagerly; the mighty consciousness is well-known to arouse desires on the hill.

Indra swells over to the brain cells. (1275)

३. एष स्य मानुषीष्वा श्येनो न विक्षु सीदति ।
गच्छं जारो न योषितम् ॥

3. New nourishment watching like a hawk flows into our home eagerly bestowing desires,

like a sweet heart going to meet her paramour. (1276)

४. एष स्य मद्यो रसोऽव चष्टे दिवः शिशुः ।
य इन्दुर्वारमाविशत् ॥

4. We seek the essence of sense activities; consciousness favours the mind also to gain them.

He moves to the brain cells to bestow the gifts on the home. (1277)

५. एष स्य पीतये सुतो हरिरर्षति धर्णसिः ।
क्रन्दन्योनिमभि प्रियम् ॥

5. He (consciousness) seeks us to swell to mind flowing boldly, to please the source resoundingly. (1278)

६. एतं त्यं हरितो दश मर्मृज्यन्ते अपस्युवः ।
याभिर्मदाय शुम्भते ॥

6. The motley sense activities are well-known to convey protection (daśa) to mortals.

They support us handsomely and joyously. (1279)

D. V.

१. एष वाजी हितो नृभिर्विश्वविन्मनसस्पतिः ।
आव्यं वारं वि धावति ॥

1. Men seek welfare in life-activity which the sense organs bestow mightily through the lord of the mind and brain cells (Activity/Soma).

The Aśvins separate the composite Activity (into individual sense activities) for Knowledge. (1280)

२. एष पवित्रे अक्षरत्सोमो देवेभ्यः सुतः ।
विश्वा धामान्याविशन् ॥

2. Soma flows beneficently seeking ideas (devas) for mind.

They (ideas) are manifested through sense organs in the home. (1281)

३. एष देवः शुभायतेऽधि योनावमर्त्यः ।
वृत्रहा देववीतमः ॥

3. Ideas from beyond seek to unite with us for our welfare, which the source releases for mortals.

Vṛtra (inertia) departing ideas bless us as desired. (1282)

४. एष वृषा कनिक्रदद्दशभिर्जामिभिर्यतः ।
अभि द्रोणानि धावति ॥

4. They (ideas) rain protection resoundingly; support their relative (mind) by uniting with him.

They bestow understanding on the brain. (1283)

५. एष सूर्यमरोचयत्पवमानो अधि द्यवि ।
पवित्रे मत्सरो मदः ॥

5. Consciousness on ascending unites with mind and blesses it from heaven beyond.

He flows to us beneficently and causes rejoicings. (1284)

६. एष सूर्येण हासते संवसानो विवस्वता ।
पतिर्वाचो अदाभ्यः ॥

6. Consciousness seeks mightily to bestow existence on all in the home and illuminates knowledge.

He is the inviolable lord of speech. (1285)

D. VI.

१. एष कविरभिष्टुतः पवित्रे अधि तोशते ।
पुनानो घ्नन्नप द्विषः ॥

1. Agni's (poets) wishes flow to us; also satisfy us from beyond beneficently.

Activity flows repeatedly with wealth for the desires of both brain cells and sense organs. (1286)

२. एष इन्द्राय वायवे स्वर्जित्परि षिच्यते ।
पवित्रे दक्षसाधनः ॥

2. Indra seeks to bestow on brain cells by winning from heaven and sprinkling them.

He bestows on us wealth beneficently and satisfies us. (1287)

३. एष नृभिर्वि नीयते दिवो मूर्धा वृषा सुतः ।
सोमो वनेषु विश्ववित् ॥

3. Consciousness seeks to support men by uniting and guiding and rains his rays on mind from the head.

Soma acquaints us with desires through the sense organs. (1288)

४. एष गव्युरचिक्रदत्पवमानो हिरण्ययुः ।
इन्दुः सत्राजिदस्तृतः ॥

4. The sense activities seek perceptions extensively; they produce them and bestow on mind arousing gladness by uniting with him.

Prāṇa (Trita) wins the wants of the brain cells in life-activity. (1289)

५. एष शुष्म्यसिष्यददन्तरिक्षे वृषा हरिः ।
पुनान इन्दुरिन्द्रमा ॥

5. Prāṇa gushes seeking to bestow the wishes of the mind and rains through consciousness.

Indra bestows on brain cells repeatedly. (1290)

६. एष शुष्म्यदाभ्यः सोमः पुनानो अर्षति ।
देवावीरघशंसहा ॥

6. Inviolable Soma flows repeatedly seeking what has dried up.

The deva blesses those who are dependent praiseworthily. (1291)

D. VII.

१. स सुतः पीतये वृषा सोमः पवित्रे अर्षति ।
विघ्नन्रक्षांसि देवयुः ॥

1. Soma flows beneficently and rains (sense perceptions) and swelling over to mind bestows them.

Through wealth you support the devotee with protection. (1292)

२. स पवित्रे विचक्षणो हरिरर्षति धर्णसिः ।
अभि योनिं कनिक्रदत् ।।

2. The tawny consciousness flows boldly; perceives instantly (or diligently); bestows beneficially.

He produces the sense activities from the source to bestow. (1293)

३. स वाजी रोचनं दिवः पवमानो वि धावति ।
रक्षोहा वारमव्ययम् ।।

3. Consciousness ascends in life-activity and honours the mind by bestowing discriminating understanding.

The Aśvins controlling wealth protect him by changes in him. (1294)

४. स त्रितस्याधि सानवि पवमानो अरोचयत् ।
जामिभिः सूर्यं सह ।।

4. Prāṇa bestows on mind coming with spoils and satisfies him,

together with the relative consciousness when he rises up to unite with. (1295)

५. स वृत्रहा वृषा सुतो वरिवोविददाभ्यः ।
सोमो वाजमिवासरत् ।।

5. And on Vṛtra's departure Soma rains to mind and bestows on him freedom for knowledge inviolably.

Soma approaches the home in life-activity and gladdens it. (1296)

६. स देवः कविनेषितो३ऽभि द्रोणानि धावति ।
इन्दुरिन्द्राय मंहयन् ।।

6. Devas (ideas) bestow at the wishes of Agni and bestow understanding on the brain.

Indra bestows abundantly on the brain cells and guides them. (1297)

D. VIII.

१. यः पावमानीरध्येत्यृषिभिः संभृतं रसम् ।
सर्वं स पूतमश्नाति स्वदितं मातरिश्वना ।।

1. The ṛṣis of the motley sense activities hasten to the dependent (mind) and support him with all essences.

They swell over to the hill to bestow on all as determined by Agni (Mātariśvan). (1298)

२. पावमानीर्यो अध्येत्यृषिभिः संभृतं रसम् ।
तस्मै सरस्वती दुहे क्षीरं सर्पिर्मधूदकम् ॥

2. Agni arouses the motley sense activities to sip (the brain cells); they all support essences (sense perceptions).

Knowledge flows from them; milk (perceptions) and sap flow from them; the sense perceptions (honey) bestow desires. (1299)

३. पावमानीः स्वस्त्ययनीः सुदुघा हि घृतश्चुतः ।
ऋषिभिः संभृतो रसो ब्राह्मणेष्वमृतं हितम् ॥

3. It is well-known that Agni himself guides; arouses sense activities to incite clarified butter to drip.

The sense activities support all perceptions (essences); bestow knowledge desired by men for welfare. (1300)

४. पावमानीर्दधन्तु न इमं लोकमथो अमुम् ।
कामान्त्समर्धयन्तु नो देवीर्देवैः समाहृताः ॥

4. Agni bestows within here by churning the external world through sense activities.

He bestows desires on mortals within to sip; the devī takes away ideas with her at the same time. (1301)

५. येन देवाः पवित्रेणात्मानं पुनते सदा ।
तेन सहस्रधारेण पावमानीः पुनन्तु नः ॥

5. Those ideas beneficently swell over by themselves constantly to sense activities repeatedly.

Agni repeatedly supports them thousands of times to bind them. (1302)

६. पावमानीः स्वस्त्ययनीस्ताभिर्गच्छति नान्दनम् ।
पुण्यांश्च भक्षान्भक्षयत्यमृतत्वं च गच्छति ॥

6. Agni guides to welfare those dependent on him and supports them for which he comes and is praised.

He swells over to the home to guide and shines; he unites with the homes of mortals, for which also he comes. (1303)

D. IX.

१. अगन्म महा नमसा यविष्ठं यो दीदाय समिद्धः स्वे दुरोणे ।
चित्रभानुं रोदसी अन्तरुर्वी स्वाहुतं विश्वतः प्रत्यञ्चम् ॥

1. The brain honours us; it honours us greatly by bestowing the desires on the brain cells, which inherit (dāya) ideas of sense objects (fuel) soaring around from their own head.

They shine in varied lights in both (brain cells and sense organs) within; the reservoir (brain) itself invokes the sense organs to nourish and adorn it. (1304)

२. स मह्ना विश्वा दुरितानि साह्वानग्निः ष्टवे दम आ जातवेदाः ।
स नो रक्षिषद्दुरितादवद्यादस्मान्गृणत उत नो मघोनः ॥

2. On being invoked Agni at his desire bestows from the highly honoured sense organs inciting them and releasing through the nerves on the home for the birth of knowledge.

He bestows gifts to protect our desires; he releases them for consumption and blesses the devotees to be closely united to them through the bounteous nerves. (1305)

३. त्वं वरुण उत मित्रो अग्ने त्वां वर्धन्ति मतिभिर्वसिष्ठाः ।
त्वे वसु सुषणनानि सन्तु यूयं पात स्वस्तिभिः सदा नः ॥

3. Agni! You foster the growth of (ideas) of the external world (Varuṇa) in the brain (Mitra) to promote his growth to support knowledge in the home as desired.

Indra easily obtains gifts from the mother through you and bestows the gifts; your path always binds us to welfare. (1306).

D. X.

१. महाँ इन्द्रो य ओजसा पर्जन्यो वृष्टिमाँ इव ।
स्तोमैर्वत्सस्य वावृधे ॥

1. Indra is great and he moves to bestow vigorously like a burst of rain from a rain cloud.

Praiseworthily he bestows on mind for his growth. (1307), (Y. V. 7, 40)

२. कण्वा इन्द्रं यदक्रत स्तोमैर्यज्ञस्य साधनम् ।
जामि ब्रुवत आयुधा ॥

2. Indra produces those in life-activity which bestow wealth and bestows them on the brain-cells.

He speaks to his relative Soma to unite (with life-activity) and bestow knowledge. (1308)

३. प्रजामृतस्य पिप्रतः प्र यद्भरन्त वह्नयः ।
विप्रा ऋतस्य वाहसा ॥

3. He nourishes births in mortals and nourishes them also; he nourishes those whom he supports within to whom he conveys and whom he guides.

Agni conveys and bestows Ṛta. (1309)

D. XI.

१. पवमानस्य जिघ्नतो हरेश्चन्द्रा असृक्षत ।
जीरा अजिरशोचिषः ॥

1. He wins wealth for our fickle mind; he carries them to mind letting them flow from the home to him.

Quickly or slowly his (minds) desires will be released. (1310)

२. पवमानो रथीतमः शुभ्रेभिः शुभ्रशस्तमः ।
हरिश्चन्द्रो मरुद्गणः ॥

2. Desires control the mind; they are attractive and handsomely praised.

Indeed they release retinues of ideas (Maruts) to Mind. (1311)

३. पवमान व्यश्नुहि रश्मिभिर्वाजसातमः ।
दधत्स्तोत्रे सुवीर्यम् ॥

3. They (ideas) arouse the mind and manifest themselves in him and praised; they support the rays (of sense activities) in life-activity continuously.

They bestow praiseworthily to arouse vigour. (1312)

D. XII.

१. परीतो षिञ्चता सुतं सोमो य उत्तमं हविः ।
दधन्वाँ यो नर्यो अप्स्व३न्तरा सुषाव सोममद्रिभिः ॥

1. They (the ideas) go around tingling along to mind as the best oblations from Soma.

They bestow wealth (of perceptions) on us men; Activity himself releases them within by arousing Soma eagerly to bestow on the hill (brain). (1313), (512), (Y. V. 19, 2)

२. नूनं पुनानोऽविभिः परि स्रवावब्धः सुरभिंतरः ।
सुते चित्त्वाप्सु मदामो अंधसा श्रीणन्तो गोभिरुत्तरम् ।।

2. 'Now, Soma goes around repeatedly to favour us; he flows to us from the ocean (of existence) for us to cross over (ignorance) pleasantly.

You arouse Activity for bestowing ideas on mind from our homes; to release him from ignorance, the sense activities are the best support to cook up within. (1314)

३. परि स्वानश्चक्षसे देवमादनः क्रतुरिन्दुर्विचक्षणः ।।

3. Soma goes around himself to perceive; achieve and bestow; the deva joyously binds us; he perceives the brain cells and produces for them instantly. (1315)

D. XIII.

१. असावि सोमो अरुषो वृषा हरी राजेव दस्मो अभि गा अचिक्रदत् ।
पुनानो वारमत्येष्यव्ययं श्येनो न योनिं घृतवन्तमासदत् ।।

1. Soma bestows during waking (day); the tawny consciousness rains his rays like a king for the sense activities to perceive and produce and bestow our wants.

The Aśvins who watch like a hawk from the source and control bestow on us gifts repeatedly through prāṇa for clarified butter which he bestows within the home. (1316), (562)

२. पर्जन्यः पिता महिषस्य पर्णिनो नाभा पृथिव्या गिरिषु क्षयं दधे ।
स्वसार आपो अभि गा उदासरन्त्सं ग्रावभिर्वसते वीते अध्वरे ।।

2. The father (Activity) is born from beyond and gladdens our desires by coming from the source like feathers (or leaves) to control the home on the hill and bestow on the sense organs.

Activity lets sense activities from his own essence to flow to all above, to support the home on the hill desirous of life-activity. (1317)

३. कविर्वेधस्या पर्येषि माहिनमत्यो न मृष्टो अभि वाजमर्षसि ।
अपसेधन् दुरिता सोम नो मृड घृता वसानः परि यासि निर्णिजम् ।।

3. Agni (poet) goes around to the desires of the devotee; arouses and honours him through Prāṇa and does not forget to flow to life-activity.

Activity releases wealth through Soma to consume; he goes

around in compassion for clarified butter in the home, ascertains and binds it. (1318)

D. XIV.

१. श्रायन्त इव सूर्यं विश्वेदिन्द्रस्य भक्षत ।
वसूनि जातो जनिमान्योजसा प्रति भागं न दीधिमः ।।

1. As if to cook the sense organs within, consciousness shines for Indra in the home.

Indra (Vasu) from the source bestows vigorously on the home for the sake of mind (son), every part of which beams down satisfaction and delight. (1319), (267), (Y. V. 33, 41)

२. अलर्षिरातिं वसुदामुप स्तुहि भद्रा इन्द्रस्य रातयः ।
यो अस्य कामं विधतो न रोषति मनो दानाय चोदयन् ।।

2. Indra desires graciously to bestow above; Indra is ready to arouse and bestow welfare praiseworthily.

He pays homage to our desires; bestows eagerly to mind; he unites above to bestow and guide. (1320)

D. XV.

१. यत इन्द्र भयामहे ततो नो अभयं कृधि ।
मघवन् छग्धि तव तन्न ऊतये वि द्विषो वि मृधो जहि ।।

1. When in great fear Indra unites with the father (Activity) and creates fearlessness and satisfaction.

Indra (Maghavan) satisfies also the hill and helps through nourishment (sense activities) the desires of both brain cells and sense organs without weariness or without forsaking. (1321), (274)

२. त्वं हि राधसस्पते राधसो महः क्षयस्यासि विधर्ता ।
तं त्वा वयं मघवन्निन्द्र गिर्वणः सुतावन्तो हवामहे ।।

2. Indra! You arouse the lord of wealth, bestow wealth and gladden us; you support it if it wanes in us.

You bestow on us desires munificently; you bestow on mind within great oblations desired from the hill. (1322)

D. XVI.

१. त्वं सोमासि धारयुर्मन्द्र ओजिष्ठो अध्वरे ।
पवस्व मंहयद्रयिः ।।

1. Indra! You bind Soma to support extensively life-activity with vigour.

He himself bestows wealth praiseworthily to drink. (1323)

२. त्व सुतो मविन्तमो दधन्वान्मत्सरिन्तमः ।
इन्दुः सत्राजिदस्तृतः ॥

2. You bestow delight on mind mightily as desired; you honour him and bestow wealth and flow mightily for desires.

Prāṇa wins the wants in life-activity for the brain cells. (1324)

३. त्वं सुष्वाणो आद्रिभिरभ्यर्ष कनिक्रदत् ।
द्युमन्तं शुष्ममा भर ॥

3. You bestow desires eagerly on the hill and flow to support fearlessness by producing sense activities and bestowing.

You gush to us within from heaven to bestow support on us. (1325)

D. XVII.

१. पवस्व देववीतय इन्दो धाराभिरोजसा ।
आ कलशं मधुमान्त्सोम नः सदः ॥

1. Indra! You yourself go to the brain cells to bestow devas (ideas) desired by them to drink and support it vigorously.

Soma bestows sweet perceptions within the head (brain) constantly and binds them. (1326), (527)

२. तव द्रप्सा उदप्रुत इन्द्रं मदाय वावृधुः ।
त्वां देवासो अमृताय कं पपुः ॥

2. Brain cells! You sprouted from water, Indra bestowed on you joyously and enveloped and roused you up.

Devas bestowed you on mortals to whom you moved to enlighten and protect as desired. (1327)

The Vedas long ago realised that life originated in water from cell organisms. These cells combine in them both the heavenly component of ideas and the earthly component of inertia or matter. The heavenly component consisted of the sense of differentiation and sense of touch besides ideas which determine the nature of the activity of the cells. The terrestrial components consist of water and dissolved substances in water. The latent heat of water furnished the energy requirements for building up the cells.

It will be noted that this earliest step in evolution is mentioned at a late stage in the Veda. It indicates that this idea was conceived at a late stage of the traditional stock of knowledge. So, the Veda comprises knowledge which was built up on tradhtion.

३. आ नः सुतास इन्दवः पुनाना धावता रयिम् ।।
वृष्टिद्यावो रीत्यापः स्वर्विदः ।।

3. The brain cells from the front (face) bestow on mind repeatedly and bestow understanding through wealth.

Activity is well-known to move to them and release from heaven a rain (of ideas) of the knowledge of heaven. (1328)

We see from this mantra that mind gets all its ideas from the brain. The sense activities first impinge on the brain and flow through the sense organs to the external world. Then the sense perceptions and reactions from the external world also go straight to the brain through the nerves. The brain then imparts all its stored information then and there to mind. So, mind is kept informed continually. The general belief that mind is responsible for all our achievements is totally wrong. This matter was discussed under mantra 852, where the primary purpose of mind was explained. Firstly the creator looks at and experiences his own creations through man's mind. Secondly it is mind that flits from life to life and maintains continued activity which is the desire of the creator.

D. XVIII.

१. परि त्यं हर्यतं हरिं बभ्रुं पुनन्ति वारेण ।
यो देवान्विश्वाँ इत्परि मदेन सह गच्छति ।।

1. The tawny consciousness is eagerly desirous of going around the enclosure repeatedly.

The devas (ideas) going to the sense organs go around together with sense activities and consciousness. (1329), (552), (1681)

२. द्वियं पञ्च स्वयशसं सखायो अद्रिसंहतम् ।
प्रियमिन्द्रस्य काम्यं प्रस्नापयन्त ऊर्मयः ।।

2. The five sense activities control both brain cells and sense organs and themselves help them famously; they bestow the needs of the brain (hill) as desired.

Indra kindly controls over desires and bathes or washes them in waves of sense perceptions (nourishment). (1330)

३. इन्द्राय सोम पातवे वृत्रघ्ने परि षिच्यसे ।
नरे च दक्षिणावते वीराय सदनासदे ॥

3. Indra moves to Soma to fulfil his needs, who envelops and supports wealth and sprinkles it (or striking down Vṛtra sprinkles (sense activities).

He moves vigorously towards men to bestow the gifts of understanding constantly in the home. (1331), (1679)

D. XIX.

१. पवस्व सोम महे दक्षायाश्वो न निक्तो वाजी धनाय ।

1. Soma himself bestows to drink greatly through prāṇa to dispel ignorance through wealth in life-activity. (1332), (430)

२. प्र ते सोतारो रसं मदाय पुनन्ति सोमं महे द्युम्नाय ॥

2. Soma repeatedly nourishes the devotees with the essence from sense activities (i.e. perceptions); Soma guides us excellently. (1333)

३. शिशुं जज्ञानं हरिं मृजन्ति पवित्रे सोमं देवेभ्य इन्दुम् ॥

3. Knowledge is born to mind from the brain cells through ideas (devas) graciously released by Soma and which mortals win from the tawny consciousness. (1334)

D. XX.

१. उपो षु जातमप्तुरं गोभिर्भङ्गं परिष्कृतम् ।
इन्दुं देवा अयासिषुः ॥

1. Activity from the source speeds along from above to the sense organs splitting up the sense activities and embelishing.

The devas assail the brain cells with their rays (missiles). (1335), (762), (487)

Activity at source comprises a single ray though intrinsically composite. It splits up into its seven components only when it meets objects and sense organs. However, it enters the head as a single ray.

In like manner light is composed of a single white ray of light. It is only when it strikes objects that dispersion into the well-known seven colours takes place.

२. तमिद्वर्धन्तु नो गिरो वत्सं संशिश्वरीरिव ।
य इन्द्रस्य हृदं सनिः ॥

2. They (Activity and ideas) foster the growth of the brain on the hill growing well with mind as if released together.

Indra moves to us to bestow gifts on brain. (1336)

३. अर्षा नः सोम शं गवे धुक्षस्व पिप्युषीमिषम् ।
वर्धा समुद्रमुक्थ्य ॥

3. Soma flows to toil for sense activities, arousing the brain (home) himself and also opening its eyes to drink eagerly.

He fosters the growth praiseworthily and bestows joys. (1337)

D. XXI.

१. आ घा ये अग्निमिन्धते स्तृणन्ति बर्हिरानुषक् ।
येषामिन्द्रो युवा सखा ॥

1. Agni indeed kindles the variegated sense activities to follow the nerves.

Indra helps the mind through them. (1338), (133), (Y. V. 7, 32)

२. बृहन्निदिध्म एषां भूरि शस्त्रं पृथुः स्वरुः ।
येषामिन्द्रो युवा सखा ॥

2. When (the variegated sense activities) are bestowed by the home greatly (to the sense organs) below, then sense perceptions (śastra) in abundance spread out by themselves ascend and flow (to the brain).

Indra helps the mind with them. (1339), (Y. V. 33, 24)

३. अयुद्ध इद्युधा वृतं शूर आजति सत्वभिः ।
येषामिन्द्रो युवा सखा ॥

3. Just irresistable in fights (Indra) enveloped the water for the Aśvins to bestow existence (births).

Indra helped the mind with them. (1340)

D. XXII.

१. य एक इद्विदयते वसु मर्ताय दाशुषे ।
ईशानो अप्रतिष्कुत इन्द्रो अङ्ग ॥

1. Indra is known to be alone to move to mortals and unite with them to serve them.

Prāṇa rules us; he nourishes the sense organs, as Indra's limb. (1341), (389)

२. यश्चिद्धि त्वा बहुभ्य आ सुतावाँ आविवासति ।
उग्रं तत्पत्यते शव इन्द्रो अङ्ग ॥

2. You move to satisfy mind greatly by bestowing to ride on existence.

He unites with the paths of Indra's limbs (nerves) powerfully. (1342)

३. कदा मर्तमराधसं पदा क्षुम्पमिव स्फुरत् ।
कदा नः शुश्रवद्गिर इन्द्रो अङ्ग ॥

3. All paths (steps) to wealth of mortals sprout up like sneezing, always.

He attends to the brain always through Indra's limbs i.e. nerves and is bound to them. (1343)

D. XXIII.

१. गायन्ति त्वा गायत्रिणोऽर्चन्त्यर्कमर्किणः ।
ब्रह्माणस्त्वा शतक्रत उद्वंशमिव येमिरे ॥

1. Indra! You guide the sense activities; you move along with them to the three states; you honour the devotees praise-worthily.

You do a hundred acts for knowledge; you support him like a cross beam and control him for our comfort. (1344), (342)

२. यत्सानोः सान्वारुहो भूर्यस्पष्ट कर्त्वम् ।
तदिन्द्रो अर्थं चेतति यूथेन वृष्णिरेजति ॥

2. Soma! You unite with the summit of the brain; you bestow freshly for growth; you produce for achieving profusely to drink. (1345)

Indra stirs up Mind and rains wealth from the host (of brain cells).

३. युंक्ष्वा हि केशिना हरी वृषणा कक्ष्यप्रा ।
अथा न इन्द्र सोमपा गिरामुपश्रुतिं चर ।।

3. The long-haired tawny consciousness bestows on the home by uniting with it; he fulfils the brain cells powerfully or diligently.

Then Indra fulfils Soma's needs on the hill by going round and listening. (1346), (Y. V. 8, 34)

BOOK VI : CHAPTER I

D. I.

१. सुषमिद्धो न आ वह देवाँ अग्ने हविष्मते ।
होतः पावक यक्षि च ॥

1. Agni bestows oblations for understanding eagerly on the brain through ideas (devas).

He presides, bestows on the head for fulfilment and speeds up also. (1347)

२. मधुमन्तं तनूनपाद्यज्ञं देवेषु नः कवे ।
अद्या कृणुहूतये ॥

2. Agni leads ideas with the sense perceptions (honey) through the sense organs (descendants) delicately.

Now he helps to produce transformations. (1348)

The transformations consist in sense activities passing through sense organs towards objects of the world and returning along the sense organs and nerves as sense perceptions as ideas to the brain.

३. नराशंसमिह प्रियमस्मिन्यज्ञ उप ह्वये ।
मधुजिह्वं हविष्कृतम् ॥

3. Men praise here the kindness of our life-activity which is invoked above,

wherein the tongues of sense activities produce oblations. (1349)

४. अग्ने सुखतमे रथे देवाँ ईडित आ वह ।
असि होता मनुर्हितः ॥

4. Agni desiring our welfare conveys ideas to sense organs for oblations.

He presides for the welfare of mind. (1350)

D. II.

१. यदद्य सूर उदितेऽनागा मित्रो अर्यमा ।
सुवाति सविता भगः ॥

1. He who now appears as hero along the spinal cord in the brain (Mitra), is Indra (Aryamā),

who arouses knowledge by stimulating consciousness. (1351), (Y. V. 33, 20)

२. सुप्रावीरस्तु स क्षयः प्र नु यामन्त्सुदानवः ।
ये नो अंहोऽतिपिप्रति ॥

2. The leaders (Vīra) arouse and fulfil (our needs); they move and bestow nourishment on the home, and are praised; they stir up the paths to bestow freshly.

They also nourish in need (aṁha). (1352)

३. उत स्वराजो अदितिरदब्धस्य व्रतस्य ये ।
महो राजान ईशते ॥

3. Also, Aditi (sense activities) herself controls, bestows on us without hurting as her duty (vow).

She bestows greatly from the source and rules us. (1353)

D. III.

१. उ त्वा मदन्तु सोमाः कृणुष्व राधो अद्रिवः ।
अव ब्रह्मद्विषो जहि ॥

1. Soma! You are joyous within, you produce wealth eagerly and bestow on the brain (hill).

You arouse the birth of knowledge from the desires of both (brain cells and sense organs and favour us. (1354), (194)

२. पदा पणीनराधसो नि बाधस्व महाँ असि ।
न हि त्वा कश्च न प्रति ॥

2. Soma! You are great in taking steps for exchange of wealth below for the devotees.

You arouse the brain (head) and gladden it with nourishment. (1355)

३. त्वमीशिषे सुतानामिन्द्र त्वमसुतानाम् ।
त्वं राजा जनानाम् ॥

3. Indra! You desire to rule over mind for which you arouse the nerves.

You are the king of the people. (1356)

D. IV.

१. आ जागृविर्विप्र ऋतं मतीनां सोमः पुनानो असदच्चमूषु ।
सपन्ति यं मिथुनासो निकामा अध्वर्यवो रथिरासः सुहस्ताः ॥

1. Ṛta inspires us through the waking state with knowledge which Soma repeatedly lets in from the sense organs to sip.

And he bestows admirably on the couple (brain cells and sense organs) and controls them at his pleasure; he bestows from the sense organs in life-activity and releases them through the nerves (hands). (1357)

२. स पुनान उप सूरे दधान ओभे अप्रा रोदसी वी ष आवः ।
प्रिया चिद्यस्य प्रियसास ऊती सतो धनं कारिणे न प्र यंसत् ॥

2. The leaders (Soma and Ṛta) repeatedly bestow gifts on both (brain and sense organs) fulfil and both bringing (āvaḥ) bestowing desires.

They are fond of mind and bestow on him in kindness and help him; they nourish the mind with wealth mightily from the brain (prison) and contrc! his existence. (1358)

३. स वर्धिता वर्धनः पूयमानः सोमो मीढ्वाँ अभि नो ज्योतिषावित् ।
यत्र नः पूर्वे पितरः पदज्ञाः स्वर्विदो अभि गा अद्रिमिष्णन् ॥

3. They swell over to him from the home and increase his prosperity; Soma bestows rewards on him which the effulgent co.isciousness acquaints us with.

There the ancient father (Savitā) binds us to steps leading to knowledge of heaven to which the sense activities open our eyes. (1359)

D. V.

१. मा चिदन्यद्वि शंसत सखायो मा रिषण्यत ।
इन्द्रमित्स्तोता वृषणं सचा सुते मुहुरुक्था च शंसत ॥

1. The two bestow on mind and guide him praiseworthily as friends; they do not hurt by uniting.

Indra establishes him (mind) powerfully by uniting with him instantly praiseworthily and toils for his existence. (1360), (242)

२. अवक्रक्षिणं वृषभं यथा जुवं गां न चर्षणीसहम् ।
विद्वेषणं संवननमुभयङ्करं मंहिष्ठमुभयाविनम् ॥

2. Indra rules over (destroys) crookedness as speedily as he is diligently active together with sense activities.

He knows and honours the desires of both (brain and sense

organs); he honours all desires of both sides and gladdens them; he blesses both munificently and mightily. (1361)

D. VI.

१. उदु त्ये मधुमत्तमा गिरः स्तोमास ईरते ।
सत्राजितो धनसा अक्षितोतयो वाजयन्तो रथा इव ॥

1. The sweet sense perceptions with my desires are well-known to move above inciting and bestowing on the brain (hill).

They win the Soma Yajña (life-activity), bestow wealth on the home; help and guide the life-activity like a vehicle (chariot). (1362), (251)

२. कण्वा इव भृगवः सूर्या इव विश्वमिद्धीतमाशत ।
इन्द्रं स्तोमेभिर्महयन्त आयवः प्रियमेधासो अस्वरन् ॥

2. The sense activities bestow on the brain cells as if to support them; they move to the sense organs to arouse as if to support the brain with food as desired.

Indra praiseworthily supports and guides the brain cells and gladdens; he bestows understanding in kindness from heaven. (1363)

D. VII.

१. पर्यू षु प्र धन्व वाजसातये परि वृत्राणि सक्षणिः ।
द्विषस्तरध्या ऋणया न ईरसे ॥

1. He goes around to sense organs to nourish them for bestowing new wealth in life-activity continually; he goes around to them to envelop and support bestowing instantly.

He is obliged to stir up the desires of both (brain cells and sense organs) dependent on him. (1364), (428)

२. अजीजनो हि पवमान सूर्यं विधारे शक्मना पयः ।
गोजीरया रंहमाणः पुरन्ध्या ॥

2. He (Indra) is victorious for men by arousing consciousness who bestows on the home for drinking through supporting skilfully sense perceptions (payaḥ).

The sense activities move quickly bestowing the needs (aṁha) of the home for the brain (pura) to sip. (1365)

३. अनु हि त्वा सुतं सोम मदामसि [महे समर्यराज्ये ।
वाजां अभि पवमान प्र गाहसे] ॥

3. Soma now arouses the mind (son) who is joyous greatly in the region of the assembly.

The sense perceptions (nourishment) plunge into the fickle mind to bestow him in life-activity. (1366), (432)

D. VIII.

१. परि प्र धन्व [इन्द्राय सोम स्वादुर्मित्राय पूष्णेभगाय] ।

1. Indra goes around and moves to Soma to bestow new nourishment, who himself moves to the brain to consume for prosperity through consciousness. (1367), (427)

२. एवामृताय महे क्षयाय स शुक्रो अर्ष दिव्यः पीयूषः ॥

2. In the early morning of creation he speeded up the (birth) of mortals, which perished greatly, by letting bright ideas flow. (1368)

In the early part of creation many species of creatures are said to have perished on account partly perhaps of inherent instability and partly due to unfavourable environment. It was undoubtedly a period of great experimentation. So new ideas were constantly implemented ushering in newer species till stable creatures were established at each stage.

३. इन्द्रस्ते सोम सुतस्य पेयात्क्रत्वे दक्षाय विश्वे च देवाः ।

3. In Indra's home Soma produces (gifts) for mind and bestows them in his path to drink and satisfies also the sense organs through ideas (devas). (1369)

D. IX.

१. सूर्यस्येव रश्मयो द्रावयित्नवो मत्सरासः प्रसुतः साकमीरते ।
तन्तुं ततं परि सर्गास आशवो नेन्द्रादृते पवते धाम किं चन ॥

1. Consciousness speeded up the rays (of Activity) to bestow new (ideas) on the slumbering (brain cells), which flowed to us (creatures) and induced the creation of new creatures jointly.

The father (Activity) went around the nerves in surges and bestowed on the sense organs (śava); now Indra gave consideration to protect understanding in the home which pleases. (1370)

२. उपो मतिः पृच्यते सिच्यते मधु मन्द्राजनी चोदते अन्तरासनि ।
पवमानः सन्तनिः सुन्वतामिव मधुमान् द्रप्सः परि वारमर्षति ॥

2. Above, the sense perceptions (madhu) nourish by uniting (with the brain) and discharge (themselves) by uniting (with mind); the sense activities are pleasant above and they bestow gifts within.

They bestow gifts on the fickle mind continually; they approach the devotees to bestow; the sense perceptions go around the brain cells in the home and let gifts flow around. (1371)

३. उक्षा मिमेति प्रति यन्ति धेनवो देवस्य देवीरूप यन्ति निष्कृतम् ।
अत्यक्रमीदर्जूनं वारमव्ययमत्कं न निक्तं परि सोमो अव्यत ॥

3. The sense activities approach us, and nourish and guide us to grow strong; bestow ideas for milch-cow (perceptions) for which the devī is guided above to the appointed place; Prāṇa duly bestows knowledge (whiteness); the Aśvins are a cloak to us and a gift against ignorance; they go around and bestow on us unwaveringly. (1372)

D. X.

१. अग्निं नरो दीधितिभिररण्योर्हस्तच्युतं जनयत प्रशस्तम् ।
दूरेदृशं गृहपतिमथव्युम् ॥

1. Agni bestows satisfaction on men; supports, gladdens extensively letting sense activities drip from the nerves to unite with men nourishing knowledge desired.

The lord of the home churns us through the sense activities for far-sightedness (i.e. confers eye-sight). (1373), (72)

२. तमग्निमस्ते वसवो न्यृण्वन्त्सुप्रतिचक्षमवसे कुतश्चित् ।
दक्षाय्यो यो दम आस नित्यः ॥

2. Agni desires to bestow on the home and envelop (vasa) it; he is obliged to guide desires; look them up; nourish and bestow his favo''rs on mind wherever he is.

He satisfies him thus from the home and everyday. (1374)

३. प्रेद्धो अग्ने दीदिहि पुरो नोऽजस्रया सूर्म्या यविष्ठ ।
त्वां शश्वन्त उप यन्ति वाजाः ॥

3. Agni incites nourishment which shines by arousing and

bestowing on the brain (city) untiringly through the nerves (pipes) as desired by the brain cells.

He guides us constantly above in life. (1375), (Y. V. 17, 76)

D. XI.

१. आयं गौः पृश्निरक्रमीदसदन्मातरं पुरः ।
पितरं च प्रयन्त्स्वः ॥

1. The path of the earth (gau) is in a reverse direction across the speckled sky to the home of its mother (region of water),

also its father who nourishes and guides it himself (Sun). (1376), (630)

२. अन्तश्चरति रोचनास्य प्राणादपानती ।
व्यख्यन्महिषो दिवम् ॥

2. The earth wanders within the space going up and coming down like prāṇa and apāna,

and known to us (manifested as) like a buffalo before the sun. (1377), (631), (Y. V. 3, 7)

३. त्रिंशद्धाम वि राजति वाक्पतङ्गाय धीयते ।
प्रति वस्तोरह द्युभिः ॥

3. The flight of speech is controlled by thirty banded steps (activities) which unite with knowledge.

Every object here is nourished by heaven (with words-ideas). (1378), (632), (Y. V. 3, 8)

Speech is governed by thirty steps or activities preceding its flow. The following organs are involved in speech: (1) lungs; (2) larynx; (3) ovula; (4) tongue; (5) lips; (6) upper and lower palate; (7) teeth; (8) nerves; (9) brain; (10) breath. Everyone of them is actuated by the following combination of devas: (1) Agni; (2) Activity; (3) Sarasvatī; (4) Aśvins, (5) Indra prāṇa; (6) Ideas; (7) Heaven. The intervention of the Aśvins between the subtle devas and terrestrial organs is reckoned as two activities at each stage.

BOOK VI: CHAPTER II

D. I.

१. उपप्रयन्तो अध्वरं मन्त्रं वोचेमाग्नये ।
आरे अस्मे च शृण्वते ॥

1. Above, sense activity nourishes and guides speech bestowing it pleasantly in life-activity.

The spokes-like nerves also cook knowledge. (1379), (Y. V. 3, 11)

We have explained in the previous mantra the number of steps and the devas involved in producing speech. An extensive area of nerves is also involved in it.

२. यः स्नीहितीषु पूर्व्यः संजग्मानासु कृष्टिषु ।
अरक्षद्दाशुषे गयम् ॥

2. The rays (missiles of sense activities) speeded in ancient times in attaching (sound-speech) to all mobile creatures in the brain (home) to arouse announcing their desires.

The sense activities control it and protect the creatures (devotees). (1380)

३. स नो वेदो अमात्यमग्नी रक्षतु शन्तमः ।
उतास्मान्पात्वंहसः ॥

3. Agni's minister (speech) bestows knowledge as gift and protects most beneficently (śantama).

Also it fulfils our needs (aṁha) by its bestowals. (1381)

४. उत ब्रुवन्तु जन्तव उदग्निर्वृत्रहाजनि ।
धनञ्जयो रणेरणे ॥

4. Also it tells us within, that creatures were born from the source in water through Agni striking down Vṛtra (inertia).

He won wealth in fight after fight (1382)

The origin of life in water is reiterated. It originated from the source. What was preventing life to sprout up was inertia which could more easily be overcome in water. When this solution was discovered life-activity took an uninterrupted course.

D. II.

१. अग्ने युंक्ष्वा हि ये तवाश्वासो देव साधवः ।
अरं वहन्त्याशवः ॥

1. Agni! You bestow on the home by uniting with it, you achieve to bestow ideas (devas) by releasing prāṇa.

You convey to the sense organs through the spoke-like nerves. (1383), (25), (Y. V. 13, 36)

२. अच्छा नो याह्या वहाभि प्रयांसि वीतये ।
आ देवान्त्सोमपीतये ॥

2. Being near and closely united you desire to support the nourishment to move and convey it.

You release ideas (devas) to us which we drink. (1384)

३. उदग्ने भारत द्युमदजस्रेण दविद्युतत् ।
शोचा वि भाह्यजर ॥

3. The heat in the water (latent heat) shines (within) and pleases the sense activities from heaven (in the head) untiringly bestowing like lightning.

It shines ever fresh without appearing externally. (1385)

The reference to water here in the head seems to indicate the brain fluids which obviously help the sense activities and perceptions to discharge to the brain like lightning. It is the latent heat of water that helps here.

D. III.

१. प्र सुन्वानायान्धसो मर्तो न वष्ट तद्वचः ।
अप श्वानमराधसं हता मखं न भृगवः ॥

1. The sense activities (pra) bestow on mortals what dispels ignorance and they newly achieved (gained) speech.

Activity honours prāṇa for wealth (for discharging it); indeed he is vigorous in supporting sense activities. (1386), (774), (553)

२. आ जामिरत्के अव्यत भुजे न पुत्र ओण्योः ।
सरज्जारो न योषणां वरो न योनिमासवम् ॥

2. The Aśvins, their relatives (i.e. sense activities) provide us protection (mantle) with their arms, like protecting one's off-

spring, like running to one's sweet heart or a young bride going to her husband, from the source to our homes. (1387)

३. स वीरो दक्षसाधनो वि यस्तस्तम्भ रोदसी ।
हरिः पवित्रे अव्यत वेधा न योनिमासदम् ।।

3. The valiant Indra accomplishes to satisfy both the brain and sense organs (heaven and earth) through the spinal cord (pillar).

The tawny consciousness beneficially and unwaveringly probes (pierces into) our homes from the source. (1388)

D. IV.

१. अभ्रातृव्यो अना त्वमनापिरिन्द्र जनुषा सनादसि ।
युधेदापित्वमिच्छसे ।।

1. Indra! You are ever our brother and also of mind; you are ancient and the origin (for manifestation).

You bestow by fighting for us and bestow our desires. (1389), (399)

२. न की रेवन्तं सख्याय विन्दसे पीयन्ति ते सुराश्वः ।
यदा कृणोषि नदनुं समूहस्यादित्पितेव हूयसे ।।

2. You help wealth within against ignorance; you bestow knowledge which swells over to us to guide; prāṇa incites and bestows it,

which fulfils us eagerly and resoundingly and praised by the multitude, which thus strives to bestow like a father on being invoked. (1390)

D. V.

१. आ त्वा सहस्रमा शतं युक्ता रथे हिरण्यये ।
ब्रह्मयुजो हरय इन्द्र केशिनो वहन्तु सोमपीतये ।।

1. You unite thousands of brain cells to the sense organs to which the tawny consciousness speeds up, Indra! You yoke us to knowledge and convey it before the long-haired consciousness who releases it to us to drink. (1391), (245)

२. आ त्वा रथे हिरण्यये हरी मयूरशेप्या ।
शितिपृष्ठा वहतां मध्वो अन्धसो विवक्षणस्य पीतये ।।

2. (Indra!) Indeed you release the sense activities, variegated like peacock's tail, to the sense organs before the tawny consciousness.

The sense perceptions convey the longed-for knowledge (whiteness) foremost dispelling ignorance; they swell over to us to teach us. (1392)

३. पिबा त्व३स्य गिर्वणः सुतस्य पूर्वपा इव ।
परिष्कृतस्य रसिन इयमासुतिश्चारुर्मदाय पत्यते ॥

3. You scatter them (sense perceptions) to drink as if to fulfil as desired by the devotee.

He (mind) adorns us tastefully; here he (Indra) bestows on mind and gladdens him through sense perceptions which unite with him, for him to drink. (1393)

D. VI.

१. आ सोता परि षिञ्चताश्वं न स्तोममप्तुरं रजस्तुरम् ।
वनप्रक्षमुदप्रुतम् ॥

1. Prāṇa goes around sprinkling Soma juice which Activity praiseworthily presses onward abundantly in varied colours.

He nourishes the desires which sprout up in the home, as wished for. (1394), (580)

२. सहस्रधारं वृषभं पयोदुहं प्रियं देवाय जन्मने ।
ऋतेन य ऋतजातो विवावृधे राजा देव ऋतं बृहत् ॥

2. Indra moves to the devas in kindness in our life for thousands of streams of sense perceptions (milk) to drink.

Then Ṛta moves to them; Ṛta from the source rides them and fosters their growth bestowing (causing) birth of ideas, Ṛta is great. (1395)

D. VII.

१. अग्निर्वृत्राणि जङ्घनद्द्रविणस्युर्विपन्यया ।
समिद्धः शुक्र आहुतः ॥

1. Agni strikes down Vṛtra resoundingly and hastens to scatter wealth extensively,

and offers satisfaction through the sense activities (perceptions) which brighten. (1396), (4)

२. गर्भे मातुः पितुष्पिता विदिद्युतानो अक्षरे ।
सीदन्नृतस्य योनिमा ॥

2. In the mother's womb the father of Activity (our father) i.e. Savitā flows in through the nerves like lightning.

The womb bestows the home for man. (1397)

३. ब्रह्म प्रजावदा भर जातवेदो विचर्षणे ।
अग्ने यद्दीदयद्दिवि ॥

3. Knowledge supports the speech of man and it is diligently active for (further) birth of knowledge.

Agni allots it in the waking state. (1398)

D. VIII.

१. अस्य प्रेषा हेमना पूयमानो देवो देवेभिः समपृक्त रसम् ।
सुतः पवित्रं पर्येति रेभन्मितेव सद्म पशुमन्ति होता ॥

1. Our mind is indeed nourished by desires which swell from the brain (home) with ideas; the devas (ideas) mingle as equals and bestow on all.

The motley sense activities go around beneficially to mind and hasten to establish him resoundingly instantly; the sense activities preside within me. (1399), (526)

२. भद्रा वस्त्रा समन्या३ वसानो महान्कविर्निवचनानि शंसन् ।
आ वच्यस्व चम्वोः पूयमानो विचक्षणो जागृविर्देववीतौ ॥

2. The brain (vastra) bestows on the mind for his welfare; the great Agni toiled to bestow the gift of speech below through the mother.

He himself moves towards speech; it swells from the home to be sipped; he is diligent in waking state desiring ideas. (1400)

३. समु प्रियो मृज्यते सानो अव्ये यशस्तरो यशसां क्षैतो अस्मे ।
अभि स्वर धन्वा पूयमानो यूयं पात स्वस्तिभिः सदा नः ॥

3. The Aśvins win from the summit of the brain in his kindness everything for mortals by uniting with it; he crosses over in splendour; he is honoured in our homes.

Heaven swells over to the home to bestow freshly; you control our paths in welfare always and bind them. (1401)

D. IX.

१. एतो न्विन्द्रं स्तवाम शुद्धं शुद्धेन साम्ना ।
शुद्धैरुक्थैर्वावृध्वांसं शुद्धैराशीर्वान्ममत्तु ॥

1. Indra bestows mightily through the motley sense activities praiseworthily in purity, pure wealth.

He supports to bestow for growth in purity praiseworthily; he bestows on us pure benedictions as desired. (1402), (350)

२. इन्द्र शुद्धो न आ गहि शुद्धः शुद्धाभिरूतिभिः ।
शुद्धो रयिं नि धारय शुद्धो ममद्धि सौम्य ॥

2. Indra arouses pure sense activities; he helps in purity to support their purity.

He moves to support the pure wealth; Soma satisfies us with the pure sense activities. (1403)

३. इन्द्र शुद्धो हि नो रयिं शुद्धो रत्नानि दाशुषे ।
शुद्धो वृत्राणि जिघ्नसे शुद्धो वाजं सिषाससि ॥

3. Indra arouses wealth to purify and bestows pure valuable wealth eagerly on devotees.

He envelops us to support in purity and win wealth to bestow; desires to bestow in purity in life-activity and bind them. (1404)

D. X.

१. अग्ने स्तोमं मनामहे सिध्रमद्य दिविस्पृशः ।
देवस्य द्रविणस्यवः ॥

1. Agni praiseworthily holds on the great mind and binds him to the intoxicating sense perceptions, during (touching) waking state.

The deva runs to our brain cells mightily. (1405)

२. अग्निर्जुषत नो गिरो होता यो मानुषेष्वा ।
स यक्षद्दैव्यं जनम् ॥

2. Agni rejoices on the hill; presides over men eagerly to bestow.

And he hurries ideas to men. (1406)

३. त्वमग्ने सप्रथा असि जुष्टो होता वरेण्यः ।
त्वया यज्ञं वि तन्वते ॥

3. Agni! You extend (spread out) far to bestow; you rejoice to preside excellently.

You move to life-activity through which you lead us to knowledge. (1407)

D. XI.

१. अभि त्रिपृष्ठं वृषणं वयोधामङ्गोषिणमवावशंत वाणीः ।
वना वसानो वरुणो न सिन्धुर्वि रत्नधा दयते वार्याणि ॥

1. To bestow health or strength on the three states foremost, Indra (bull) favours eagerly the desire for sounds (speech) through his limbs (nerves).

Sindhu (the sense activities) bestows valuable wealth from the external world (Varuṇa) desired by the brain (home) and divides (daya) them in the enclosure. (1408), (528)

२. शूरग्रामः सर्ववीरः सहावान् जेता पवस्व सनिता धनानि ।
तिग्मायुधः क्षिप्रधन्वा समत्स्वषाढः साह्वान्पृतनासु शत्रून् ॥

2. A community of heroes, all vigorous together desire to bestow gifts of wealth themselves to be consumed (drunk).

They bestow cheekful of wealth passionately through the nerves (weapons); they are all equally unconquerable and overcome their enemies in fights. (1409)

३. उरुगव्यूतिरभयानि कृण्वन्त्समीचीने आ पवस्वा पुरन्धी ।
अपः सिषासन्नुषसः स्वऽ३र्गाः सं चिक्रदो महो अस्मभ्यं वाजान् ॥

3. The sense activities seize the sense organs and help them extensively; they all turn to create desires together (in the brain) and themselves bestow understanding in the brain (city) to drink.

Activity bestows desires eagerly as gifts from heaven; they all perceive us produce and bestow greatly in life-activity. (1410)

D. XII.

१. त्वमिन्द्र यशा अस्यृजीषी शवसस्पतिः ।
त्वं वृत्राणि हं स्यप्रतीन्येक इत्पुर्वनुत्तश्चर्षणीधृतिः ॥

1. Indra! You are honoured by us; as lord of the brain cells and sense organs you rush to us.

You encounter Vṛtra (inertia) all alone indeed since ancient times invincibly with diligence and steadfastness. (1411), (248)

२. तमु त्वा नूनमसुर प्रचेतसं राधो भागमिवेमहे ।
महीव कृत्तिः शरणा त इन्द्र प्र ते सुम्ना नो अश्नुवन् ॥

2. Indra! You bestow also now on mind his portion of wealth (sense perceptions) from the sense organs (asura) and nourish him greatly by approaching him; you bestow on the sense organs (mahī) clad in a hide for protection.

You nourish them excellently as they desire from the hill (brain). (1412)

D. XIII.

१. यजिष्ठं त्वा ववृमहे देवं देवत्रा होतारममर्त्यम् ।
अस्य यज्ञस्य सुक्रतुम् ॥

1. Indra! You are fond of life-activity. You bestow ideas greatly on it by enveloping it (or remaining concealed); you support the devas and presiding over them gladden mortals.

You do good to us in our Yajña. (1413), (112)

२. अपां नपातं सुभगं सुदीदितिमग्निमु श्रेष्ठशोचिषम् ।
स नो मित्रस्य वरुणस्य सो अपामा सुम्नं यक्षते दिवि ॥

2. Activity highly favours (Subhaga) the sense organs (descendants); Agni shines on them excellently so that they flame up in the best manner.

He bestows gifts from Varuṇa (external world) to Mitra (brain); Activity bestows on them excellently and speeds them up in waking state. (1414)

D. XIV.

१. यमग्ने पृत्सु मर्त्यमवा वाजेषु यं जुनाः ।
स यन्ता शश्वतीरिषः ॥

1. Agni controls the nourishing (pṛ) and favours mortals by arousing them to it.

And he guides them constantly as desired. (1415)

२. न किरस्य सहन्त्य पर्येता कयस्य चित् ।
वाजो अस्ति श्रवाय्यः ॥

2. You do not grudge (irasya) to go around together with the motley sense activities to the head and from there to mind.

You are praiseworthy in life-activity. (1416)

३. स वाजं विश्वचर्षणिरर्वद्भिरस्तु तरुता ।
विप्रेभिरस्तु सनिता ॥

3. You are diligently active with sense organs in life and hasten to support them which grow like a tree.

You stir them up, support and bestow gifts. (1417)

D. XV.

१. साकमुक्षो मर्जयन्त स्वसारो दश धीरस्य धीतयो धनुत्रीः ।
हरिः पर्यद्रवज्जाः सूर्यस्य द्रोणं ननक्षे अत्यो न वाजी ॥

1. Together (Agni and sense organs) they arouse the home and gain within for the mortals lasting protection from their own ability (essence); the three states (dhanu-islands) bestow knowledge.

The tawny consciousness runs to go around and win for the brain (pot) by arousing him; prāṇa now approaches it in life. (1418), (598)

२. सं मातृभिर्न शिशुर्वावशानो वृषा दधन्वे पुरुवारो अद्भिः ।
मर्यो न योषाम भि निष्कृतं यन्त्सं गच्छते कलश उस्रियाभिः ॥

2. The mother (sense activities) supports all, bestows on the mind from the brain (home); Indra bestows on him freshly abundant gifts as food.

Indra bull goes from the brain (head) to guide all like a young man going to meet his girl friend at the appointed place. (1419)

३. उत प्र पिप्य ऊधरघ्न्याया इन्दुर्धाराभिः सचते सुमेधाः ।
मूर्धानं गावः पयसा चमूष्वभि श्रीणन्ति वसुभिर्न निक्तैः ॥

3. Also he bestows nourishment to drink by way of sense perceptions (milk); he supports the brain cells with wealth and unites with them to arouse understanding.

The sense perceptions bestow on the head (brain) to drink which it licks eagerly when bestowed; Indra supports the cooking within against ignorance. (1420)

D. XVI.

१. पिबा सुतस्य रसिनो मत्स्वा न इन्द्र गोमतः ।
आपिर्नो बोधि सधमाद्ये वृधे३ऽस्मां अवन्तु ते धियः ॥

1. Mind drinks with relish from my panting Indra rich in cows (perceptions).

He teaches his associate mind and fosters the growth of his comrade; he blesses him and satisfies. (1421)

२. भूयाम ते सुमतौ वाजिनो वयं मा न स्तरभिमातये।
अस्मां चित्राभिरवतादभिष्टिभिरा नः सुम्नेषु यामय॥

2. They are the paths for my existence, arousing understanding in life, bestowing and controlling the home and scattering hostility.

They support us in a variety of ways, bestow us understanding as desired; thew bestow excellently the paths to bind us. (1422)

D. XVII.

१. त्रिरस्मै सप्त धेनवो दुदुह्रिरे सत्यामाशिरं परमे व्योमनि।
चत्वार्यन्या भुवनानि निर्णिजे चारूणि चक्रे यदृतैरवर्धत॥

1. Our three states consume sense perceptions (milk) from the seven milch-cows for their comfort; the path for existence in the head is from the distant heaven.

The four states (including heaven) determine the creatures; they are welcome here below; they go around determining the growth of the creatures. (1423), (560)

२. स भक्षमाणो अमृतस्य चारुण उभे द्यावा काव्येना वि शश्रथे।
तेजिष्ठा अपो महना परि व्यत यदी देवस्य श्रवसा सदो विदुः॥

2. They bestow food for consumption on the homes of mortals; heaven bestows to please both the brain cells and sense organs and knowledge on mind through sense organs.

Activity desires to illumine (reveal) objects and goes around to give gifts which ideas (devas) manifest, flowing and bestowing knowledge always. (1424)

३. ते अस्य सन्तु केतवोऽमृत्यवोऽदाभ्यासो जनुषी उभे अनु।
येभिर्नृम्णा च देव्या च पुनत आदिद्राजानं मनना अगृभ्णत॥

3. He bestows on us desires as gifts; bestows on the brain cells of mortals inviolably; now both (brain cells and sense organs) cause births (of ideas).

He supports manfully and the devas too repeatedly; the

sense activities ran down from the source in ancient times to seize mind. (1425)

D. XVIII.

१. अभि वायुं वीत्यर्षा गृणानो३ऽभि मित्रावरुणा पूयमानः ।
अभि नरं धीजवनं रथेष्ठामभीन्द्रं वृषणं वज्रबाहुम् ॥

1. Desires flow to the devotees through the nerves; Varuṇa swells over to the brain Mitra in the home.

Understanding takes birth in men from desires; Indra powerfully conveys desires, through the nerves to the sense organs. (1426)

२. अभि वस्त्रा सुवसनान्यर्षाभि धेनूः सुदुघाः पूयमानः ।
अभि चन्द्रा भर्तवे नो हिरण्याभ्यश्वान्रथिनो देव सोम ॥

2. The milch-cow (sense activities) flow to the brain (vastra) and are guided to adorn it; good milk (perceptions) swell over to the brain (home).

They give support to mind as well as the golden consciousness and ideas from sense organs coming from Soma. (1427)

३. अभी नो अर्ष दिव्या वसून्यभि विश्वा पार्थिवा पूयमानः ।
अभि येन द्रविणमश्नवामाभ्यार्षेयं जमदग्निवन्नः ॥

3. Now ideas (devas) flow (to the brain); wealth (vasu—sense perceptions) from the earthly sense organs swell over to the brain.

This wealth is bestowed and flows here to the hill (brain); Agni bestows sense activities for the birth of food (perceptions). (1428)

D. XIX.

१. यज्जायथा अपूर्व्य मघवन्वृत्रहत्याय ।
तत्पृथिवीमप्रथयस्तदस्तभ्ना उतो दिवम् ॥

1. Life-activity came into being correctly in ancient times after Indra overcame Vṛtra (inertia).

He spreads it out on earth, and established life-process, consciousness also (accompanied). (1429)

२. तत्ते यज्ञो अजायत तदर्क उत हस्कृतिः ।
तद्विश्वमभिभूरसि यज्जातं यच्च जन्त्वम् ॥

2. Life-activity was born out of it; consciousness also blossomed and created it.

From that sense organs came into existence; from them desires were born from which (fresh) creatures came into being. (1430)

३. आमासु पक्वमैरय आ सूर्यं रोहयो दिवि ।
घर्मं न सामं तपता सुवृक्तिभिर्जुष्टं गिर्वणसे बृहत् ॥

3. The crude (āma) organs were cooked and aroused; consciousness rose up to produce waking state.

Dharma was affluent and was the path and supported it praiseworthily and released great desires in the devotees joyously. (1431)

D. XX.

१. मत्स्यपायि ते महः पात्रस्येव हरिवो मत्सरो मदः ।
वृषा ते वृष्ण इन्दुर्वाजी सहस्रसातमः ॥

1. Fishes fulfilled and gladdened us as if they were the instruments (vessels); consciousness released sense activities to flow to us (i.e. the creatures).

Indra rained powerfully to their brain cells in life-activity thousands of desires. (1432)

२. आ नस्ते गन्तु मत्सरो वृषा मदो वरेण्यः ।
सहावाँ इन्द्र सानसिः पृतनाषाडमर्त्यः ॥

2. They are associated with sense activities which flow to us and rain joyousness excellently.

Indra, the unconquerable in fights, at the same time bestows victoriously on mortals. (1433)

३. त्वं हि शूरः सनिता चोदयो मनुषो रथम् ।
सहावान्दस्युमव्रतमोषः पात्रं न शोचिषा ॥

3. Indra! You arouse us valiantly to bestow gifts which take birth also in the mind which arise from the sense organs.

At the same time Umā (sense activities), in accordance with her duty (vow), bestows willingly our wants eagerly as suitable subjects (vessels) and shines. (1434)

BOOK VI: CHAPTER III

D. I.

१. पवस्व वृष्टिमा सु नोऽपामूर्मिं दिवस्परि ।
अयक्ष्मा बृहतीरिषः ॥

1. Waves of Activity go around in waking state by themselves, rain to our minds bestowing to drink.

They speed us bestowing a great many desires. (1435)

२. तया पवस्व धारया यया गाव इहागमन् ।
जन्यास उप नो गृहम् ॥

2. They themselves bestow on us to drink and come here hurriedly to support the sense perceptions.

They move in from the sourcc to the head above to bestow on the home. (1436)

३. घृतं पवस्व धारया यज्ञेषु देववीतमः ।
अस्मभ्यं वृष्टिमा पव ॥

3. In life-activity ideas (devas) favour our desires and support them by bestowing themselves for clarified butter to drink.

They are rained to bestow protection on us. (1437)

४. स न ऊर्जे व्य३व्ययं पवित्रं धाव धारया ।
देवासः शृणवन् हि कम् ॥

4. The Aśvins beneficially run to us to support us with gifts of nourishment. They bestow ideas to cook up new ones to arouse desires. (1438)

५. पवमानो असिष्यदद्रक्षांस्यपजङ्घनत् ।
प्रत्नवद्रोचयन्रुचः ॥

5. They bestow such desires of the fickle mind which support to protect the drinks of mobile creatures.

They nourish and guide speech; they guide hymns and shine. (1439)

D. II.

१. प्रत्यस्मै पिपीषते विश्वानि विदुषे भर ।
अरङ्गमाय जग्मयेऽपश्चादध्वने नरः ॥

1. It is well-known also that what swells over from the sense organs in existence nourishes knowledge and supports it eagerly.

It (knowledge) supported variegated species of mobile creatures (at first) then later on me, in life-activity. (1440), (352)

The whole of creation is the expression of knowledge which is incorporated in their being and activities. The creatures did not come out of nothing. Knowledge was there prior to all types of existences. All this knowledge arose out of the browsings of the creator who fills up all space.

२. एमेनं प्रत्येतन सोमेभिः सोमपातमम् ।
अमत्रेभिर्ऋजीषिणमिन्द्रं सुतेभिरिन्दुभिः ॥

2. It is well-known that Soma nourished this mighty course through the motley sense activities; Soma fulfilled (furnishing) the knowledge desired.

Indra rushed to support our three states; the brain cells supported the mind. (1441)

३. यदी सुतेभिरिन्दुभिः सोमेभिः प्रतिभूषथ ।
वेदा विश्वस्य मेधिरो धृषत्तन्तमिदेषते ॥

3. What supported mind from the brain cells was all nourished by Soma for coming into existence.

Knowledge is bestowed on us through the sense organs satisfying us; they are boldly guided through the nerves to the brain as desired by it. (1442)

४. अस्माअस्मा इदन्धसोऽध्वर्यो प्र भरा सुतम् ।
कुवित्समस्य जेन्यस्य शर्धतोऽभिशस्ते रवस्वरत् ॥

4. Man after man is released from ignorance thus in life-activity which nourishes and supports mind.

All our knowledge arises from sense organs (Ku); it arises there boldly; heaven praiseworthily blesses it (or to be praised and blessed by heaven). (1443)

D. III.

१. बभ्रवे नु स्वतवसेऽरुणाय दिविस्पृशे ।
सोमाय गाथमर्चत ॥

1. The ruddy Sun (consciousness) himself nourishes with his rays, the home caressing it with the waking state.

Soma honours the devotee. (1444)

२. हस्तच्युतेभिरद्रिभिः सुतं सोमं पुनीतन ।
मधावा धावता मधु ॥

2. From the nerves drip (sense perceptions) to support mind from the brain (hill), bestowed repeatedly by Soma.

Sense perceptions (honey) run to us and bestow understanding (1445)

३. नमसेदुप सीदत दध्नेदभि श्रीणीतन ।
इन्दुमिन्द्रे दधातन ॥

3. Indra dwelling in the home honours and bestows above (on the brain) wealth to guide to prosperity.

Indra bestows on the brain cells and guides them. (1446)

४. अमित्रहा विचर्षणिः पवस्व सोम शं गवे ।
देवेभ्यो अनुकामकृत् ॥

4. Soma is diligently active in looking to unfriendly ideas departing and he toils himself to bestow sense perceptions to drink.

Ideas (devas) now produce desires. (1447)

५. इन्द्राय सोम पातवे मदाय परि षिच्यसे ।
मनश्चिन्मनसस्पतिः ॥

5. Indra moves to Soma to fulfil his needs and goes around to sense activities to sprinkle them.

I achieve ideas from (Soma) lord of the mind and brain cells. (1448)

६. पवमान सुवीर्यं रयिं सोम रिरीहि णः ।
इन्दविन्द्रेण नो युजा ॥

6. Soma arouses the fickle mind and releases wealth to him to arouse vigour.

Indra unites with the brain cells and bestows mightily on them. (1449)

D. IV.

१. उद्धेदभि श्रुतामघं वृषभं नर्यापसम् ।
अस्तारमेषि सूर्य ॥

1. Though proud to listen to us, Indra (bull) is diligently active for men to bestow gifts (magha).

He moves in to arouse us and gladdens our desires in the home. (1450), (125)

२. नव यो नवतिं पुरो बिभेद बाह्वोजसा ।
अहिं च वृत्रहावधीत् ॥

2. Newer and newer species of creatures (cities) without distinction, he conveyed vigorously to earth on invocation.

The spinal cord too strikes down Vṛtra who departs. (1451)

The invocation is from the subtle world where newer and newer species of creatures already conceived awaited manifestation.

३. स न इन्द्रः शिवः सखाश्वावद्गोमद्यवमत् ।
उरुधारेव दोहते ॥

3. Indra bestows gifts for prosperity; he tells his friend prāṇa to bestow the joyous sense activities on us.

He supports extensively to hasten the milking. (1452)

D. V.

१. विभ्राड्बृहत्पिबतु सोम्यं मध्वायुर्दधद्यज्ञपतावविह्रुतम् ।
वातजूतो यो अभिरक्षति त्मना प्रजाः पिपर्ति बहुधा वि राजति ॥

1. Soma drinks much (sense activities) without glitter, bestows them extensively through the nerves in the path of life-activity to increase it.

He incites the nerves himself to protect them (sense activities); he rules also the paths of the devotees greatly. (1453), (628)

२. विभ्राड्बृहत्सुभृतं वाजसातमं धर्मं दिवो धरुणे सत्यमर्पितम् ।
अमित्रहा वृत्रहा दस्युहन्तमं ज्योतिर्जज्ञे असुरहा सपत्नहा ॥

2. Soma without glitter, supports life-activity well greatly bestowing desires; consciousness supports him as his duty and dedicates to existence.

Unfriendly (ideas) depart; Vṛtra departs; desires transform our wants through knowledge born of consciousness indeed through sense organs (asura) bestowing the paths tied to one another. (1454)

३. इदं श्रेष्ठं ज्योतिषां ज्योतिरुत्तमं विश्वजिद्धनजिदुच्यते बृहत् ।
विश्वभ्राड्भ्राजो महि सूर्यो दृश उरु पप्रथे सह ओजो अच्युतम् ॥

3. Here the highest deva is the effulgent consciousness; consciousness wins the best gifts from the sense organs; wins wealth accustomed to unite with them greatly.

The sense organs glitter and shine much; consciousness looks them up extensively; spreads out victoriously and vigorously in an abiding manner. (1455)

D. VI.

१. इन्द्र क्रतुं न आ भर पिता पुत्रेभ्यो यथा ।
शिक्षा णो अस्मिन्पुरुहूत यामनि जीवा ज्योतिरशीमहि ॥

1. Indra is power and supports the father (Activity) like supporting one's son.

He instructs us abundantly on call about the course which he wins and bestows; the motley sense activities win us greatly from slumber. (1456), (259)

२. मा नो अज्ञाता वृजना दुराध्यो३ माशिवासोऽव क्रमुः ।
त्वया वयं प्रवतः शश्वतीरपोऽति शूर तरामसि ॥

2. Knowledge envelops the brains (homes) of men by consuming wealth (of perceptions) which bestows prosperity by bestowing favours duly.

Indra nourishes us with knowledge constantly through Activity, a great hero; he gladdens us. (1457)

D. VII.

१. अद्याद्या श्वःश्व इन्द्र त्रास्व परे च नः ।
विश्वा च नो जरितॄन्त्सत्पते अहा दिवा नक्तं च रक्षिषः ॥

1. Again and again Indra himself supports prāṇa from beyond to gladden us.

The lord of existence gladdens devotees through the sense organs which indeed protect us night and day as desired. (1458)

२. प्रभङ्गी शूरो मघवा तुवीमघः सम्मिश्लो वीर्याय कम् ।
उभा ते बाहू वृषणा शतक्रतो नि या वज्रं मिमिक्षतुः ॥

2. The hero Indra (Maghavā) crushes his foes for mighty wealth and mingles vigorously with all our desires.

Indra (Vṛṣaṇā) conveys to both brain cells and sense organs

doing a hundred things below moving through the vigorous nerves by approaching and mingling with them. (1459)

D. VIII.

१. जनीयन्तो न्वग्रवः पुत्रीयन्तः सुदानवः ।
सरस्वन्तं हवामहे ॥

1. Indra! You bestow first a new (gift) on women (janī); you arouse the girl and bestowing the gift guide it.

The great oblation flows within by itself. (1460)

The reference here is to the act of impregnating a woman for the sake of offspring.

D. IX.

१. उत नः प्रियः प्रियासु सप्तस्वसा सुजुष्टा ।
सरस्वती स्तोभ्या भूत् ॥

1. Also you bind her with kindness, and arousing bestow or introduce the seven-pronged Activity into her in kindness, very well acceptable.

You flow in her yourself praiseworthily for birth. (1461)

D. X.

१. तत्सवितुर्वरेण्यं भर्गो देवस्य धीमहि ।
धियो यो नः प्रचोदयात् ॥

1. That Savitā of excellent vigour, whose effulgence is great with ideas (conceptions) for us,

satisfies us from the source and also nourishes us above with the course of life. (1462), (Y. V. 3, 35)

D. XI.

१. सोमानां स्वरणं कृणु हि ब्रह्मणस्पते ।
कक्षीवन्तं य औशिजः ॥

1. Soma gladdens us himself; as lord of knowledge he arouses us and produces it for us.

He bestows eagerly on the (brain cells) hiding within. (1463), (139), (Y. V. 3, 28)

D. XII.

१. अग्न आयूंषि पवसे आसुवोर्जमिषं च नः ।
आरे बाधस्व दुच्छुनाम् ॥

1. Agni! You protect our lives from the home eagerly; you stimulate nourishment and, opening our eyes to it, gladden us.

He himself drives away the host of enemies (āra) who plague us. (1464), (627), (1518)

D. XIII.

१. ता नः शक्तं पार्थिवस्य महो रायो दिव्यस्य ।
महि वा क्षत्रं देवेषु ॥

1. The nerves have the power to control the terrestrial sense organs greatly through ideas (devas).

The devas bestow on them great power. (1465)

२. ऋतमृतेन सपन्तेषिरं दक्षमाशाते ।
अद्रुहा देवौ वर्धेते ॥

2. Ṛta bestows admirably on mortals mighty desires to gladden and satisfies them with food.

Without (hurting) he fosters the growth of ideas through the motley sense activities. (1466)

३. वृष्टिद्यावा रीत्यापेषस्पती दानुमत्याः ।
बृहन्तं गर्तमाशाते ॥

3. Activity and the lord of desires Soma move to our brain cells (dānu) and rain night and day,

which swallow much food as desired. (1467)

D. XIV.

१. युञ्जन्ति ब्रध्नमरुषं चरन्तं परि तस्थुषः ।
रोचन्ते रोचना दिवि ॥

1. The ruddy rays of consciousness move around within and unite (with the brain) eagerly and abidingly.

He shines within and bestows gladness in waking. (1468), (Y. V. 23, 5)

२. युञ्जन्त्यस्यकाम्या हरी विपक्षसा रथे ।
शोणा धृष्णू नृवाहसा ॥

2. It is well-known that he unites with our desires; the tawny consciousness inspires the home (or scatters to the home) (ideas from) the sense organs.

The ruddy rays boldly convey and bestow them on men. (1469), (Y. V. 23, 6)

३. केतुं कृण्वन्नकेतवे पेशो मर्या अपेशसे ।
समुषद्भिरजायथाः ॥

3. The rays (of consciousness) produce the desires of perceptions and bestow the (forms of objects) forms of men.

Uṣas (Dawn) supports all of them eagerly from the source. (1470), (Y. V. 29, 37)

D. XV.

१. अयं सोम इन्द्र तुभ्यं सुन्वे तुभ्यं पवते त्वमस्य पाहि ।
त्वं ह यं चकृषे त्वं ववृष इन्दुं मदाय युज्याय सोमम् ॥

1. Indra is the path for Soma; both of them are the paths for the devotee; both of them protect understanding; they arouse us and fulfil (our needs).

They indeed cultivate and control; they bestow on the brain cells by raining; Soma moves to sense activities and unites with them. (1471)

२. स इं रथो न भुरिषाडयोजि महः पुरूणि सातये वसूनि ।
आदीं विश्वा नहुष्याणि जाता स्वर्षाता वन ऊर्ध्वा नवन्त ॥

2. Then they bestow on the sense organs abundantly; they win victoriously and gladden us abundantly continually with wealth (of perceptions).

In ancient times the sense organs were bestowed by Nahuṣa (matter) from the source; heaven bestowed them within newly at the desire of the brain (head). (1472)

It is said here that matter was in heaven in ancient times i.e. before the manifestation took place. Matter prevailed over ideas from which it arose. This is the basis of the frequent references in the purāṇas about asuras (matter) having conquered the three worlds and subordinating devas (ideas) to their rule. Indra overcomes the asuras with his divine armies and initiates manifestation.

This manifestation took place at the desire of heaven. At the same time we must remember that matter (or packed ideas) too tried to release itself as evidenced by the radioactivity of the higher periodic elements like radium, uranium etc.

३. शुष्मी शर्धो न मारुतं पवस्वानभिशस्ता दिव्य यथा विट्।
आपो न मक्षू सुमतिर्भवा नः सहस्राप्साः पृतनाषाण् न यज्ञः ।।

3. Then breath (vital air) boldly rushed by itself to bestow protection praiseworthily like an attendant of devas.

Then Activity honoured the food (sense perceptions) to arouse understanding in existence and bind it. Activity guides food thousands of times to fulfil in life-activity. (1473)

D. XVI.

१. त्वमग्ने यज्ञानां होता विश्वेषां हितः।
देवेभिर्मानुषे जने ।।

1. Agni! You preside over life-activity and arouse desires through the sense organs.

Ideas (devas) support the homes of men eagerly. (1474)

२. स नो मन्द्राभिरध्वरे जिह्वाभिर्यजा महः।
आ देवान्वक्षि यक्षि च ।।

2. You bestow gifts and support life pleasantly; you support life-activity with your tongues (rays) and gladden us.

The devas (ideas) strengthen and speed it up. (1475)

३. वेत्था हि वेधो अध्वनः पथश्च देवाञ्जसा।
अग्ने यज्ञेसु सुक्रतो ।।

3. They (the devas) pierce into our life-journey and arouse us thus; the devas adorn the path of life and bestow,

Agni's missiles do good in life. (1476)

D. XVII.

१. होता देवो अमर्त्यः पुरस्तादेति मायया।
विदथानि प्रचोदयन् ।।

1. Ideas hasten to mortals to preside over them; the motley sense activities in their forefront hasten to bestow.

They direct the nourishment and also guide above. (1477)

२. वाजी वाजेषु धीयतेऽध्वरेषु प्र णीयते।
विप्रो यज्ञस्य साधनः ।।

2. They win for us and bestow on us in life-activity; they unite for understanding with the missiles of sense activities in life and honour them by uniting.

They inspire our yajña and bestow wealth. (1478)

३. धिया चक्रे वरेण्यो भूतानां गर्भमा दधे ।
दक्षस्य पितरं तना ॥

3. The ideas go around excellently within the creatures; bestow from the source and satisfy.

The father (Activity) guides us and satisfies by gladdening. (1479)

D. XVIII.

१. आ सुते सिञ्चत श्रियं रोदस्योरभिश्रियम् ।
रसा दधीत वृषभम् ॥

1. The ideas tingle along to mind for prosperity, from the brain cells and sense organs (fulfilling) their prosperity too.

Indra bestows their essence for knowledge. (1480)

२. ते जानत स्वमोक्यं ३ सं वत्सासो न मातृभिः ।
मिथो नसन्त जामिभिः ॥

2. They take their births by themselves for the sense activities praiseworthily to control; the mother bestows them all on mind.

Then they (the ideas) associate themselves with their relative mind within. (1481)

३. उप स्रक्वेषु बप्सतः कृण्वते धरुणं दिवि ।
इन्द्रे अग्ना नमः स्वः ॥

3. Above, the rays of sense activities are devoured by the brain cells for existence; consciousness boldly produces understanding from them.

They bow to Indra and Agni themselves. (1482)

D. XIX.

१. तदिदास भुवनेषु ज्येष्ठं यतो जज्ञ उग्रस्त्वेषनृम्णः ।
सद्यो जज्ञानो नि रिणाति शत्रूनन् यं विश्वे मदन्त्यूमाः ॥

1. The eldest Indra bestows them (on the brain cells of creatures) with the rays (of sense activities) and unites with life-activity powerfully and courageously and is praised.

Knowledge is born immediately which he releases; the enemies are now controlled; the sense organs rejoice through the sense activities. (1483)

२. वावृधानः शवसा भूर्योजाः शत्रुर्दासाय भियसं दधाति ।
अव्यनच्च व्यनच्च सस्नि सं ते नवन्त प्रभृता मदेषु ॥

2. He bestows by enveloping the brain (head) with might, abundantly and vigorously; he serves against enemies extensively and he strives to bestow fearlessly.

We honour the Aśvins also; we honour the brain cells which are enveloped by the rays of sense activities, nourished by them all freshly within and supported by them. (1484)

३. त्वे क्रतुमपि वृञ्जन्ति विश्वे द्विर्यदेते त्रिर्भवन्त्यूमाः ।
स्वादोः स्वादीयः स्वादुना सृजा समदः सु मधु मधुनाभि योधीः ॥

3. Indra! You are a power; you enfold the sense organs; what is two (brain and sense organs) becomes three (states) through the motley sense activities, including mind.

The sweet (sense perceptions) themselves speed up to bestow themselves to be consumed; the sense activities flow in to bestow and arouse sense perceptions; the sense perceptions are the centres of knowledge. (1485)

D. XX.

१. त्रिकद्रुकेषु महिषो यवाशिरं तुविशुष्मस्तृम्पत्सोममपिबाद्विष्णुना
सुतं यथावशम् ।
स ईं ममाद महि कर्म कर्तवे महामुरुं सैनं
सश्चद्देवो देवं सत्य इन्दुः सत्यमिन्द्रम् ॥

1. The rays (iṣu of sense activities) hasten from the sense organs (Kadru) to the brain (head-ka) for the sake of the three states to gladden their desires; they rush mightily to the brain cells in the head to satisfy them which drink Soma juice from Viṣṇu.

The mind likewise drinks from the home. They give us great purposeful activities (karma) to carry out with great and extensive troops (of ideas).

The devas (ideas) unite with us; the devas are well-known to bestow; Indra is well-known just to bestow them. (1486), (457)

२. साकं जातः क्रतुना साकमोजसा ववक्षिथ
साकं वृद्धो वीर्यैः सासहिर्मृधो विचर्षणिः।
दाता राध स्तुवते काम्यं वसु
प्रचेतन सैनं सश्चद्देवो देवं सत्य इन्दुः सत्यमिन्द्रम् ॥

2. Together (Indra and Ideas) from the source inspire us; together they bestow powerfully; they bestow for strengthening.

Together they promote vigour; they are victorious in fights and diligently active.

Indra bestows on their (ideas) wealth praiseworthily for knowledge as desired and controls them.

The troops (of ideas) nourish mind uniting with the deva (Indra); the devas are well-known to bestow; Indra is well-known just to bestow them. (1487)

३. अध त्विषीमाँ अभ्योजसा क्रिविं युधाभवदा
रोदसी अपृणदस्य मज्मना प्र वावृधे।
अधत्तान्यं जठरे प्रेमरिच्यत प्र चेतय
सैनं सश्चद्देवो देवं सत्य इन्दुः सत्यमिन्द्रम् ॥

3. Then he bestows our desires fearlessly and vigorously; through carrying out fights he bestows on us existence.

He nourishes the wants of brain cells and sense organs (heaven and earth); magnanimously nourishes them to grow. He bestows on and guides the brain cells with love, which he empties (or from which he removes) to bestow on mind by uniting with him.

The troops of ideas unite with the deva Indra; the devas are well-known to bestow; Indra is well-known just to bestow them. (1488)

(Alt—third line). Then he bestows another body when the loved one is released (at death) and nourishes mind to unite with another.

Death does not terminate existence to mind. It is carried to an afterlife with another body. The main purpose of mind is to continue existence for ever so that activity can never come to an end.

BOOK VII: CHAPTER I

D. I.

१. अभि प्र गोपतिं गिरेन्द्रमर्च यथा विदे ।
सूनुं सत्यस्य सत्पतिम् ॥

1. Indra honours the lord of subjects (cows) Agni on the hill to nourish, as enjoined.

The lord of existence Indra (does so) for the sake of existence of mind (son). (1489), (168)

२. आ हरयः ससृज्रिरेऽरुषीरधि बर्हिषि ।
यत्राभि संनवामहे ॥

2. He hastens to convey and flows to go and release the ruddy consciousness from beyond to the nerves,

who moves to support all afresh greatly. (1490)

३. इन्द्राय गाव आशिरं दुदुह्रे वज्रिणे मधु ।
यत्सीमुपह्वरे विदत् ॥

3. Indra moves to bestow sense activities on the head (brain) through the nerves for the spinal cord to consume for the sake of sense perceptions (honey).

They unite with the spinal cord above and are bound up as knowledge. (1491)

D. II.

१. आ नो विश्वासु हव्यमिन्द्रं समत्सुभूषत ।
उप ब्रह्माणि सवनानि वृत्रहन्परमज्या ऋचीषम ॥

1. Indra arouses the sense organs for oblations all of which adorn well.

Above, knowledge is stimulated through the sense activities, after Vṛtra is struck down by Indra for winning from beyond. (1492), (269)

२. त्वं दाता प्रथमो राधसामस्यसि सत्य ईशानकृत् ।
तुविद्युम्नस्य युज्या वृणीमहे पुत्रस्य शवसो महः ॥

2. Indra! You bestow them foremost to release wealth to us in existence and to rule and produce for us.

You move to unite with us like lightning and envelop the mind greatly with might and gladden him. (1493)

D. III.

१. प्रत्नं पीयूषं पूर्व्यं यदुक्थ्यं महो गाहाद्दिव आ निरधुक्षत ।
इन्द्रमभि जायमानं समस्वरन् ॥

1. The earliest creatures of ancient times were very old, which the sense activities brought to light (waking) praiseworthily on whom their brains (homes) depended.

Indra came to their homes from the source and gladdened them all himself. (1494)

२. आदीं के चित्पश्यमानास आप्यं वसुरुचो दिव्या अभ्यनूषत ।
दिवो न वारं सविता व्यूर्णुते ॥

2. In ancient times the intelligence (cit) of Prajāpati (ka) perceived homes (cell bodies) in water and to control them Indra who shone with ideas and to whom they were attached,

consciousness gladdened them newly and stimulated manifestation in waves. (1495)

३. अध यदिमे पवमान रोदसी इमा च विश्वा भुवनाभि मज्मना ।
यूथे न निष्ठा वृषभो वि राजसि ॥

3. It bestowed protection on the homes (cells) lightning like (rodasī) and bestowed existence on the homes from the source in its greatness.

Indra controlled and bound the multitude of cells at the desire of sense activities. (1496)

D. IV.

१. इमम् षु त्वमस्माकं सनिं गायत्रं नव्यांसम् ।
अग्ने देवेषु प्र वोचः ॥

1. You bestow gifts for our sake on the sense organs where the sense activities bestow fresh support.

Agni is accustomed to bestow ideas (devas) with the rays of sense activities (nourishment). (1497), (28)

२. विभक्तासि चित्रभानो सिन्धोरूर्मा उपाक आ ।
सद्यो दाशुषे क्षरसि ॥

2. The waves of Sindhu (sense activities) separate themselves in variegated colours (rays) in the head above.

They flow in to bestow instant service eagerly. (1498)

३. आ नो भज परमेष्वा वाजेषु मध्यमेषु ।
शिक्षा वस्वो अन्तमस्य ॥

3. The sense activities control life activity with their missiles (rays) bestowing the desires of heaven to honour (worship).

They instruct us by bestowing on the home within us. (1499)

D. V.

१. अहमिद्धि पितुष्परि मेधामृतस्य जग्रह ।
अहं सूर्य इवाजनि ॥

1. Activity (father) goes around the brain in waking state for understanding to be born in the homes of mortals.

Like consciousness the waking state is born of the source. (1500), (152)

२. अहं प्रत्नेन जन्मना गिरः शुम्भामि कण्ववत् ।
येनेन्द्रः शुष्ममिद्दधे ।

2. In ancient births (creatures) Activity adorned the hill (brain) and approached the brain cells for the sake of understanding,

for which Indra rushed to the brain to bestow. (1501)

३. ये त्वामिन्द्र न तुष्टुवुर्ऋषयो ये च तुष्टवुः ।
ममेद्वर्धस्व सुष्टुतः ॥

3. Indra! You bestow satisfaction to the ṛṣis extensively; they too bestow satisfaction.

You foster our growth yourself appropriately. (1502)

D. VI.

१. अग्ने विश्वेभिरग्निभिर्जोषि ब्रह्म सहस्कृत ।
ये देवत्रा य आयुषु तेभिर्नो महया गिरः ॥

1. Agni supports the sense organs which eagerly support the birth of knowledge producing it with might.

He supports ideas (devas); moves to prāṇa (life) to support him on the hill and gladden him. (1503)

२. प्र स विश्वेभिरग्निभिरग्निः स यस्य वाजिनः ।
तनये तोके अस्मदा सम्यङ्वाजैः परीवतः ।।

2. Agni bestows nourishment on the sense organs to support them, which support our ardour (agni), which he bestows in life-activity.

He bestows on our family and progeny; he comes together with them in life, and goes round for knowledge. (1504)

३. त्वं नोअग्ने अग्निभिर्ब्रह्म यज्ञं च वर्धय ।
त्वं नो देवतातये रायो दानाय चोदय ।।

3. You are Agni; as Agni you support knowledge and promote the growth of Yajña.

The father of devas Savitā control you and bestowed you as a gift on us and moved you up. (1505)

D. VII.

१. त्वे सोम प्रथमा वृक्तबर्हिषो महे वाजाय श्रवसे धियं दधुः ।
स त्वं नो वीर वीर्याय चोदय ।

1. Soma! You are the foremost to move to the life-activity along the nerves spread out to hear and bestow satisfaction.

You bestow vigour moving vigorously above. (1506)

२. अभ्यभि हि श्रवसा ततर्दिथोत्सं न कं चिज्जनपानमक्षितम् ।
शर्याभिर्न भरमाणो गभस्त्योः ।।

2. Soma! You listen to this and that and arouse to bestow, half of all of which are without desires which men perceive and drink in the home as desired.

The rays (arrows) are supported and they support the home through the nerves. (1507)

Half the sense activities coming in contact with objects are said to be untinged by desires. These are the true and pure perceptions.

३. अजीजनो अमृत मर्त्याय कमृतस्य धर्मन्नमृतस्य चारुणः ।
सदासरो वाजमच्छा सनिष्यदत् ।।

3. Soma! You win for men i.e. for mortals from the immortal source; Prajāpati gladdens mortals in accordance with dharma from the immortal source.

You flow constantly in life-activity and bestow gifts on the wishes of those near you. (1508)

D. VIII.

१. एन्द्रुमिन्द्राय सिञ्चत पिबाति सोम्यं मधु ।
प्र राधांसि चोदयते महित्वना ॥

1. Indra tingles along to the brain cells which drink sense perceptions (honey) controlled by Soma.

He supports nourishment for wealth and unites above for much desires. (1509), (386)

२. उपो हरीणां पतिं राधः पृञ्चन्तमब्रवम् ।
नूनं श्रुधि स्तुवतो अश्व्यस्य ॥

2. Above the tawny consciousness is the lord of wealth (or protects prosperity); he mingles with our desires and communicates to us.

Prāṇa now learns about it and satisfies us with understanding praiseworthily. (1510)

३. नह्यं३ग पुरा च न जज्ञे वीरतरस्त्वत् ।
न की राया नैवथा न भन्दना ॥

3. Indra controls sense activities in the city (brain) and gladdens us in life by enabling us to cross (ignorance) vigorously and praiseworthily.

Heaven controls and speeds up and is praised. (1511)

D. IX.

१. नदं व ओदतीनां नदं योयुवतीनाम् ।
पतिं वो अघ्न्यानां धेनूनामिषुध्यसि ॥

1. Indra (Nada) bestows the clouds (of sense activities); Indra unites with knowledge.

He bestows wealth (of sense perceptions) to drink; he strives to bestow the missiles of the milch-cow to sip. (1512)

D. X.

१. देवो वो द्रविणोदाः पूर्णां विवष्ट्वासिचम् ।
उद्वा सिञ्चध्वमुप वा पृणध्वमादिद्वो देव ओहते ॥

1. Devas (ideas) bestow wealth, bestow to fulfil, through the dwellers, by sipping them eagerly.

They run to tingle along and bestow; the two ancient devas (Agni and Indra) run to bestow, nourish and effect transformations. (1513)

The transformations consist in sense activities turning to sense perceptions and in the brain and mind getting new ideas and so forth.

२. तं होतारमध्वरस्य प्रचेतसं वह्नि देवा अकृण्वत ।
दधाति रत्नं विधते सुवीर्यमग्निर्जनाय दाशुषे ।।

2. Ideas preside over our desires for life-activity and gladden us; they nourish mind; ideas convey all for producing knowledge.

They bestow valuable wealth and pay homage (Vidha) to us; Agni bestows services to men by arousing vigour. (1514)

D. XI.

१. आदर्शि गातुवित्तमो यस्मिन्व्रतान्यादधुः ।
उपो षु जातमार्यस्य वर्धनमग्निं नक्षन्तु नो गिरः ।।

1. Knowing the desires of the devotees to see, Agni bestows and guides the devotees vows.

Above, heaven bestows (ideas) for the sense organs of man. Agni approaches them on the hill, honours them and fosters their growth. (1515), (47)

२. यस्माद्रेजन्त कृष्टयश्चर्कृत्यानि कृण्वतः ।
सहस्रसां मेधसाताविव त्मनाग्निं धीभिर्नमस्यत ।।

2. He is excited over the devotees within; goes around to cultivate (the brain) through the sense organs creating knowledge.

Agni himself bestows thousands (of ideas) on the brain (medha) by riding over it continually and honours it by bestowing and supporting it. (1516)

३. प्र दैवोदासो अग्नि [र्देव इन्द्रो न मज्मना] ।
[अनु मातरं पृथिवीं वि वावृते तस्थौ नाकस्य शर्मणि] ।।

3. Ideas (devas) do service for Agni [Mind honours Indra and wins ideas].

[Now the mother envelops the sense organs by riding them and protects them abidingly from heaven.] (1517), (51)

D. XII.

१. अग्न आयूंषि पवस [आसुवोर्जमिषं च नः] ।
[आरे बाधस्व दुच्छुनाम्] ॥

1. Agni protects life (prāṇa) in the home [he arouses and opens our eyes to the nourishment and gladdens us].

[He himself dispels any calamities to us through the spoke-like nerves]. (1518), (627), (1464)

२. अग्निर्ऋषिः पवमानः पाञ्चजन्यः पुरोहितः ।
तमीमहे महागयम् ॥

2. Agni bestows to drink (or protect) on the home through the ṛṣis (Activity); the five sense activities from the source are the presiding priests.

The sense activities greatly control our great desires. (1519), (Y. V. 26, 9)

३. अग्ने पवस्व स्वपा अस्मे वर्चः सुवीर्यम् ।
दधद्रयिं मयि पोषम् ॥

3. Agni himself bestows and protects; he himself fulfils our needs of vigour and arouses illuminating power (Varcas).

He bestows on us wealth for our prosperity. (1520)

D. XIII.

१. अग्ने पावक रोचिषा मन्द्रया देव जिह्वया ।
आ देवान्वक्षि यक्षि च ॥

1. Agni bestows on the brain (head) for fulfilment and brings our desires to light pleasantly through the rays (tongues of sense activities).

The devas (ideas) strengthen and speed up life-activity. (1521), (Y. V. 17, 8)

२. तं त्वा घृतस्नवीमहे चित्रभानो स्वर्दृशम् ।
देवां आ वीतये वह ॥

2. Agni! You are greatly desirous of new clarified butter (mental reactions) and look to heaven for variegated lustres.

The devas (ideas) convey them eagerly. (1522)

३. वीतिहोत्रं त्वा कवे द्युमन्त समिधीमहि ।
अग्ने बृहन्तमध्वरे ॥

3. Agni! You desire to preside and support from heaven and approaching me bestow much knowledge within.

Agni! You bestow (bṛh) desires in life-activity. (1523)

D. XIV.

१. अवा नो अग्न ऊतिभिर्गायत्रस्य प्रभर्मणि ।
विश्वासु धीषु वन्द्य ।।

1. Agni! You favour us now; you help and support sense activities by whom our brain cells (maṇi) are nourished and supported.

They arouse the sense organs for knowledge and are praised. (1524)

२. आ नो अग्ने रयिं भर सत्रासाहं वरेण्यम् ।
विश्वासु पृत्सु दुष्टरम् ।।

2. Agni! Now you support wealth and are victorious in life-activity (Soma Yajña) excellently.

You arouse the sense organs to nourish and consume eagerly to gladden us. (1525)

३. आ नो अग्ने सुचेतुना रयिं विश्वायुपोषसम् ।
मार्डीकं धेहि जीवसे ।।

3. Agni! Now you incite the mind for the wealth in want and unite with the sense organs and fulfil him eagerly with all.

You bestow victoriously on him in compassion. (1526)

D. XV.

१. अग्निं हिन्वन्तु नो धियः सप्तिमाशुमिवाजिषु ।
तेन जेष्म धनंधनम् ।।

1. Agni arouses us within and bestows for satisfaction the seven-pronged Activity quickly for life-activity.

From his wealth are born our desires which honour and bestow on us. (1527)

२. यया गा आकरामहे सेनयाग्ने तवोत्या ।
तां नो हिन्व मघत्तये ।।

2. The sense activities hasten to the brain (head) to bestow greatly as the troops of Agni whom the latter helps.

They arouse those longing for them and bestow bounties. (1528)

३. आग्ने स्थूरं रयिं भर पृथुं गोमन्तमश्विनम् ।
अङ्घि खं वर्तया पविम् ।।

3. Agni supports wealth stoutly; the Aśvins spread out the sense activities within.

The roots of the brain cells subsist in the rim of the brain. (1529)

४. अग्ने नक्षत्रमजरमा सूर्यं रोहयो दिवि ।
दधज्ज्योतिर्जनेभ्यः ।।

4. Agni approaches me to support ever fresh and bestows consciousness who releases the waking state through prāṇa.

The effulgence of consciousness bestows it on men. (1530)

५. अग्ने केतुर्विशामसि प्रेष्ठः श्रेष्ठ उपस्थसत् ।
बोधा स्तोत्रे वयो दधत् ।।

5. Agni! You nourish the desires of the brain (home) at your wish; you are the best leader in existence.

You bestow on us knowledge praiseworthily. (1531)

D. XVI.

१. अग्निर्मूर्धा दिवः ककुत्पतिः पृथिव्या अयम् ।
अपां रेतांसि जिन्वति ।।

1. Agni bestows consciousness on mortals, who is the lord of the summit bestowing the path on the sense organs.

Activity is supported by him to win knowledge. (1532)

२. ईशिषे वार्यस्य हि दात्रस्याग्ने स्वः पतिः ।
स्तोता स्यां तव शर्मणि ।।

2. Agni! You rule over our desires for wealth; you arouse us yourself to wealth (property) as its lord.

You protect us praiseworthily. (1533)

३. उदग्ने शुचयस्तव शुक्रा भ्राजन्त ईरते ।
तव ज्योतींष्यर्चयः ।।

3. Agni! You glow brightly above (or you glow in water as latent heat); you shine brightly to stir us up.

You honour the effulgence of consciousness. (1534)

BOOK VII: CHAPTER II

D. I.

१. कस्ते जामिर्जनानामग्ने को दाश्वध्वरः ।
को ह कस्मिन्नसि श्रितः ॥

1. Agni! Who is your kinsman in the home? Who bestows services on men in life-activity?

Who indeed are you? Where do you rest? (1535)

२. त्वं जामिर्जनानामग्ने मित्रो असि प्रियः ।
सखा सखिभ्य ईड्यः ॥

2. Agni! You are a kinsman of men; you are a friend and kind.

You are a comrade whose comradeship is praised. (1536)

३. यजा नो मित्रावरुणा यजा देवाँ ऋतं बृहत् ।
अग्ने यक्षि स्वं दमम् ॥

3. Mitra (brain) and Varuṇa (external world) worship you; ideas worship you and the great Ṛta.

Agni! You speed up life-activity in the home. (1537), (Y. V. 33, 3)

D. II.

१. ईडेन्यो नमस्यस्तिरस्तमांसि दर्शतः ।
समग्निरिध्यते वृषा ॥

1. We offer you fresh prayers and make obeisances in the home for supporting our home on your visits.

Agni rains and releases all for sipping. (1538)

२. वृषो अग्निः समिध्यतेऽश्वो न देववाहनः ।
तं हविष्मन्त ईडते ॥

2. Agni rains (gifts); unites with sense objects (Samidh); prāṇa is the vehicle of the Devas.

We pray for oblations desired within us. (1539)

३. वृषणं त्वा वयं वृषन्वृषणः समिधीमहि ।
अग्ने दीद्यतं बृहत् ।

3. You are powerful; you rain to us powerfully much sense objects (fuel-sticks).

Agni! You unite with us to bestow much. (1540)

D. III.

१. उत्ते बृहन्तो अर्चय समिधानस्य दीदिवः ।
अग्ने शुक्रास ईरते ॥

1. They also hasten to bestow (bṛha) much and honour us with sense objects (kindling fuel) which shine in waking state.

Agni incites them and bestows knowledge (brightness). (1541)

२. उप त्वा जुह्वो३ मम घृताचीर्यन्तु हर्यत ।
अग्ने हव्या जुषस्व नः ॥

2. Above you convey to us also streams of clarified butter through your rays (tongues).

Agni! You yourself bind us to the oblations rejoicingly. (1542)

३. मन्द्रं होतारमृत्विजं चित्रभानुं विभावसुम् ।
अग्निमीडे स उ श्रवत् ॥

3. Indra presides over the devotees and gladdens them with variegated lustres shining brilliantly.

Agni bestows oblations which cooks up knowledge. (1543)

D. IV.

१. पाहि नो अग्न एकया पाह्यु३त द्वितीयया ।
पाहि गीर्भिस्तसृभिरूर्जां पते पाहि चतसृभिर्वसो ॥

1. Agni! You arouse us and fulfil (our needs) firstly; secondly you hasten to bestow our path; thirdly you arouse the hill (brain) to support it with nourishment and fulfil; fourthly you support the home by arousing, fulfilling and protecting it. (1544), (36), (Y.V.27. 43)

२. पाहि विश्वस्माद्रक्षसो अराव्णः प्र स्म वाजेषु नोऽव ।
त्वामिद्धि नेदिष्ठं देवतातय आपि नक्षामहे वृधे ॥

2. You arouse our sense organs to bestow on us protection and fulfil (our needs); you bestow our desires, nourish us with our wants (una) in life-activity and bless us.

You are near the brain; you are a friend (āpi) of the father of the devas whom you approach greatly and foster our growth. (1545)

D. V.

१. इनो राजन्नरतिः समिद्धो रौद्रो दक्षाय सुषुमाँ अदर्शि ।
चिकिद्वि भाति भासा बृहतासिक्नीमेति रुशतीमपाजन् ॥

1. Consciousness (sun) controls men; sense objects (fuel-sticks) from the south (or front) move violently towards him to visit our minds.

Knowing the two lustres (brain cells and sense organs) he clarifies them. which are bound up greatly with the girl namely motley sense activities, whose birth Activity browses on. (1546)

२. कृष्णां यदेनीमभि वर्पसाभूज्जनयन्योषां बृहतः पितुर्जाम् ।
ऊर्ध्वं भानुं सूर्यस्य स्तभायन् दिवो वसुभिररतिर्वि भाति ॥

2. The mighty consciousness, as a relative of the great Activity, draws out the assumed form (varpasā) (of savitā) for existence among men whom the sense activities guide; consciousness shines in the head and establishes the waking state which Indra (Vasu) supports and gladdens us through the waking state. (1547)

Man is said to have been conceived in the image of the father of all creatures Viṣṇu by the Veda and hence he is named dwarf Viṣṇu. This fact is brought out by the purāṇic story relating to the Vāmana avatāra. It indicates the advent of man on earth after the animal creation had been completed. The asura Bali typified the brute strength and courage of the animal kingdom which held sway over the three worlds till man appeared with superior intelligence and knowledge.

३. भद्रो भद्रया सचमान आगात्स्वसारं जारो अभ्येति पश्चात् ।
सुप्रकेतैर्द्युभिरग्निर्वितिष्ठन्रुशद्भिर्वर्णैरभि राममस्थात् ॥

3. The motley sense activities arrive with their own essential natures to unite with the home (brain) auspiciously and move in for our prosperity; they are followed by their lovers (sense reactions).

Agni supports and nourishes the desires of heaven (head) who, through browsing on them as he desires, supports their variegated demands and gladdens us abidingly. (1548)

D. VI.

१. कया ते अग्ने अङ्गिर ऊर्जो नपादुपस्तुतिम् ।
वराय देव मन्यवे ॥

1. Agni! They (the sense activities) move to the head; these Aṅgiras nourish the sense organs (dependents) praiseworthily.

Ideas move as gifts from the brain cells to the mind. (1549)

२. दाशेम कस्य मनसा यज्ञस्य सहसो यहो ।
कदु वोच इद नमः ॥

2. The head (brain) gives us service, bestows on the mind in life with might and speeds up.

The head is accustomed to bestow for its consumption and honour thus. (1550)

३. अधा त्वं हि नस्करो विश्वा अस्मभ्यं सुक्षितीः ।
वाजद्रविणसो गिरः ॥

3. (Agni!) Then you associate with our sense organs arouse and bestow by arousing (inducing the home).

You bestow wealth through them in life on the brain (hill). (1551)

D. VII.

१. अग्न आ याह्यग्निभिर्होतारं त्वा वृणीमहे ।
आ त्वामनक्तु प्रयता हविष्मती यजिष्ठं बर्हिरासदे ॥

1. Agni! You preside over the closely united ardour (agni) and nourish us greatly.

You unite with mind and nourish him with understanding as oblations; you release knowledge as you desire in life constantly and bestow them through the nerves. (1552)

२. अच्छा हि त्वा सहसः सूनो अङ्गिरः स्रुचश्चरन्त्यध्वरे ।
ऊर्जो नपातं घृतकेशमीमहेऽग्निं यज्ञेषु पूर्व्यम् ॥

2. Agni! You arouse the mind near you with might; the Aṅgiras (sense activities) go around to him in life whom you ladle out to him.

You toil greatly in the head for clarified butter through nourishing the sense organs (descendants).

Agni was there earlier than life-activity. (1553)

D. VIII.

१. अच्छा नः शीरशोचिषं गिरो यन्तु दर्शतम् ।
अच्छा यज्ञासो नमसा पुरूवसुं पुरुप्रशस्तमूतये ॥

1. Agni! You visit the desires of the brain which shine on the hill to guide them well.

You honour life-activity well and bestow abundant wealth in it; you help it much to be praised. (1554)

२. अग्नि सूनुं सहसो जातवेदसं दानाय वार्याणाम् ।
द्विता यो भूदमृतो मर्त्येष्वा होता मन्द्रतमो विशि ॥

2. You bestow with might on mind so that all knowledge may be born to him and accordingly move to the brain cells with the gifts from sense organs.

You bestow both (to the brain cells and sense-organs) and support their existence; bestow men's desires and preside pleasantly over these desires in the home. (1555)

D. IX.

१. अदाभ्यः पुरएता विशामग्निर्मानुषीणाम् ।
तुर्णी रथः सदा नवः ॥

1. The motley sense activities bestow on my brain (city) inviolably through Agni so that men

have their waves from sense organs ever new. (1556)

२. अभि प्रयांसि वाहसा दाश्वाँ अश्नोति मर्त्यः ।
क्षयं पावकशोचिषः ॥

2. The motley sense activities bestow services on mortals on the hill by conveying nourishment.

They control the home and bestow glowing desires in the head to fulfil. (1557)

३. साह्वान्विश्वा अभियुजः क्रतुर्देवानाममृक्तः ।
अग्निस्तुविश्रवस्तमः ॥

3. They bestow on the sense organs on call and unite with the might of ideas (devas) to cross them.

Agni listens to their powerful desires. (1558)

D. X.

१. भद्रो नो अग्निराहुतो भद्रा रातिः सुभग भद्रो अध्वरः ।
भद्रा उत प्रशस्तयः ॥

1. Agni bestows for our welfare; he is ready to bestow propitiously; he arouses consciousness for our welfare in life.

He helps in our welfare praiseworthily. (1559), (111), (Y.V. 15, 38)

२. भद्रं मनः कृणुष्व वृत्रतूर्ये येना समत्सु सासहिः ।
अव स्थिरा तनुहि भूरि शर्धतां वनेमा ते अभिष्टये ॥

2. He himself produces (gifts) for the welfare of mind and sends Vṛtra (inertia) to the fourth state and arouses mind to all (gifts) victoriously.

He favours us abidingly, arouses delicately releasing us boldly to existence longed for which bestows our forest of desires. (1560)

D. XI.

१. अग्ने वाजस्य गोमत ईशानः सहसो यहो ।
अस्मे देहि जातवेदो महि श्रवः ॥

1. Agni! in life-activity the sense activities rule us with might and speed us up.

They bestow on us knowledge to take birth in us from much hearing. (1561), (99), (Y.V.15, 35)

२. स इधानो वसुष्कविरग्निरीडेन्यो गिरा ।
रेवदस्मभ्यं पुर्वणीक दीदिहि ॥

2. Indra kindles and bestows the compositions which Agni bestows as oblations on the hill.

He transfers them as wealth of speech from the city to us and shines. (1562), (Y.V.15, 36)

३. क्षपो राजन्नुत त्मनाग्ने वस्तोरुतोषसः ।
स तिग्मजम्भ रक्षसो दह प्रति ॥

3. Agni! You control ignorance also; you yourself bestow eagerly through Uṣas extensively,

who devours (ignorance) passionately and bestows protection indeed by bestowing nourishment in its place. (1563), (Y.V.15, 37)

D. XII.

१. विशोविशो वो अतिथिं वाजयन्तः पुरुप्रियम् ।
अग्निं वो दुर्यं वच स्तुषे शूषस्य मन्मभिः ॥

1. The guests (sense activities) bestow on creature after creature (home after home) guidance in life with great love.

Agni opens the door to speech praiseworthily and to mind resoundingly. (1564), (87)

२. यं जनासो हविष्मन्तो मित्रं न सर्पिरासुतिम् ।
प्रशंसन्ति प्रशस्तिभिः ॥

2. Agni! You control men and bestow oblations of ideas on the brain (Mitra) which creep along to bestow on mind.

They nourish him praiseworthily and are praised. (1565)

३. पन्यांसं जातवेदसं यो देवतात्युद्यता ।
हव्यान्यैरयद्दिवि ॥

3. He supports admirably for the birth of all knowledge; ideas (devas) unite with it to march in step.

The waking state incites the oblations. (1566)

D. XIII.

१. समिद्धमग्निं समिधा गिरा गृणे शुचिं पावकं पुरो अध्वरे ध्रुवम् ।
विप्रं होतारं पुरुवारमद्रुहं कविं सुम्नैरीमहे जातवेदसम् ॥

1. Agni bestows on us sense objects (fuel) and approaches us to bestow on the hill (brain); flames up in the devotees; bestows desires for fulfilment in the city abidingly in life.

The wise Agni presides and gladdens us with much wealth without hurting; the poet releases graciously for all knowledge to be born. (1567)

२. त्वां दूतमग्ने अमृतं युगेयुगे हव्यवाहं दधिरे पायुमीड्यम् ।
देवासश्च मर्तासश्च जागृविं विभुं विश्पतिं नमसा नि षेदिरे ॥

2. Agni! You are a messenger from immortal heaven, you convey oblations to us day after day of curds which unite as oblations to fulfil.

Devas follow you; mortals follow you in the waking state; you are pervasive, lord of the home; you honour and bestow on the home for our comfort. (1568)

३. विभूषन्नग्न उभयाँ अनु व्रता दूतो देवानां रजसी समीयसे ।
यत्ते धीतिं सुमतिमावृणीमहेऽध स्मा नस्त्रिवरूथः शिवो भव ॥

3. Agni! Through adorning both (the brain and sense organs) now according to your duty (vow) you rouse up ideas and bind them to strive together.

They unite for understanding; they envelop us and bestow much good knowledge; then they associate with all our three states to help to an auspicious existence. (1569)

D. XIV.

१. उप त्वा जामयो गिरो देदिशतीर्हविष्कृतः ।
वायोरनीके अस्थिरन् ॥

1. Agni! Prāṇa springs from you above on the hill to whom you give directions to produce oblations.

The nerves below stabilise them. (1570), (13).

२. यस्य त्रिधात्ववृतं बर्हिस्तस्थावसन्दिनम् ।
आपश्चिन्नि दधा पदम् ॥

2. They bestow on the three states enveloping their desires through the nerves abidingly in the home in the waking state.

Activity bestows ideas in the home to drink. (1571)

३. पदं देवस्य मीढुषोऽनाधृष्टाभिरूतिभिः ।
भद्रा सूर्य इवोपदृक् ॥

3. The devas (ideas) bestow rewards on us eagerly in the home to protect (or to drink); the unconquerable Indra supports and helps them.

Consciousness looks at us above for our welfare. (1572)

BOOK VII: CHAPTER III

D. I.

१. अभि त्वा पूर्वपीतय इन्द्र स्तोमेभिरायवः ।
समीचीनास ऋभवः समस्वरन्रुद्रा गृणन्त पूर्व्यम् ॥

1. Indra! You swelled over to the brain cells in ancient times to support them praiseworthily.

Turning to us together with the Ṛbhus (the three primary nerves), you bestowed on us from heaven; Rudra (master of the nervous system) within the devotee is ancient. (1573), (256)

Rudra is the controller of the nervous system under Indra and is said to be his younger brother.

२. अस्येदिन्द्रो वावृधे वृष्ण्यं शवो मदे सुतस्य विष्णवि ।
अद्या तमस्य महिमानमायवोऽनु ष्टुवन्ति पूर्वथा ॥

2. Whatever Indra bestows on us he fosters their growth; he controls the sense organs powerfully (or he rains to them and controls); the sense activities work afresh for the mind.

Now, a great many desires are bestowed on the mind from the home (brain) and praised as in olden times. (1574)

D. II.

१. प्र वामर्चन्त्युक्थिनो नीथाविदो जरितारः ।
इन्द्राग्नी इष आ वृणे ॥

1. Indra! I honour (worship) and unite with you, for bestowal of nourishment; you guide the devotee to knowledge to cross over (ignorance).

Agni desires to choose Indra for this. (1575), (1703)

२. इन्द्राग्नी नवतिं पुरो दासपत्नीरधूनुतम् ।
साकमेकेन कर्मणा ॥

2. When Indra serves Agni in the city (brain) for knowledge, he is dependent on the sense activities (woman) now for his desires.

Together they have common duties (Karman). (1576), (1704)

३. इन्द्राग्नी अपसस्पर्युप प्र यन्ति धीतयः ।
ऋतस्य पथ्या३ अनु ॥

3. Indra and Agni work to go around to the brain cells above to nourish and guide them to understanding.

Now it is for Ṛta to move along the path. (1577)

४. इन्द्राग्नी तविषाणी वां सधस्थानि प्रयांसि च ।
युवोरप्तूर्यं हितम् ॥

4. Indra and Agni bestow desires on us and move to support us in the assembly to nourish us also.

Activity does much good to mind from the fourth state. (1578)

D. III.

१. शग्ध्यू३ षु शचीपत इन्द्र विश्वाभिरूतिभिः ।
भगं न हि त्वा यशसं वसुविदमनु शूर चरामसि ॥

1. Indra takes the path of might for food (sense perceptions) from the sense organs and helps to support them.

Consciousness arouses him excellently and Indra now valiantly goes around for the knowledge. (1579), (253)

२. पौरो अश्वस्य पुरुकृद्गवामस्युत्सो देव हिरण्ययः ।
न किर्हि दानं परि मर्धिषत्त्वे यद्यद्यामि तदा भर ॥

2. Prāṇa produces much for the brain (city), bestows the sense activities on it and also runs to release the deva golden consciousness.

He goes around to arouse and scatter his gifts and bestows the desires of mortals as and when they need and supports them. (1580)

D. IV.

१. त्वं ह्येहि चेरवे विदा भगं वसुत्तये ।
उद्वावृषस्व मघवन्गविष्टय उदिन्द्राश्वमिष्टये ॥

1. Prāṇa! You incite also heaven (head) to bestow knowledge; consciousness is gracious to you.

Indra desiring sense activities himself showers and bestows them; above Indra is fond of prāṇa. (1581), (240)

२. त्वं पुरू सहस्राणि शतानि च यूथा दानाय मंहसे ।
आ पुरंदरं चकृम विप्रवचस इन्द्रं गायन्तोऽवसे ॥

2. You bestow abundantly and munificently to thousands of sections and in fact millions of brain cells.

Indra (destroyer of forts) also produces speech for me by inspiring and bestowing it; Indra guides the sense activities in the home for this. (1582)

D. V.

१. यो विश्वा दयते वसु होता मन्द्रो जनानाम् ।
मघोर्न पात्रा प्रथमान्यस्मै प्र स्तोमा यन्त्वग्नये ॥

1. Indra divides (daya) (the sense activities) among the sense organs; presides over men pleasantly.

He is our foremost and munificent instrument to nourish us praiseworthily, whom Agni guides. (1583), (44)

२. अश्व न गीर्भी रथ्यं सुदानवो मर्मृज्यन्ते देवयवः ।
उभे तोके तनये दस्म विश्पते पर्षि राधो मघोनाम् ॥

2. Prāṇa controls the sense organs from the hill; arouses and bestows gifts on them which cleanse the deceased cells by winning within ideas (devas) for them.

The lord of the home dexterously nourishes (parṣi) both the brain cells and sense organs (descendants) with munificent wealth. (1584)

D. VI.

१. इमं मे वरुण श्रुधी हवमद्या च मृडय ।
त्व मवस्युरा चके ॥

1. Here Varuṇa (external world) bestows oblations of knowledge from hearing through sense perceptions (madyā) also in compassion.

You favour our brain (head); the Aśvins too. (1585), (Y. V. 21, 1)

D. VII.

१. कया त्वं न ऊत्याभि प्र मन्दसे वृषन् ।
कया स्तोतृभ्य आ भर ॥

1. Varuṇa! You move to the head and help to nourish through Indra when dull (or bestow gladness).

You move praiseworthily to the head to support. (1586), (Y. V. 36, 7)

D. VIII.

१. इन्द्रमिद्देवतातय इन्द्रं प्रयत्यध्वरे ।
इन्द्रं समीके वनिनो हवामह इन्द्रं धनस्य सातये ॥

1. Indra runs from the father of the devas to the brain to nourish it by uniting with it in life-activity.

Indra encounters the sense activities in the head; Indra gladdens us with oblations of wealth continually. (1587)

२. इन्द्रो मह्ना रोदसी पप्रथच्छव इन्द्रः सूर्यमरोचयत् ।
इन्द्रे ह विश्वा भुवनानि येमिर इन्द्रे स्वनास इन्दवः ॥

2. Indra in his greatness spreads out to the brain cells and sense organs to bestow for drinking; Indra unites with consciousness when he rises.

Indra controls the sense organs of creatures for their comfort; Indra himself associates with the brain cells. (1588)

D. IX.

१. विश्वकर्मन्हविषा वावृधानः स्वयं यजस्व तन्वा३ स्वा हि ते ।
मुह्यन्त्वन्ये अभितो जनास इहास्माकं मघवा सूरिरस्तु ॥

1. The duty (activity) of the sense organs is to bestow oblations which envelop the brain (head); they themselves control life-activity; they themselves guide us to cross (ignorance) and they themselves are for our welfare.

They guide us to rejoicings by bestowing on us; here Indra is our leader. (1589), (Y. V. 17, 22)

D. X.

१. अया रुचा हरिण्या पुनानो विश्वा द्वेषांसि तरति
सयुग्वभिः सूरो न सयुग्वभिः ।
धारा पृष्ठस्य रोचते पुनानो अरुषो हरिः ।
विश्वा यद्रूपा परियास्यृक्वभिः सप्तास्येभिर्ऋक्वभिः ॥

1. The tawny consciousness shines over the paths to guide; again and again he supports the wishes of both brain cells and

sense organs to cross over (ignorance) by bestowing (his rays) to the home.

United to (sense activities) he bestows; he associates and unites with sense activities to bestow.

The tawny consciousness shines repeatedly to support us foremost.

In whatever form the objects of the world go around he bestows whatever they present; Activity supports it and bestows, whatever it be. (1590), (463)

२. प्राचीमनु प्रदिशं याति चेकितत्सं रश्मिभिर्यतते दर्शतो
रथो दैव्यो दर्शतो रथः ।
अग्मन्नुक्थानि पौंस्येन्द्रं जैत्राय हर्षयत
वज्रश्च यद्भवथो अनपच्युता समत्स्वनपच्युता ।।

2. Consciousness appearing on the east (face) nourishes all directions in which (the rays) move; on their appearance all rays support by uniting with whatever they visit.

Indra nourishes the mind with sense perceptions; he moves victoriously and joyously guides.

Whatever happens in the nerves they unite with the sense organs; they cook all of them by uniting with them themselves. (1591)

३. त्वं ह त्यत्पणीनां विदो वसु सं मातृभिर्मर्जयसि स्व आ दमं
ऋतस्य धीतिभिर्दमे ।
परावतो न साम तद्यत्रा रणन्ति धीतयः ।
त्रिधातुभिररुषीभिर्वयो दधे रोचमानो वयो दधे ।

3. It is well-known that Indra (Vasu) parts with (sells) the knowledge to you (nerves); the mother supports all from whom you win yourself from the home.

Ṛta supports our knowledge in the home. We associate with the distant world for knowledge which gladdens us.

He bestows eagerly on the three states and supports them and supports us; he bestows that the home may shine and bestow on us. (1592)

D. XI.

१. उत नो गोषणिं धियमश्वसां वाजसामुत ।
नृवत्कृणुह्यूतये ।।

1. Also the sense activities bestow gifts; prāṇa bestows them on us and satisfies by bestowing life-activity as well.

You help to produce knowledge for men. (1593)

D. XII.

१. शशमानस्य वा नरः स्वेदस्य सत्यशवसः ।
विदा कामस्य वेनतः ॥

1. Prāṇa! You bestow on the mind of men; from the home you bestow on us yourself in existence with might.

The sense activities bestow the knowledge desired by us. (1594)

D. XIII.

१. उप नः सूनवो गिरः शृण्वन्त्वमृतस्य ये ।
सुमृडीका भवन्तु नः ॥

1. Above, the brain (hill) bestows on mind and binds it; it cooks up desires for mortals.

It is very compassionate and bound to us. (1595). (Y. V. 33, 77)

D. XIV.

१. प्र वां महि द्यवी अभ्युपस्तुतिं भरामहे ।
शुची उप प्रशस्तये ॥

1. Heaven (head) blesses us and bestows much nourishment and supports us above greatly and praiseworthily.

It is flaming praiseworthily. (1596)

२. पुनाने तन्वा मिथः स्वेन दक्षेण राजथः ।
ऊह्याथे सनादृतम् ॥

2. Brain! You bestow repeatedly on mind; then you two satisfy us mightily and rule us yourselves.

You transform the course determining it from ancient practices. (1597)

३. मही मित्रस्य साधथस्तरन्ती पिप्रती ऋतम् ।
परि यज्ञं नि षेदथुः ॥

3. The brain has achieved much from the sense organs (mahī) and they gladden us, also Ṛta nourishes them.

He goes around the home in life-activity. (1598)

D. XV.

१. अयमु ते समतसि कपोत इव गर्भंधिम् ।
वचस्तच्चिन्न ओहसे ॥

1. Brain! You bestow also a path for ideas; the head (brain) also fulfils (the idea) of the source and satisfies us.

It transforms the ideas and bestows them on speech. (1599), (183)

२. स्तोत्रं राधानां पते गिर्वाहो वीर यस्य ते ।
विभूतिरस्तु सूनृता ॥

2. The lord of wealth praiseworthily conveys to the hill and approaching eagerly bestows on it.

He is pervading all and arouses men (to activity). (1600)

३. ऊर्ध्वंस्तिष्ठा न ऊतयेऽस्मिन्वाजे शतक्रतो ।
समन्येषु ब्रवावहै ॥

3. Indra, doer of a hundred deeds gives help in the head above as he desires in our life-activity.

And the missiles (of sense activities) convey speech to mind. (1601)

D. XVI.

१. गाव उप ववावटे मही यज्ञस्य रप्सुवा ।
उभा कर्णा हिरण्यया ॥

1. The sense activities above communicate what the sense organs (mahī) yield to the brain cells in life; they arouse and bestow by whispering to them.

Both the ears are roused speedily to gladden us. (1602), (117)

२. अभ्यारमिवद्रयो निषिक्तं पुष्करे मधु ।
अवटस्य विसर्जने ॥

2. The sense perceptions yield nourishment in effusions from below and fearlessly bestow on the brain cells their rays (streams).

They surge towards the brain cells. (1603)

३. सिञ्चन्ति नमसावटमुच्चाचक्रं परिज्मानम् ।
नीचीनबारमक्षितम् ॥

3. The sense perceptions go around above tingling along, honour and bestow on the brain cells being everywhere (parijmān).

Wealth from below is desired by the home. (1604).

D. XVII.

१. मा भेम मा श्रमिष्मोग्रस्य सख्ये तव ।
महत्ते वृष्णो अभिचक्ष्यं कृतं पश्येम तुर्वशं यदुम् ।।

1. You bestow formidably; do not be weary of my desires. You help me powerfully.

To perceive (objects) and to produce sense perceptions, the sense activities rain greatly and control them; they unite and bestow speedily on the home. (1605)

२. सव्यामनु स्फिग्यं वावसे वृषा न दानो अस्य रोषति ।
मध्वा संपृक्ताः सारघेण धेनवस्तूयमेहि द्रवा पिब ।।

2. Now, from the left side of the hip (buttocks) the bestowal (of the sense activities) is controlled; they now rain to the brain cells eagerly bestowing our desires.

The sense perceptions hovering about like bees about flowers mingle with all cells and bestow on them; the milch-cow bestows on the home quickly which flow to be drunk (by the cells). (1606)

The two long nerves from either side of the spinal cord, commencing from the buttocks level, run parallel to near neck level where they cross each other and mingle with the spinal system of nerves and excite the brain cells of opposite sides. It is only then the sense activities are ready for flowing out to the external world to apprehend objects. The right nerve is said to be under the control of Indra and normally in operation. The left side nerve controlled by Viṣṇu comes into operation when the right section of the brain is rendered inoperative due to damage to it.

Normally all perceptions flowing in from outside are divided and received by both sections of the brain so that one section only need be operative at a time. The right section of the brain controlled by Viṣṇu holds also the records from the previous life remaining to be fulfilled in the current cycle. They break out and take effect when the proper time comes for their fruition.

D. XVIII.

१. इमा उ त्वा पुरूवसो गिरो वर्धन्तु या मम ।
पावकवर्णाः शुचयो विपश्चितोऽभि स्तोमैरनूषत ।।

1. Here the sense activities also move to us and grow abundantly in the home on the hill.

They flame up in varied colours (for various sense organs) in the head and fulfil their functions; they inspire the mind to whom they are attached praiseworthily. (1607), (250). (Y. V. 33. 81)

२. अयं सहस्रमृषिभिः सहस्कृतः समुद्र इव पप्रथे ।
सत्यः सो अस्य महिमा गृणे शवो यज्ञेषु विप्रराज्ये ।।

2. The paths for the ṛṣis (sense activities) are in thousands; they produce (perceptions) with might, extending like an ocean to drink.

They bestow existence on us; they arouse the sense organs and bestow (the results) to devotee in life-activity in Agni's empire. (1608)

D. XIX.

१. यस्यायं विश्व आर्यो दासः शेवधिपा अरिः ।
तिरश्चिदर्ये रुशमे पवीरवि तुभ्येत्सो अज्यते रयिः ।।

1. The sense activities control the sense organs of man; the kind and faithful lord Indra serves them.

Men indeed browse on crossing over; the vigorous (Indra) favours them to drink; the two bestow the wealth of clarified butter. (1609), (Y. V. 3382)

२. तुरण्यवो मधुमन्तं घृतश्चतं विप्रासो अर्कमानृचुः ।
अस्मे रयिः पप्रथे वृष्ण्यं शवोऽस्मे स्वानास इन्दवः ।।

2. The sense perceptions hasten to the brain cells to let clarified butter to drip; consciousness releases them to stir up men and be released to them.

Wealth (of perceptions) spread out to us to be drunk; the rain of perceptions from the sense organs control us and they by themselves associate with the brain cells. (1610)

D. XX.

१. गोमन्न इन्दो अश्ववत्सुतः सुदक्ष धनिव ।
शुचिं च वर्णमधि गोषु धारय ॥

1. Our sense perceptions are food to the brain cells; prāṇa acquaints the mind with them and arouses satisfaction in him as if it were wealth.

They shine and their varied colours (activities) satisfy us; the sense perceptions support us. (1611), (574)

२. स नो हरीणां पत इन्दो देवप्सरस्तमः ।
सखेव सख्ये नर्यो रुचे भव ॥

2. The tawny consciousness bestows the paths on the brain cells as gifts to whom the deva Activity flows as desired.

He bestows help as a friend on men and shines in existence. (1612)

३. सनेमि त्वमस्मदा अदेवं कं चिदत्रिणम् ।
साह्वाँ इन्दो परि बाधो अप द्वयुम् ॥

3. You approach me and bestow gifts; you bestow on me ideas (devas) for my desires indeed to the three states.

At the call of the brain cells you go around and bestow and drink up any bother from both (brain cells and sense organs) through sense activities. (1613)

D. XXI.

१. अञ्जते व्यञ्जते समञ्जते क्रतुं रिहन्ति मध्वाभ्यञ्जते ।
सिन्धोरुच्छ्वासे पतयन्तमुक्षणं हिरण्यपावाः पशुमप्सु गृभ्णते ॥

1. Ṛta anoints us, causes manifestation, anoints all equally, caresses the sense activities and releases them to anoint.

He releases Sindhu in the home above, guides her to the paths and honours and sprinkles; the golden consciousness releases him to fulfil by grabbing the sense activities from Activity. (1614), (564)

२. विपश्चिते पवमानाय गायत मही न धारात्यन्धो अर्षति ।
अहिर्न जूर्णामति सर्पति त्वचमत्यो न क्रीडन्नसरद्वृषा हरिः ॥

2. The sense activities move into the home and bestow to inspire the mind to drink; they are well-known to support the sense organs by flowing to them against ignorance.

Understanding takes birth in the spinal cord in waves and flows in them; prāṇa sports with it also; consciousness associates with it (spinal cord) and rains his rays. (1615)

३. अग्रेगो राजाप्यस्तविष्यते विमानो अह्नां भुवनेष्वर्पितः ।
हरिर्घृतस्नुः सुदृशीको अर्णवो ज्योतीरथः पवते राय ओक्यः ॥

3. With the sense activities in the forefront, the King Activity is active in the home and unites with them, through the home; he bestows the desires of the creatures in the waking state and dedicates to them.

Consciousness arouses clarified butter at sight on the hill and bestows it in waves in the head; the effulgent consciousness protects understanding arising from sense organs and controls them praiseworthily. (1616)

BOOK VIII: CHAPTER I

D. I

१. विश्वेभिरग्ने अग्निभिरिमं यज्ञमिदं वचः ।
चनो धाः सहसा यहो ॥

1. Agni supports the sense organs (or Agni) bestows support on the home (brain); Agni supports speech in life-activity here.

He bestows gladness and hastens life-activity with might. (1617)

२. यच्चिद्धि शश्वता तना देवंदेवं यजामहे ।
त्वे इद्धूयते हविः ॥

2. Who indeed satisfies continually and guides but ideas (devas); devas take birth in us greatly.

They unite and stir up oblations. (1618)

३. प्रियो नो अस्तु विश्पतिर्होता मन्द्रो वरेण्यः ।
प्रियाः स्वग्नयो वयम् ॥

3. They are kind; the lord of the home presides pleasantly and excellently over them.

They themselves guide sense activities in kindness for us. (1619)

D. II.

१. इन्द्रं वो विश्वतस्परि हवामहे जनेभ्यः ।
अस्माकमस्तु केवलः ॥

1. Indra goes around to the sense organs and bestows much oblations on people.

He is all to us. (1620)

२. स नो वृषन्नमुं चरुं सत्रादावन्नपा वृधि ।
अस्मभ्यमप्रतिष्कुतः ॥

2. Activity honours and rains his gifts in life-activity and fosters its growth.

He nourishes our desires and produces them. (1621)

३. वृषा यूथेव वंसगः कृष्टीरियर्त्योजसा ।
ईशानो अप्रतिष्कुतः ॥

3. Indra (bull) rains and bestows on millions of brain cells; he releases them and cultivates (enriches them).

He rules; nourishes the desires of the sense organs. (1622)

D. III.

१. त्वं नश्चित्र ऊत्या वसो राधांसि चोदय।
अस्य रायस्त्वमग्ने रथीरसि विदा गाधं तुचे तु नः॥

1. Agni! You associate with various (Devas) and help them graciously; you move up and support wealth also.

You rule us; you are our charioteer; you control sense activities; you bind us to knowledge in the home from sense activities. (1623), (41)

२. पर्षि तोकं तनयं पर्तृभिष्ट्वमदब्धैरप्रयुत्वभिः।
अग्ने हेडांसि दैव्या युयोधि नोऽदेवानि ह्वरांसि च॥

2. You nourish your progeny and family from beyond, bestow the desires of the three states without hurting and nourish them by uniting and bestowing.

Agni! You support the oblations of ideas (devas) and unite with them to satisfy us; the spinal cord also supports the ideas. (1624)

D. IV.

१. किमित्ते विष्णो परिचक्षि नाम प्र यद्ववक्षे शिपिविष्टो अस्मि।
मा वर्पो अस्मदप गूह एतद्यदन्यरूपः समिथे बभूथ॥

1. Why does Viṣṇu go around looking for, honouring and nourishing to bestow strength by enveloping us?

Let not the form of my body be changed to another form by Activity through the motley sense activities together with you (Viṣṇu) in existence. (1625)

This is a reference to what had taken place continually during the evolution of various creatures on earth. A new species could come into existence only by introducing transformations in an existing creature without its knowledge. Activity with its limbs namely sense of differentiation and sense of touch together with new ideas of the subtle world, i.e. new creatures in heaven awaiting manifestation, exercised their potency on some selected species. Structural changes were introduced in the brains of the creatures as ideas which were reflected in the offspring. Man also emerged in this manner from an earlier animal species.

२. प्र तत्ते अद्य शिपिविष्ट हव्यमर्यः शंसामि वयुनानि विद्वान् ।
तं त्वा गृणामि तवसमतव्यान्क्षयन्तमस्य रजसः पराके ॥

2. Viṣṇu (śipiviṣṭa) now nourished these creatures with oblations; Indra (arya) approached the creatures and toiled and bestowed to achieve the goal which he knew (namely a new creature).

He approached the creatures (devotees) and the Aśvins worked with ideas in the home and guided the desires from heaven (space) beyond to the head. (1626)

३. वषट् ते विष्णवास आ कृणोमि तन्मे जुषस्व शिपिविष्टहव्यम् ।
वर्धन्तु त्वा सुष्टुतयो गिरो मे यूयं पात स्वस्तिभिः सदा नः ॥

3. They (Indra and Aśvins) terminated their work in the brain; they now approached the (new) creatures to guide and rejoice at Viṣṇu's own oblations.

They promote growth in such suitable creatures in their brains (hill); the paths controlled by you are always for our welfare. (1627)

D. V.

१. वायो शुक्रो अयामि ते मध्वो अग्रं दिविष्टिषु ।
आ याहि सोमपीतये स्पार्हो देव नियुत्वता ॥

1. The sense activities bestow at first to their relatives i.e. nerves which brighten the desires in the waking state.

Soma swells over to them and arouses them charmingly to move; he unites them to ideas for knowledge. (1628), (Y. V. 27, 30)

२. इन्द्रश्च वायवेषां सोमानां पीतिमर्हथः ।
युवां हि यन्तीन्दवो निम्नमापो न सध्र्यक् ॥

2. Indra also bestows the desires of the brain cells. Soma swells over to them as being competent (to bestow).

He arouses mind and guides to him what the brain cells bestow; Activity associates with the low lying (nimna—brain cells) who support. (1629)

३. वायविन्द्रश्च शुष्मिणा सरथं शवसस्पती ।
नियुत्वन्ता न ऊतय आ यातं सोमपीतये ॥

3. Indra also riding the same chariot (i.e. together) with the lord of the sense organs and brain cells (Soma) rush mightily to bestow on the brain cells.

They bestow within on millions of brain cells and help them, Soma swells over to them along their paths. (1630)

D. VI

१. अध क्षपा परिष्कृतो वाजाँ अभि प्र गाहसे ।
यदी विवस्वतो धियो हरिं हिन्वन्ति यातवे ॥

1. Then he goes around and fulfils (the needs) of the home (brain); then he plunges (gāha) into life-activity to produce and bestow nourishments,

which riding on understanding satisfies us; consciousness arouses desires for it bestowing the course. (1631)

२. तमस्य मर्जयामसि मदो य इन्द्रपातमः ।
यं गाव आसभिर्दधुः पुरा नूनं च सूरयः ॥

2. You win the desires for us mortals; sense activities move towards Indra for him to fulfil our desires.

He controls the sense activities and supports them to bestow now as in olden times arousing streams of them. (1632)

३. तं गाथया पुराण्या पुनानमभ्यनूषत ।
उतो कृपन्त धीतयो देवानां नाम बिभ्रतीः ॥

3. He desired to move to the devotees in olden times to guide them and was repeatedly attached to them.

Also he produced knowledge within for them to drink by honouring ideas (devas) without delusion. (1633)

D. VII

१. अश्वं न त्वा वारवन्तं वन्दध्या अग्निं नमोभिः ।
सम्राजन्तमध्वराणाम् ॥

1. Prāṇa! You bestow wealth (of sense activities) within desiring curds and move to Agni to honour him,

in his dominion for gifts from sense activities (or in the supreme ruler's life-activity. (1634)

२. स घा नः सुनुः शवसा पृथुप्रगामा सुशेवः ।
मीढ्वाँ अस्माकं बभूयात् ॥

2. And indeed he (prāṇa) binds mind with might and spreads out to nourish us by arousing us in kindness.

He bestows us rewards in the path of existence. (1635)

३. स नो दूराच्चासाच्च नि मर्त्यादघायोः ।
पाहि सदमिद्विश्वायुः ।

3. And whether far or near you bestow gifts on mortals to sip.

You arouse and fulfil the (needs of) home by uniting the sense organs to the brain. (1636)

D. VIII.

१. त्वमिन्द्र प्रतूर्तिष्वभि विश्वा असि स्पृधः ।
अशस्तिहा जनिता वृत्रतूरसि त्वं तूर्य तरुष्यतः ॥

1. Indra! You help to nourish and bestow the desires of the sense organs which gain by bestowing.

As they are born powerless, you overcome Vṛtra; you send him to unite with the fourth state quickly. (1637), (311), (Y. V. 33, 66)

२. अनु ते शुष्मं तुरयन्तमीयतुः क्षोणी शिशुं न मातरा ।
विश्वास्ते स्पृधः श्नथयन्त मन्यवे वृत्रं यदिन्द्र तूर्वसि ॥

2. Now they (sense organs) are parched; you guide speedily a host (of sense activities) to unite with them for their needs; the mother releases to Mind.

The sense organs gain by bestowals from the home; Indra strikes down Vṛtra and guides (bestowals) from brain cells to mind and bestows quickly. (1638), (Y. V. 33, 67)

D. IX.

१. यज्ञ इन्द्रमवर्धयद्यद्भूमिं व्यवर्तयत् ।
चक्राण ओपशं दिवि ॥

1. Indra fosters the growth of such creatures as subsist, in life-activity, by uniting with them.

Also he lets others become extinct in consciousness willingly. (1639), (121)

२. व्य१न्तरिक्षमतिरन्मदे सोमस्य रोचना ।
इन्द्रो यदभिनद्वलम् ।।

2. The sense activities gladden our mind; Soma bestows and gladdens him.

Indra moves to the brain cells and bestows resoundingly. (1640)

३. उद्गा आजदङ्गिरोभ्य आविष्कृण्वन्गुहा सतीः ।।
अर्वाञ्चं नुनुदे वलम् ।।

3. Above the sense activities are born, being bestowed by Aṅgirasas (Agni, Aśvins, Activity) who work to create desires secretly in existence.

Now they turn to the brain cells to bestow and are praised (nu). (1641)

D. X.

१. त्यमु वः सत्रासाहं विश्वासु गीर्ष्वायतम् । आ च्यावयस्यूतये ।

1. Indra! You convey yourself from the brain (hill) in life-activity (Soma yajña) and bestow on the sense organs in waking state after arousing them.

Also you strive to help the brain cells. (1642), (170)

२. युध्मं सन्तमनर्वाणं सोमपामनपच्युतम् ।
नरमवार्यक्रतुम् ।।

2. Soma unites with the home to bestow gifts on mind for which he hastens and honours him and fulfils the mind by cooking and uniting with him.

He produces wealth for men. (1643)

३. शिक्षा ण इन्द्र राय आ पुरु विद्वाँ ऋचीषम ।
अवा नः पार्ये धने ।।

3. Indra controls and teaches us and bestows abundant knowledge and desire for sacred hymns.

He favours us and binds us with wealth from beyond. (1644)

D. XI.

१. तव त्यदिन्द्रियं बृहत्तव दक्षमुत क्रतुम् ।
वज्रं शिशाति धिषणा वरेण्यम् ।।

1. Indra! You are well-known to bestow much on the sense organs and also create satisfaction in them.

The vigorous nerves are bounteous to the brain (head) and are desirable. (1645)

२. तव द्यौरिन्द्र पौंस्यं पृथिवी वर्धति श्रवः ।
त्वामापः पर्वतासश्च हिन्विरे ॥

2. Indra! You bestow from heaven, nourish and control the sense organs and foster the growth of the sense of hearing.

You unite with Activity in the brain (hill) and also arouse and bestow to its comfort. (1646)

३. त्वां विष्णुर्बृहन्क्षयो मित्रो गृणाति वरुणः ।
त्वां शर्धो मदत्यनु मारुतम् ॥

3. Indra! You work extensively to bestow to the home through the sense activities from Varuṇa to the brain (Mitra) in the waking state (gṛ).

Now you boldly bestow ideas (Maruts) on sense activities. (1647)

D. XII.

१. नमस्ते अग्न ओजसे गृणन्ति देव कृष्टयः ।
अमैरमित्रमर्दय ॥

1. Agni! Obeisances for bestowing ideas vigorously to cultivate the devotees (brain).

You distribute them on the hill (brain) of mortals. (1648), (11)

२. कुवित्सु नो गविष्टयेऽग्ने संवेषिषो रयिम् ।
उरुकृदुरु णस्कृधि ॥

2. Agni! You acquaint the mind with sense organs which desire sense activities to bestow all desires for wealth.

They produce and bestow extensively; they associate extensively with us to produce satisfaction. (1649)

३. मा नो अग्ने महाधने परा वर्ग्भारभृद्यथा ।
संवर्गं सं रयिं जय ॥

3. Agni! You bestow much wealth from beyond on the home (brain) (or I do not need much wealth from beyond which is a group of burdens, likewise to support it).

All collections, all wealth (is a burden) to win. (1650)

D. XIII

१. समस्य मन्यवे विशो विश्वा नमन्त कृष्टयः ।
समुद्रायेव सिन्धवः ॥

1. All our thoughts (ideas) of the brain cells in the home arise from the sense organs which cultivate and honour them.

The sense activities (Sindhu) move in and bestow them and gladden it (the home). (1651), (137)

२. विचिद्वृत्रस्य दोधतः शिरो बिभेद वृष्णिना ।
वज्रेण शतपर्वणा ॥

2. Indeed through enveloping us the mighty (Vṛṣṇi) Sindhu divide themselves and bestow on the head without any differences.

The vigorous nerves sub-divide (Sata) them into sections. (1652)

३. ओजस्तदस्य तित्विष उभे यत्समवर्तयत् ।
इन्द्रश्चर्मेव रोदसी ॥

3. They excite vigorously both (our brain cells and sense organs); unite evenly with them to subsist.

Indra envelops them both internally (through the nerves) like the skin (externally). (1653)

D. XIV

१. सुमन्मा वस्वी रन्ती सूनरी ॥

1. (Indra) arouses the mind and bestows (mā) on him from the home; seeks him eagerly (Vī) for gladness to blossom in him. (1654)

२. सरूप वृषन्ना गहीमौ भद्रौ धुर्यावभि ।
ताविमा उप सर्पतः ॥

2. The sense activities (annā) of the same species (as mind) bestow against his ignorance and for welfare to the brain cells by arousing them.

The sense activities creep up (from the brain cells) above and bestow on him (mind). (1655)

३. नीव शीर्षाणि मृढ्वं मध्य आपस्य तिष्ठति ।
शृङ्गेभिर्दशभिर्दिशन् ॥

3. Activity at his desire moves to the sense activities to bestow on the head in compassion and guides them,

which support the brain (hill), support to protect (daśa—armour) by directing them. (1656)

BOOK VIII: CHAPTER II

D. I.

१. पन्यंपन्यमित्सोतार आ धावत मद्याय ।
सोमं वीराय शूराय ॥

1. Soma controls us admirably, stabilises admirably and bestows to cross ignorance by bestowing knowledge through the sense activities.

Soma, a hero, procures for us like a King. (1657), (123)

२. एह हरी ब्रह्मयुजा शग्मा वक्षतः सखायम् ।
इन्द्रं गीर्भिर्गिर्वणसम् ॥

2. Here, on earth, the tawny consciousness unites with knowledge bounteously and helps it to bestow on the home.

Indra supports the brain (hill) and all its desires. (1658)

३. पाता वृत्रहा सुतमा घा गमन्नारे अस्मत् ।
नि यमते शतमूतिः ॥

3. The sense activities come to us to bestow on mind and fulfil (his needs) on Vṛtra's departure.

They help a hundred observances of ours (or they control what is below sense organs) and help in a hundred ways. (1659)

D. II.

१. आ त्वा विशन्त्विन्दवः समुद्रमिव सिन्धवः ॥
न त्वामिन्द्राति रिच्यते ॥

1. Sindhu! You bestow knowledge on the home and are extensive like the ocean.

Indra releases you to unite. (1660), (197)

२. विव्यक्थ महिना वृषन्भक्षं सोमस्य जागृवे ।
य इन्द्र जठरेषु ते ॥

2. Soma bestows on us in the waking state and rains much for consumption and manifests mightily.

Indra moves the missiles to the brain cells. (1661)

३. अरं त इन्द्र कुक्षये सोमो भवतु वृत्रहन् ।
अरं धामभ्य इन्दवः ॥

3. After Vṛtra is struck down Indra moves along the spoke-like nerves from Soma in the home to the sense organs.

The nerves bestow on the brain cells in our homes. (1662)

D. III.

१. जराबोध तद्विविड्ढि विशोविशे यज्ञियाय ।
स्तोमं रुद्राय दृशीकम् ।।

1. Old age in life bestows some wisdom on every man.

Our desires flee by resoundingly and we look on them desirably. (1663), (15)

२. स नो महाँ अनिमानो धूमकेतुः पुरुश्चन्द्रः ।
धिये वाजाय हिन्वतु ।।

2. From (the sense organs) below come great desires to the brain (home), in a hazy form like smoke in abundance which satisfies the mind in life by arousing (his curiosity). (1664)

३. स रेवाँ इव विश्पतिर्दैव्यः केतुः शृणोतु नः ।
उक्थैरग्निर्बृहद्भानुः ।।

3. The lord of the home (Agni) rushes ideas (devas) like a river and bestows on them to cook desires through the motley sense activities and binds them.

Agni then shines brightly and praiseworthily. (1665)

D. IV

१. तद्वो गाय सुते सचा पुरुहूताय सत्वने ।
शं यद्गवे न शाकिने ।।

1. The sense activities move to both (the brain cells and sense organs) for uniting them to mind which invokes greatly desires in his existence.

The sense activities toil for him to be helpful. (1666), (115)

२. न घा वसुर्नि यमते दानं वाजस्य गोमतः ।
यत्सीमुपश्रवद्गिरः ।।

2. Indra (Vasu) indeed controls (these activities) and bestows on them as gifts in life activities through the ideas accompanying sense activities.

They unite with us to be bound and cooked on the hill. (1667)

३. कुवित्सस्य प्र हि वज्रं गोमन्तं दस्युहा गमत् ।
शचीभिरप नो वरत ॥

3. The brain cells know the sense organs (ku) which arouse them through the vigorous nerves through which the sense activities come within to bestow the wants and transform or bring changes in it.

Activity supports it with his might to bestow joy (or for gifts). (1668)

D. V.

१. इदं विष्णुर्वि चक्रमे त्रेधा नि दधे पदम् ।
समूढमस्य पांसुले ॥

1. Here Viṣṇu perceives us in due course and bestow on the three states in their homes to drink.

And he grasps and arouses us, who are in bewilderment to fulfil. (1669), (222), (Y. V. 5, 15)

२. त्रीणि पदा वि चक्रमे विष्णुर्गोपा अदाभ्यः ।
अतो धर्माणि धारयन् ॥

2. Three are the states which Viṣṇu perceives in due course inviolably as the protector of creatures.

Then he supports them and guides us in accordance with dharma. (1670), (Y. V. 34, 43)

३. विष्णोः कर्माणि पश्यत यतो व्रतानि पस्पशे ।
इन्द्रस्य युज्यः सखा ॥

3. Viṣṇu perceives our activities with purposes (karmas); unites with them as his duty (vrata) and protects on beholding.

Indra hastens to unite and help. (1671), (Y. V. 6, 4)

४. तद्विष्णोः परमं पदं सदा पश्यन्ति सूरयः ।
दिवीव चक्षुराततम् ॥

4. This Viṣṇu from his station beyond looks into us constantly inciting us with the streams of rays of his looks.

Like consciousness he looks at and is ready to bestow our desires. (1672), (Y. V. 6, 5)

५. तद्विप्रासो विपन्यवो जागृवांसः समिन्धते ।
विष्णोर्यत्परमं पदम् ॥

5. He inspires us and bestows on the brain cells by stirring them up in waking state; he supports the bestowal of sense objects (kindling fuel).

Viṣṇu unites with us from his station beyond in heaven. (1673), (Y. V. 34, 44)

६. अतो देवा अवन्तु नो यतो विष्णुर्विचक्रमे ।
पृथिव्या अधि सानवि ।।

6. Then the deva blesses us by uniting with us and working extensively after he perceives us in due course.

From beyond the cosmos he bestows afresh (or he satisfies the sense organs by bestowing new ideas). (1674)'

D. VI.

१.. मो षु त्वा वाघतश्च नारे अस्मन्निरीरमन् ।
आरात्ताद्वा सधमादं न आ गहीह वा सन्नुप श्रुधि ।।

1. You bestow on us sense organs and destroy them too; the sense activities release them to us from below and gladden us.

These two are comrades; they two come to us here to bestow as gift above satisfaction from the sense of hearing. (1675), (284)

२. इमे हि ते ब्रह्मकृतः सु ते सचा मधौ न मक्ष आसते ।
इन्द्रे कामं जरितारो वसूयवो रथे न पादमा दधुः ।।

2. Here they produce knowledge for our welfare; unite with mind who venerates sense perceptions (honey) in existence.

Indra releases for the desires of the devotees; he graciously bestows from the dependents i.e. sense organs on the brain cells. (1676)

D. VII.

१. अस्तावि मन्म पूर्व्यं ब्रह्मेन्द्राय वोचत ।
पूर्वीर्ऋतस्य बृहतीरनूषत स्तोतुर्मेधा असृक्षत ।।

1. In ancient times when the home (i.e. cells) was without a mind, Indra used to move to bestow the impulses (knowledge).

In ancient times Ṛta followed up greatly all activities. Intelligence flowed into the homes (cells) praiseworthily. (1677)

The mantra refers to the period in creation when plant life alone existed without any mobile creatures. These trees and plants do not have a mind for the cells to associate with and to make known the needs of the plants. Indra was the one to establish communication. The needs of the plants were ascertained by the all-pervading intelligence direct who maintained them. The activities initiated by Intelligence were followed up by Activity and Ṛta. And of the seven limbs of Activity only two are functioning in trees and plants namely: (1) the sense of differentiation and (2) the sense of touch. The role of Ṛta in existence is to repeat the activities initiated by other devas. Now, since in trees other sense faculties are latent, those in operation were greatly strengthened. This accounts for their growth to mighty proportions such as not to be met with in mobile life, in which the activity is dissipated, as it were, among more sense activities. Ṛta is like a flywheel in machines.

२. समिन्द्रो रायो बृहतीरधूनुत सं क्षोणी समु सूर्यम् ।
सं शुक्रासः शुचयः सं गवाशिरः सोमा इन्द्रममन्दिषुः ॥

2. Indra ruled over all who were greatly dependent for their wants, over all senses and also over consciousness (Sūryam).

He bestows on them all when bright and glowing, awake as it were, all sense activities with their missiles, released by Soma and Indra mingled with all the cells when in a dull state. (1678).

D. VIII

१. इन्द्राय सोम पातवे वृत्रघ्ने परि षिच्यसे ।
नरे च दक्षिणावते वीराय सदनासदे ॥

1. Indra moves to Soma to fulfil (his needs) who envelops wealth and strives to sprinkle,

and satisfies man also mightily with understanding vigorously in the home constantly. (1679), (1331)

२. तं सखायः पुरूरुचं वयं यूयं च सूरयः ।
अश्याम वाजगन्ध्यं सनेम वाजपस्त्यम् ॥

2. You speed up helping our desires abundantly and shine; you bestow on us and control and also arouse streams (of sense activities),

against ignorance in the mobile creature by bestowing gifts to sip in the home in life-activity. (1680)

३. परि त्यं हर्यतं हरिं [बभ्रुं पुनन्ति वारेण ।
यो देवान्विश्वां इत्परि मदेन सह गच्छति] ॥

3. It is well-known that you go around eagerly to consciousness; the tawny consciousness repeatedly goes around for mighty gifts (or in the enclosure),

and thus go around to the devas of sense organs together with sense activities. (1681), (552), (1329)

D. IX.

१. कस्तमिन्द्र त्वा वस [वा मर्त्यो दधर्षति ।
श्रद्धा हि ते मघवन्पार्ये दिवि वाजी वाजं सिषासति] ॥

1. Indra! You reside in the home in the head; you flow in to bestow on mortals.

Indra (Maghavan) fulfils us for welfare with confidence in waking state and in life-activity victoriously bestows our desires in existence. (1682)

२. मघोनः स्म वृत्रहत्येषु चोदय ये ददति प्रिया वसु ।
तव प्रणीती हर्यश्व सूरिभिर्विश्वा तरेम दुरिता ॥

2. When Vṛtra is struck down the missiles (of sense activities) appear and Indra bestows them on us in kindness which bind us to wealth.

You nourish us by guiding them; you arouse, release and support the sense organs to cross ignorance quickly. (1683)

D. X.

१. एदु मधोर्मदिन्तरं सिञ्चाध्वर्यो अन्धसः ।
एवा हि वीर स्तवते सदावृधः ॥

1. Behold the bounteous intoxicating and mighty sense activities tingling along and crossing over in life-activity to releases us from ignorance.

They speed up and arouse vigorously knowledge praiseworthily and let it grow continually. (1684), (385)

२. इन्द्र स्थातर्हरीणां न किष्टे पूर्व्यस्तुतिम् ॥
उदानंश शवसा न भन्दना ॥

2. Indra abidingly crosses over to the tawny Consciousness at the desire of heaven as in olden times praiseworthily.

His Udāna aspect from the summit cells for gifts from the sense organs (Śava). (1685)

Indra is a five-aspected deva which are (1) Udāna, (2) Prāṇa, (3) Apāna, (4) Vyāna, and (5) Samāna. As Udāna he came down from heaven, entered the ocean waters and overcoming its inertia organised cell life and developed a brain with the help of other devas. Now, it is as Udāna Indra enters the brain via the skull. As Prāṇa he excites the brain cells both to receive sense activities from heaven and sense perceptions and reactions from Varuṇa through the sense organs. Prāṇa also feeds mind. As Apāna he conveys messages from the brain to all parts of the body to actuate the cells. As Samāna he looks after blood circulation to maintain a uniform temperature. As Vyāna he regulates the breathing process.

३. तं वो वाजानां पतिमहूमहि श्रवस्यवः ।
अप्रायुभिर्यज्ञेभिर्वावृधेन्यम् ॥

3. In life-activity the lord Indra is invoked much by brain cells at hearing which he bestows as desired.

He unites with us to support and fulfil and he supports life and bestows for growth and guides. (1686)

D. XI.

१. तं गूर्धया स्वर्णरं देवासो देवमरतिं दधन्विरे ।
देवत्रा हव्यमूहिषे ॥

1. Heaven praises the desires of men and bestows ideas (devas); the devas gladden us by bestowing wealth which bestows on us comfort.

The devas support oblations which transform desires. (1687).

२. विभूतरातिं विप्र चित्रशोचिषमग्निमीडिष्व यन्तुरम् ।
अस्य मेधस्य सोम्यस्य सोभरे प्रेमध्वराय पूर्व्यम् ॥

2. Agni is all-pervading and is ready to bestow by inspiring us, and flames up in variegated hues, bestows desire for oblations and guides speedily.

Soma bestows on us understanding and supports out of love for which he runs and controls us as in olden times. (1688)

D. XII.

१. आ सोम स्वानो अद्रिभिस्तिरो वाराण्यव्यया ।
जनो न पुरि चम्वोर्विशद्धरिः सदो वनेषु दध्रिषे ।

1. Soma pantingly crosses over to the brain (hill); the Aśvins guide his wealth.

He bestows mightily in the city (brain) for men to sip; supports the home; the Ṛṣis (sense activities) constantly bestow desires with their missiles. (1689), (513)

२. स मामृजे तिरो अण्वानि मेष्यो मीढ्वांत्सप्तिर्न वाजयुः ।
अनुमाद्यः पवमानो मनीषिभिः सोमो विप्रेभिर्ऋक्वभिः ।।

2. The Aśvins win the fingers (rays) (of sense activities) evenly for men to cross (ignorance); they bestows us rewards through the seven-pronged Activity by uniting with life-activity.

Men hail the fickle mind whom Soma inspires, supports and on whom he bestows wherever he be. (1690)

D. XIII.

१. वयमेनमिदा ह्योऽपीपेमेह वज्रिणम् ।
तस्मा उ अद्य सवने सुतं भरा नूनं भूषत श्रुते ।।

1. Our mind gets fat from drinking what overflows from heaven here through the vigorous nerves.

On his (mind's) account, heaven bestows the desires of the mind now and adorns with the sense of hearing. (1691)

We learn from this mantra that the sense organs have been released from heaven to fulfil the demands of the mind. So, one of the primary functions of the mind is to complain and cry for what it needs like a child. And heaven fulfils such demands. The sense organs have been gifted in this manner.

२. वृकश्चिदस्य वारण उरामथिरा वयुनेषु भूषति ।
सेमं न स्तोमं जुजुषाण आ गहीन्द्र प्र चित्रया धिया ।।

2. Our mind indeed envelops the brain (head) and bestows on us gladness; the Aśvins (ura) churn (the sense activities) and bestows the aims of the mind which adorns us. (1692)

He gladdens us praiseworthily; Indra nourishes him variedly through Aditi.

D. XIV.

१. इन्द्राग्नी रोचना दिवः परि वाजेषु भूषथः ।
तद्वां चेति प्र वीर्यम् ॥

1. Indra and Agni bestow us gladness (or shine) in the waking state and go around adorning life-activity with the rays of sense activities.

These two nourish the mind with vigour. (1693)

२. इन्द्राग्नी अपसस्प [र्युप प्र यन्ति धीतयः ।
ऋतस्य पथ्या३ अनु] ॥

2. Indra and Agni go around the brain cells to protect and guide nourishment to it for understanding.

And now it is in Ṛta's path to complete. (1694)

३. इन्द्राग्नी तविषाणि वां [सधस्थानि प्रयांसि च ।
युवोरप्तूर्यं हितम] ॥

3. Indra and Agni bestow our desires and support also our nourishment in the assembly by going to it.

Activity bestows welfare on mind quickly. (1695)

D. XV.

१. कईं वेद सुते सचा [पिबन्तं कद्वयो दधे ।
अयं यः पुरो विभिनत्त्योजसा मन्दानः शिप्रयन्धसः] ॥

1. The mind unites with the brain for knowledge, and drinks what the two (Indra-Agni) bestow.

He hasten along the path to the brain (city), through the appearance of the mighty prāṇa, who bestows on the mind vigorously which sharpens him against ignorance. (1696), (297)

२. दाना मृगो न वारणः पुरुत्रा चरथं दधे ।
न किष्ट्वा नि यमदा सुते गमो महाँश्चरस्योजसा ॥

2. The gift of an animal body bestows gladness to a great extent and has also bestowed a vehicle (to move).

Heaven at its desire has bestowed some restraints on the mind on its arrival; the great one goes around vigorously. (1697)

३. य उग्रः सन्ननिष्टृतः स्थिरो रणाय संस्कृतः ।
यदि स्तोतुर्मघवा शृणवद्धवं नेन्द्रो योषत्या गमत् ॥

3. The stationary plants and trees are sunk in fearful dependence and they rejoice to grow collectively,

which Indra praiseworthily crushed by running to the devi (Aditi).

Thus mobile creatures are ushered in. (1698)

D. XVI.

१. पवमाना असृक्षत सोमाः शुक्रास इन्दवः ।
अभि विश्वानि काव्या ।।

1. Soma flows from the home to the fickle mind to bestow from the brain cells to brighten him,

with knowledge from the sense organs. (1699)

२. पवमाना दिवस्पर्यन्तरिक्षादसृक्षत ।
पृथिव्या अधि सानवि ।।

2. The fickle mind goes around in the waking state; from the home (gifts) flow to mind (antarikṣa.)

The sense organs satisfy him by bestowing new (ideas). (1700)

३. पवमानास आशवः शुभ्रा असृग्रमिन्दवः ।
घ्नन्तो विश्वा अप द्विषः ।।

3. The brain cells bestow (sense activities) which flow first radiantly to the sense organs which bestow on the fickle mind.

Activity bestows wealth within on the desires of both (brain cells and sense organs) from the home. (1701)

D. XVII.

१. तोशा वृत्रहणा हुवे सजित्वानापराजिता ।
इन्द्राग्नी वाजसातमा ।।

1. Satisfied with striking down Vṛtra Indra invoked desires from beyond and won and bestowed them victoriously.

Indra-Agni bestow on us desires in life. (1702)

२. प्र वामर्चन्त्युक्थिनो [नीथाविदो जरितारः ।
इन्द्राग्नी इष आ वृणे] ।।

2. Indra bestows on us nourishment for which we worship him; he leads knowledge to the devotees.

Indra-Agni desire knowledge and envelop it. (1703), (1575)

३. इन्द्राग्नी नवतिं पुरो [दासपत्नीरधूनुतम् ।
साकमेकेन कर्मणा] ॥

3. Indra-Agni bestow knowledge on the brain (city) [and guide those dependent on it by bestowing the path as desired.
They have together a common duty (purpose)]. (1704), (1576)

D. XVIII.

१. उप त्वा रण्वसंदृशं प्रयस्वन्तः सहस्कृत ।
अग्ने ससृज्महे गिरः ॥

1. Agni! You bestow gladness on all above, whom you see; you strive to bestow nourishment within producing it victoriously.
Agni! You flow much to the brain (hill) to bestow. (1705)

२. उप च्छायामिव घृणेरगन्म शर्म ते वयम् ॥
अग्ने हिरण्यसंदृशः ॥

2. Above, the sense activities honour the devotees and protect him as if giving a shade; they bestow and control us.
Agni indeed sees all and arouses gladness. (1706)

३. य उग्र इव शर्यहा तिग्मशृङ्गो न वंसगः ।
अग्ने पुरो रुरोजिथ ॥

3. Indra (bull) moves passionately to the brain (hill) like a powerful arrow.
Agni won him resoundingly and released him to the brain (city). (1707)

D. XIX.

१. ऋतावानं वैश्वानरमृतस्य ज्योतिषस्पतिम् ।
अजस्रं घर्ममीमहे ॥

1. Ṛta desires Activity (Vaiśvānara) from the immortal source (or in mortals) to protect the brain cells through the effulgent consciousness,
who untiringly warms up greatly by making up for what the brain loses. (1708)

२. य इदं प्रतिपप्रथे यज्ञस्य स्वरुत्तिरन् ।
ऋतूनुत्सृजते वशी ॥

2. Ṛta moves into and spreads out our life-activity from his exalted position in heaven to nourish and protect.

Ṛta flows also in the home to win for it what it wants. (1709)

३. अग्निः प्रियेषु धामसु कामो भूतस्य भव्यस्य ।
सम्राडेको विराजति ।।

3. Agni fondly arouses desires, both present and future ones in the home (brain).

He reigns all alone in his sovereign region. (1710)

BOOK VIII: CHAPTER III

D. I.

१. अग्निः प्रत्नेन जन्मना शुम्भानस्तन्वां३ स्वाम् ।
कविर्विप्रेण वावृधे ।।

1. In very ancient births Agni adorned the lives of the species himself, associated with, guided and bestowed on them.

The wise (Agni) inspired them, bestowed and fostered their growth. (1711)

The mantra refers to the period when not even herbs and trees inhabited the earth. The seas and earth were overrun by cell organisms. This period, the earliest in evolution is referred to in our purāṇas as padma kalpa, the padma referring to the lotus of brain. The earliest species of cells were asexual and multiplied by continued subdivision. Sex life was introduced in them as a first step to diversify life-activity and break up the monotony. Agni carried out all activity in them with the sense of differentiation and sense of touch alone to assist him. Agni in these low forms of life indicated the zest for manifestation of the jīvas from heaven active within the cells.

२. ऊर्जो नपातमा हुवेऽग्निं पावकशोचिषम् ।
अस्मिन्यज्ञे स्वध्वरे ।।

2. Our sense organs invoke nourishment; Agni releases from the head to their glowing desires and fulfils,

in our life-activity with desirable gifts. (1712)

३. स नो मित्रमहस्त्वमग्ने शुक्रेण शोचिषा ।
देवैरा सत्सि बर्हिषि ।।

3. Agni! You bestow gifts on the brain (Mitra) and gladden him who glows bright with desires.

You bestow on him devas (ideas) and bind them in existence to the motley sense activities (barhiṣi). (1713)

D. II.

१. उत्ते शुष्मासो अस्थू रक्षो भिन्दन्तो अद्रिवः ।
नुदस्व याः परिस्पृधः ।।

1. They (ideas) also rush in and bestow protection abidingly on the brain cells within on the hill.

They move by themselves and going around push away (enemies) in fights. (1714)

२. अया निजघ्निरोजसा रथसङ्गे धने हिते ।
स्तवा अबिभ्युषा हृदा ॥

2. The indwelling (nija) path sets in motion (the ideas) vigorously and bestows wealth to the brain cells for welfare by meeting the sense organs,

which they bestow eagerly and fearlessly on the brain. (1715)

३. अस्य व्रतानि नाधृषे पवमानस्य दूढ्या ।
रुज यस्त्वा पृतन्यति ॥

3. Our vows (duties) are dependent on the ṛṣis (sense activities) and the ill-disposition of the mind.

They strive to shatter by enveloping and uniting with it and guiding. (1716)

४. तं हिन्वन्ति मदच्युतं हरिं नदीषु वाजिनम् ।
इन्दुमिन्द्राय मत्सरम् ॥

4. Desires arouse the sense activities afresh and drip from them; the missiles release them indeed resoundingly in life-activity.

Indra moves and flows to the brain cells with them. (1717)

D. III.

१. आ मन्द्रैरिन्द्र हरिभिर्याहि मयूररोमभिः ।
मा त्वा के चिन्न येमुरिन्न पाशिनोऽति धन्वेव ताँ इहि ॥

1. The tawny consciousness pleasantly supports Indra who moves and arouses the motley sense activities like a peacock's plumage.

They bestow thoughts (ideas) in the head who control us extensively as though by mighty strings from beyond like a bow-string here. (1718), (246)

२. वृत्रखादो वलं रुजः पुरां दर्मो अपामजः ।
स्थाता रथस्य हर्योरभिस्वर इन्द्रो दृढा चिदारुजः ॥

2. After Vṛtra is shattered and devoured the Aśvins turn

round to Activity for the home in accordance with established rules (dharma).

They convey abidingly from heaven to the bodies extensively; Indra establishes them on perceiving, by bestowing on them resoundingly after birth. (1719)

३. गम्भीरौँ उदधीरिव क्रतुं पुष्यसि गा इव ।
प्र सुगोपा यवसं धेनवो यथा ह्रदं कुल्या इवाशत ॥

3. Indra! You produce from the depths of the ocean of heaven as if lastingly and nourish us with the sense perceptions.

The protector of creatures arouses and nourishes all brain cells like the milch-cow; the brain cells are in hundreds of families like pools of water. (1720)

D. IV.

१. यथा गौरो अपा कृतं तृष्यन्नेत्यवेरिणम् ।
आपित्वे नः प्रपित्वे तूयमा गहि कण्वेषु सु सचा पिब ॥

1. The motley sense activities are released to honour the brain cells like leading buffaloes to water to satisfy their thirst.

You are a friend (āpi); you also nourish us; you arouse the brain cells with their missiles to unite with them and drink. (1721), (252)

२. मन्दन्तु त्वा मघवन्निन्द्रेन्दवो राधोदेयाय सुन्वते ।
आमुष्या सोममपिबश्चमू सुतं ज्येष्ठं तद्दधिषे सहः ॥

2. Indra! You bestow bounteously to the brain cells and gladden them within; you hasten to bestow prosperity to the devotees.

Soma moves carrying off (ideas) for mind to sip and drink; the eldest Indra gives him satisfaction together with his desires. (1722)

D. V.

१. त्वमङ्ग प्र शंसिषो देवः शविष्ठ मर्त्यम् ।
न त्वदन्यो मघवन्नस्ति मर्डितेन्द्र ब्रवीमि ते वचः ॥

1. Indra! Your limb prāṇa praiseworthily nourishes the desires of mortals for devas (ideas) with might and controls.

Indra! there is no one like you who is as bounteous and

compassionate; I tell them so in my talks. (1723), (247), (Y.V. 6, 37)

२. मा ते राधांसि मा त ऊतयो वसोऽस्मान्कदा चना दभन्।
विश्वा च न उपमिमीहि मानुष वसूनि चर्षणिभ्य आ ॥

2. They (the ideas) bestow support on our prosperity; they bestow on us help graciously; they gladden us always by bestowing speech.

They gladden the sense organs; they approach me above and when they dry up Indra arouses the home eagerly and with diligent activity. (1724)

D. VI.

१. प्रति ष्या सूनरी जनी व्युच्छन्ती परि स्वसुः।
दिवो अदर्शि दुहिता ॥

1. Uṣas (Dawn), the daughter of consciousness joyously (Sunarī) nourished the desires of creatures (Janī) and terminated her rounds herself to arouse,

for consciousness to visit (men). (1725)

The feeble light of Dawn was adequate to bring to light the ideas which dawned in creatures other than men. That light was however inadequate when it came to man. So the daughter terminated her rounds by herself and gave place to consciousness.

२. अश्वेव चित्रारुषी माता गवामृतावरी।
सखा भूदश्विनोरुषाः ॥

2. Prāṇa hastens the variegated ṛṣis (sense activities) and bestows them on us; the sense activities are wealth to mortals.

The ruddy consciousness helps the Aśvins as a friend in existence. (1726)

३. उत सखास्यश्विनोरुत माता गवामसि।
उतोषो वस्व ईशिषे ॥

3. Also, the Aśvins help us, also the mother to bestow sense perceptions.

Also they themselves bestow eagerly and rule our desires. (1727)

D. VII.

१. एषो उषा अपूर्व्या व्युच्छति प्रिया दिवः ।
स्तुषे वामश्विना बृहत् ॥

1. In ancient times Uṣas sought to cut out her own activities in kindness to consciousness,

whom the great Aśvins released to us. (1728).

२. या दस्रा सिन्धुमातरा मनोतरा रयीणाम् ।
धिया देवा वसुविदा ॥

2. Sindhu (sense activities) move and wondrously bestows on us for crossing (ignorance); bestows also wealth on mind.

Indra (Vasu) moves to satisfy us with ideas (devas) for knowledge. (1729)

३. वच्यन्ते वां ककुहासो जूर्णायामधि विष्टपि ।
यद्वां रथो विभिष्पतात् ॥

3. He guides speech within by bestowing from the head and sense organs by inspiring them in their paths and bestowing and satisfying the three worlds,

through what the sense organ(s) bestows through the appearance of desires in its path. (1730)

D. VIII.

१. उषस्तच्चित्रमा भरास्मभ्यं वाजिनीवति ।
येन तोकं च तनयं च धामहे ॥

1. Uṣas bestows (mā) on a variety of creatures; supports them among us with understanding in life-activity.

She bestows greatly on the family and descendants of the creatures. (1731), (Y.V. 34, 33)

२. उषो अद्येह गोमत्यश्वावति विभावरि ।
रेवदस्मे व्युच्छ सूनृतावति ॥

2. Uṣas now hastens sense activities to our prāṇa (i.e. creatures) for knowledge against ignorance (Vibhāvari).

She interrupts herself for the sake of wealth for us (men) to arouse understanding in men. (1732)

During the progress of animal evolution Uṣas hastened the sense activities for rapid progress, endowing them with more sense organs that the ultimate creature man may appear. Uṣas terminates her activity in animal life.

३. युंक्ष्वा हि वाजिनीवत्यश्वाँ अद्यारुणाँ उषः ।
अथा नो विश्वा सौभगान्या वह ॥

3. Now, it is the ruddy consciousness instead of Uṣas with whom prāṇa unites and bestows knowledge by arousing the home.

Then he guides the sense organs and conveys them for our welfare. (1733)

D. IX.

१. अश्विना वर्तिरस्मदा गोमद्दस्रा हिरण्यवत् ।
अर्वाग्रथं समनसा नि यच्छतम् ॥

1. The Aśvins are like a lamp wick bestowing on us the exhilarating sense activities dexterously arousing gladness from knowledge.

They turn towards the sense organs and release them to mind from below whose desires they control. (1734)

२. एह देवा मयोभुवा दस्रा हिरण्यवर्तनी ।
उषर्बुधो वहन्तु सोमपीतये ॥

2. The deva (Aśvins) hastens to conduct us to gladness dexterously through the golden consciousness to whom they are like a lamp wick.

With eagerness they convey (sense activities) to the wonderful Soma to drink. (1735)

३. यावित्था श्लोकमा दिवो ज्योतिर्जनाय चक्रथुः ।
आ न ऊर्जं वहतमश्विना युवम् ॥

3. They acquaint us with the fame of the waking state which the radiant consciousness produces in men.

The Aśvins now convey nourishment to mind. (1736)

D. X.

१. अग्निं तं मन्ये यो वसुरस्तं यं यन्ति धेनवः ।
अस्तमर्वन्त आशवोऽस्तं नित्यासो वाजिन इषं स्तोतृभ्य आ भरा ॥

1. Agni desires to move to mind in Indra's home which he controls to guide sense activities (perceptions) to him.

He hastens to the home within to bestow food to the home on whom he bestows constantly in life-activity and supports its desires praiseworthily. (1737), (425)

२. अग्निर्हि वाजिनं विशे ददाति विश्वचर्षणिः ।
अग्नी राये स्वाभुवं स प्रीतो याति वार्यमिषं स्तोतृभ्य आ भर ॥

2. Agni arouses the home in life-activity and with diligent activity bestows (ideas) through sense activities to it.

Agni is king; himself bestows existence and pleases; opens our eyes to the paths for gifts and praiseworthily supports them. (1738)

३. सो अग्निर्यो वसुगृंणे सं यमायन्ति धेनवः ।
समर्वन्तो रघुद्रुवः सं सुजातासः सूरय इषं स्तोतृभ्य आ भर ॥

3. Agni moves and bestows the retinue of Indra (i.e. ideas) whom he controls and guides to sense activities.

At the same time he hastens to consider and convey speedily all well born (ideas) and bestow them; he arouses streams of desires and supports them praiseworthily. (1739), (Y.V.15, 42)

D. XI.

१. महे नो अद्य बोधयोषो राये दिवित्मती ।
यथा चिन्नो अबोधयः सत्यश्रवसि वाय्ये सुजाते अश्वसूनृते ॥

1. Now, Uṣas instructs us (i.e. creatures) greatly; controls understanding in walking state.

Likewise ideas (thoughts) instruct us in existence; sense of hearing is bound to the brain (Vāyya) which arouses mind and prāṇa induces him to dance. (1740), (421)

२. या सुनीथे शौचद्रथे व्यौच्छो दुहितर्दिवः ।
सा व्युच्छ सहीयसि सत्यश्रवसि वाय्ये सुजाते अश्वसूनृते ॥

2. Dawn, the daughter of consciousness, terminated for activity to arouse guidance and purification of sense organ.

By terminating her activity a more mighty presence strove for existence flowing from the brain arousing the mind through prāṇa who arouses him to dance. (1741)

Uṣas gave way to consciousness when man was evolved and appeared on earth endowed with a new faculty, namely speech.

३. सा नो अद्याभरद्वसुर्व्युच्छा दुहितर्दिवः ।
यो व्यौच्छः सहीयसि सत्यश्रवसि वाय्ये सुजाते अश्वसूनृते ।।

3. On the daughter of consciousness terminating her activity, Indra now supports the summit.

On her termination a more mighty presence (Speech) strove for existence which flowed from the brain arousing the mind through prāṇa who arouses him to dance. (1742)

D. XII.

१. प्रति प्रियतमं रथं वृषणं वसुवाहनम् ।
स्तोता वामश्विनावृषि स्तोमेभिर्भूषति प्रति
माध्वी मम श्रुतं हवम् ।।

1. The sense organ (of speech) fondly desires to nourish it; Indra Vṛṣaṇa honours it and graciously conveys it.

The lovely Aśvins praiseworthily bestow the sense activity (ṛṣi), which praiseworthily adorns and supports it and runs to bestow on me hearing as an oblation. (1743), (418)

२. अत्यायातमश्विना तिरो विश्वा अहं सना ।
दस्रा हिरण्यवर्तनी सुषुम्णा सिन्धुवाहसा
माध्वी मम श्रुतं हवम् ।।

2. Prāṇa moves at the desire of the Aśvins and crosses over to the sense organ in waking as of olden times.

Sindhu conveys it graciously (Suṣumṇā) in the path of consciousness wondrously and runs and bestows on me hearing as an oblation. (1744)

३. आ नो रत्नानि बिभ्रतावश्विना गच्छतं युवम् ।
रुद्रा हिरण्यवर्तनी जुषाणा वाजिनीवसू माध्वी मम श्रुतं हवम् ।।

3. The Aśvins go to mind at his desire for valuable presents to be given without rivalry.

Rudra (nervous system) arouses gladness along its paths guiding life-activity joyously; Indra sets up the sense activity of hearing as an oblation to me. (1745)

D. XIII.

१. अबोध्यग्निः समिधा जनानां प्रति धेनुमिवायतीमुषासम् ।
यह्वा इव प्र वयामुज्जिहानाः प्र भानवः सस्रते नाकमच्छ ।।

1. Agni instructs men through sense objects (fuel-sticks); he nourishes them as if with milk; all these (ideas) are the off-spring (āyati) of Uṣas.

He moves as though invoked and bestows nourishment along his path victoriously; consciousness from heaven nourishes the brain cells near it and gladdens it. (1746), (Y.V.15, 24)

२. अबोधि होता यजथाय देवानूर्ध्वो अग्निः सुमनाः प्रातरस्थात् ।
समिद्धस्य रुशददर्शि पाजो महान् देवस्तमसो निरमोचि ।।

2. The presiding Agni instructs us in life-activity through ideas (deva) from above (heaven—head); Agni kindled the home (brain) with them in the early morning of creation.

He bestowed sense objects (fuel-sticks) cooked by him on the jīvas (from heaven) who were browsing, for them to visit (see); the great one bestowed devas (ideas) desired down below and gladdened them suitably. (1747)

Alt. : In the early morning of creation, Agni presiding over life-activity, instructed the devas (in heaven) above about the various plants (Sumana) of an abiding nature intended in creation.

The great Agni visited the browsing jīvas (in heaven) over their want of fuel-sticks (i.e. objects to think about) and cooked up inertia (tamas) with the ideas (devas) who did not relish it.

Many illuminating facts are revealed by the mantra. That the external material world with its sun, moon, stars and the sky and the planets as well as earth, water and air had all been created before manifestation is a natural inference. The mantra, however, says that this material world or inertia was cooked up with its opposite i.e. ideas which are most active: Inertia is only absence of natural activity. In matter activity is inhibited, driven underground as it were. In matter ideas are very very closely packed and the great natural activity of ideas is latent in matter and this accounts for the release of tremendous amount of energy when the inertia is suddenly destroyed as in on atom bomb.

Then we learn that the jīvas who manifested themselves as various types of creatures subsequently on earth were already in heaven browsing over their state of inactivity for which Agni found them a remedy by way of manifestation on earth.

Then we are told that ideas in heaven were informed of the

impending creation of plant life on earth which incorporated the ideas in their make-up. The universal devas participated in the manifestation process.

Then we learn that manifestation had to wait till tamas (inertia) could form an integral part of life. There are various reasons for this. In the first place ideas by themselves are so extraordinarily quick that life-process would come to a quick end. The idea of the creator is to maintain unending activity to avoid non-existence which is invitable if activity came to an end. The association of ideas and inertia in a joint enterprise like the life process ensures continued activity by the opposing tendencies resulting in a struggle. Ideas have the upper hand for about half a life-time and then inertia predominates in the latter part of life.

Another feature of this association is that effort and result do not coincide in time. Our desires, ambitions etc. are mental whereas their results have to be translated in the material plane which takes place only after a lapse of varying intervals of time, sometimes after several years. Often the efforts of one life-time are realised only in succeeding lives. This feature contributes to continued activity as desired by the creator.

Then the association of matter with life-process contributes to memory in the brain cells. Life-process is unthinkable without memory. Matter has the characteristic of preserving whatever it is endowed with and it lends this feature to the brain.

३. यदीं गणस्य रशनामजीगः शुचिरङ्क्ते शुचिभिर्गोभिरग्निः ।
आद्दक्षिणा युज्यते वाजयंत्युत्तानामूर्ध्वो अधयज्जुहूभिः ॥

3. So, followers of Agni (i.e. ideas) were won and roped together to form impenetrable ignorance giving diverse guileless (śuci) objects honestly supporting sense activities which are supported by Agni.

They united together dexterously and marched harmoniously together; it is well-known that there are extensive (uttāna) brain cells in the head controlling life-activity which sip the tongues of sense activities. (1748)

It is clearly mentioned here that ideas were densely packed to form matter which took various forms such as earth, water, air, sun, moon, stars etc. also round, heat, light radiations etc. all of which were derived from ideas and variously and in varying proximities packed together to form various forms of matter. So, everything in the world has both the features of ideas and matter. Light behaving both as a wave and a particle is accounted for by this basic principle of its genesis.

D. XIV.

१. इदं श्रेष्ठं ज्योतिषां ज्योतिरागाच्चित्रः प्रकेतो अजनिष्ट विभ्वा ।
यथा प्रसूता सवितुः सवायैवा रात्र्युषसे योनिमारैक् ।।

1. Here, the highest deva is the effulgent consciousness; his effulgence bestows on the sense activities the variegated nourishing rays (Ketu) desired in men (creatures) throughout their existence.

Savitā likewise created night and day (ignorance and knowledge) and bestowed them on the brain cells in our heads (Ka) from the source. (1749)

The seven prongs of Activity are said to be derived from consciousness i.e. from the creator who reveals his undisclosed form in existence as consciousness while revealing his manifested forms as the objects of the world. Thus the creator continually reveals both his forms to the mind i.e. man. It is wrong then to say that the creator is beyond speech and thought. He is continually in evidence to all the senses.

Savitā endows the brain cells with ideas and matter producing knowledge and the means of storing them.

२. रुशद्वत्सा रुशती श्वेत्यागादारैगु कृष्णा सदनान्यस्याः ।
समानबन्धू अमृते अनूची द्यावा वर्णं चरत आमिनाने ।।

2. The mind browses; he browses on knowledge (whiteness) which the sense activities bestow through the sense organs (gu) against ignorance, which they bestow in the home (i.e. to the brain cells).

He (Mind) is a relative, of the same species as the immortals, following after them (anūcī), the mother bestows from heaven variegated (wealth) also to please him. (1750)

३. समानो अध्वा स्वस्रोरनंतस्तमन्यान्या चरतो देवशिष्टे ।
न मेथेते न तस्थतुः सुमेके नक्तोषासा समनसा विरूपे ।।

3. Alike to one another as sisters and running around, delighted with and desirous of one another, being the remains (śiṣṭa)

of the deva (consciousness), not alternately (but continually), not staying still, remaining as one (continuous phenomenon) either as night or day, of the same genus but of varied hues (shades). (1751)

The phenomena referred to here is the exclusive feature of the Arctic Circle where, after the long-continued winter nights extending up to hundred days at a particular latitude, the sun tries to emerge above the horizon preceded by the Dawns numbering 30. This is an unmistakable evidence of the Arctic origin of the Veda.

Tilak cites from the Taittrīya Saṁhitā that the thirty sisters are divided into six groups of five each. These figures may well indicate six species of creatures everyone of which was endowed with five sense perceptions some latent and some expressed. The six species of lives are (1) plants and trees; (2) fishes; (3) amphibious creatures; (4) reptiles; (5) mammals; and (6) man.

D. XV.

१. आ भात्यग्निरुषसामनीकमुद्विप्राणां देवया वाचो अस्थुः ।
अर्वाञ्चा नूनं रथ्येह यातं पीपिवांसमश्विना धर्ममच्छ ॥

1. Agni! it is well-known that Uṣas appears below to inspire and gladden ideas who move strongly to speech.

Now, she turns towards the sense organs here, swells over the path of the Aśvins nearby also to help and to bestow support in accordance with her dharma. (1752)

२. न संस्कृतं प्र मिमीतो गविष्ठान्ति नूनमश्विनोपस्तुतेह ।
दिवाभिपित्वेऽवसागमिष्ठा प्रत्यवर्ति दाशुषे शम्भविष्ठा ॥

2. Where the ideas diminish (to inspire speech) She (Uṣas) meets them to nourish as the sense activities desire within for which the Aśvins are praised above.

She comes to reside also in the home in the waking state as desired by the sense activities to nourish as well-known and to incite them to serve by toiling for existence as desired. (1753)

३. उता यातं संगवे प्रातरह्नो मध्यन्दिन उदिता सूर्यस्य ।
दिवा नक्तमवसा शन्तमेन नेदानीं पीतिरश्विना ततान ॥

3. Also, all the paths of sense activities were released in the

early morning of creation in the waking state, consciousness arose in the midday (of creation in man).

Consciousness blesses us by releasing us from ignorance mightily beneficently; just now the Aśvins swell and cross over to Activity. (1754)

The paths for the sense activities to the brain cells and sense organs were all established even in the early creatures which appeared in evolution and they are followed even in the higher species of creatures namely the nervous system.

D. XVI.

१. एता उ त्या उषसः केतुमक्रत पूर्वे अर्धे रजसो भानुमञ्जते ।
निष्कृण्वाना आयुधानीव धृष्णवः प्रति गावोऽरुषीर्यन्ति मातरः ।।

1. It is well-known that the motley sense activities eagerly bestowed on our (creature's) heads to produce powerful atmospheric creatures (rajasā) to appear (bhā) and adorn and praised in the earlier half of creative period.

They were produced to satisfy new desires (from the creatures) with instruments (weapons) (i.e. the beaks) to bestow and guide boldly, the sense activities bestowed nourishment through them; the mother guided them in good humour (aruṣa). (1755)

The mammoth bird life is said to have been produced in the earlier half of creative period. It is further stated that this bird life came into existence at the desire of the creatures which preceded. To get an insistent desire to take to the air deserting land could have arisen only in the then existing crawling creatures. The land must have become too hot for these creatures to survive on land. And perhaps there was no water too nearby. The only recourse was to take to the air.

२. उदपप्तन्नरुणा भानवो वृथा स्वायुजो अरुषीर्गा अयुक्षत ।
अक्रन्नुषासो वयुनानि पूर्वथा रुशन्तं भानुमरुषीरशिश्रयुः ।।

2. The ruddy light of Uṣas protects the paths of sense perceptions (food) which appears newly in these new creatures at their pleasure; the ruddy rays of Uṣas by themselves unite with the sense activities which unite with the brain (home).

Uṣas arranged and bestowed their aims in ancient times when the creatures browsed over them and had recourse to the ruddy rays of Uṣas. (1756)

The sense activities in these creatures are largely guided by Uṣas. This is what we call instinct which guides the birds over long distances to their summer and winter haunts.

३. अर्चन्ति नारीरपसो न विष्टिभिः समानेन योजनेना परावतः ।
इषं वहन्तीः सुकृते सुदानवे विश्वेदह यजमानाय सुन्वते ।।

3. Activity honours Dawn (nārī) to bestow on new creatures (new desires) by bestowing to the mighty brain (home) by uniting with knowledge from beyond.

Activity conveys the desires (of the ear-marked creatures for transformation) to do them good; he arouses them to bestow newly from the sense organs in the waking state; Indra the master moves then to the devotee. (1757)

D. XVII.

१. अबोध्यग्निर्ज्म उदेति सूर्यो व्यु३षाश्चन्द्रा मह्यावो अर्चिषा ।
आयुक्षातामश्विना यातवे रथं प्रासावीद्देवः सविता जगत्पृथक् ।।

1. Agni honours consciousness when he rises and awakes us; our mind eagerly honours the sense activities from the brain cells.

The Aśvins bestow the path of the sense organs for the yearning brain (home); Savitā creates the ideas separately for (everything) on earth. (1758)

२. यद्युञ्जाथे वृषणमश्विना रथं घृतेन नो मधुना क्षत्रमुक्षतम् ।
अस्माकं ब्रह्म पृतनासु जिन्वतं वयं धना शूरसाता भजेमहि ।।

2. Indra yokes them (ideas) to the sense organs through the Aśvins for clarified butter and he supports the sense perceptions in the home and sprinkles as desired.

He arouses and guides us to knowledge by enveloping and wins us understanding; the hero honours us with wealth continually and greatly for the purpose. (1759)

३. अर्वाङ त्रिचक्रो मधुवाहनो रथो जीराश्वो अश्विनोर्यातु सुष्टुतः ।
त्रिबन्धुरो मघवा विश्वसौभगः शं न आ वक्षद्द्विपदे चतुष्पदे ।।

3. The three-wheeled vehicle of the sense perceptions turns towards the sense organs; prāṇa sets them suitably in the path of the Aśvins quickly.

Indra bestows on his three relatives (brain, mind and sense

organs) bestowing from the home for their welfare; he toils to strengthen bipeds and quadrupeds. (1760)

D. XVIII.

१. प्र ते धारा असश्चतो दिवो न यन्ति वृष्टयः ।
अच्छा वाजं सहस्रिणम् ॥

1. He nourishes and supports them by uniting with them in waking state and guides the raining rays speedily.
He wins a thousand things from being near life-activity. (1761)

२. अभि प्रियाणि काव्या विश्वा चक्षाणो अर्षति ।
हरिस्तुञ्जान आयुधा ॥

2. Indra flows to the sense organs in kindness to perceive the knowledge (kāvya) emerging from them.
Consciousness praiseworthily bestows by uniting with the source. (1762)

३. स मर्मृजान आयुभिरिभो राजेव सुव्रतः ।
श्येनो न वंसु षीदति ॥

3. And the mortal leading a family (ebho) life like a king observing his vows (duties) is removed (mṛja).
Watching like a hawk he is induced to a new home (new life). (1763)

४. स नो विश्वा दिवो वसूतो पृथिव्या अधि ।
पुनान इन्दवा भर ॥

4. Consciousness bestows on him from beyond the earth as gift a body (Viśva).
He repeatedly bestows on the brain cells and supports them (in the new life). (1764)

BOOK IX: CHAPTER I

D. I.

१. प्रास्य धारा अक्षरन्वृष्णः सुतस्यौजसः ।
देवाँ अनु प्रभूषतः ॥

1. Indra (bull) flows to us and fulfils us with streams (of sense perceptions) and bestows them vigorously on Mind.

Ideas (devas) now nourish and adorn him. (1765)

२. सप्तिं मृजन्ति वेधसो गृणन्तः कारवो गिरा ।
ज्योतिर्जज्ञानमुक्थ्यम् ॥

2. The seven-pronged Activity crushes (enemies) and wins within by piercing (Vedhा) and bestowing on the devotees; they produce and bestow on the hill.

Knowledge takes its birth from consciousness praiseworthily. (1766)

३. सुषहा सोम तानि ते पुनानाय प्रभूवसो ।
वर्धा समुद्रमुक्थ्य ॥

3. Soma arouses his friend (mind) and repeatedly guides him along the nerves to the home of the lord (Indra).

He fosters growth; gladdens us praiseworthily. (1767)

D. II.

१. एष ब्रह्मा य ऋत्विय इन्द्रो नाम श्रुतो गृणे ॥

1. Indra moves seeking knowledge for the devotees honouring the sense of hearing of devotees (or which are sung by tradition). (1768), (438)

२. त्वामिच्छवसस्पते यन्ति गिरो न संयतः ॥

2. The lord of the home (Agni) desires you to guide the brain (hill) continually. (1769)

३. वि स्रुतयो यथा पथा [इन्द्र त्वद्यन्तु रातयः] ॥

3. Indra! Your path is like that of a flood; you guide along it ready to bestow. (1770), (453)

D. III.

१. आ त्वा रथं यथोतये [सुम्नाय वर्तयामसि ।
तुविकूर्मिमृतीषहमिन्द्रं शविष्ठ सत्पतिम्] ॥

1. Indra! You help the sense organs likewise [you move along the path of wealth to subsist].

Indra, the lord of existence, moves with might and approaches the sense organs mightily for the desires of mortals. (1771), (354)

२. तुविशुष्म तुविक्रतो शचीवो विश्वया मते ।
आ पप्राथ महित्वना ॥

2. He rushes in mightily to us; he creates knowledge mightily through the sense organs and bestows with might.

Activity spreads out much for desires. (1772)

३. यस्य ते महिना महः परि ज्मायन्तमीयतुः ।
हस्ता वज्रं हिरण्ययम् ॥

3. He strives greatly for them and gladdens; he speeds around everywhere; guides to unite for what is wasted.

With the vigorous hands he arouses, gladdens and controls. (1773)

D. IV.

१. आ यः पुरं नार्मिणीमदीदेदत्यः कविर्नभन्यो३ नार्वा ।
सूरो न रुरुक्वां छतात्मा ॥

1. Agni (poet) from the centre of existence hastens to the brain (city) of man, guides, bestows on men and approaches to guide understanding through prāṇa.

He is the hero of the body (ruru) wherever the ātmā is hidden. (1774)

२. अभि द्विजन्मा त्री रोचनानि विश्वा रजांसि शुशुचानो अस्थात् ।
होता यजिष्ठो अपां सधस्थे ।

2. Three flaming activities bestow on the homes of the twice born creatures, gladden and support them and please the mind abidingly.

Activity desiring life-course presides over the assembly. (1775)

The first birth of creatures is from heaven and the second birth when consciousness reveals them. The three activities are (1) Agni, Activity and Soma.

३. अयं स होता यो द्विजन्मा विश्वा दधे वार्याणि श्रवस्या ।
मर्तो यो अस्मै सुतुको ददाश ॥

3. The presiding devas bestow the paths to the sense organs on the twice-born and guide the wealth of the sense of hearing.
They have given the child mind, to serve mortals. (1776)

D. V.

१. अग्ने तमद्याश्वं न स्तोमैः क्रतुं न भद्रं हृदिस्पृशम् ।
ऋध्यामा त ओहैः ॥

1. Agni! Prāṇa praiseworthily produces the intoxicating sense perceptions for welfare by contacting the brain.
He makes transformations for the road to prosperity. (1777), (434), (Y.V.15, 44)

२. अधा ह्यग्ने क्रतोर्भद्रस्य दक्षस्य साधोः ।
रथीर्ऋतस्य बृहतो बभूथ ॥

2. Then Agni produces our welfare and enables us to achieve satisfaction.
Ṛta controls us greatly in existence. (1778), (Y.V.15, 45)

३. एभिर्नो अर्कैर्भवा नो अर्वाङ्स्व३र्ण ज्योतिः ।
अग्ने विश्वेभिः सुमना अनीकैः ॥

3. Consciousness supports Ṛta in existence and turns his effulgent rays on him wherever he is.
Agni is of a good disposition to mind below or Fire is in plants (sumanā) below on earth. (1779)

D. VI.

१. अग्ने विवस्वदुषसश्चित्रं राधो अमर्त्य ।
आ दाशुषे जातवेदो वहा त्वमद्या देवां उषर्बुधः ॥

1. Agni! Through the sweet sense activities you bestow eagerly varied wealth on the brain cells of mortals.
You serve eagearly for the birth of knowledge and now you convey ideas (devas) to the wonderful Uṣas. (1780), (40)

२. जुष्टो हि दूतो असि हव्यवाहनोऽग्ने रथीरध्वराणाम् ।
सजूरश्विभ्यामुषसा सुवीर्यमस्मे धेहि श्रवो बृहत् ॥

2. Agni! You are an agreeable messenger; you convey oblations from the sense organs in life-activity (or as charioteer in life-activity).

Attaching prāṇa to Uṣas extensively, you arouse and bestow vigour; you bestow on us the hearing organ (or hearing much you bestow us vigour). (1781)

D. VII.

१. विधुं दद्राणं समने बहूनां युवानं सन्तं पलितो जगार ।
देवस्य पश्य काव्यं महित्वाद्या ममार स ह्यः समान ॥

1. Agni! All alone you bestowed many youthful creatures freeing them from their slumber in the fight for life and honoured them with gifts born of and bestowed by sense activities to which they clung for protection.

The deva sensed (perceived) us in the story of creation (Kāvya); you bestowed many creatures beginning with us and at once bestowed a home (on earth) on them (from heaven). (1782), (325)

It is clearly stated here that evolution took place first in the subtle world or world of ideas. And this evolution began with man, who was later to be the most important being. After man all the lower orders of creatures were created one after another in the world of ideas. These slumbering ideas or creatures were now visualized in an ascending order on earth and provided with an encasing material body for the protection and play of ideas within. These were provided by Agni through sense activities.

२. शाक्मना शाको अरुणः सुपर्ण आ यो महः शूरः सनादनीडः ।
यच्चिकेत सत्यमित्तन्न मोघं वसु स्पार्हमुत जेतोत दाता ॥

2. The ruddy rays of the sun are helpful to the Vegetable Kingdom (Śāko); they gladdened these valiant creatures (being manifested) as from olden times with a nest (or shelter).

The sense activities perceived their desires and established them in existence; Indra did not strike them down; they were agreeable; he won for them and bestowed them also. (1783)

The rays of the sun are said to have been helpful not only to the plant world but also to the mobile creatures, which were created, by providing them with a shelter which means that matter, which formed the shelter, was derived from the rays of the sun. The fact is that both energy or the various types of radiations and matter have been derived from their parent i.e. ideas. Both are forms of ideas differing in the density of ideas with which they are packed. The ideas are much more densely packed in matter than in other forms like energies. The fact is that ideas constitute the basic material for everything in the universe. And all these ideas are the objective counterparts of the universal and intelligent subject, the creator.

३. एमिद्वंदे वृष्ण्या पौंस्यानि येभिरौक्षद् वृत्रहत्याय वज्री ।
ये कर्मणः क्रियमाणस्य मह्न ऋतेकर्ममुदजायन्त देवाः ॥

3. Indra (bull) moved to them (creatures) to bestow support by eagerly fulfilling their needs through the sense organs; he supported them to grow strong by striking down Vṛtra (inertia) through his vigorous nerves.

These (ideas from sense organs) produced in the home (brain) activities with definite aims.

The highly honoured (mahna) Ṛta gives rise (birth) to such Karmas and guides them by devas and gladdens them. (1784)

Karmas arise out of sense reactions tinged with desires and these desires are based on objects of the world. Ideas form the basis for desires.

D. VIII.

१. अस्ति सोमो अयं सुतः पिबन्त्यस्य मरुतः ।
उत स्वराजो अश्विना ॥

1. Soma is there as the path (or good fortune) for mind who drinks ideas (Maruts) from him.

There is also the self-controlled Aśvins for him. (1785), (174)

२. पिबन्ति मित्रो अर्यमा तना पूतस्य वरुणः ।
त्रिषधस्थस्य जावतः ॥

2. The brain (Mitra) drinks what swells over from Varuṇa (outer world) lead in by Indra (Aryamā).

Understanding flows in to us from the tree homes. (1786)

३. उतो न्वस्य जोषमा इन्द्रः सुतस्य गोमतः ।
प्रातर्होतेव मत्सति ॥

3. Also Indra gives rise to new ideas eagerly to take birth in mind through the sense activities.

He presided in the early morning of creation and he hastened existence for us (men) (1787)

D. IX.

१. बण्महाँ असि सूर्य बडादित्य महाँ असि ।
महस्ते सतो महिमा पनिष्टम मह्ना देव महां असि ।।

1. Consciousness is spoken of as great; Aditi is powerful and great.

They gladden us in the home in existence by bestowing great and admirable desires; the honoured devas are great. (1788), (276)

२. बट् सूर्य श्रवसा महाँ असि सत्रा देव महाँ असि ।
मह्ना देवानामसुर्यः पुरोहितो विभु ज्योतिरदाभ्यम् ।।

2. Truly consciousness is great by releasing the sense of hearing; the deva is great; is great in life-activity (Soma yajña).

Devas honour consciousness who presides [or does good to the brain (city)]; is all-pervading; his effulgence are channels (rada) of fearlessness. (1789), (Y. V. 33, 40)

D. X.

१. उप नो हरिभिः सुतं याहि मदानां पते ।
उप नो हरिभिः सुतम् ।।

1. Above, now consciousness moves to mind to arouse him to sense activities who protect him (or for him to drink).

Above, now consciousness arouses him to desires. (1790), (150)

२. द्विता यो वृत्रहन्तमो विद इन्द्रः शतक्रतुः ।
उप नो हरिभिः सुतम् ।।

2. Secondly he strikes down ignorance (Vṛtra) giving him desire for knowledge through Indra, doer of a hundred deeds.

Above now consciousness arouses him to desires. (1791)

The hundred deeds were performed in winter in the Arctic Circle in bringing the sun above the horizon after the hibernation for hundred days below the oceans, as already explained.

३. त्वं हि वृत्रहन्नेषां पाता सोमानामसि ।
उप नो हरिभिः सुतम् ॥

3. You strike down Vṛtra and arouse him (mind) eagerly and fulfil (his needs) through Soma.

Above now consciousness arouses him to desires. (1792)

D. XI.

१. प्र वो महे महेवृधे भरध्वं प्रचेतसे प्र सुमतिं कृणुध्वम् ।
विशः पूर्वीः प्र चर चर्षणिप्राः ॥

1. Indra! You bestow much nourishment (on mind) [or you hover about (the brain) much] and foster his growth; you run to support and bestow nourishment on mind; you run to create good understanding and nourish him.

Earlier you go around the home (brain) and nourish it with great diligence. (1793), (328)

२. उरुव्यचसे महिने सुवृक्तिमिन्द्राय ब्रह्म जनयन्त विप्राः ।
तस्य व्रतानि न मिनन्ति धीराः ॥

2. He bestows on us extensive comprehension greatly to be praised (Suvṛkti); Indra moves to knowledge and guides and inspires men to it.

His duty (vow) is to approach us within and bestow understanding. (1794)

३. इन्द्रं वाणीरनुत्तमन्युमेव सत्रा राजानं दधिरे सहध्यै ।
हर्यश्वाय बर्हया समापीन् ॥

3. Indra hastens Sarasvatī (Vāṇī) to bestow the best on us by uniting in life-activity (Sattra—Soma yajña) who honours, controls and bestows curds (sense reactions) jointly for tasting (sipping).

Consciousness moves to the motley sense activities (barha) to complete (the bestowal). (1795)

D. XII.

१. यदिन्द्र यावतस्त्वमेतावदहमीशीय ।
स्तोतारमिद्दिधिषे रदावसो न पापत्वाय रंसिषम् ॥

1. What Indra moves for is understanding which the motley sense activities praiseworthily bestow and burn away slumber.

Praiseworthily he bestows curds on the brain along the channels (nerves) to the home; he bestows on the sense organs (descendants) and supports their desires. (1796), (310)

२. शिक्षेयमिन्महयते दिवेदिवे राय आ कुहचिद्विदे ।
न हि त्वदन्यन्मघवन्न आप्यं वस्यो अस्ति पिता च न ॥

2. Indra! You control us mightily and instruct us much by uniting day after day and you move indeed from the sense organs (Ku) to Mind to bestow knowledge.

There is no one like you obtainable to bestow wealth from food (sense activities) and to gladden us like a father at home. (1797)

D. XIII.

१. श्रुधी हवं विपिपानस्याद्रेर्बोधा विप्रस्यार्चतो मनीषाम् ।
कृष्वा दुवांस्यन्तमा सचेमा ॥

1. Also through drinking oblations of hearing closely united with knowledge one gets understanding for which men worship Agni (the wise).

He honours us by being intimate and uniting; he cultivates and bestows knowledge. (1798)

२. न ते गिरो अपि मृष्ये तुरस्य न सुष्टुतिमसुर्यस्य विद्वान् ।
सदा ते नाम स्वयशो विवक्मि ॥

2. I praise (gira) the sense activities and quickly forget them also; I am spiritually (asurya) competent to be desirous of knowledge.

I bow to it constantly and speak of its fame. (1799)

३. भूरि हि ते सवना मानुषेषु भूरि मनीषी हवते त्वामित् ।
मारे अस्मन्मघवं ज्योक्कः ॥

3. The missiles of (sense activities) bestow abundant welfare eagerly on the home (brain) as desired; they establish indeed abundant understanding in men.

They bestow on the brain lasting love for wealth. (1800)

D. XIV.

१. प्रो ष्वस्मै पुरोरथमिन्द्राय शूषमर्चत ।
अभीके चिदु लोककृत्सङ्गे समत्सु वृत्रहा ।

अस्माकं बोधि चोदिता नभन्तामन्यकेषां
ज्याका अधि धन्वसु ॥

1. Indra moves and resoundingly honours the sense organs and fulfils us eagerly in the city. All the devas meet opportunely (abhīka) indeed to produce worlds.

Understanding dawns in us from within the centre of existence in the head as desired by mind. (1801)

२. त्वं सिधूँरवासृजोऽधराचो अहन्नहिम् ।
अशत्रुरिन्द्र जज्ञिषे विश्वं पुष्यसि वार्यम् ।
तं त्वा परि ष्वजामहे नभन्तामन्यकेषां ज्याका अधि धन्वसु ॥

2. You favour us with Sindhu which flows and which the spinal cord also supports and arouses. Indra is acquainted with his enemies; he nourishes the desires of the sense organs and controls the gifts.

You desire to go round yourself for many births (of ideas) from within the centre of existence; you move from the brain (head) to win for mind his desires from beyond and bestow wealth by arousing him. (1802)

३. वि षु विश्वा अरातयोऽर्यो नशन्त नो धियः ।
अस्तासि शत्रवे वधं यो न इन्द्र जिघांसति ।
या ते रातिर्ददिर्वसु नभन्तामन्यकेषां ज्याका अधि धन्वसु ॥

3. The sense organs are ready to bestow from all around; Indra gains them within to satisfy (others).

He destroys the enemies in the home with the intention to slay them at source. He bestows the path to cross (ignorance); he arouses and bestows in waking state; he moves from the centre of existence to the head winning the desires of the mind and bestows on him the wealth from beyond by arousing him. (1803)

D. XV.

१. रेवाँ इन्द्रेवत स्तोता स्यात्त्वावतो मघोनः ।
प्रेदु हरिवः सुतस्य ॥

1. You bestow even wealth resoundingly; you bind us to understanding through wealth praiseworthily.

Behold the nourishment which the tawny consciousness bestows on mind. (1804)

२. उक्थं च न शस्यमानं नागो रयिरा चिकेत ।
न गायत्रं गीयमानम् ।।

2. The spinal cord (snake) praiseworthily gladdens the brain cells in the home by bestowing wealth perceiving their desires.

The spinal cord supports them and honours and controls them. (1805)

३. मा न इन्द्र पीयत्नवे मा शर्धते परा दाः ।
शिक्षा शचीवः शचीभिः ।।

3. Indra swells over to the brain (home), unites with it freshly and bestows on us boldly from beyond.

He instructs us, bestows powerfully and he is powerful. (1806)

D. XVI.

१. एन्द्र याहि हरिभिरुप कण्वस्य सुष्टुतिम् ।
दिवो अमुष्य शासतो दिवं यय दिवावसो ।।

1. Indra moves to arouse consciousness above to support our brain cells suitably.

The waking state eagerly releases us to existence; waking state moves speedily; the waking state bestows on us favours. (1807)

२. अत्रा वि नेमिरेषामुरां न धूनुते वृकः ।
दिवो अमुष्य शासतो दिवं यय दिवावसो ।।

2. There on the rim of the brain desires pulsate like the trembling sheep at sight of wolf.

The waking state eagerly releases us to existence; waking state moves speedily; the waking state bestows favours on us. (1808)

३. आ त्वा ग्रावा वदन्निह सोमी घोषेण वक्षतु ।
दिवो अमुष्य शासतो दिवं यय दिवावसो ।।

3. Indra! You bestow (produce) on me first (agra) and inform me here about Soma who proclaims bestowing mightily through you on the home.

The waking state eagerly releases us to existence; waking state moves speedily; the waking state bestows on us favours. (1809)

D. XVII.

१. पवस्व सोम मन्दयन्निन्द्राय मधुमत्तमः ।

1. Soma himself bestows on us to drink (sense perceptions and activities). When dull, Indra guides sense perceptions (honey) as desired by us. (1810)

२. ते सुतासो विपश्चितः शुक्रा वायुमसृक्षत ।।

2. They bestow on mind; inspire the mind brightly flowing through the nerves from the home. (1811)

३. असृग्रं देववीतये वाजयन्तो रथा इव ।।

3. They flow first desiring ideas (devas) to guide life-activity like conducting a chariot. (1812)

D. XVIII.

१. अग्निं होतारं मन्ये दास्वन्तं वसोः सूनुं
सहसो जातवेदसं विप्रं न जातवेदसम् ।
य ऊर्ध्वया स्वध्वरो देवो देवाच्या कृपा ।
घृतस्य विभ्राष्टिमनु शुक्रशोचिष आजुह्वानस्य सर्पिषः ।।

1. Agni presides and gladdens mind; Indra bestows the wants of the mind within.

He bestows with might so that all knowledge may be born to mind; he inspires him with all knowledge from the source.

He moves to the head for the sweet gifts of ideas (devas); the devas honour in compassion.

Now he produces clarified butter without a frying pan; flames up brightly; bestows desires to flow to us through his tongues. (1813). (465)

२. यजिष्ठं त्वा यजमाना हुवेम ज्येष्ठमङ्गिरसां विप्र
मन्मभिर्विप्रेभिः शुक्र मन्मभिः ।
परिज्मानमिव द्यां होतारं चर्षणीनाम् ।
शोचिष्केशं वृषणं यमिमा विशः प्रावन्तु जूतये विशः ।।

2. Agni! You are fond of life-activity; you invoke Indra, our elder, for us, to inspire the Aṅgirasas.

You support mind and inspire him brightly we honour him.

Like going around the home victoriously, you preside in heaven and gladden us with diligent activity.

The flaming haired consciousness controls us powerfully in the home; bestows fulfilment within by inspiring the brain (home). (1814)

३. स हि पुरु चिदोजसा विरुक्मता दीद्यानो
भवति द्रुहन्तरः परशुर्न द्रुहन्तरः ।
वीडु चिद्यस्य समृतौ श्रुवद्वनेव यत्स्थिरम् ।
निष्षहमाणो यमते नायते धन्वासहा नायते ॥

3. Agni arouses mind and bestows abundantly and vigorously through the golden consciousness who turns towards him,

and gives him existence by slaying enemies quickly and to cross ignorance; consciousness is a hatchet to slay enemies quickly to cross over.

He firms up mind and bestows on mortals the sense of hearing speech, extensive like a forest to stabilise (knowledge).

He (consciousness) controls him (mind) jointly with the home (brain); restrains and guides him; bestows wealth by uniting at the same time. (1815)

BOOK IX: CHAPTER II

D. I.

१ अग्ने तव श्रवो वयो महि भ्राजन्ते अर्चयो विभावसो ।
बृहद्भानो शवसा वाजमुक्थ्यां३ दधासि दाशुषे कवे ।।

1. Agni! We hear much from you; you shine much within, you honour us through bestowing existence.

You shine much with might (or bestowing on the sense organs) in life-activity praiseworthily; you bestow knowledge on the devotees. (1816), (Y. V. 12, 106)

२. पावकवर्चाः शुक्रवर्चा अनूनवर्चा उदियर्षि भानुना ।
पुत्रो मातरा विचरन्नुपावसि पृणक्षि रोदसी उभे ।

2. Consciousness flows on rising, bestows speech and honours us by fulfilling, honours by brightening us and now honours us newly.

Like a mother caring for her son you look after us; fulfil by residing with us. (1817), (Y. V. 12, 107)

३. ऊर्जो नपाज्जातवेदः सुशस्तिभिर्मन्दस्व धीतिभिर्हितः ।
त्वे इषः सं दधुर्भूरिवर्पसश्चित्रोतयो वामजाताः ।।

3. The sense organs nourish us with knowledge from the source; they support us praiseworthily (Suśasti) themselves when it is dull (or/and gladden us); they support understanding for welfare.

They bestow all our desires abundantly; they help the brain cells in their assumed forms (Varpasa) variously; they bestow on us from the source. (1818), (Y. V. 12, 108)

४. इरज्यन्नग्ने प्रथयस्व जन्तुभिरस्मे रायो अमर्त्य ।
स दर्शतस्य वपुषो वि राजसि पृणक्षि दर्शतं क्रतुम् ।।

4. Agni! You guide (iraj) the sense perceptions; spread out yourself among the creaturcs like us; rule the mortals.

You bestow on man (Vapuṣa) a lookable form; rule him; approach and nourish him and produce a beautiful form. (1819), (Y. V. 12, 109)

५. इष्कर्तारमध्वरस्य प्रचेतसं क्षयन्तं राधसो महः ।
रातिं वामस्य सुभगां महीमिषं दधासि सानसिं रयिम् ॥

5. You produce desires; bestow gifts through sense-activities; nourish the mind; guide wealth to the home as desired and gladden him.

You bestow welfare on us graciously; open our eyes to the sense organs which bestow on us wealth victoriously. (1820), (Y. V. 12, 110)

६. ऋतावानं महिषं विश्वदर्शतमग्निं सुम्नाय दधिरे पुरो जनाः ।
श्रुत्कर्णं सप्रथस्तमं त्वा गिरा दैव्यं मानुषा युगा ॥

6. Agni desires Ṛta to gladden the desires of the sense organs by visiting them and to bestow curds (sense reactions) on the brains (cities) of men graciously.

You have spread out the desires from the head by bestowing ears to hear ideas which control men by uniting with them. (1821), (Y. V. 12, 111)

D. II.

१. प्र सो अग्ने तवोतिभिः सुवीराभिस्तरति वाजकर्मभिः ।
यस्य त्वं सख्यमाविथ ॥

1. Agni! Ṛta bestows nourishment and helps to arouse vigour and gladden praiseworthily in the duties of life-activity.

You help him with fore-knowledge (āvitha) (1822)

२. तव द्रप्सो नीलवान्वाश ऋत्विय इन्धानः सिष्णवा ददे ।
त्वं महीनामुषसामसि प्रियः क्षपो वस्तुषु राजसि ॥

2. You desire the brain cells of the devotees lowing in darkness, and kindle them to bestow new desires and bind them.

You bestow on them through Uṣas with love; you control ignorance (Tchapo) and satisfy the home. (1823)

D. III.

१. तमोषधीर्दधिरे गर्भमृत्वियं तमापो अग्निं जनयन्त मातरः ।
तमित्समानं वनिनश्च वीरुधोऽन्तर्वतीश्च सुवते च विश्वहा ॥

1. Agni! You bestow curds on the thoughtful man eagerly desirous; Activity controls the rituals connected with the desires at the source; Agni guides and releases the mother to men.

He gains the desires scattered like forest trees in the home and establishes them; he conveys to the home the knowledge within (from the sense organs) and also wealth (Suvat). (1824)

D. IV.

१. अग्निरिन्द्राय पवते दिवि शुक्रो वि राजति ।
महिषीव वि जायते ॥

1. Agni moves Indra to protect understanding; the waking state with its brightness rules over it.

He bestows much desires by winning them by uniting (with sense activities). (1825)

D. V.

१. यो जागार तमृचः कामयन्ते यो जागार तमु सामानि यन्ति ।
यो जागार तमयं सोम आह तवाहमस्मि सख्येन्योकाः ॥

1. Agni desires to shine in the waking state; he guides the desires in the waking state; he bestows them on the home and guides.

Soma controls the desires in the waking state; he comes to us in the waking state and helps to guide the home (1826).

D. VI.

१. अग्निर्जागार तमृचः कामयन्तेऽग्निर्जागार तमु सामानि यन्ति ।
अग्निर्जागार तमयं सोम आह तवाहमस्मि सख्ये न्योकाः ॥

1. Agni praises the desires in the waking state; guides the desires; Agni bestows the desires in the waking state and guides them.

Agni controls the desires in the waking state; Soma comes to us; he conveys (the desires) to us and helps to guide them in the home. (1827)

D. VII.

१. नमः सखिभ्यः पूर्वसद्भ्यो नमः साकंनिषेभ्यः ।
युञ्जे वाचं शतपदीम् ॥

1. Obeisances to friends; obeisances to the ancient fearless creatures (homes); their families are together in the homes (i.e. the brain cells).

They unite for speech over hundreds of stanzas. (1828)

२. युञ्जे वाचं शतपदीं गाये सहस्रवर्तनि ।
गायत्रं त्रैष्टुभं जगत् ॥

2. The sense activity moves and unites with speech for hundreds of stanzas along a thousand paths; the sense activity supports them among the three states to move. (1829)

३. गायत्रं त्रैष्टुभं जगद्विश्वा रूपाणि सम्भृता ।
देवा ओकांसि चक्रिरे ॥

3. The sense activities support through all the three states all forms of objects of the world passing through the sense organs.

Alt. Gāyatrī, Tṛṣṭubh and Jagatī metres support all forms of hymns which support all (ideas) in the world.

The sense activities go around the brain (head), support it and set it going. (1830)

D. VIII.

१. अग्निर्ज्योतिर्ज्योतिरग्निरिन्द्रो ज्योतिर्ज्योतिरिन्द्रः ।
सूर्यो ज्योतिर्ज्योतिः सूर्यः ॥

1. Agni enlightens us and the effulgent consciousness reveals Agni; Indra is flaming activity and the effulgence of consciousness reveals Indra.

Consciousness is effulgent and effulgence is consciousness. (1831)

२. पुनरूर्जा नि वर्तस्व पुनरग्न इषायुषा ।
पुनर्नः पाह्यंहसः ॥

2. Repeated nourishment quickens life-activity by itself (or repeated vigorous activity causes one to turn back on life); Agni repeatedly bestows desires in life.

Agni repeatedly controls the sense organs (descendants) and indeed bestows on them. (1832)

३. सह रय्या नि वर्तस्वाग्ने पिन्वस्व धारया ।
विश्वप्स्न्या विश्वतस्परि ॥

3. Agni himself sets activity in motion together with wealth (rayya); he himself gives abundant support.

Activity guides the sense organs and gladdens us; he goes round to the sense organs for it. (1833)

D. IX.

१. यदिन्द्राहं यथा त्वमीशीय वस्व एक इत् ।
स्तोता मे गोसखा स्यात् ॥

1. Agni! You rule Indra as he rules us; he is all alone in bestowing on the home.

He supports our sense activities praiseworthily. (1834)

२. शिक्षेयमस्मै दित्सेयं शचीपते मनीषिणे ।
यदहं गोपतिः स्याम् ॥

2. Agni! You instruct us here (or you instruct by controlling me); you desire to give (ditsa) and control along the path of might all men mightily,

by which I am the lord of the creatures. (1835)

३. धेनुष्ट इन्द्र सूनृता यजमानाय सुन्वते ।
गामश्वं पिप्युषी दुहे ॥

3. Indra loves the milch-cow (sense activities) which arouse men to life-activity in the home of the devotees.

Prāṇa also eagerly comes to bestow on me milk (sense perceptions) to drink. (1836)

D. X.

१. आपो हि ष्ठा मयोभुवस्ता न ऊर्जे दधातन ।
महे रणाय चक्षसे ॥

1. Water is indeed desired; bestows welfare (or refreshes us) in the home; gives nourishment to the brain to guide.

He gives us much pleasure to look at him. (1837), (Y. V. 11, 50, 36, 14)

२. यो वः शिवतमो रसस्तस्य भाजयतेह नः ।
उशतीरिव मातरः ॥

2. He gives us gracious desires; he unites with our taste when drunk.

He is desired like a mother who bestows. (1838), (Y. V. 11, 51, 36, 15)

३. तस्मा अरं गमाम वो यस्य क्षयाय जिन्वथ ।
आपो जनयथा च नः ॥

3. He is colourless and blesses us; by his disappearance within us (when drunk), we gain (vigour).

Water likewise gladdens men. (1839), (Y. V. 11, 52, 36, 16)

D. XI.

१. वात आ वातु भेषजं शम्भु मयोभु नो हृदे ॥
प्र न आयूंषि तारिषत् ।

1. The nerves which are powerful nourish the brain beneficently toiling for existence.

They nourish us eagerly through prāṇa and release our desires. (1840), (184)

२. उत वात पितासि न उत भ्रातोत नः सखा ।
स नो जीवातवे कृधि ॥

2. Also the nerves are bound to our father (Activity) (or are our father), are also our brother and bound to us as a friend.

They bestow gifts on the jīva and produce satisfaction. (1841)

३. यददो वात ते गृहे३ऽमृतं निहितं गुहा ।
तस्य नो धेहि जीवसे ॥

3. What the nerves bestow on the home (brain) of mortals down here for their welfare is in secret.

They are bestowed to arouse and bestow on the jīva. (1842)

D. XII.

१. अभि वाजी विश्वरूपो जनित्रं हिरण्ययं बिभ्रदत्कं सुपर्णः ।
सूर्यस्य भानुमृतुथा वसानः परि स्वयं मेधमृज्रो जजान ॥

1. In life-activity the sense organs support the forms of objects born from the source which the golden consciousness controls without rivalry; the golden-winged consciousness bestows them as desired.

The effulgence of consciousness bestows on the summit (of the brain) of mortals; they revolve by themselves and cleansing the knowledge of mortals born from the source releases it. (1843)

२. अप्सु रेतः शिश्रिये विश्वरूपं तेजः पृथिव्यामधि यत्संबभूव ।
अन्तरिक्षे स्वं महिमानं मिमानः कनिक्रन्ति वृष्णो अश्वस्य रेतः ।।

2. The rays of Activity sharpen (promote) prosperity illumining the forms of objects through the sense organs from beyond the earth and uniting with all in existence.

The mind by itself approaches the brain (home) much; the brain rains the rays of sense activities produced on the mind through prāṇa. (1844)

३. अयं सहस्रा परि युक्ता वसानः सूर्यस्य भानुं यज्ञो दाधार ।
सहस्रदाः शतदा भूरिदावा धर्ता दिवो भुवनस्य विश्पतिः ।।

3. The sense activities go around a thousand paths to unite with the home and bind; consciousness bestows his effulgence to support them in life-activity.

Consciousness bestows liberally (bhūridā) on thousands of cells and hundreds of their families its support; consciousness is the lord of the homes of creatures. (1845)

D. XIII.

१. नाके सुपर्णमुप यत्पतन्तं हृदा वेनन्तो अभ्यचक्षत त्वा ।
हिरण्यपक्षं वरुणस्य दूतं यमस्य योनौ शकुनं भुरण्युम् ।।

1. The golden-winged consciousness from heaven above flies down to the brain within desiring to perceive within.

With golden-wings (brain and sense organs) he controls the restless sense activities, who are the messengers with good omens from heaven to Varuṇa (external world). (1846), (320)

२. ऊर्ध्वो गन्धर्वो अधि नाके अस्थात्प्रत्यङ्चित्रा बिभ्रदस्यायुधानि ।
वसानो अत्कं सुरभिं दृशे कं स्वा३र्ण नाम जनत प्रियाणि ।।

2. Ideas (gandharvas) from heaven beyond are well-known to nourish from the brain every organ in a variety of ways without rivalry in our life, by bestowing on us.

Residing within the mantle of the head, they look at our desires themselves pleasantly; born with the sense activities they honour us lovingly in waves. (1847)

३. द्रप्सः समुद्रमभि यज्जिगाति पश्यन् गृध्रस्य चक्षसा विधर्मन् ।
भानुः शुक्रेण शोचिषा चकानस्तृतीये चक्रे रजसि प्रियाणि ।।

3. The brain cells win sense activities to give us rejoicings; the latter watching like a hawk observe; they look into us and bestow following dharma.

Consciousness shines brightly; goes around the three forest-like states from the sky (heaven) out of love. (1848)

BOOK IX: CHAPTER III

D. I.

१. आशुः शिशानो वृषभो न भीमो घनाघनः क्षोभणश्चर्षणीनाम् ।
सङ्क्रन्दनोऽनिमिष एकवीरः शतं सेना अजयत्साकमिन्द्रः ॥

1. Indra (bull), quick, bounteous, powerful whether he strikes (enemies) or not, is agitated and he is diligent.

A single hero with a retinue of hundreds meets his enemies resoundingly and jointly wins over them in a moment. (1849), (Y.V.17, 33)

२. सङ्क्रन्दनेनानिमिषेण जिष्णुना युत्कारेण दुश्च्यवनेन धृष्णुना ।
तदिन्द्रेण जयत तत्सहध्वं युधो नर इषुहस्तेन वृष्णा ॥

2. He meets the sense activities resoundingly in a moment; unites to produce mightily even in inaccessible places victoriously.

There Indra wins running together (with others) to fight for men with missiles in his hands (nerves) powerfully. (1850) (Y.V.17, 34)

३. स इषुहस्तैः स निषङ्गिभिर्वशी संस्रष्टा स युध इन्द्रो गणेन ।
संसृष्टजित्सोमपा बाहुशर्ध्यू३ग्रधन्वा प्रतिहिताभिरस्ता ॥

3. He releases the missiles through the nerves (hands) and supports the quivers in the home; he initiates all fights with his retinue and bestows (gifts).

He creates all and wins to fulfil Soma's (needs) with his defiant arms; earlier he bestows wealth (of sense activities) and nourishes and supports the home for welfare. (1851). (Y.V.17, 35)

D. II.

१. बृहस्पते परि दीया रथेन रक्षोहामित्राँ अपबाधमानः ।
प्रभञ्जन्त्सेनाः प्रमृणो युधा जयन्नस्माकमेध्यविता रथानाम् ॥

1. Bṛhaspati (Soma) goes around to the sense organs and bestows on us much, protects and causes changes in the brain (Mitra) and dispels annoyance in the home through Activity.

He shatters the enemy troops; he crushes them in the fight for nourishment; wins the sense activities for us and blesses the sense organs therewith. (1852), (Y.V.17, 36)

२. बलविज्ञायः स्थविरः प्रवीरः सहस्वान्वाजी सहमान उग्रः ।
अभिवीरो अभिसत्वा सहोजा जैत्रमिन्द्र रथमा तिष्ठ गोवित् ॥

2. He (Soma) is strong in discernment; he is mighty; he vigorously nourishes desires in life-activity with might and the home at the same time powerfully.

He is victorious and strong to be a hero and to bestow existence; Indra wins for the sense organs as desired by them the sense activities who know them. (1853), (Y.V.17, 37)

३. गोत्रभिदं गोविदं वज्रबाहुं जयन्तमज्म प्रमृणन्तमोजसा ।
इमं सजाता अनु वीरयध्वमिन्द्रं सखायो अनु सं रभध्वम् ॥

3. He has knowledge of sense activities to support them in the home through his vigorous hands (nerves) by winning majestically after crushing the enemies within vigorously.

Indra now runs and sets up a stream (of sense activities) to his kinsman (Soma); now he runs to embrace all (through the nerves). (1854), (Y.V.17, 38)

D. III.

१. अभि गोत्राणि सहसा गाहमानोऽदयो वीरः शतमन्युरिन्द्रः ।
दुश्च्यवनः पृतनाषाडयुध्यो३ऽस्माकं सेना अवतु प्र युत्सु ॥

1. He (Indra) plunges into the sense activities in the home to bestow together with his relative Soma, who sets up and releases hundreds of ideas by uniting with Indra.

The unconquerable (Indra) in fights desires to nourish inaccessible places; he favours them with his troops and nourishes them by arousing and uniting with them. (1855), (Y.V.17, 39)

२. इन्द्र आसां नेता बृहस्पतिर्दक्षिणा यज्ञः पुर एतु सोमः ।
देवसेनानामभिभञ्जतीनां जयन्तीनां मरुतो यन्त्वग्रम् ॥

2. Indra from his seat guides Soma (Bṛhaspati) and satisfies him mightily in life-activity in the home with the motley sense activities.

To crush the enemies he has troops of ideas (devas) and guiding the Maruts (ideas) to the community (village) he is victorious. (1856), (Y.V.17, 40)

३. इन्द्रस्य वृष्णो वरुणस्य राज्ञ आदित्यानां मरुतां शर्ध उग्रम् ।
महामनसां भुवनच्यवानां घोषो देवानां जयतामुदस्थात् ॥

3. Indra rains ideas (Maruts) boldly with Aditi from Varuṇa's dominion vigorously.

The great mind of creatures proclaims their desires which the devas (ideas) win for him and gladden him abidingly. (1857), (Y.V.17, 41)

D. IV.

१. उद्धर्षय मघवन्नायुधान्युत्सत्वनां मामकानां मनांसि ।
उद्वृत्रहन्वाजिनां वाजिनान्युद्रथानां जयतां यन्तु घोषाः ॥

1. Indra assaulted (dharṣa) the water for the sake of live cells desiring existence (for the jīvas) which the egoistic mind supported.

He struck down Vṛtra (inertia) in the water for life-activity; in this life-activity he won another thing namely sense organs from the water, guided them and proclaimed. (1858), (Y.V.17, 42)

In keeping with modern science this Veda realised in preglacial times, i.e. nearly 12,000 years ago, that life originated in water as cell-organisms. This manifestation comprises providing a form and substance for the creatures already created as ideas in heaven i.e. the unperceivable subtle world for their activity on earth. Rudiments of mind were there to bring about progressive changes and evolution of successive species of creatures. Inertia was the stumbling block for life to sprout up which was overcome by Indra. In this connection mantras 1327 and 1382 may be referred to.

२. अस्माकमिन्द्रः समृतेषु ध्वजेष्वस्माकं या इषवस्ता जयन्तु ।
अस्माकं वीरा उत्तरे भवन्त्वस्माँ उ देवा अवता हवेषु ॥

2. Indra bestows on this sense of egoism (mind) of mortals through the missiles (of sense activities); egoism releases the banner of desires which he wins from the home (brain) which bestows the desires.

Egoism is a hero of superior grade existing in our home; ideas favour it with oblations through the rays (of sense activities). (1859), (Y.V.17, 43)

३. असौ या सेना मरुतः परेषामभ्येति न ओजसा स्पर्धमाना ।
तां गूहत तमसापव्रतेन यथैतेषामन्यो अन्यं न जानात् ॥

3. As such the troops of ideas (Maruts) move to him, as

desires from beyond, to the motley sense activities bestowing vigour on the home in emulation.

They (the ideas) are indeed the longings of the sense organs to drink up ignorance (tamas) according to their duty; like the motley sense activities these ideas from the source love one another. (1860)

D. V.

१. अमीषां चित्तं प्रतिलोभयन्ती गृहाणाङ्गान्यप्वे परेहि ।
अभि प्रेहि निर्दह हृत्सु शोकैरन्धेनामित्रास्तमसा सचन्ताम् ॥

1. Let not the mind desire to be greedy for everything which the limbs of Activity lead in from beyond arousing the home.

Let him not torment the brain (heart) by arousing to nourish him; the milch-cow unites with the brain within releasing him from ignorance and gladdens his grief. (1861), (Y.V.17, 44)

२. प्रेता जयता नर इन्द्रो वः शर्म यच्छतु ।
उग्रा वः सन्तु बाहवोऽनाधृष्या यथासथ ॥

2. Indra conveys nourishment to man by winning the motley sense activities, protects and controls, or Indra wins a dead body (or sense organs) to man for protection and controls it (them).

He conveys them mightily; bestows gifts through his arms (nerves); he is unconquerable likewise in existence. (1862), (Y.V.17, 46)

३. अवसृष्टा परा पत शरव्ये ब्रह्मसंशिते ।
गच्छामित्रान्प्र पद्यस्व मामीषां कं च नोच्छिषः ॥

3. He creates the path to the father world and favours us with the knowledge, all of which he sharpens.

He goes along his own paths to nourish the brain (Mitra) as we wish; desires please us; we seek desires. (1863), (Y.V.17, 45)

D. VI.

१. कङ्काः सुपर्णा अनु यन्त्वेनान् गृध्राणामन्नमसावस्तु सेना ।
मैषां मोच्यघहारश्च नेन्द्र वयांस्येनाननुसंयन्तु सर्वान् ॥

1. The golden-winged consciousness is a limb of Prajāpati whom he guides as he desires, who smells the mind in the waking state (or watches like a vulture), honours him and bestows troops of objects to him.

The Aśvins release them indeed like a garland to gladden Indra; then they support us. now they praise all continually. (1864)

२. अमित्रसेनां मघवन्नस्मां छत्रुयतीमभि ।
उभौ तामिन्द्र वृत्रहन्नग्निश्च दहत प्रति ॥

2. Indra associates with the troops of Mitra (brain cells) to marshal and protect like an umbrella.
He strikes down Vṛtra as longed for by both (the brain and sense organs) and even burns them in turn. (1865)

३. यत्र बाणाः संपतन्ति कुमारा विशिखा इव ।
तत्र नो ब्रह्मणस्पतिरदितिः शर्म यच्छतु ।
विश्वाहा शर्म यच्छतु ॥

3. There all the missiles (of sense activities) drop down like flameless fires.
There Soma (Brahmaṇaspati) protects Aditi and controls her.
Indeed he protects and controls the sense organs. (1866)

D. VII.

१. वि रक्षो वि मृधो जहि वि वृत्रस्य हनू रुज ।
वि मन्युमिन्द्र वृत्रहन्नमित्रस्याभिदासतः ॥

1. Without protection, without a fight Vṛtra departs through being struck down and shattered.
Indra strikes down the unfriendly Vṛtra without resentment to give his services to us. (1867)

२. वि न इन्द्र मृधो जहि नीचा यच्छ पृतन्यतः ।
यो अस्माँ अभिदासत्यधरं गमया तमः ॥

2. Without weariness Indra now goes down below to nourish and guide (the sense organs) by uniting with them and controlling.
It is well-known that to serve us he supports and gladdens the sense activities through prāṇa as desired. (1868), (Y.V.8, 44, 18, 70)

३. इन्द्रस्य बाहू स्थविरौ युवानावनाधृष्यौ सुप्रतीकासह्यौ ।
तौ युञ्जीत प्रथमौ योग आगते याभ्यां
जितमसुराणां सहो महत् ॥

3. Indra's arms (nerves) are mighty, which turns towards the mind unconquerably to bestow mind's desires at once.

They (the nerves and mind) are yoked together primarily; they come to unite with him (mind) after winning from the sense organs (asuras) and together they gladden him. (1869)

D. VIII.

१. मर्माणि ते वर्मणा च्छादयामि सोमस्त्वा राजामृतेनानु वस्ताम् ।
उरोर्वरीयो वरुणस्ते कृणोतु जयन्तं त्वानु देवा मदन्तु ॥

1. The nerves honour man; protect like an armour (or bestow gifts to the home) well in compassion; they approach (the brain and sense organs) and bestow praiseworthily; they control the mortals mightily and now (look to) longings of the home.

The motley sense activities produce much from Varuṇa's home (in the shape of) extensive gifts which they (nerves) win within; now these ideas gladden us within. (1870), (Y.V. 17, 49)

२. अन्धा अमित्रा भवताशीर्षाणोऽहय इव ।
तेषां वो अग्निनुन्नानामिन्द्रो हन्तु वरंवरम् ॥

2. In the state of ignorance, the brain (Mitra) is restive like a horse.

Agni bestows on it now a variety of gifts in the enclosure through Indra to strike down (ignorance). (1871)

३. यो नः स्वोऽरणो यश्च निष्ठ्यो जिघांसति ।
देवास्तं सर्वे धूर्वन्तु ब्रह्म वर्म ममान्तरं शर्म वर्म ममान्तरम् ॥

3. The source itself is glad that it depends on ignorance being devoured to (establish) existence (on earth).

The devas in the home, all of them agitate to bestow knowledge within to shelter and protect us and gladden in our enclosure; they gladden us within. (1872)

D. IX.

१. मृगो न भीमः कुचरो गिरिष्ठाः परावत आ जगन्था परस्याः ।
सृकं संशाय पविमिन्द्र तिग्मं वि शत्रून् ताढि वि मृधो नुदस्व ॥

1. The sense activities in mortals are formidable and move round the sense organs at the desire of the brain (hill); the yonder world bestows them and they move within to protect us.

Alt. Indra moves around the body like a formidable animal

and is desirous to understand the yonder world through the birth of sense activities within us from beyond.

They (sense activities) run swiftly to the head; they are released from the rim (Summit) by Indra passionately through striking down the enemies without weariness and pushes them away himself. (1873). (Y.V. 18, 71)

२. भद्रं कर्णेभिः शृणुयाम देवा भद्रं पश्येमाक्षभिर्यजत्राः ।
स्थिरैरंगैस्तुष्टुवांसस्तनूभिर्व्यशेमहि देवहितं यदायुः ॥

2. May the path to our ears shout welfare; Agni! may our eyes see safely and support life-activity.

May the sense activities gladden and give satisfaction abidingly, bestow delicately to the brain cells and support manifestation greatly in which the devas (ideas) arouse desires in life. (1874), (Y.V. 25, 21)

३. स्वस्ति न इन्द्रो वृद्धश्रवाः स्वस्ति नः पूषा विश्ववेदाः ।
स्वस्ति नस्तार्क्ष्यो अरिष्टनेमिः स्वस्ति नो बृहस्पतिर्दधातु ॥
स्वस्ति नो बृहस्पतिर्दधातु ॥

3. May Indra foster our sense of hearing for welfare and protect our eagerness for knowledge through the sense organs.

May we be associated with the home and the summit to cross over (ignorance) scathelessly for welfare; may Soma bestow it for our welfare; Soma bestows it for our well-being. (1875)

APPENDIX I

Sāma Veda and Tradition

This Veda is not attributed to any particular ṛṣis. Many mantras of this Veda are cited in Ṛg Veda, 1443 in fact, by the ṛṣis although these did not originate from them. The Veda grew out of tradition in pre-glacial times. No one can escape the conclusion, after going through the Veda, that the Veda grew out of a tradition, as the same ideas are repeated several times in different words. Then the mantras on evolution are presented in such a disorderly fashion that we must come to the conclusion that new ideas on the early part of evolution dawned on men's minds later and such knowledge has been added on from time to time.

Then there are a few pointed references to it in the Veda itself which are set out here.

Sl. no.	M. no.	
1.	438/1768	Tradition sings of you by the name Indra.
2.	822	Men protect ancient knowledge from wise men.
3.	1105	He strives for us to hear the guidance of traditional knowledge.
4.	1768/438	Indra moves seeking knowledge for the devotees which are sung by Tradition. (Or Traditional knowledge sings the name of Indra as one who seeks the knowledge of ritual of life-activity.

APPENDIX II

References to Arctic Phenomena

Sl. no.	M. no.	
1.	173	Indra of a hundred deeds supports nourishment.
2.	257	He strikes down Vṛtra and carries out a hundred deeds in a hundred days.
3.	271	Indra, the destroyer of forts, produces nourishment etc.
4.	1086	What the doer of a hundred deeds bestows for consumption of the devotees is desires.
5.	1582	Indra destroyer of forts etc.
6.	1751	Alike to one another as sisters and running around etc. etc.
7.	1791	Indra doer of a hundred deeds.

This subject is discussed in detail in the introduction. Further, the explanations given under mantras 116, 1751 may be referred to.

There are similar references in the Yajur Veda also. That these two Vedas originated and were fostered by tradition in the Arctic area in pre-glacial times cannot be doubted. The repositories of these Vedas were the devas and asuras who passed on their tradition, language and culture to our forefathers, headed by the patriarchs Marīci, Atri, Bhṛgu etc. and to the Parsees of the present day Iran, when these peoples came in contact with one another in Central Asia.

APPENDIX III

Mantras on Evolution

Sl.no.	M. no.	
1.	4	Agni strikes down Vṛtra...and offers sense objects.
2.	11	Agni ! You cultivate the devotee with ideas.
3.	13	Above prāṇa is born of you (Agni).
4.	18	Agni invoked and announced his desire to water to give support to bodies with the latent heat in waters.
5.	20	In the early morning of creation in ancient times the effulgent consciousness looked within the head which gave the waking state.
6.	55	The devas bestow wealth from waters by over-flowing and riding them which the brain cells sip.
7.	67	Vaiśvānara has his source in Agni; man is a guest.
8.	69	Agni in ancient times ran to create many forms of creatures and bestowed his favours on Mind through nerves.
9.	77	The sense activities from the source preside and bestow mightily from heaven.
10.	85	In the early morning of creation Agni let in the motley sense activities as guests.
11.	89	Consciousness honours the sense activities and strikes down Vṛtra through Indra.
12.	90	Birth is the dharma of the yonder world which unites with us (life) and grows with existence.
13.	121	Indra fosters life-activity in whatever creature which subsists which he envelops.
14.	126	What now honours the head after striking down and pushing away Vṛtra is consciousness.
15.	143	Above, the spinal cord unites with the brain like a river; the source heaven unites with it.
16.	145	The footless brain cells release us from ignorance.
17.	160	Indra arouses the sense activites to bestow sense perceptions creating forms of objects.
18.	170	It is well-known that ideas attach themselves to the hill; unite with and strive to help the brain cells.
19.	172	Their (i.e. the ideas) paths are below consciousness.

Sl.no.	M.no.	
20.	179	Indra bestows understanding and supports it by opposing Vṛtra whom he struck down to give newer and newer forms of creatures.
21.	181	Indra, after striking down Vṛtra makes him from the other half of creatures.
22.	211	Indra cut off the head of Namuci with the foam from water of the oceans; he won him for the bodies of creatures.
23.	244	According to sacred ordinances of old times the bones of creatures were split and jointed for (new forms of creatures).
24.	303	The great Activity chose the sense of sight as desired; the effulgence of consciousness gladdened sense activity.
25.	321	From the depths of heaven hundreds of images like us are released.
26.	324	Ideas praiseworthily nourish the sense organs.
27.	325	Alone Indra ran to the conflict of life and bestowed many youthful creatures as gifts.
28.	352	Various colourful creatures are born of sense activities and then man enters.
29.	356	The brain drinks the intoxicating honey; there you (Indra) support the sense of hearing.
30.	359	When the brain cells were young Agni established mammoth creatures.
31.	440	Prāṇa carves out new forms in the home with Tvaṣṭā.
32.	467	From heaven above the jīvas were born in ignorance.
33.	524	Soma tells us that we belong to the shining ones i.e. devas and have descended along the line of animals (boar).
34.	529	The first step in producing creatures taken by the creator was in the ocean waters.
35.	594	My "Self" was born foremost in ancient times prior to Ṛta.
36.	597	Indra supports us by uniting with us; he mingles with all for yoking them to speech.
37.	619	All this here is the puruṣa, all that exists and which may come into existence.

Sl. no.	M. no.	
38.	621	The puruṣa bestows births and unites with them, then he created the worlds, then the brain.
39.	622	The brain and sense organs bestow on Mind.
40.	629	Agni from above visualized a variety of creatures in the waters through ideas.
41.	636	Every organ of the body is the home of ideas.
42.	913	Indra strikes down Vṛtra for newer and newer creatures.
43.	1116	The devas tell us that we men were born among the devas with great duties.
44.	1250	In ancient times when the brain cells (earth) were (was) young, Agni established odd creatures from the source.
45.	1264	Ancient creatures sought ideas and they hastened to Mind.
46.	1301	Agni bestows by churning the external world through sense activities.
47.	1327	Brain cells ! You sprouted from water Indra bestowed on you, enveloped and roused you up.
48.	1348	Agni helps to produce transformations.
49.	1382	Agni's minister speech tells us that creatures were born from the source in water.
50.	1385	The (latent) heat in water (brain fluids) shines and pleases the sense activities bestowing untiringly like lightning.
51.	1429	Life-activity came into being when Vṛtra was overcome who was hindering it.
52.	1430	Life-activity was born out of it and consciousness also took a hand at it. Sense organs were born of Vṛtra.
53.	1432	Fishes fulfilled (the purpose of life-activity) and gladdened, as if they were the instruments.
54.	1460	Indra ! You bestow a new gift on women; you arouse the girl and bestowing it guide it.
55.	1494	The earliest creatures of ancient times were very old which the sense activities brought to light (cell organisms), on whom the brain depended.
56.	1495	In ancient times the intelligence of Prajāpati per-

Sl. no.	M. no.	
		ceived homes (cells) in water and bestowed Activity to control them.
57.	1496	Consciousness bestowed protection on the cells like lightning as well as existence.
58.	1547	Consciousness as a relative of Activity draws out the image of Savitā for existence as men.
59.	1625	Let not the form of my body be changed to another form by Activity.
60.	1626	Viṣṇu nourished these new creatures with oblations; Indra approached the creatures and the Aśvins worked with ideas.
61.	1639	Indra fosters the growth of only such creatures which have to subsist and lets others become extinct.
62.	1641	The sense activities are bestowed by the Aṅgiras (Agni, Aśvins and Activity).
63.	1652	Sindhu envelops us and subdivides itself and bestows on the head impartially.
64.	1677	In ancient times when the cells were without a mind Indra used to move to release knowledge (as impulses) in Vegetable Kingdom.
65.	1678	Indra ruled over them, over the sense activity and consciousness.
66.	1691	The Mind gets fat from drinking what spills over from heaven.... On mind's account heaven bestows hearing sense.
67.	1698	The stationary plants and trees are sunk in fearful dependence and they rejoice to grow collectively.
68.	1711	In very ancient births Agni adorned the lives of the species himself (cell life).
69.	1719	After Vṛtra is shattered and devoured the Aśvins turn round to Activity for the home; Indra establishes them.
70.	1720	The protector of creatures nourishes all brain cells like the milch-cow.
71.	1725	Dawn terminated herself in favour of consciousness when man appeared.
72.	1728	In ancient times Uṣas sought to cut out her own activities.
73.	1747	In the early morning of creation Agni bestowed

Sl. no.	M. no.	
		sense objects on the jīvas in heaven, who were browsing; he bestowed them ideas.
74.	1748	So, followers of Agni (ideas) were roped together to form impenetrable ignorance (matter) giving diverse guileless objects. They united together dexterously etc.
75.	1749	The highest deva is consciousness bestowing the variegated rays on the sense activities. Savitā likewise created night and day.
76.	1754	All paths of sense activities were released in the early morning of creation in the waking state. Consciousness arose in midday in man.
77.	1755	The motley sense activities eagerly bestowed powerful atmospheric creatures in the earlier half of creative period.
78.	1756	The ruddy light of Uṣas protects the paths of sense perceptions in these new creatures. They are said to be guided by instinct.
79.	1782	Agni ! All alone you bestowed many youthful creatures freeing from their slumber in the fight for life and honoured them with gifts from sense activities. The deva sensed us in the story of creation and bestowed many creatures beginning with us men.
80.	1783	The ruddy rays of the Sun are helpful to the vegetable kingdom and they gladdened the valiant creatures with a nest (made of matter).
81.	1857	Indra rains ideas boldly with Aditi in Varuṇa's dominion vigorously.
82.	1858	Indra assaulted water for the sake of live cells desiring existence for the jīvas.
83.	1860	Troops of ideas move to Indra from the beyond emulating sense activities.
84.	1871	In the state of ignorance the brain is restive like a horse; Agni bestows a variety of gifts on it.
85.	1872	The source itself is glad that it depends on ignorance being devoured to establish existence (on earth).

Sl. no.	M. no.	
86.	617	The puruṣa, creator, has a thousand heads, a thousand eyes etc. enveloping the entire world and transcending it.
87.	618	Three parts of the puruṣa are above; we are at his feet taking repeated existences.
88.	770	In ancient times troops of ideas supported the body watching over like a swan and the brain with knowledge.
89.	625	Indra overpowers Vṛtra to initiate life-activity.
90.	1010	In ancient times prāṇa was not the cause of delighting manifestations (plants); the sense of touch was the comrade of the sap.

APPENDIX IV

Sāma Veda Mantras Repeated twice

Sl. no.	M. no.	Name of the Ṛṣis from Ṛg Veda		Devas
1.	487	Amahīyu	Āṅgirasa	Pavamāna-Soma
	762	,,	,,	,, ,,
	1335	,,	,,	,, ,,
2.	552	Ambarīṣa	Vārṣāgira	,, ,,
	1329	,,	,,	,, ,,
	1681	,,	,,	,, ,,
3.	553	Prajāpati	Viśvāmitra	,, ,,
	774	,,	,,	,, ,,
	1386	,,	,,	,, ,,
4.	627	Śatam	Vaikhānasāḥ	Agni-Pavamāna
	1464	Bhārgava	Prāgātha	Savitā
	1681	,,	,,	,,

APPENDIX V

Mantras from S.V. and Y.V. Included in R.V.
and
No. of Ṛṣis who have Contributed to Ṛg Veda

Maṇḍala No.	Total No. Mantras in R.V.	Mantras from S.V.	Mantras from Y.V.	Mantras of R.V. alone	No. of Ṛṣis contributed	
1.	2006	186	134	1687	21	various ṛṣis
2.	429	10	20	399	8	Gṛtsamada etc.
3.	617	39	32	545	11	Viśvāmitra etc.
4.	589	22	32	536	3	Vāmadeva etc.
5.	727	50	20	656	43	Atri family etc.
6.	765	74	40	654	10	Bharadvāja etc.
7.	841	73	24	742	3	Vasiṣṭha family
8.	1716	356	27	1336	59	various ṛṣis
9.	1108	543	8	557	85	do
10.	1754	89	144	1517	151	do
	10552	1442	481	8629	394	

APPENDIX VI

Hymns Common to S.V., Y.V. & R.V.

Maṇḍala I

	S.V.	Y.V.	R.V.
1.	14	3-22	I-1-7
2.	847	33-57	I-2-7
3.	1146	20-87	I-3-4
4.	1147	20-88	I-3-5
5.	1148	20-89	I-3-6
6.	189	20-84	I-3-10
7.	1468	33,5	I-6-1
8.	1469	33,6	I-6-2
9.	1470	29,37	I-6-3
10.	180	33,25	I-9-1
11.	1346	8,34	I-10-3
12.	343,827	12,56 15,61 17,61	I-11-1
13.	139,1463	3,28	I-18-1
14.	171	32,13	I-18-6
15.	1669	5,15	I-22-17
16.	1670	34,43	I-22-18
17.	1671	6,4	I-22-19
18.	1672	6,5	I-22-20
19.	1673	34,44	I-22-21
20.	795	33,46	I-23-6
21.	1585	21,1	I-25-19
22.	1415	27,7	I-27-7
23.	163,743	11,14	I-30-7
24.	50	33,15	I-44-13
25.	31	7,41	I-50-1
26.	1379	3,11	I-74-1
27.	637	33,32	I-74-6
28.	1537	33,3	I-75-5
29.	1561	15,35	I-79-4
30.	1562	15,36	I-79-5

31.	1563	15,37	I-79-6
32.	424	3,52	I-82-3
33.	1030	8,35	I-84-2
34.	247,1723	6,37	I-84-19
35.	1875	25,19	I-89-6
36.	1874	25,21	I-89-8
37.	1731	34,33	I-92-13
38.	417	33,90	I-105-1

Maṇḍala II

	S.V.	Y.V.	R.V.
1.	910	7, 9	II-41-4

Maṇḍala III

	S.V.	Y.V.	R.V.
1.	76	12,51	III-1-23
2.	669	7,31	III-12-1
3.	24,1718	20,53	III-45-1
4.	1462	3,35	III-62-10

Maṇḍala IV

	S.V.	Y.V.	R.V.
1.	1777	15,44	IV-10-1
2.	1778	15,40	IV-20-2
3.	169,682	27,39	IV-31-1
4.	683	27,40	IV-31-2
5.	684	27,41	IV-31-3
6.	181	33,65	IV-32-1
7.	358	23,32	IV-39-6
8.	1628	27,30	IV-47-1

Maṇḍala V

	S.V.	Y.V.	R.V.
1.	1746	15,24	V-1-1
2.	1739	15,42	V-6-2

3.	1024	15,43	V-6-9
4.	907	15,27	V-11-1
5.	908	15,28	V-11-6
6.	448,1107	3,25,15,48	V-24-1
7.	1108	3,25,15,48	V-24-2
8.	1109	3,26,15,48	V-24-4
9.	86	26,12	V-25-7
10.	1521	17,8	V-26-1

Maṇḍala VI

	S.V.	Y.V.	R.V.
1.	67	7,24	VI-7-1
2.	661	3,3	VI-16-11
3.	9	11,32	VI-16-13
4.	1383	13,36	VI-16-43
5.	234,809	27,37	VI-46-1
6.	810	27,38	VI-46-2
7.	333	20,50	VI-47-11
8.	35,703	27,42	VI-48-1
9.	704	27,44	VI-48-2
10.	1595	33,77	VI-52-9
11.	854	33,61	VI-60-5
12.	378	34,45	VI-70-1
13.	1863	17,45	VI-75-16
14.	1856	17,40	VI-75-17
15.	1870	17,49	VI-75-18

Maṇḍala VII

	S.V.	Y.V.	R.V.
1.	1375	17,76	VII-1-3
2.	1220	15,62	VII-3-2
3.	45,749	15,32	VII-16-1
4.	750	15,33	VII-16-2
5.	38	33,14	VII-16-7
6.	233,680	27,35	VII-32-22
7.	682	27,39	VII-32-23
8.	1351	33,20	VII-66-4

Maṇḍala VIII

	S.V.	Y.V.	R.V.
1.	250,1607	33,81	VIII-3-3
2.	1608	33,83	VIII-3-4
3.	1574	33,97	VIII-3-8
4.	1307	7,40	VIII-6-1
5.	143	26,15	VIII-6-28
6.	8,1166	12,115	VIII-11-7
7.	211	19,71	VIII-14-13
8.	111,1559	15,38-39	VIII-19-19
9.	133,1338	7,32	VIII-45-1
10.	1339	33,24	VIII-45-2
11.	300	3,34	VIII-51-7
12.	1609	33,82	VIII-51-9
13.	36,1544	27,43	VIII-60-9
14.	988	8,39	VIII-76-10
15.	1246	13,52	VIII-84-3
16.	236,685	26-11	VIII-88-1
17.	257	33,96	VIII-89-3
18.	126	33,35	VIII-93-4
19.	1586	36,7	VIII-93-19
20.	267,1319	33,41	VIII-99-3
21.	1637	33,66	VIII-99-5
22.	1638	33,67	VIII-99-6
23.	1789	33,40	VIII-101-12

Maṇḍala IX

	S.V.	Y.V.	R.V.
1.	690	26-26	IX-1-2
2.	651,763	33,62	IX-11-1
3.	499,1225	20,31	IX-51-1
4.	755	3,16	IX-54-1
5.	467,672	26,16	IX-61-10
6.	593,674	26,18	IX-61-11
7.	592,673	26,17	IX-61-12
8.	627,1464,1518	19,38	IX-66-19
9.	1519	26,9	IX-66-20

10.	1313	19-2	IX-107-1
11.	1365	22-18	IX-110-3

Maṇḍala X

	S.V.	Y.V.	R.V.
1.	1837	11,50,36,14	X-9-1
2.	1838	11,51,36,15	X-9-2
3.	1839	11,52,36,16	X-9-3
4.	33	36,12	X-9-4
5.	1589	17,22	X-81-6
6.	617	31-1	X-90-1
7.	618	31-4	X-90-4
8.	619	31-2	X-90-2
9.	1849	17-33	X-103-1
10.	1850	17-34	X-103-2
11.	1851	17-35	X-103-3
12.	1852	17-36	X-103-4
13.	1853	17-37	X-103-5
14.	1854	17-38	X-103-6
15.	1855	17-39	X-103-7
16.	1856	17-40	X-103-8
17.	1857	17-41	X-103-9
18.	1858	17-42	X-103-10
19.	1859	17-43	X-103-11
20.	1861	17-44	X-103-12
21.	1862	17-46	X-103-13
22.	1816	12-106	X-140-1
23.	1817	12-107	X-140-2
24.	1818	12-108	X-140-3
25.	1819	12-109	X-140-4
26.	1820	12-110	X-140-5
27.	1821	12-111	X-140-6
28.	1868	8,44 18,70	X-152-4
29.	452,1110	25,46	X-157-1
30.	1873	18,71	X-180-2
31.	192	3,31	X-185-1
32.	1376	3,6	X-189-1
33.	631,1377	3,7	X-189-2

Summary

Maṇḍala	
1	38
2	1
3	4
4	8
5	10
6	15
7	8
8	23
9	11
10	13
	151

APPENDIX VII

Different Translations

Sl. No.	Mantra No.	R.T.H. Griffith	Swami Dayanand Sarasvati Devichand	S.V. Ganapati
1.	690	Fiend-queller, Friend of all men, he hath with the wood attained unto his place, his iron-fashioned home.	The fiend queller and the friend of all in his country attains to reverance and a dignified position and lives happily in his house filled with gold.	He protects him (mind) by modifications through the sense organs with whom he is busy to effect the transformations from the source through Prāṇa. He bestows on the languishing assembly (of brain cells) in the head.
2.	755	After his ancient splendour, they, the bold, have drawn the bright milk from the sage who wins a thousand gifts.	The venerable sages following the vedic splendour of God acquire knowledge, which is the bestower of a thousand fruits, immaculate and expositor of objects	Consciousness bestows perceptions (milk) straight, as desired by heaven, as of old. We drink thousands of them bestowed by the ṛṣis.

Sl. No.	Mantra No.	R.T.H. Griffith	Swami Dayanand Sarasvati Devichand	S.V. Ganapati
			beyond the cognisance of the senses.	
3.	1246	Drink Soma to inspire thee, juice, Indra, which the Falcon brought : For, thou art King and Sovereign Lord of all the families of men.	O Omnipotent God, do thou protect men who are charitably disposed; hear their say; preserve even the tiniest creature.	Agni ! Being fond of the brain cells you give services to men eagerly; you crush creatures surprisingly on the hill to arouse (new ones) and fulfil. You protect the offspring yourself.
4.	1313	Hence sprinkle forth the juice effused, Soma, the best of sacred gifts, who, friend of man, hath run amid the water-streams. He hath pressed Soma out with stones.	The semen is the best life-infusing support, the friend of man, the lender of strength and perseverance to the organs of senses. It is created out of complete devices of celibacy. O learned persons ! Let it flow upward to the head from beneath.	They (the ideas) go around tingling along to Mind as the best oblations from Soma. They bestow wealth (of perceptions) on us men. Activity himself releases them within by arousing Soma eagerly to bestow on the hill (brain).

Sl. No.	Mantra No.	R.T.H. Griffith	Swami Dayanand Sarasvati Devichand	S.V. Ganapati
5.	1365	O Pavamāna, thou didst generate the Sun, and spread the moisture out with power, hastening to us with plenty vivified with milk.	O God, ever active, motivation of all through the power of sustaining the universe, thou dost beget the sun to support water in the atmosphere through his rays.	He (Indra) is victorious for men by arousing consciousness who bestows on the home, for drinking, through skillfully supporting sense perceptions. The sense activities move quickly bestowing the needs of the brain to sip.
6.	1375	Shine thou before us, Agni, well-enkindled, with flame, Most Youthful God that never fadeth. To thee come all our sacrificial viands.	Shine thou before us with constant flame of knowledge. O God, most youthful and enkindled through yogic practices. Austere learned persons since times immemorial, mortals attain unto thee.	Agni incites nourishment which shines by arousing and bestowing on the brain untiringly through the nerves as desired by the brain cells. He guides us constantly above in life.
7.	1519	Agni is Pavamāna, Sage, Chief Priest of all the Races Five : To him whose wealth	God is the revealer of all verses, the purifier of all, thel over of all five sorts of	Agni bestows to drink (or protect) on the home through the ṛṣis (Activity);

Sl. No.	Mantra No.	R.T.H. Griffith	Swami Dayanand Sarasvati Devichand	S.V. Ganapati
		is great we pray.	men, present in the universe before its creation. To him we pray whose knowledge is great.	the five sense activities from the source are the presiding priests. The sense activities greatly control our great desires.
8.	192	Great, unassailable must be the heavenly favour of Three Gods, Varuṇa, Mitra Aryaman.	May great unassailable heavenly favour of god possessing the triple qualities of love, praiseworthiness and justice, shower on us.	Indra (Aryamā) bestows on the brain (Mitra) heavenly gifts and blesses the three states by bestowing mightily. He opens the door to flow to Varuṇa (the external world.)

APPENDIX VIII

Sāma Veda Mantras in Ṛg Veda

Maṇḍala 1

3, 14, 16, 31, 32, 50, 54, 56, 59, 66, 96, 97	12
129, 135, 166, 171, 180, 185, 189	7
205, 214, 218, 221, 287	5
306, 341, 363, 367, 368, 373, 376, 377, 380	9
410, 412, 413, 415, 416, 417, 423, 424, 459, 461, 465	11
612, 637	2
740, 741, 742, 743, 744, 745, 790, 791, 792, 793, 794, 795, 796, 797, 798, 799	16
827, 828, 829, 844, 845, 846, 847, 848, 849, 850, 851, 852	12
913, 914, 915, 949, 950, 951	6
1002, 1003, 1004, 1005, 1006, 1007, 1028, 1029, 1030, 1064, 1065, 1066, 1084, 1085, 1086, 1087, 1088, 1089	18
1146, 1147, 1148	3
1250, 1251, 1252	3
1304, 1341, 1342, 1343, 1344, 1345, 1346, 1347, 1348, 1349, 1350, 1379, 1380, 1381	14
1415, 1416, 1417, 1432, 1433, 1463, 1468, 1469, 1470, 1497, 1498, 1499	12
1524, 1525, 1526, 1535, 1536, 1537, 1561, 1562, 1563, 1585, 1594, 1599	12
1600, 1601, 1618, 1619, 1620, 1621, 1622, 1630, 1634, 1635, 1636, 1663, 1664, 1665, 1669, 1670, 1671, 1672, 1673, 1674	20
1723, 1724, 1728, 1729, 1730, 1731, 1732, 1733, 1734, 1735, 1736, 1749, 1750, 1751, 1755, 1756, 1757, 1758, 1759, 1760, 1774, 1775, 1776, 1780, 1781	25
1814, 1815, 1874, 1875	4
	191

Repetitions not included—25

Maṇḍala 2

94, 200, 466, 607, 875, 885, 910, 911, 912, 1486 10

Repetitions not included—1

Maṇḍala 3

53, 60, 62, 76, 79, 98, 100, 195, 210, 338, 374, 663, 664, 665, 669, 670, 671, 737, 738, 739, 1462, 1477, 1478, 1479, 1538, 1539, 1540, 1556, 1557, 1558, 1694, 1695, 1696, 1702, 1703, 1704, 1718, 1719, 1720 39

Repetitions not included—4

Maṇḍala 4

12, 23, 30, 69, 82, 83, 84, 181, 203, 335, 358, 682, 683, 684, 1596, 1597, 1598, 1628, 1629, 1630, 1725, 1726, 1727, 1777, 1778, 1779 26

Repetition not included—1

Maṇḍala 5

81, 85, 86, 88, 141, 315, 366, 439, 440, 462 10

907, 908, 909, 985, 986, 987, 1022, 1023, 1024 9

1107, 1108, 1109, 1143, 1144, 1165, 1166, 1167, 1172, 1173, 1174 11

1405, 1406, 1407, 1521, 1522, 1523 6

1737, 1738, 1739, 1740, 1741, 1742, 1743, 1744, 1745 9

1746, 1747, 1748, 1752, 1753, 1754, 1826, 1827 8

53

Repetitions not included—8

Maṇḍala 6

22, 67, 68, 75, 83, 84, 105, 127, 146, 148 10

202, 262, 266, 281, 286, 322, 333, 351, 357, 365, 378 11

454, 660, 661, 662, 703, 704, 705, 706, 707 9

809, 810, 853, 854, 855, 991, 992, 993 8

1142, 1149, 1150, 1151, 1181, 1383, 1384, 1385, 1396 9

1397, 1398 2

49

	49
1440, 1441, 1442, 1443, 1461, 1474, 1475, 1476	8
1567, 1568, 1569, 1593, 1595, 1623, 1624, 1666, 1667, 1668	10
1705, 1707, 1863, 1866, 1870, 1872	6
	73

Repetitions not included—5

Maṇḍala 7

24, 36, 38, 61, 70, 78, 132, 241, 270, 285, 293	11
309, 313, 314, 318, 330, 433, 680, 681	8
716, 749, 750, 751, 752, 753, 754	7
800, 801, 802, 867, 868, 916, 917, 918, 927, 928, 929	11
1067, 1068, 1069, 1219, 1220, 1221	6
1304, 1305, 1306, 1351, 1352, 1353, 1373, 1374, 1375, 1381	10
1456, 1457, 1513, 1514	4
1625, 1626, 1627, 1675, 1676, 1682, 1683	7
1793, 1794, 1795, 1796, 1797, 1798, 1799, 1800	8
	72

Repetitions not included—13

Maṇḍala 8

6, 18, 19, 20, 29, 34, 39, 42, 43, 46, 48, 49, 52, 58, 89	15
102, 103, 104, 106, 113, 114, 116, 118, 120, 126, 128, 131, 136, 138, 140, 142, 143, 144, 145, 149, 151, 162, 173, 186, 187, 188, 193, 199	28
204, 206, 208, 209, 211, 213, 215, 216, 217, 219, 223, 227, 230, 244, 254, 255, 257, 258, 260, 263, 264, 271, 275, 277, 279, 282, 283, 289, 291, 292, 295, 296	32
300, 301, 307, 308, 312, 323, 324, 326, 355, 360, 364, 382, 384, 390, 391, 394, 395, 396	18
400, 401, 402, 403, 404, 407, 447, 460	8
666, 667, 668, 685, 686, 687, 688	7
	108

108

708, 709, 710, 711, 712, 713, 714, 715, 719, 720, 721, 722, 723, 724, 725, 726, 727, 728, 729, 730, 732, 733, 734, 735, 736, 738, 746, 747, 748 29

811, 812, 813, 814, 824, 825, 826, 862, 863, 864, 865, 878, 879, 880, 881, 882, 883, 884, 885 19

915, 930, 931, 932, 933, 934, 946, 947, 948, 988, 989, 990 12

1025, 1026, 1027, 1047, 1070, 1071, 1072, 1073, 1074, 1075 10

1155, 1156, 1166, 1167, 1168, 1169, 1170, 1171 8

1222, 1223, 1224, 1232, 1233, 1234, 1244, 1245, 1246, 1247, 1248 11

1307, 1308, 1309, 1319, 1320, 1321, 1322, 1338, 1339, 1340, 1354, 1355, 1356, 1360, 1361, 1362, 1363, 1389, 1390, 1391, 1392, 1393 22

1402, 1403, 1404, 1411, 1412, 1413, 1414, 1421, 1422, 1429, 1430, 1431, 1450, 1451, 1452, 1458, 1459, 1480, 1481, 1482, 1489, 1490, 1491, 1492, 1493 25

1500, 1501, 1502, 1510, 1511, 1512, 1515, 1516, 1517, 1532, 1533, 1534, 1541, 1542, 1543, 1544, 1545, 1549, 1550, 1551, 1552, 1553, 1554, 1555, 1559, 1560, 1564, 1565, 1566, 1570, 1571, 1572, 1573, 1574, 1575, 1579, 1580, 1581, 1582, 1583, 1584, 1586, 1587, 1588 44

1602, 1603, 1604, 1605, 1606, 1607, 1608, 1609, 1610, 1637, 1638, 1639, 1640, 1641, 1642, 1643, 1644, 1645, 1646, 1647, 1648, 1649, 1650, 1651, 1652, 1653, 1657, 1658, 1659, 1660, 1661, 1662, 1677, 1684, 1685, 1686, 1687, 1688, 1691, 1692, 1697, 1698 42

1711, 1712, 1713, 1721, 1722, 1732, 1771, 1772, 1773, 1785, 1786, 1787, 1788, 1789, 1790, 1791, 1792 17

1804, 1805, 1806, 1807, 1808, 1809, 1822, 1823, 1834, 1835, 1836 11

358

Repetitions 78 not included in the above list

Maṇḍala 9

18, 23, 80, 84, 101, 191 6

428, 429, 430, 431, 432, 436, 463, 467, 468, 469, 470,

471, 472, 473, 474, 475, 476, 477, 478, 479, 480, 481, 482, 483, 484, 485, 486, 487, 488, 489, 490, 491, 492, 493, 494, 495, 496, 497, 498, 499, 500, 501, 502, 504, 505, 506, 507, 508, 509, 510, 511, 513, 514, 515, 516, 517 56

524, 526, 527, 528, 532, 533, 534, 535, 536, 537, 538, 539, 540, 542, 543, 544, 547, 548, 549, 550, 551, 552, 553, 555, 557, 560, 561, 562, 563, 565, 566, 567, 568, 569, 570, 571, 573, 574, 575, 576, 577, 578, 581, 582, 583, 584, 592, 593 48

627, 651, 652, 653, 654, 655, 656, 657, 658, 659, 672, 673, 674, 675, 676, 677, 678, 679, 689, 690, 692, 693, 694, 695, 696, 697, 698, 699 28

700, 701, 702, 755, 756, 757, 758, 759, 760, 761, 762, 763, 764, 765, 766, 767, 768, 769, 770, 771, 772, 773, 775, 776, 777, 778, 779, 780, 781, 782, 784, 785, 786, 787, 788, 789 36

803, 804, 805, 806, 807, 808, 815, 816, 817, 818, 819, 820, 821, 822, 823, 830, 831, 832, 833, 834, 835, 836, 837, 838, 839, 840, 842, 843, 856, 857, 858, 859, 860, 861, 869, 870, 871, 872, 873, 874, 875, 876, 877, 886, 887, 888, 889, 890, 891, 892, 893, 894, 895, 896, 897, 898, 899 57

900, 901, 902, 903, 904, 905, 906, 919, 920, 921, 922, 924, 925, 926, 935, 936, 937, 938, 939, 940, 941, 942, 943, 944, 945, 955, 956, 957, 958, 959, 960, 961, 962, 963, 964, 965, 966, 967, 968, 969, 970, 971, 972, 973, 974, 975, 976, 977, 978, 979, 980, 981, 994, 995, 996, 997, 998, 999 58

1000, 1001, 1008, 1009, 1010, 1011, 1012, 1013, 1014, 1015, 1016, 1017, 1018, 1019, 1020, 1029, 1031, 1032, 1033, 1034, 1035, 1036, 1037, 1038, 1039, 1040, 1041, 1042, 1043, 1044, 1045, 1046, 1047, 1048, 1049, 1050, 1051, 1052, 1053, 1054, 1055, 1056, 1057, 1058, 1059 1060, 1061, 1062, 1063, 1076, 1077, 1078, 1079, 1080, 1081, 1082, 1083, 1084, 1085, 1093, 1094, 1095, 1096, 1097, 1098, 1099 66

355

1100, 1101, 1102, 1103, 1104, 1105, 1106, 1116, 1117, 1118, 1119, 1120, 1121, 1122, 1123, 1124, 1125, 1126, 1127, 1128, 1129, 1130, 1131, 1132, 1133, 1134, 1135, 1136, 1137, 1138, 1139, 1152, 1153, 1154, 1157, 1158, 1159, 1160, 1161,

	355
1162, 1163, 1164, 1165, 1175, 1176, 1177, 1178, 1179, 1180, 1181, 1182, 1183, 1184, 1185, 1186, 1187, 1188, 1189, 1190, 1191, 1192, 1193, 1194, 1195, 1196, 1197, 1198, 1199	68
1200, 1201, 1202, 1203, 1204, 1205, 1206, 1207, 1208, 1209, 1210, 1211, 1212, 1213, 1214, 1215, 1216, 1217, 1218, 1225, 1226, 1227, 1228, 1229, 1230, 1235, 1236, 1237, 1238, 1239, 1240, 1241, 1242, 1243, 1253, 1254, 1255, 1256, 1257, 1258, 1259, 1260, 1261, 1262, 1263, 1264, 1265, 1266, 1267, 1268, 1269, 1270, 1271, 1272, 1273, 1274, 1275, 1276, 1277, 1278, 1279, 1280, 1281, 1282, 1283, 1284, 1285, 1286, 1287, 1288, 1289, 1290, 1291, 1292, 1293, 1294, 1295, 1296, 1297, 1298, 1299	81
1310, 1311, 1312, 1313, 1314, 1315, 1316, 1317, 1318, 1323, 1324, 1325, 1326, 1327, 1328, 1329, 1330, 1331, 1332, 1333, 1334, 1335, 1336, 1337, 1357, 1358, 1359, 1364, 1365, 1366, 1367, 1368, 1369, 1370, 1371, 1372, 1386, 1387, 1388, 1394, 1395, 1399	42
1400, 1401, 1408, 1409, 1410, 1418, 1419, 1420, 1423, 1424, 1425, 1426, 1427, 1428, 1435, 1436, 1437, 1438, 1439, 1444, 1445, 1446, 1447, 1448, 1449, 1464, 1471, 1472, 1473, 1494, 1495, 1496	32
1506, 1507, 1508, 1518, 1519, 1590, 1591, 1592	8
1611, 1612, 1613, 1614, 1615, 1616, 1631, 1632, 1633, 1679, 1680, 1681, 1689, 1690, 1699	15
1700, 1701, 1714, 1715, 1716, 1717, 1761, 1762, 1763, 1764, 1765, 1766, 1767	13
1810, 1811, 1812	3
	617
Less Mantras repeated	79
	538

Maṇḍala 10

33, 64, 65, 71, 74, 77, 91, 95, 120, 184, 192	11
316, 317, 319, 325, 331, 332, 334, 339, 371, 379, 420, 422, 426, 443, 451	15
617, 619, 628, 982, 983, 984, 1090, 1091, 1092, 1110, 1111, 1112	12

1376, 1377, 1378, 1454, 1455, 1484, 1485	7
1505, 1527, 1528, 1529, 1530, 1531, 1546, 1547, 1548, 1589	10
1782, 1783, 1784	3
	58
1801, 1802, 1803, 1816, 1817, 1818, 1819, 1820, 1821, 1824, 1837, 1838	12
1839, 1840, 1842, 1846, 1847, 1848, 1849, 1850, 1851, 1852	10
1853, 1854, 1855, 1856, 1857, 1858, 1859, 1861, 1862, 1867, 1868	11
1873	1
	90

Repetitions not included—7

Summary

Sl. No.	S.V. Mantras	Repetition not included
1.	191	25
2.	10	1
3.	39	4
4.	26	1
5.	53	8
6.	73	5
7.	72	13
8.	358	78
9.	538	79
10.	90	7
	1450	221

APPENDIX IX

Sāmans Arranged According to Every Deva Separately

1. *Savitā*, *Viṣṇu*

141, 177, 222, 321, 435, 528, 529, 617, 618, 619, 620, 621, 911, 912, 1359, 1462, 1495, 1497, 1625, 1626, 1627, 1669, 1670, 1671, 1672, 1673, 1674, 1675, 1872. 29

2. *Aśvins*

169, 304, 305, 306, 377, 378, 639, 886, 887, 1056, 1079, 1080, 1133, 1134, 1160, 1199, 1207, 1274, 1387, 1388, 1438, 1485, 1641, 1642, 1692, 1727, 1729, 1734, 1745, 1753, 1754. 31

3. *Consciousness Uṣas* (*Dawn*)

20, 33, 34, 52, 66, 67, 75, 102, 126, 127, 178, 224, 267, 276, 319, 320, 352, 365, 368, 372, 451, 463, 464, 467, 476, 497, 530, 558, 562, 576, 596, 609, 614, 623, 624, 625, 632, 633, 634, 635, 637, 657, 672, 753, 755, 756, 757, 773, 774, 817, 833, 876, 877, 900, 935, 950, 960, 1031, 1032, 1042, 1043, 1044, 1077, 1083, 1109, 1112, 1140, 1183, 1186, 1204, 1216, 1217, 1218, 1227, 1228, 1229, 1262, 1263, 1270, 1273, 1284, 1285, 1293, 1294, 1316, 1319, 1391, 1392, 1468, 1469, 1490, 1546, 1547, 1548, 1590, 1591, 1612, 1658, 1660, 1661, 1693, 1725, 1728, 1731, 1732, 1733, 1741, 1742, 1749, 1751, 1755, 1756, 1761, 1762, 1764, 1783, 1784, 1788; 1789, 1843, 1845, 1846, 1847, 1864, 1866. 125

4. *Agni*

1, 2, 3, 4, 5, 6, 7, 8, 9, 10, 11, 12, 13, 14, 15, 16, 17, 18, 19, 21, 22, 23, 24, 25, 26, 27, 28, 29, 30, 31, 32, 35, 36, 37, 38, 39, 40, 41, 42, 43, 44, 45, 46, 47, 48, 49, 50, 53, 54, 59, 60, 61, 62, 63, 64, 65, 68, 71, 72, 73, 74, 76, 77, 78, 79, 80, 81, 82, 83, 84, 85, 86, 87, 88, 93, 95, 96, 97, 98, 99, 100, 104, 105, 106, 108, 109, 110, 111, 112, 113, 114, 133, 136, 137, 146, 151, 164, 165, 171, 193, 419, 420, 421, 423, 425, 426, 434, 447, 448, 449, 461, 462, 465, 486, 499, 500, 526, 533, 579, 605, 613, 615, 627, 646, 649, 659, 660, 661, 662, 665, 667, 668, 669, 670, 671, 703, 704, 705, 707,

708, 709, 737, 749, 761, 791, 792, 845, 846, 907, 908, 909, 944, 946, 947, 948, 982, 984, 991, 992, 993, 1011, 1012, 1022, 1030, 1064, 1065, 1066, 1074, 1107, 1108, 1116, 1130, 1131, 1141, 1142, 1143, 1144, 1145, 1149, 1150, 1167, 1168, 1169, 1170, 1171, 1172, 1174, 1202, 1208, 1219, 1221, 1250, 1251, 1280, 1286, 1306, 1318, 1338, 1350, 1373, 1374, 1375, 1382, 1383, 1384, 1386, 1389, 1396, 1400, 1401, 1405, 1406, 1407, 1408, 1409, 1410, 1415, 1416, 1417, 1464, 1465, 1467, 1474, 1475, 1476, 1503, 1504, 1505, 1514, 1515, 1519, 1520, 1521, 1523, 1524, 1525, 1526, 1527, 1528, 1529, 1530, 1531, 1532, 1533, 1534, 1535, 1536, 1539, 1540, 1541, 1542, 1543, 1544, 1545, 1552, 1553, 1554, 1555, 1556, 1557, 1559, 1561, 1562, 1563, 1564, 1566, 1567, 1568, 1569, 1587, 1595, 1596, 1597, 1617, 1618, 1619, 1623, 1624, 1648, 1649, 1650, 1666, 1677, 1706, 1710, 1711, 1712, 1713, 1717, 1719, 1720, 1721, 1722, 1723, 1737, 1738, 1739, 1740, 1746, 1747, 1752, 1758, 1774, 1775, 1776, 1777, 1778, 1779, 1780, 1781, 1782, 1813, 1814, 1815, 1816, 1818, 1819, 1820, 1821, 1822, 1823, 1825, 1827, 1831, 1833, 1834, 1835. 327

5. *Aditi*, *Sarasvatī*

56, 57, 58, 64, 101, 189, 221, 380, 442, 443, 444, 498, 514, 531, 534, 560, 564, 565, 607, 608, 658, 686, 723, 760, 830, 942, 979, 1033, 1061, 1062, 1063, 1075, 1112, 1125, 1128, 1129, 1165, 1176, 1177, 1192, 1198, 1317, 1353, 1354, 1355, 1356, 1362, 1363, 1368, 1370, 1419, 1424, 1425, 1461, 1498, 1499, 1608, 1614, 1708, 1709, 1726, 1766. 62

6. *Activity*

397, 510, 539, 1023, 1071, 1213, 1214, 1215, 1237, 1238, 1239, 1257, 1258, 1259, 1260, 1261, 1414, 1844. 18

7. *Indra*, *Prāṇa*

115, 116, 118, 119, 120, 121, 122, 123, 124, 125, 128, 129, 130, 131, 132, 142, 144, 148, 153, 156, 157, 158, 159, 160, 161, 162, 163, 166, 167, 168, 170, 173, 175, 176, 179, 180, 181, 182, 183, 187, 188, 192, 194, 195, 196, 197, 198, 199, 200, 201, 202, 203, 205, 206, 207, 209, 211, 212, 213, 214, 215, 216, 217, 226, 228, 229, 231, 232, 233, 234, 235, 236, 237,

238, 239, 240, 241, 242, 243, 244, 245, 246, 247, 248, 249,
250, 251, 252, 253, 254, 255, 256, 257, 258, 259, 260, 261,
262, 263, 264, 265, 266, 269, 270, 271, 272, 273, 274, 275,
277, 278, 279, 280, 281, 282, 283, 284, 286, 289, 290, 100
291, 292, 293, 294, 295, 296, 297, 298, 300, 301, 302, 303,
307, 308, 309, 310, 311, 312, 313, 314, 315, 316, 317, 318,
325, 326, 327, 328, 329, 330, 333, 334, 335, 337, 338, 339,
340, 342, 343, 344, 345, 346, 347, 348, 349, 350, 351, 354,
355, 356, 357, 359, 363, 366, 373, 374, 375, 376, 379, 381,
382, 383, 384, 385, 386, 387, 388, 389, 390, 391, 392
393, 394, 395, 396, 398, 399, 400, 402, 403, 405,
406, 408, 410, 411, 412, 413, 414, 416, 424, 438, 439, 446, 200
453, 456, 459, 460, 466, 472, 482, 483, 490, 491, 492, 493,
494, 496, 520, 521, 540, 541, 544, 556, 559, 566, 567, 568,
570, 578, 580, 585, 586, 587, 591, 592, 593, 597, 598, 599,
602, 603, 612, 631, 640, 641, 643, 644, 645, 647, 648, 653,
666, 673, 680, 681, 683, 684, 685, 687, 688, 689, 692,
693, 694, 695, 696, 697, 698, 710, 713, 715, 716, 718, 719,
720, 722, 725, 726, 727, 728, 729, 730, 731, 733, 734,
736, 740, 742, 743, 744, 745, 746, 747, 748, 750, 751, 752,
754, 762, 763, 766, 769, 771, 772, 775, 776, 777, 778, 779, 300
780, 783, 784, 785, 786, 796, 797, 798, 799, 800, 803, 804,
805, 806, 808, 809, 810, 811, 812, 813, 814, 815, 821,
823, 824, 825, 826, 827, 828, 829, 836, 837, 838, 841, 843,
850, 853, 854, 857, 858, 862, 863, 864, 865, 867, 868,
879, 880, 883, 884, 885, 895, 896, 897, 898, 899, 903, 913,
919, 923, 924, 925, 927, 928, 929, 931, 934, 936, 937, 949,
951, 952, 953, 954, 955, 956, 957, 966, 970, 971, 972, 973,
974, 977, 978, 980, 989, 995, 1002, 1003, 1004, 1005, 1010, 400
1013, 1014, 1015, 1016, 1017, 1025, 1026, 1027, 1028, 1029,
1034, 1036, 1039, 1045, 1050, 1052, 1053, 1054, 1055, 1057,
1058, 1059, 1060, 1070, 1072, 1076, 1082, 1084, 1085, 1086,
1087, 1088, 1090, 1091, 1092, 1093, 1094, 1095, 1096, 1097,
1098, 1100, 1106, 1110, 1111, 1113, 1114, 1115, 1119, 1120,
1121, 1122, 1123, 1124, 1126, 1127, 1146, 1147, 1148, 1151,
1156, 1157, 1158, 1159, 1164, 1173, 1184, 1185, 1190, 1191,
1194, 1211, 1212, 1220, 1222, 1223, 1224, 1230, 1231,
1233, 1234, 1235, 1247, 1248, 1249, 1252, 1272, 1275, 1276,
1277, 1279, 1283, 1287, 1295, 1307, 1308, 1315, 1321, 1322, 500

1326, 1327, 1331, 1332, 1333, 1336, 1340, 1341, 1342, 1344, 1345, 1346, 1358, 1361, 1364, 1365, 1366, 1367, 1369, 1377, 1378, 1393, 1394, 1395, 1402, 1403, 1404, 1411, 1413, 1421, 1428, 1434, 1437, 1446, 1448, 1450, 1452, 1453, 1454, 1455, 1456, 1458, 1459, 1472, 1484, 1487, 1488, 1489, 1491, 1493, 1494, 1502, 1510, 1511, 1513, 1516, 1517, 1570, 1573, 1574, 1576, 1577, 1578, 1579, 1580, 1581, 1582, 1583, 1584, 1588, 1589, 1592, 1593, 1607, 1610, 1620, 1621, 1622, 1634, 1635, 1636, 1637, 1638, 1639, 1643, 1644, 1645, 1646, 1652, 1653, 1655, 1662, 1664, 1665, 1667, 1668, 1678, 1679, 1680,
1681, 1682, 1683, 1684, 1685, 1694, 1695, 1696, 1704, 1705, 600
1718, 1724, 1744, 1750, 1759, 1765, 1768, 1769, 1770, 1771, 1772, 1787, 1791, 1794, 1795, 1796, 1797, 1798, 1802, 1803, 1806, 1807, 1809, 1836, 1849, 1850, 1851, 1854, 1855, 1856,
1857, 1858, 1859, 1862, 1865, 1868, 1869, 1873, 1875. 648

8. *Soma, Mind*

70, 91, 94, 139, 140, 154, 174, 190, 191, 223, 285, 286, 299, 364, 417, 427, 428, 429, 430, 431, 432, 436, 468, 469, 475, 477, 478, 479, 480, 484, 485, 501, 503, 504, 505, 506, 507, 508, 509, 511, 513, 515, 516, 517, 518, 519, 522, 523, 524, 525, 527, 532, 536, 537, 538, 542, 543, 545, 546, 547, 548, 549, 554, 555, 561, 569, 571, 572, 573, 575, 577, 581, 583, 590, 604, 606, 651, 654, 655, 656, 675, 676, 677, 678, 699, 700, 711, 712, 764, 767, 781, 782, 787, 788, 789,
790, 818, 819, 820, 834, 844, 856, 860, 861, 871, 873, 874, 100
889, 890, 892, 893, 894, 904, 905, 906, 916, 917, 921, 922, 926, 932, 933, 938, 940, 943, 958, 959, 961, 962, 963, 964, 965, 967, 976, 981, 988, 994, 997, 998, 999, 1000, 1001, 1006, 1007, 1018, 1019, 1020, 1021, 1038, 1039, 1040, 1041, 1047, 1048, 1049, 1051, 1099, 1101, 1102, 1103, 1104, 1105, 1132, 1152, 1153, 1154, 1162, 1163, 1175, 1178, 1179, 1180, 1181, 1182, 1187, 1188, 1189, 1193, 1195, 1196, 1197, 1200, 1203, 1209, 1225, 1226, 1236, 1240, 1241, 1242, 1243,
1244, 1245, 1246, 1255, 1281, 1289, 1290, 1291, 1292, 1298, 200
1299, 1300, 1301, 1303, 1310, 1311, 1312, 1323, 1324, 1325, 1328, 1329, 1330, 1334, 1337, 1420, 1435, 1436, 1439, 1440, 1441, 1443, 1444, 1449, 1457, 1463, 1496, 1506, 1507, 1509, 1560, 1611, 1613, 1615, 1616, 1640, 1654, 1689, 1691,

1699, 1700, 1701, 1702, 1767, 1785, 1790, 1793, 1810, 1852, 1853. 251

9. *Mitra, Viśvedevas (Brain)*

117, 145, 220, 225, 317, 323, 457, 502, 557, 610, 616, 663, 739, 793, 801, 802, 835, 847, 866, 881, 882, 910, 975, 985, 987, 1046, 1067, 1069, 1135, 1136, 1210, 1271, 1376, 1447, 1482, 1483, 1486, 1512, 1537, 1538, 1599, 1600, 1601, 1602, 1603, 1604, 1605, 1647, 1651, 1786, 1808, 1848, 1871. 53

10. *Varuṇa*

185, 218, 288, 588, 589, 795, 1585, 1586. 8

11. *Jīva*

152, 155, 230, 321, 353, 362, 371, 401, 409, 458, 535, 582, 594, 642, 664, 679, 690, 691, 714, 732, 816, 832, 840, 842, 851, 852, 918, 969, 1073, 1078, 1089, 1117, 1118, 1137, 1138, 1139, 1232, 1278, 1288, 1347, 1357, 1360, 1372, 1379, 1380, 1397, 1399, 1418, 1422, 1423, 1432, 1471, 1500, 1501, 1508, 1550, 1551, 1558, 1565, 1575, 1594, 1687, 1690, 1703, 1757, 1763, 1773, 1799, 1801, 1805, 1861, 1874. 72

12. *Ṛta (Established Pattern of working of human system)*

107, 341, 701, 765, 794, 848, 849, 1035, 1466, 1598. 10

13. *Devas, Maruts (Ideas)*

55, 92, 138, 149, 332, 445, 452, 454, 470, 563, 629, 636, 652, 721, 738, 758, 759, 770, 920, 1256, 1264, 1282, 1297, 1302, 1460, 1473, 1477, 1481, 1522, 1572, 1714, 1735, 1736, 1812, 1860, 1870. 36

14. *Soma, juice, curdled milk, Desires*

150, 358, 437, 441, 489, 495, 512, 550, 551, 552, 553, 584, 735, 741, 768, 872, 891, 901, 902, 914, 986, 996, 1024, 1155, 1205, 1313, 1314, 1320, 1433, 1442, 1445, 1480, 1800, 1811, 1824, 1826. 36

15. *Tvaṣṭṛ (sense of touch)*

147. 1

16. *Water*

1837, 1838, 1839. 3

17. *Vṛtra* (*Inertia*)

324, 337, 855, 1296, 1412, 1659, 1792, 1867. 8

18. *Miscellaneous*

89, 90, 103, 135, 172, 204, 208, 227, 322, 331, 336, 360, 367, 369, 415, 595, 650, 706, 717, 807, 822, 831, 839, 915, 941, 968, 1068, 1161, 1253, 1265, 1266, 1267, 1268, 1269, 1304, 1305, 1309, 1343, 1348, 1349, 1371, 1381, 1385, 1390, 1398, 1478, 1479, 1606, 1663, 1676, 1686, 1688, 1697, 1698, 1715, 1716, 1748, 1804, 1830, 1832. 60

19. *Speech*

471, 859, 869, 870, 875, 945, 990, 1201, 1206, 1817, 1828, 1829. 12

20. *Nervous System*

69, 143, 184, 422, 433, 473, 474, 600, 601, 630, 724, 983, 1008, 1009, 1254, 1339, 1351, 1352, 1426, 1451, 1571, 1628, 1629, 1630, 1631, 1632, 1633, 1657, 1840, 1841, 1842. 31

21. *Head and Body* (*Heaven and Earth*)

134, 186, 210, 219, 268, 272, 361, 370, 404, 407, 418, 440, 450, 451, 487, 488, 574, 611, 622, 626, 674, 682, 702, 878, 888, 930, 939, 1335, 1427, 1429, 1430, 1431, 1470, 1492, 1609, 1656, 1730, 1743, 1760. 39

Summary

1.	Savitā	29
2.	Aśvins	31
3.	Consciousness	125
4.	Agni	327
5.	Aditi	62
6.	Activity	18
7.	Indra	648
8.	Soma	251
9.	Mitra	53
10.	Varuṇa	8
11.	Jīva	72
12.	Ṛta	10
13.	Devas	36
14.	Soma Juice	36
15.	Tvaṣṭṛ	1
16.	Water	3
17.	Vṛtra	8
18.	Miscellaneous	60
19.	Speech	12
20.	Nerves	31
21.	Head and Body	39
		1860